Saved by the 'Ligl

# Buddha Within!

## Tommy Beaumont

WARNING: contains some coarse language and sexually explicit content..

First published by the author Tom Bird 2019


ISBN: 978-0-6487555-9-3



Cover, title design and internal picture arranging: Co Ogita.
Editing: Tom Bird with some help from friends.

I'd like to say that working with Angel Key Publications
has been an absolute pleasure.
Their professional help, support and friendliness is second to none.

NATIONAL LIBRARY OF AUSTRALIA

A catalogue record for this book is available from the National Library of Australia

For contact and enquiries: buddhawithin@yahoo.com

I dedicate this book to Co and Masami, and to all those who from their hearts express, compassion, love and a desire to help to achieve World Peace, and who share my respect for all living things.

My sincere wish is for my story to help s many others as possible to face, challenge and overcome their difficulties by learning to change their poions into medicine.

*The pure lotus flower blooms out of the muddy pond, the fragrant sandalwood grows from the soil, the graceful cherry blossoms come forth from trees, the beautiful Yang Kuei-fei was born from a woman of low station, and the moon rises from behind the mountains to shed light on them. Misfortune comes from one's mouth and ruins one, but fortune comes from one's heart and makes one worthy of respect.*

*(The fifth day of the first month, Nichiren).*

# Contents


INTRODUCTION . . . . . . . . . . . . . . . . . . . . . . . . . vii

*Chapter 1*
THE 'LIGHT' . . . . . . . . . . . . . . . . . . . . . . . . . 1

*Chapter 2*
THE BEGINNING . . . . . . . . . . . . . . . . . . . . . . . . 7

*Chapter 3*
GROWING UP . . . . . . . . . . . . . . . . . . . . . . . . . 11

*Chapter 4*
RADICAL CHANGES . . . . . . . . . . . . . . . . . . . . . . 19

*Chapter 5*
HOUSE OF TORTURE! . . . . . . . . . . . . . . . . . . . . . 23

*Chapter 6*
INTO AN EVEN BIGGER FIRE . . . . . . . . . . . . . . . . 29

*Chapter 7*
INCARCERATED . . . . . . . . . . . . . . . . . . . . . . . . 37

*Chapter 8*
DIFFICULT READJUSTMENTS . . . . . . . . . . . . . . . . 45

*Chapter 9*
CLIMBING THE ROCK 'N' ROLL LADDER . . . . 53

*Chapter 10*
SURF CITY – MYSTERY LIGHTS – BEE GEES . 61

*Chapter 11*
TURBULENCE . . . . . . . . . . . . . . . . . . . . . . . . . 67

*Chapter 12*
AFTER THE '*LIGHT*' . . . . . . . . . . . . . . . . . . . . 77

*Chapter 13*
HORROR WEEKEND! . . . . . . . . . . . . . . . . . . . . . 89

*Chapter 14*
THE BLACK-EYED MAN! . . . . . . . . . . . . . . . . . . 97

*Chapter 15*
RUNNING FOR MY LIFE! . . . . . . . . . . . . . . . . 105

*Chapter 16*
MULTIPLE CATASTROPHES . . . . . . . . . . . . . . 115

*Chapter 17*
NAM-MYOHO-RENGE-KYO. . . . . . . . . . . . . . . 131

*Chapter 18*
G'DAY HIROSHIMA . . . . . . . . . . . . . . . . . . . . 139

*Chapter 19*
NICHIREN . . . . . . . . . . . . . . . . . . . . . . . . . . . 149

*Chapter 20*
FREE AT LAST . . . . . . . . . . . . . . . . . . . . . . . 159

*Chapter 21*
THE GREAT MYSTIC REFLECTION . . . . . . . . 167

*Chapter 22*
WISDOM OF THE '*LIGHT*'. . . . . . . . . . . . . . . . *175*

*Chapter 23*
A MOST SIGNIFICANT LESSON . . . . . . . . . . . 181

*Chapter 24*
KEEPING THE FAITH . . . . . . . . . . . . . . . . . . . 193

*Chapter 25*
SNAKES AND WITCHES . . . . . . . . . . . . . . . . . 203

*Chapter 26*
VENOM OF THE SNAKE-DANCER! . . . . . . . . . 211

*Chapter 27*
HONOLALALAND-SAN FRANSYDNEY . . . . . 219

*Chapter 28*
FAMILY REUNION . . . . . . . . . . . . . . . . . . . . . 233

*Chapter 29*
CHANGING POISON INTO MEDICINE . . . . . . 243

*Chapter 30*
DESTINATION LONDON . . . . . . . . . . . . . . . . 251

*Chapter 31*

UFO - PREMONITIONS OR JUST A DREAM? 263

*Chapter 32*

DRAGS, DRUGS
AND CRAZY HOTEL GUESTS . . . . . . . . . . . . . 271

*Chapter 33*

CAMBRIDGEMAN. . . . . . . . . . . . . . . . . . . . . . 283

*Chapter 34*

ROOM WITH A VIEW TO MURDER! . . . . . . . . 297

*Chapter 35*

CH-CH-CH-CHANGES AND
SOME UNAVOIDABLE COMPLAINING. . . . . . 309

*Chapter 36*

CO SAN . . . . . . . . . . . . . . . . . . . . . . . . . . . 317

*Chapter 37*

POSITIVES & NEGATIVES . . . . . . . . . . . . . . . 325

*Chapter 38*

HURTFUL CONFRONTATIONS. . . . . . . . . . . . . 337

*Chapter 39*

BEST REUNION OF ALL . . . . . . . . . . . . . . . . . 345

*Chapter 40*

MODERN FAMILY. . . . . . . . . . . . . . . . . . . . . . 355

*Chapter 41*

SINCE THEN . . . . . . . . . . . . . . . . . . . . . . . . . 361

*Chapter 42*

AFTERTHOUGHTS-IDEAS-OPINIONS
& SOME TRIVIAL STUFF . . . . . . . . . . . . . . . . 369

# INTRODUCTION

Back in 1993, I was informed by my doctor that signs of cancer had shown up in a test and decided that it was time to share as much of what has happened in my life as I could. For years, people have been telling me to write a book on my life, especially those people who've witnessed some of the extraordinary events along the way. Concerned that my days could be numbered, and while I was in the process of enduring various medical tests, I finally sat and put pen to paper. As I began to investigate the hidden corridors of my past, there were days when I laughed and other days when I almost wept, but on most days there were surprises and even shocks by what I discovered. Memories that had been hidden from my mind's eye for decades were manifesting relentlessly and causing my deep-rooted emotions to run amok.

On a more positive note, because I was so involved with my memories, I completely forgot my present dilemma, and it was such a joy when new tests revealed that the signs of cancer had disappeared. The only explanation that my doctor could give me was that sometimes cancer can be eliminated by one's immune system. At the time, there'd been no signs of cancer with any other member of my family, but that was about to change dramatically! Now, 26 years later, I've finally completed the book...

My early childhood was filled with sadness, suffering and cruel, extreme abuse, and while what is written about it may be upsetting for some, sympathy isn't the reason that I've chosen to expose my life and share my story with the world. I now consider my unhappy childhood as an amazing gift, an education filled with valuable lessons that have since allowed me to grow stronger than my obstacles and become the compassionate and caring person that I try to be today, after having gained a greater understanding of human suffering from what I experienced myself. My deepest underlying wish is that my story will help others who are suffering to climb up from the depths of their torment, as I did, and turn their poisons into medicine.

From the very start, my life has been an outrageous and extraordinary journey, a story that not everyone will find easy to understand or accept, or, in some cases, believe. I even struggle to accept and understand some of what I've experienced, but it's all true, nonetheless. Some who've read my story have said that whether one believes all of it or not, it's still mind-boggling, thought-provoking, exiting and a fascinating read.

As a taste of things to come in my story, back in the 70s, while I was struggling to become a Rock 'n' Roll star I was struck by lightning and suddenly taken on a cosmic journey to where 'real stars' are born and where my life was changed forever, after an NDE (Near Death Experience) that I experienced cracked open the vault that I was living in and triggered off a whole new awareness and understanding of mine and all life in general. Later, my singing career took me around the world, and like millions of others who have done so, including celebrities such as Tina Turner, Herbie Hancock, Boy George and Orlando Bloom, just to name a few, I discovered the 'key' to life, the true reality of our existence and the real reason for why we're all here.

*When you read the first few chapters of a book you usually*
*learn about the main characters of a story*
*and what they are doing at the time.*
*Then if you jump ahead to the final chapters of the*
*book you are likely to find them in entirely different*
*circumstances that make little or no immediate sense.*
*You'll need to read the entire story in order to link*
*the front and back together.*
*Life in many ways is similar to this.*
*Due to the past good or bad causes made by*
*humankind, certain future effects have already been*
*put into place and are waiting to manifest.*
*However, nothing is ever set in stone and anything*
*can be changed for the better or worse in accordance*
*with causes that are made before manifestation.*
*Everyone is capable of tapping into deeper areas of*
*their mind's potential to see what the future has in*
*store, not only for themselves, but also for others*
*and even the entire world.*
*This process could involve things about to happen*
*within seconds or many years or even lifetimes into the*
*future.*

*To bring peace to the Earth, please strive to*
*make your own life peaceful.*
*As it's not the absence of fear and despair,*
*but the strength to conquer them.*

# Chapter 1

# THE 'LIGHT'

September the 1ST 1970 was a miserable and chilly wet day in Sydney. I woke up very early in the morning with the weirdest feeling – a strong sense of foreboding. It's awful to wake up and not be able to trust a day's beginning for no apparent reason, but that's precisely how I felt. I had nothing much to do, so I spent most of the morning hanging around the house, practising new songs and waiting for the all-important phone calls regarding future gigs. As the day dragged on, it became increasingly colder, and by mid-afternoon, I needed to switch on the heater. The clouds that had been gathering in the southeast throughout most of the morning had formed into a massive, thick cluster over the nearby Georges River, making a thunderstorm seem imminent. I can usually tell when a storm is about to break, even without looking outside. I often sense the build-up of intense energy, and my skin starts tingling. That's how I felt by late afternoon, but there was a difference, I had a dreadful gnawing sensation that something weird was going on, and it was making me feel increasingly irritable and uneasy. I was lodging with a friend's parents, Mr and Mrs Deedy at the time, who lived in East Hills, part of the Bankstown municipality of Sydney. Their fibro cottage was only a short distance from the river and was surrounded by thick native bush and gum trees. It was a pleasant enough place to be on a sunny day, but in a storm, it could be quite chilly and intimidating. To try to ease my growing buildup of fear, I went into the kitchen and got busy preparing the vegetables for dinner. When I glanced out of the window and noticed that the sky had turned to a horrid mixture of shades of grey and black, I instantly felt worse. The cloud formation had the shape of a giant devilish creature, hunched up and ready to strike, and its aggressive appearance gave me a sudden dose of the creeps. I was overwhelmed by a feeling of urgency to prepare myself, but for what, I didn't yet know. In a moment of panic, I raced down the hall, grabbed a couple of sheets from the closet and quickly hung them across the kitchen windows. I didn't think that it would make much difference, but it still felt better than doing nothing. Still feeling no safer, I put on a pair of rubber-soled house scuffs that Mum had paid a dollar for at Vinnies and given me a week earlier. The waves of fear racing through my body became so intense that they were starting to feel painful. As lightning flashed and the massive booms of thunder shook the house, my heart almost stopped, and my stomach was doing somersaults. I had the scariest feeling that something was about to happen and how I wished that I had someone else in the house with me to help me get through it…

"That's it!" I thought, "I'll bring in the dogs."

My behaviour was becoming bizarre, which I put that down to why the dogs were acting so unusually strange. I kept telling myself that they were picking up my anxious vibes, which I'm sure they were. Suddenly the strong winds howled, the gum trees swayed, and as giant forks of lightning raced across the sky like spider legs, I felt the hairs on my body standing on end. I was almost levitating with fear as I sprinted around the house in circles, and when the phone suddenly rang, I almost hit the ceiling…

"Hello?" I answered in a failing voice.

Knock-kneed, I stumbled backwards towards the big square box-heater that was stationed in the middle of the room. The caller was the manager of a gay dance club called *Isadora's*, and at first, his effeminate voice sounded like a woman. My agent had given him my number, and he wanted to book me for a show the following week. I knew that there were several gay venues around Sydney's inner-city area, but I'd never actually performed at one. As I sat down on the back of the heater to hear more about it, the tension in my legs began to ease, and it felt so good to have someone other than the dogs and the walls to talk to. Whenever I used the phone, I'd usually sit on a little stool next to it, and the smaller of the two dogs would lay his head on my lap while I talked. Because the heater stood higher than the stool, the dog compromised by resting his nose gently on the front of my leg, and as the manager of Isadora's continued explaining all the details of the gig, I began to feel relaxed for the first time in hours...

**THEN IT HAPPENED!!!**

With a tumultuous roar in my head, that sounded like a great gush of water, I was sucked upwards, burst through a sort of film or barrier and then I was in the silence of outer space, moving at a tremendous speed. I couldn't see my body at all, and it was similar to the sensation of travelling in a dream. The view all around me was amazing – it looked like black velvet covered in millions of tiny illuminating platinum white lights. Those that I saw up close as I whizzed by were like crystal-clear discs. Then there was a much brighter and far more distinct light in the distance, rapidly increasing in size. It was positioned directly ahead of me and it almost instantly expanded out into a magnificent and seemingly endless array of countless luminous colours that were more vibrant and beautiful than any that I'd ever seen. The closer I came to the shimmering display of light, the larger it grew, and the more everything around me began to have a ring of familiarity about it. Then it all suddenly slowed down to a snail's pace, as I began to gently descend into the glow of the magnificent display of countless colours beneath me. I was then embraced by an overwhelming feeling of peace and inner security, and it was as if I'd made this incredible journey many times before – as if I'd finally found my way back to the safety of my loving home after being lost and all alone in the wilderness for the longest time. As I basked in the warmth and immense wonder of it all, I felt wave after wave of indescribable love reaching up to greet me – softly soothing me and washing away any remaining fears and concerns that I had. It was such a magnificent and beautiful experience and one that I've never forgotten – pure grandeur, an all-embracing state of loving-kindness and acceptance which far exceeded anything that I've ever known or experienced before or since. I was almost close enough to touch the beautiful display of what looked like multicoloured dust cloud particles, and each speck was radiating its own, unique, loving welcome. This giant maze of wonder was more vibrant and intense than anything that I'm able even to remotely compare it to. Blended as one entity, it appeared to be alive and intelligent, and it gave me an astounding feeling of *déjàvu* – I felt like I knew exactly where I was and so happy and at home. In fact, it seemed more real to me than anything else that I've ever known or experienced.

I was only with the beautiful Light for a few moments, before I was suddenly sucked away from it and into a state of complete reversal. In the blink of an eye, I was leaving the light at what seemed like the same speed as when I'd approached it. After I burst feet-first back through the same barrier that I'd passed through when leaving, everything instantly slowed down again and then stopped. The next thing that I knew, was being hit in the face by a large, wooden object! From that point on, I only have segmental memories of what happened, such as throwing water over my face at the kitchen sink, feeling my skin tingle and hearing distant cries for help and loud groaning, which later turned out to be me, and outrageous visions of the living room in all sorts of distorted shapes and positions. I must have been in a state of psychedelic disorientation, caught between two realms of existence. At some point during my 'out-of-this-world' experience, I'd fallen onto the living-room floor. I can clearly remember lying there feeling so sleepy that I could barely keep on breathing. It was similar to the sensation of fatigue that one feels after a hectic day or an exhausting climb and the relief of finally lying down and letting go at the end of it, but I couldn't. Every time I started falling off to sleep, a deep, emotionless, disembodied voice permeated my body, causing it to jolt! It felt like a series of electric shocks…

"WAKE UP! WAKE UP!" The voice kept yelling.

Thank goodness my neighbours managed to force their way into the house in time to save me from potentially being burned alive. The heater was still switched on and face down on the carpet next to my head, and when a neighbour lifted it and discovered a huge scorch mark, there was a loud sigh of relief in the room. Mr and Mrs Deedy arrived home just as the ambulance men were carrying me out of their house to rush me off to Bankstown City Hospital, and were stunned by all the commotion, and they got another big shock when they saw my hair standing on end. Most people who knew me were aware that I was overly vain and forever trying to look as outrageous as I possibly could. The Deedy's must have thought that I'd finally cracked the jackpot that night! As soon as Mr Deedy entered his house, he picked up his landline phone from the floor, to check if anyone was there, and was surprised to find Mr Isadora still hanging on in anticipation. He'd heard everything, including the deafening roar and all of the screaming afterwards. Mr Isadora's description of what happened was a big help to us later when we were trying to put the pieces together and make sense of it all. I spoke to him the following day, and with a cheeky giggle, he told me that he'd thought I was a mentally impaired screaming queen doing my *thang*. The reason he hadn't hung up was that he didn't want to miss out on the grand finale. I have only vague recollections of arriving at the hospital that night, but I do remember the sight of the doctors' faces peering down at me each time that I opened my eyes. They were all staring at me with astonished looks on their faces and telling each other how unbelievable it was that I'd survived...

"It's a miracle he's still with us!"

"It is ... it's absolutely incredible!"

"A one in a million chance if you ask me!"

After I was eventually able to talk, I tried my best to explain to them about the beautiful Light and the journey that I'd taken through the stars to reach it, but none of them seemed to know what I was talking about, let alone, where I'd been. It was my home doctor who later suggested that I may have been momentarily dead. During the days that followed, I wandered endlessly around the house in a stupor, remembering vivid, momentary flashes of the incredible Light, but I still couldn't make much sense out of it. I also saw flashes of the dog's eyes bulging out at me and his hair and ears standing up as you do in a cartoon. He must have absorbed a fair amount of the shock as well because he wasn't able to keep any of his food down for days, and he also wouldn't come anywhere near me! My body was still radiating excess energy when Mrs Deedy applied a soothing cream to some bruises on my back, she felt a tingling sensation from the left-over static charge. After that, whenever we crossed paths, she couldn't resist the thrill of running her fingers up and down my spine to experience the magic of it all over again and again. The only apparent injuries that I'd sustained were an aching ear, a few bruises and some swelling on one side of my tongue, which was slightly uncomfortable but only for a couple of hours. It was a very much-welcomed relief when all of the swellings eventually subsided, and my ear finally stopped aching.

Two electricity department officials completed an investigation, and we were able to fill in some more of the gaps. The men couldn't determine for certain exactly where the lightning had hit, but because several light bulbs had exploded in the house next door, they concluded that it had probably struck the telegraph pole that supplied electricity to both houses. The men also reminded me of how lucky I'd been, as had I not been wearing the one-dollar rubber-soled scuffs, I potentially could have been incinerated. The metal disc torn from its casing inside the ear-piece of the phone could have almost done the job anyway if the dominant force of the shock hadn't thrown me away from it. The men also discovered where I'd crashed, head first, into the thick end of a Venetian blind – it had acted as a buffer and prevented me from smashing through a full-length glass window. If the dog's head had been resting on my lap, as it usually was, either of us may not have survived. All of the doors throughout the house were wood-grain, and Mr Deedy later found a gaping hole where the kitchen doorknob had ploughed through a small section of a partition wall, and we all agreed that I must have fallen against it while I was careering through the house in a panic. We were sorting out most of the mundane things, but we hadn't even begun to solve the greatest mystery of all. As absurd as it may seem, the memory of my mysterious encounter with the magnificent Light was growing more vivid by the day. Each time I thought about it, its wonders would briefly radiate through my body all over again. Like a giant wave, it would lift me into a state of sheer bliss, and I'd leave my troubles behind, and my life condition would momentarily seem perfect, carefree and happy. It really was like existing in two places at once.

Whenever I mentioned the Light to Mr and Mrs Deedy, the disapproving looks on their faces gave me the impression that they didn't want to hear anything about it. They'd refrain from commenting and turn their heads the other way or abruptly change the subject until, in the end, they became so upset with me about it that they ordered me never to mention it again in their house or presence. The Deedy's were non-active Jehovah's Witnesses, and my experience with the Light conflicted with their belief that everyone is confined to remain in their grave after death until God decides to resurrect them or not. I've since learnt that if something doesn't fit in with the J W version and interpretation of the Bible, then it's automatically considered to be the work of the Devil. Be that as it may, the Deedy's opposing reaction made no difference to me whatsoever. As far as I was concerned, and still am, the Light was the 'real deal', and I still can't get it or the journey through space to reach it out of my mind. I tried explaining what had happened to my older brother, Denis, a compulsive sceptic about anything that he hasn't seen, heard or experienced for himself and then some. His reaction was predictable, he was cynical, angry, abusive and dogmatic and considered the whole incident was nothing more than a load of bullshit! When my photograph and a story about my experience was published on the front page of the newspaper, it still made no difference to Denis. He not only refused to believe that I'd been struck by lightning but also dogmatically insisted that it was all just a publicity stunt. For as long as I can remember, Denis has had a difficult time admitting that he's wrong about anything, he'd rather argue with you instead until he's blue in the face, and as a last resort, he'll try to convince you that he said the opposite.

Having experienced many bizarre and unexplainable situations during my life, I already knew in my heart that there was much more to the meaning of life than anyone had ever taught me. It was an instinct that had developed from within my subconscious during my earliest childhood years and never left me. Consequently, I'd spent my life subconsciously searching for answers that I could never find, but all that was about to change significantly. My visit to the Light that night had intensified these underlying instincts and made them the essence of my every thought. I felt more convinced than ever that there was something spectacular waiting to be found and to be understood by all of us. My biggest obstacle back then was that I didn't have a clue what it was or where to start looking for it.

WHILE LIFE FOR the rest of the Deedy household got back to normal, my life would never be the same. I wasn't aware of its full impact at the time, but what had happened to me that night would have an ongoing and ever-increasing profound effect on my entire adult future. However, to put it into perspective, I need to return to the week that I first came into this world, and was greeted by another violent storm that almost took my life...

# Chapter 2

# THE BEGINNING

I was born in December 1946, at a private hospital in Punchbowl, a small village on the western outskirts of Sydney, Australia. My parents, Eddy and Vivian, and my six older siblings shared a small fibro cottage on the corner of Chiswick and Waterloo Roads, in the nearby suburb of East Bankstown. Just a few days later, on January 2$^{nd}$, 1947, and while I was in the hospital's small courtyard with several other newborns for some fresh air and sunshine, one of the region's worst-ever hailstorms erupted directly above the city and left thousands of people injured. More than 300 of the seriously injured were hospitalised, and many of them had fractured skulls. In those days, there were no satellite warning devices in existence, and storms often crept up out of the blue – literally! When the doctors and nurses rushed out and grabbed all the other babies, they were overwhelmed by the storm's fury, and accidentally overlooked me. My birth had been a difficult one – my mother was still feeling very weak and sore, and by the time that she'd realised and then struggled to get out to the courtyard to rescue me herself, a large clay tile from the hospital roof had already smashed across the foot of my bassinet, showering slivers of clay all over me – it was a miracle that I survived! During the ferocious storm, hunks of ice weighing up to 2.5 kilograms had crashed to the ground. The media stated that it was one of the worst hail storms to hit the area in recorded history.

It was shortly after the Second World War had ended and when Australia's CSIRO had picked up some of thc first radio waves from outer space, later found to be coming directly from the sun. The population of Australia was a mere 7.5 million people, and the basic wage was four pounds and eighteen shillings a week. Horse-drawn carts were still a common sight, and owning a telephone where we lived was almost as rare as owning a Rolls Royce, a very scarce and expensive luxury indeed. These were difficult times for many of the post-war parents, including mine. Nevertheless, my earliest memories are very vivid and happy ones. I'd been gifted with a photographic memory, and I can still clearly recall being spoilt and pampered, wheeled around in a cream cane pram, suckling on my mother's breasts and so much more. It had been a life of peaceful bliss until the time came to give up my beloved dummy (pacifier). I put up a hell of a fight to keep it until my brother-in-law, Herb, offered to buy it for two shillings and let me know how many chocolates I'd be able to buy. I've always had a love for horses, and I'm still fascinated by them, even though the thunderous noise of a herd of wild horses galloping towards our house each day never failed to terrify the life out of me, especially when they got too close. Yet despite this, I was drawn in by their beauty and strength. I especially loved watching them in their quieter times when they'd graze on the delicious long, green grass that grew outside of our front gate. I'd also sit for hours waiting impatiently for the baker, the milkman, ginger-beer man and the clothes-prop man to pass by with their horse and carts.

A far more dangerous obsession of mine was playing around with matches, and it was on one freezing winter's night that I almost burnt the house down. In a crazy attempt to warm up Mum's bedroom for her, I built a little fireplace and filled it with kindling wood before setting it alight. Thank goodness Mum smelt something burning just in time to put the fire out before there was any real damage. The only evidence that remained was a slight scorch mark on her carpet. Winters must have been long back then, or just plain dull. Early in the morning on another bitterly cold day, while I was searching through the kitchen cupboards to find some lollies that I knew Mum had hidden, I suddenly decided to create a very different kind of upheaval, when I noticed a tap dripping in the sink and decided to create my own little indoor beach. I climbed up on a chair, put the plug in the plughole, turned the tap on and just left the water running. In no time at all, I became mesmerised by the cascading water as my homemade waterfall flooded onto the kitchen floor. Everything was going great guns until I was jolted back to reality by a scream coming from Hazel, the wife of my brother George. She'd woken up and stepped straight into the icy-cold water which, by then, had spread throughout the whole house. Her terrified reaction woke the entire family up and a state of chaos and panic instantly erupted. It was all hands on deck as holes were drilled in the wooden floor to let some of the water out and floating mats and furniture were quickly salvaged or put on the higher ground to try to save them. No wonder I had the nickname 'little bugger of a kid?' Someone must have told me that tiny devils lived in our backyard toilet to keep me from using it as a cubby-house. Their method of persuasion not only failed dismally but had a reverse effect on me. While most other kids were busy trying to find fairies in their gardens, I was obsessed with searching for miniature devils in our dunny. What on earth was I thinking!? My infant years were full of loving attention from both my parents and other members of my family, I was spoilt rotten until shortly after my fifth birthday, when my younger brother, Billy, was born, and that's when my life was turned upside down. While Mum was away in the hospital giving birth, Fred, my eldest brother, and his wife, Edna, moved in temporarily to take care of things. Mum still hadn't enrolled me in school because she liked having me at home with her, but Edna soon brought a sudden end to all of that. On the very first day, she hastily enrolled me in the kindergarten at East Bankstown Primary School, and didn't I kick up a stink about it! I absolutely hated it and ran home several times in a row, only to be marched straight back each time by an increasingly pissed-off Edna. Many of the ladies in our village wore fancy hats and fox furs, especially to church on Sundays, which was my favourite day for being naughty and having fun. I must have been destined to be an animal rights campaigner before the term ever existed, as I used to hide behind a large pine tree that grew in our front yard and hose them down as they walked past our house. The sudden shock would usually make them splutter and scream, particularly if the water hit them square in the face and blasted their fancy hats off. Whenever that happened, it never failed to give me an enormous thrill, and I'd almost turn inside out with hysterical laughter. After Mum brought Billy home, I'd often climb the same pine tree and hide in it when it was time to go to school. Mum and other family members would gather at the foot of the tree and offer me different things to entice me down, and only if they offered chocolate would it become completely irresistible. Like most people's toilets back then, ours was way down the backyard, as sewerage pipes still hadn't been laid in many parts of Sydney. Once a week the *toilet men* would come in their big green truck that reeked of a mixture of phenyl and excrement to replace our and everybody else's black-tarred pan, and if the wind or a strong enough breeze happened to blow in my direction, I'd smell their truck coming from blocks away.

When I was five, I tripped on a damaged public footpath and broke my leg in three places. Following that, I spent several months stuck in Canterbury Hospital with my leg up in a sling', and then I had to learn to walk all over again. I was an overly energetic child by nature, and my incarceration was a torturous ordeal that often brought me to the point of screaming my lungs out. By the time I got back home, Billy was about six months old and had stolen most of my limelight in my absence. This caused me to become bitterly jealous, and I threw quite a few noisy tantrums over it before my father's firm hand brought it to an abrupt and painful ending. Mum took legal action over my injury and sued the Bankstown Council, winning a substantial settlement. Dad was against her doing it, but when she received the money, he immediately took control of it and investing it in his furniture factory for when I turned 21. During the months that followed, I faced far worse ordeals in my life, beginning with when I found our beautiful family dog, *Gunner,* lying dead at the side of our house, after being poisoned by a piece of baited meat. The ghastly sight of dried blood covered all over in ants and seeping from Gunner's mouth and nose was a horrific experience that's remained vivid in my memory ever since. I cried my eyes out for days afterwards because I didn't want to accept that Gunner couldn't be fixed and brought back to life. On another equally horrifying occasion, I was utterly devastated after watching my pet Joey kangaroo grow weak and die. Not long after that, a little lamb I was given to replace Joey was torn to pieces by neighbourhood dogs. I was the one who discovered his remains scattered all over our front lawn, and I almost screamed myself unconscious that day. I also had quite a fiery temper and was often stricken with prolonged, agonising headaches. My older brother, Denis, has since suggested that I may have suffered from Attention Deficit Hyperactivity Disorder, about which little was known at the time. I certainly got up to more than my fair share of mischief, so he's probably right. The buses to and from Bankstown that passed our house each hour looked like trucks and sounded like army tanks. You could hear one coming from blocks away, and they had an additive in their fuel that I must have been addicted to, and the moment I heard one coming, I'd drop everything and race frantically to the front fence as though my life depended on it, for a heavenly whiff of the fumes. Just thinking about it now still gives me an imaginary thrill – it was always such a mind-blowing experience. Then there was the scary old man that everyone referred to as 'German Dick'. He had a long fuzzy beard, always wore a big black overcoat and lived in a tiny shack hidden behind bushes further down Waterloo Road. I'd watch him coming along the footpath up until he reached a certain distance and then, in a state of panic, I'd run like mad into the house, usually in a flood of tears. Like with the horses, it was a bizarre love-hate ritual that I just couldn't resist. One day while I was watching him and had almost reached beyond the point of my ability to cope, he suddenly stopped, looked up at the sky and then collapsed backwards onto the footpath. German Dick was a very tall and solidly built man, and the sight of his large body crashing onto the ground and his head bouncing gave me such a fright that I was too afraid to venture back outside of the house alone for weeks. Sadly, I never saw poor old German Dick again after that, but my sister, Flo, has since told me that he survived and lived to see a few more years.

My earliest sexual experience of any kind took place when I was about four years old with a young woman that would sometimes babysit me while Mum was out shopping. She'd join me in some games with my toys, get me to brush her silky, long brown hair and then take me into my sister, Flo's, bedroom, where she'd lay on the bed with her legs apart while I played with her clitoris. Whenever I started to become bored, which was most of the time, she'd offer me more lollies, and like a monkey or a dog doing tricks, I'd happily keep going. All of these bizarre incidents had a penetrating effect on my early conceptions of life, but the worst of my problems started in 1954 when I was seven years old, and my parents' marriage came to an abrupt and traumatic ending. It happened after my father was caught having an affair with our new neighbour, Beatty, who was sixteen years his junior.

# Chapter 3

# GROWING UP

For me, the worst of the severe arguments between Mum and Dad started before Billy was born and got progressively worse after Beatty and her family moved into the house next door to us. However, my older siblings had since told me that they suffered them long before I was born. I could never understand what any of the arguments were about, and I dreaded the evenings when Dad would return home from work. He'd usually become violently abusive at the dinner table, and would often throw his meal across the room at Mum – the reason for which I've never been able to figure out, as Mum was an excellent cook. But even if she wasn't, no man has the right to treat his wife in such a disgusting and bullying way. Sometimes he'd hit Mum, and that would upset me so much that I'd run for my life in tears and hide under a bed with my older brother, Denis, where Dad's terrible shouting and screaming would have us both shuddering with fear. Our neighbours, Earnest and Beatty, had two daughters, Joy, who was about my age and Glynis, who was around the same age as Billy. Earnest spent a lot of time away working, and his daughters hardly ever got to see him. After school and at weekends, I'd spend hours playing *mothers and fathers* with Joy, in her little cubby-house that her Dad had built for her at the bottom of her yard. For some odd reason, whenever we played together, Joy always insisted on me being the mother and she the father. Sometimes, while we were down the yard playing in Joy's cubby-house, Dad would pop in and visit Beatty up in the main house, and if we ever tried to go into the house while Dad was there, Beatty would quickly stop us in our tracks, usher us out and order us to go back to the cubby-house and play. It was on a very cold and wet Saturday morning during the winter of 1954, that Earnest returned home to find his house empty and his wife, Beatty, living with her elder brother, Ron, down the far-end of Waterloo Road. It was also then when the gates of Hell burst open. I can still clearly recall overhearing Earnest telling Mum that Dad was having an affair with Beatty, and the horror that followed afterwards. Mum kept her raging anger undercover just long enough to convince Beatty to come out onto the front porch of her brother's house and speak with her. Then, as Billy and I watched in utter shock and terror, Mum exploded, thumping the living daylights out of Beatty and knocking her to the ground. Beatty's brother, Ron, tried to defend her, attacking Mum in the process, and Mum grabbed hold of him and shoved him up against the wall. I can still hear Beatty begging Mum not to hurt him because he had a metal plate in his skull. As Ron and his wife helped Beatty back into the house, Mum grabbed a hand full of slime from the gutter and threw it all over them, while calling Beatty a barrage of hateful names, including a *filthy gutter slut*. For me, it was another scary and very disturbing example of life on Earth.

During WW2, Mum had sold her grand piano to buy a car so that the family could use it to escape to the countryside if the Japanese army invaded Sydney. To add insult to injury, Mum had also found out that Dad was using the family car to take Beatty on secret dates, and as soon as we got back home, Mum not only threw Dad's belongings out onto the street but set fire to the car. Dad somehow managed to put the fire out just in time with his bare hands, which were severely burned in the process. It's another catastrophe from my childhood years that's lingered in the back of my mind ever since. There were also some zany moments back then, including when I stuck my finger into a fly-sprayer, and I couldn't get it back out. With the fly-sprayer hanging off my hand and me screaming my lungs out, Mum raced me all over the neighbourhood trying to get help, until eventually, some men at our local bus depot were able to file it off, but not without a barrage of high-pitched screams and a flood of tears from me. It taught a valuable lesson never to stick my fingers into strange holes. The next day, a Sydney newspaper printed a large cartoon about it.

MY THREE ELDEST siblings were married and in their own homes when Dad and Mum parted, and there were only my brothers, Denis and Billy, my sister, Flo, and myself still living at home. Flo must have been going through hormonal changes because she was forever pissed off about something or rather and snapping my head off. Having to deal with our family break up and my annoying behaviour at the same time had probably helped to push her to the edge. Denis, on the other hand, was old enough to escape from most of it and free to go off gallivanting around Bankstown with his mates to his heart's content. It was also common back then for siblings to share the same bathwater, and Denis, being the eldest, always had his bath before me. He loved playing battleships with little empty glass bottles that he'd float around in the water, and my favourite habit was propelling the water with my hands and making mountains of soapsuds. One night when I couldn't make enough suds and spotted a piece of string hanging from a tack on the wall, I decided to play a Tarzan game instead. I climbed up onto the edge of the bathtub, grabbed hold of the string, hollered out a loud Tarzan jungle cry and then went crashing down onto one of Denis's sunken battleships, cutting my bum open. That night as the local doctor stitched me up without any anaesthetic, I cursed Denis and bellowed out screams that are probably still hurtling through the cosmos. We had an old gramophone player and a collection of 78 RPM records with songs that I knew most of the lyrics to. My favourites were *Aba-Daba-Honeymoon; K-K-K-Katy; The Donkey Serenade;* and *Old Shep,* which reminded me of my dog Gunner and always brought tears to my eyes. My older cousin, Donny Boylan, was a famous singer at the time, and he'd made several records. Some of his fellow artists and many of his devoted fans considered him to be Australia's answer to Frank Sinatra. Just when he was about to head off to perform in the USA, a reporter caught him in bed with another woman, cheating on his wife. In those days adultery was a highly frowned upon crime, and after the incident became public, it brought a very hasty ending to Donny's career. I can still hear members of my family exclaiming that I was going to be another Donny when I grew up...

"You just wait 'n' see!" They'd tell each other repeatedly.

They were right about the singing side of their prediction but certainly not the women.

EVERY SECOND Sunday, Dad would take Billy and me for a little luncheon and a swim at Picnic Point, located on the George's River near Bankstown. We shared a lot of happy hours with him there, but sadly it nearly always ended up a miserable disaster. When we arrived back home, there'd often be a row between Dad and Mum and our day would be instantly ruined. Mum was building a new life for herself and had started dating other men, but I believe the main reason behind the rows was more about Dad not contributing enough towards our upkeep. I vividly recall a dreadful row one Christmas morning when Dad delivered a tiny box of food items for our Christmas dinner, Mum threw them all straight back at him and called him every nasty name that she could think of for the lousy bit of food that he'd provided. The next thing that I knew, my treasured black and white Cocker Spaniel dog ornament that I'd won at a local circus, went hurtling through the air, just missing Dad and then smashing to smithereens on the front porch – it almost broke my heart in two. At age eight, I joined forces with a local gang and spent a lot of my time helping them to build secret forts in the surrounding bushland, and if I wasn't doing that, I'd either be busy building cubby-houses down my backyard or collecting empty lemonade bottles from around the neighbourhood to sell back to the corner shop for the money that I needed to buy lollies. Another one of my favourite things that I loved doing was going to the local picture theatre in Punchbowl on Saturday afternoons to see the latest Cowboy and Indian or pirate movies. We'd line up for blocks sometimes waiting to get in, and then, as soon as our national anthem *God Save the Queen* was over, all the shouting, cheering, clapping and loud foot-stomping would commence as we responded excitedly to the main feature and all the crazy goings-on that it presented. Back then, Kids from broken homes were often highly frowned upon and treated as though they were contagious. Consequently, I spent a lot of my time playing alone after my parents separated, as most of the neighbourhood kids that lived close by weren't allowed anywhere near our house to play with me. It was also around this time that Rock 'n' Roll was having its significant initial effect throughout much of the world. In Australia, along with it came a whole new generation of devoted fans that called themselves *Bodgies* (boys) and *Widgies* (girls). While most of the Widgies wore their hair in a ponytail, with flared skirts or three-quarter-length pants (pedal pushers), many of the Bodgies wore thick grease in their hair, ripple sole shoes, tight-legged jeans and heaps of colourful badges pinned to their caps and jackets. Denis was one of them and also starting to chase after girls – something that I just couldn't make heads or tails of. The first confrontation that I had with members of the Bodgie and Widgie generation happened one day when my sister, Flo, and I were travelling back home from the Sydney CBD on a train, after seeing the original version of the film *The Blue Lagoon*. Our carriage was bursting with noisy Bill Hayley fans after they'd been to see his new movie *Rock Around the Clock*. I was still too young to understand that what I was witnessing was the beginning of one of the most powerful impressions of modern life that humankind had ever known. At around the same time, things in our house were changing by the day, Mum was rarely ever at home anymore, and when she was, there were lots of her new-found friends constantly popping in and out. To escape from the boredom of all of the adult talk, I'd spend entire days roaming up and down the narrow concrete canal system that stretched out for miles, around Bankstown and its surrounding area. I had my own little world down there, and if I wasn't there, I'd be off hiding out with fellow gang members in one of the secret forts that we'd built in the bush area, where we'd wait to attack the members of other gangs as they passed by, who were mainly made up of Italian, Maltese, German and Greek boys who'd not long immigrated to Australia. As much as I'm ashamed to admit it now, motivated by our self-centred ignorance and prejudice, we home-born Aussies were sometimes very cruel and nasty towards these *wogs*, *dagos* and *new Australians*, as we so rudely called them, and participated in a lot of dangerous *Shanghai* (sling-shot) fights with them. Many of the UK immigrants were forever running Australia down for lagging so far behind the times, and their constant comparisons and negative complaining not only did damage to our self-esteem but rightly earned them the reputation of being *whingeing poms*. Be that as it may, most of my closest friends throughout my childhood were whingeing poms.

I'm not sure of how it all came about, but Mum acquired ownership of a small ice cream-come fruit and vegetable shop on Rawson Road, near where we lived. She also later opened a second-hand furniture shop in Bankstown proper. From some of the profits that she made, she was able to give my sister, Flo, and her fiancé, John, a nice wedding and a substantial deposit on a block of land for a wedding present. During this same prosperous period, our small, fibro Housing Commission house became one of the best-furnished and up-to-date homes in the district. Along with a plush, new, silver-grey carpet throughout the house, red velvet curtains and a matching lounge, we had a brand-new Pianola and were also one of the first in the neighbourhood to own a state-of-the-art stereo-radiogram (record player). At around the same time, Mum bought a small beach cottage at Kurnel, located on the southern side of Botany Bay and just across a park from where Captain Cook first set foot on Australian soil in 1770 and officially stole the country from its rightful owners. Unlike today, back then, the water in the bay was crystal-clear, and much of the surrounding landscape still looked like it had done for thousands of years. I loved being there, especially swimming beneath the waves among the abundance of colourful fish. I remember with love and affection how my favourite Aunt, Madge, had spent an entire afternoon there searching the beachfront for me – her hollowing, squeaky voice in the distance sounded hilarious. When she finally caught up with me and scolded me for not coming home when I should have, declaring in a huff that she'd been forced to officially request all the mermaids to search Botany Bay for me, it tickled me to the point where I laughed so hard that I almost fainted.

MUM DEVELOPED a gambling addiction which got way out of control and soon brought a whole new level of despair and misery to our lives. Every Saturday there'd be a horse-race commentator's voice blaring out from our radio, and the horses that won or lost would usually determine what the rest of the weekend and the following week would turn out to be like. I still can't listen to a horse-race commentary without cringing and falling into a mood variation. Aunt Madge would sometimes rescue me and take me home to her place to spend a few days with her and her family, where I'd watch Charlie Chaplin black and white silent movies, go picnicking at the beach with my cousins, Shirley and Maxi or spend a great day at the zoo, which was always such a fresh experience of normality. After WW2 finished, while my uncle Jack served as a member of the Australian Occupational Forces, Aunt Madge and my cousins lived in Japan for a year. Upon their return, they brought back heaps of Japanese dolls and various ornaments, and the one thing that interested me the most, and always caught my undivided attention, was a large painting of Mount Fuji that hung on Aunt Madge's living room wall. It was like a magnet drawing me to it, and I must have spent hours staring at it. Looking back now, I can't help but wonder if I may have even sensed something relating to my far distant past. Sadly, Mum was eventually forced to sell our beach cottage due to her gambling, and I was shattered. However, because the government was the owner of the land that it stood on at Kurnel, it would have happened whether or not Mum had gambled. Soon afterwards, all the other cottage owners were forced to sell up and leave to make way for progress. Oh, how I'd love to go back in time and re-live some of those unique adventures and beautiful, happy moments of my childhood there again.

e Company, 47 Allingham Street, Bankstown, N.S.W. 2200

970 Registered under the Newspaper Act, 1898. Gratis

# Pop singer struck by lightning

**Rubber shoes almost certainly saved the life of an East Hills "pop" singer when he was struck by lightning during the height of a violent thunderstorm last week.**

Thomas Bird, 21, an EMI recording artist, television and club singer known professionally as Tommy Beaumont, of Matthews Avenue, East Hill was sitting on a large radiator, when lightning struck a cable outside the house.

The lightning bolt shattered light globes in the adjoining house, came up through the radiator and hurled him 10 or 11 feet across the room.

It paralised half his face, deadened one ear drum and left him semi-conscious on the floor alone in the house except for a small French poodle.

Tommy said he was apparently in a dazed delirium but after a while must have got to his feet for he later recalled searching for an opening to escape from the room.

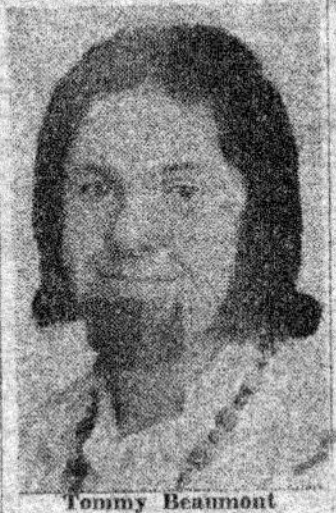

Tommy Beaumont

## Hotel

Afterwards he discovered a hole in the wall near the door where he evidently had tried to barge through.

On hearing the terrific [illegible] local doctor he was taken to Bankstown hospital by ambulance.

Both the doctor and the ambulance attendants said he survived the lightning strike by a million to one chance.

He was saved because he was wearing rubber scuffs at the time.

Next day Tommy had to cancel his appearance in a Melbourne television show, his doctor had advised against travel while he was still suffering pain from a severely bruised eardrum.

Another fortunate circumstance saved the outcome from being more serious.

But for the quick arrival on the scene by neighbours the house could have been burned down. On entering they found Tommy practically collapsed on the floor near the entrance to the kitchen with the radiator face-down on the floor still burning.

## Flashback

Tommy, now recovering from the ordeal and shock has a strong sense of humour and recounted a comical 'flash-back' when the lightning struck.

"As I was hurled up into the air, I saw the reaction of the French poodle alongside me.

"Poodles have long droopy ears, and curly hair, but I vividly recall seeing the dog with his ears pointing to the ceiling, and his hair bristling straight up like one sees in a cartoon," Tommy said.

*Oh, such stormy weather.*

NET SALES *Exceed* 155,000 DAILY

FORECAST: SCATTERED SHOWERS.

# The Courier-Mail

'Phone B0111. BRISBANE, THURSDAY, JANUARY 2, 1947. (Registered in Australia for Transmission by Post as a Newspaper.)

# 300 PEOPLE WOUNDED AS HAIL STORM HITS SYDNEY

**SYDNEY, Wednesday.—More than 300 people were wounded when Sydney was lashed by a violent barrage of large hail for 10 minutes about 2.30 this afternoon. Hundreds of others did not seek aid for minor injuries.**

*Bigger than cricket balls, with sharp, jagged edges, some pieces of hail measured more than seven inches across.*

**Many injuries were caused by flying glass and broken tiles which were ripped from the roofs of houses.**

Several people had their skulls fractured by the weight of the hail. As victims were rushed to hospitals some emergency wards were crowded with people awaiting attention.

To-night it was estimated that the storm has caused £250,000 worth of damage to property in the Eastern Suburbs.

Thousands of homes, flats, and shops were battered as the hail, followed by torrential rain, broke tiles, flattened gardens, and lopped branches from trees.

## Shower Of Glass

**A cordon of 30 police had to surround part of Central Station when a skylight covering the entire assembly platform was shattered.**

Jagged glass showered down among a crowd of 100 people, but no one was hurt.

Rain was heavier in some suburbs than others, but at Surry Hills cars were under water almost to their bonnets.

The storm delayed the start of the Australian 12ft. skiff championship, and dismasted the Queensland entrant, Renaissance, which took no part in the race.

The Queensland skiff Resolve, after finishing third in the race, was overturned by the strong wind.

The crew was rescued by the water police.

## Traffic Stops

City traffic came to a standstill during the worst of the hail. Passengers in trams huddled together as many women and children became almost hysterical at the ferocity of the storm. Trains also were delayed.

The city streets were white as the hail piled up.

"Storm damage priority"—the highest possible—will be given by the State Government to materials required for repairs. Tiles and glass, and labour to fix them, are very scarce.

# Gale Barrage Cost £250,000

## *Cyclone Whips Up Big Seas*

ROUGH seas and winds of gale force are being whipped up by a cyclone operating off the far north coast.

A special weather bureau storm warning has been broadcast to ships, giving details of the disturbance.

The cyclone, the first of the season, is operating [illegible] miles east-south-east of Willis Island. It is causing disturbances within [illegible] miles radius of its centre.

The Weather Bureau reported

## Panic On Beach

**More than 50,000 people at Bondi Beac[h] were caught by the full force of the storm.**

There was panic as bathers raced out of the surf to dodge the driving hail.

Three ambulance loads of surfers were taken to hospitals within half an hour, and others followed. Most of the injured suffered [illegible] and back wounds, and severe [illegible] Bondi police station became a casualty clearing station. [illegible] than 1000 people sought

## Stunned In Surf

Hundreds collapsed on the edge of the water and on the beach. Twenty injured people, including four serious cases were admitted to hospital.

Many people had to be rescued from the surf after having been stunned at Bondi and at other beaches.

Edna Menzies, 15, of Randwick, a niece of the Federal Opposition Leader (Mr. Menzies) was knocked unconscious at Coogee, where

The storm, one of the worst e[x]perienced in Sydney, whipped from the sea and drove throu[gh] a central belt of suburbs. Northe[rn] areas and suburbs south of M[a]roubra escaped.

Residents in suburbs in the pa[th] of the storm could hear the ro[ar] of the belting hail for nearly fi[ve] minutes before the storm reach[ed] them.

In most places the hail barra[ge] lasted only about 10 minutes, a[nd] was followed by rain, which clear[ed] away quickly.

The New South Wales vers[us] Queensland Sheffield Shi[eld] cricket match at the Sydn[ey] Cricket Ground, and many oth[er] New Year's Day sporting fixtu[res] had to be abandoned about 2 p.m.

The Tasman flying-boat fr[om] New Zealand arrived during t[he] storm, but climbed out of its pa[th] and circled the city until t[he] weather settled.

A number of planes at Masc[ot] were forced down and damaged

Mum and me (3 weeks old).

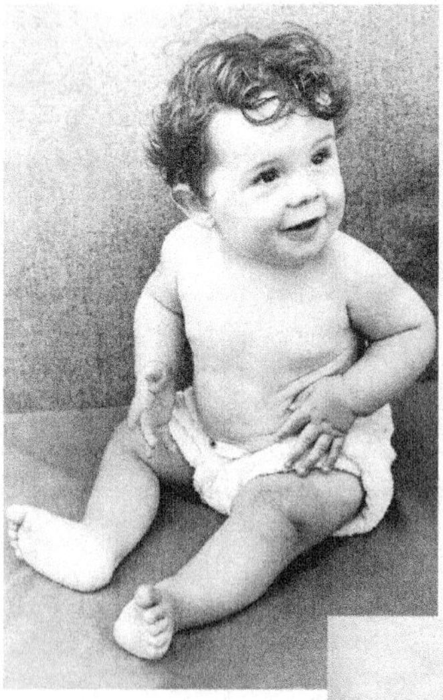

*My infant years.*

. . .

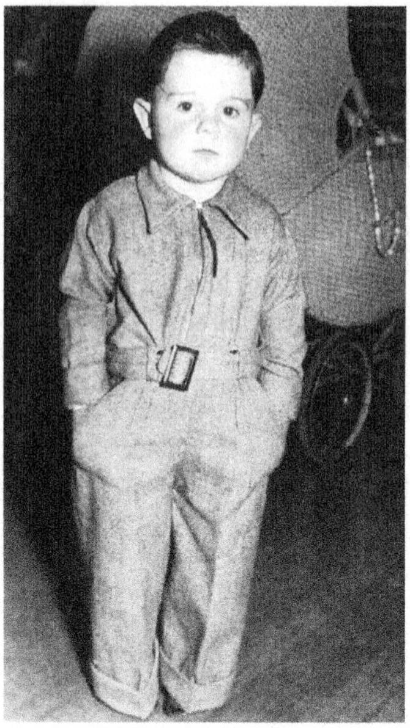

*Billy and me having a race.*

# Chapter 4

# RADICAL CHANGES

So many things were changing in my life, including the suburb of East Bankstown, which was renamed Greenacre. Things changed even more dramatically when the newly-built Greenacre Hotel opened – so much so that nothing in our friendly little suburb was ever quite the same again. Not only were drunks wobbling around and mumbling meaninglessly to themselves, and falling asleep along public footpaths, often with half-empty beer bottles in their hands. Each night, a lot of us neighbourhood kids would gather outside the hotel's beer garden, and watch through the large windows as our parents and other local adults had fun dancing and getting intoxicated. My brother, Denis, would sometimes be there singing and rocking up a storm, in his Presley-purple jacket and *rockabilly-ducks-arse* hairdo. I reckon he must have gone through a jar of thick *Spruso* hair grease a week keeping that thing in place and under control. The horse-drawn carts were disappearing fast, and being replaced by streamlined cars, including America's Ford Customlines and our own F.J.Holdens, making Waterloo Road more dangerous by the day to cross. One night Mum sent me across the road to her friend, Mrs Russell's, place to borrow a cup of sugar and my beautiful collie dog, Lassie, was hit and killed by a Ford Customline right in front of me. When I spotted the car's bright lights speeding towards us, I called out to Lassie to stay put, but she must have thought that I was calling her to come to me. There was a sudden loud thump and, then, almost as if in slow motion, I saw Lassie's body hurtle high up into the air and come crashing down with a crunch at my feet. As my beautiful Lassie looked up at me with tear-filled eyes and then died, I almost went out of my mind. It was another painful and sad lesson in life, and it took a very long time to get over it. In my class at school, there were twin brothers that I felt helplessly drawn toward. So much so, that I'd often hang around the street where they lived for hours, hoping that one of them would come out and play with me. I was only eight years old at the time, but that didn't stop me from fantasising about being kissed by them or cuddling up in their arms. I also felt attracted in this way to several of the other boys at school, yet I can't recall ever having the same sort of fantasies or feelings towards any of the girls. An older man that babysat Billy and I would sometimes get us to play with his penis. Billy was never interested, but I was utterly intrigued by the man's mass of thick pubic hair and how his penis would grow larger whenever I touched it or gently combed it. Perhaps it was this that stirred up my interest in other older men, as I can clearly remember following some of them along public footpaths and wondering what their penises and pubes might look like. In contrast, I was never curious about women's vaginas, even though I'd so often been paid in sweets to fondle one. There was an older neighbourhood boy who'd sometimes take me into the bushes after school and get me to play with his penis. I enjoyed doing it until the day that he tried to penetrate me with it. I let out such a scream of horror from the pain that he never came anywhere near me again after that. I also often played a game called doctors and nurses with my best mate Terry Kemp. We were still way too young to know anything about the delights of sex, and it was just touching each other and fumbling around, but even so, it was still an infatuation that I eagerly looked forward to whenever we were at home alone together – it was never anything other than two kids experimenting with the natural feelings and desires that they'd been born to express.

AFTER MUM LOST or sold almost everything that we owned owing to her reckless gambling, she fled our family home and took Billy and me with her into hiding. We were very poor and moved into a small, rented, disused soap factory in the outer western Sydney suburb of Riverstone. The surrounding area was rich farmland, and the scenery was breathtaking, but the ever-present smell of blood and flesh that came from a nearby abattoir constantly made me feel like I wanted to puke. To help make ends meet, Mum made paper flowers, which was a popular new trend at the time, and I went around selling them after school to the local farmers. If I'd been lucky and had sold enough by the weekend, Mum would give us a treat by taking us to see a movie at the local picture theatre and buying us our favourite ice creams. It might not sound much by today's standards, but for us back then it was an exciting event that still remains among some of my fondest memories. It was also during the same period that the world was entering the space age, and I can clearly remember the historical sight of the neighbours coming out onto the street each night to get a glimpse of Russia's Sputnik, the first module to reach space. Even though it was a tiny dot in the night sky, it was still a fascinating experience for everyone to witness as it whizzed by. At the Catholic school that I attended in Riverstone, I was the local poor boy accepted into the convent without charge. Unable to afford the cost of a proper school uniform and no longer being in possession of her sewing machine, Mum sat for hours on end sewing me one by hand. We may have had very little compared with everybody else around us, but we were abundantly wealthy with love, and I cherished that uniform and wore it with enormous pride. It wasn't long after we'd moved to Riverstone that Terry's mother, Mrs Kemp, was shot to death by the sixteen-year-old son of her next-door neighbour. The boy, who was part of an immigrant family, had waited in a local telephone booth on the corner of Rawson and Waterloo Roads in Greenacre, and his deadly plan was to shoot the first person that walked by. He later confessed to the police that he'd seen people killed in the movies, and wanted to experience what it was like in real life. After a long wait without any passersby, Waterloo Road filled up with the bumper-to-bumper traffic as cars exited the nearby Chullora Twin Drive-in. Abandoning his initial plan, the young would-be killer took the gun home and shot his mother dead in her bedroom, then went next door and shot Mrs Kemp in the head, before pushing her down her back steps. Terry tripped over his mother's bleeding body on their footpath as he was returning home from the movies. I visited Terry several years later, and his father was still caring for him – watching my best mate stare at the wall as though I wasn't even there, was a truly heartbreaking experience. Terry had never recovered from the shock of finding his murdered mother the way that he did.

TELEVISION first commenced transmission in Australia during 1956 – the same year that the Olympic Games were held in Melbourne. Many of the local farmers had bought TV sets to watch it, but for us, having a TV was still only a pipe dream until some of the shops started offering one-week free trials. Mum, being the creative and adaptable woman that she was, managed to keep us entertained with a selection of TVs for months. After she'd been through all the shops in the area offering the free trials, she dyed her hair from black to blonde, changed her name and then started all over again. Back then television was only in black and white, but even so, for me, it was pure magic, and such an enormous improvement from sitting for hours staring into a dial and listening to serials on the radio. By the time that the shop-owners woke up and got wise to Mum's little scam, we must have sampled just about every shape and size TV that was available. One day Mum won some money on a horse race and was able to buy me a proper school uniform to wear, and I was ecstatic! It was a freezing winter's morning when she rugged Billy and me up to the hilt and took us on our local steam train to Windsor, the nearest major shopping centre. When the saleslady handed Mum the bag with my brand new, authentic school uniform in it, I felt like all my Christmases had come at once. I barely slept a wink that night from excitement and the thought of proudly showing off the uniform at school, it felt like it used to feel when I was little on Christmas Eve, but when I wore it the next morning, and nobody seemed to even notice, it was a massive disappointment to me. But I was wrong, as it actually had been noticed. During the lunch break, some of the bigger kids gathered around me and proceeded to tear my new uniform to shreds on my back. It all happened so fast that it took my breath away. My first thoughts were how to tell Mum and how much it was it going to hurt her. When the Mother Superior marched swiftly across the schoolyard towards me and then scolded me for causing the fight, I was still feeling stunned and struggling to take in what had just happened. The moment she turned around to leave, I exploded with rage and started smashing the classroom windows with rocks, as I screamed out abuse at everyone in sight, including the cranky, old Mother Superior. The nuns had already ordered most of the other kids into the classrooms to hide from me and that made me even madder. I continued chucking more rocks and abusing everyone until I eventually ran out of steam and collapsed onto the muddy ground, sobbing uncontrollably. Sometime after that, a policeman arrived, lifted me into the sidecar of his motorbike and took me home to Mum. A lot of the other kids were from wealthy homes, and their parents gave substantial financial support to the convent and the adjoining Catholic Church. Those who'd attacked me lied through their teeth and left me to take the full blame for it all. The policeman had asked to hear my side of the story, but my head was aching so badly that I could hardly speak, let alone defend myself and give him a detailed account of the truth. Mum didn't know what to do, so she called my eldest brother, Fred, and asked for his help. Fred had never been the least bit interested in me and chose not to get involved, phoning our Dad and telling him about it instead. Dad arrived an hour or so later and took me to live with him, Beatty and Glynis.

Ever since my parents had split up, Mum had been ear-bashing me about her hatred of Beatty and Dad, which had only helped to create a monster within me, and I think I ended up hating Beatty more than Mum did. Consequently, I objected to Dad and Beatty's relationship in any way that I could throughout most of my childhood. In doing so, I got myself into some perilous situations that always brought about violent and painful repercussions. I was definitely out of control and in need of some strong discipline, but what I went on to endure in Dad and Beatty's care reached so far beyond the codes of discipline that, nowadays, it would be considered severe child abuse. Be that as it may, it was play-school, compared to what was waiting for me up ahead...

# Chapter 5

# HOUSE OF TORTURE!

The isolated homesteader that Dad and Beatty bought for their secret love nest in the upmarket North Sydney suburb of Frenchs Forest soon became a house of torture and horror for me. On the very first night that I spent there, I felt as though my heart and soul were being ripped out, especially when I witnessed Dad kissing Beatty passionately. It was something that I'd never seen him do before, not even with Mum. As I was struggling to hold back my tears and take it all in, and Dad caught me staring at him and Beatty, he became enraged, yanking me by my arm and dragging me into a scarcely furnished bedroom to ponder alone in the darkness. Dad had changed so much that he seemed more like a stranger to me – bewitched by Beatty, who was already making plans in the back of her mind to turn me into her servant. While I sat in the darkness and tried to come to terms with the upheaval in my life, I soon fell into a state of depression. By the next morning, my depression had turned into immense hatred and anger, and regardless of what it took, I intended to do everything that I could to get Dad away from Beatty and back home with Mum, where I believed that he belonged. Beatty, on the other hand, must have sensed my intentions because she became just as determined to make sure that I didn't succeed.

Back in those days, a couple living together out of wedlock was highly frowned upon and condemned, especially if either of them was someone else's husband or wife, which was considered to be an unforgivable sin or a punishable crime. I was under strict instructions not to say a word to anyone about their 'den of iniquity', and to make sure that I kept my mouth shut, I wasn't permitted to play after school with any neighbourhood kids. Instead, I was forced to chop wood each night until it got dark and then do homework. I was also forbidden from going on any school excursions, and sometimes I even had to ask for Beatty's permission to use the toilet. I'd have probably have been kept away from school altogether if it hadn't been compulsory. Consequently, I spent most of my time alone, chopping wood under a willow tree at the back of the house, scrubbing floors, washing, ironing, cleaning the yard or doing the shopping. Those constant and prolonged hours of loneliness and isolation almost drove me nuts and hearing the distant laughter of other kids playing with Glynis was torturous. When Dad and Beatty needed to go out, I'd sometimes be left at home in the care of the Lovelace family, who rented a self-contained flat at the end of our house. They had a teenage daughter named Dawn, who was a Country and Western singer, and a very close friend of Australian Country Music singing sensation at the time, Frank Ifield, who often popped in to see her. The Lovelaces were a warm and loving modern Aussie family who shared a life that seemed like another world compared to how I was being forced to live a short distance away. The rare and happy occasions that I was lucky enough to spend time with them always lifted my spirits no end. They had a TV set and sometimes when Dad and Beatty were late getting back home, I'd get to watch Australia's number one variety show, *In Melbourne Tonight* with Graham Kennedy and Bert Newton. Being with the Lovelaces felt like I'd escaped into another dimension and I hated having to leave. When they eventually bought a house of their own and moved away, I was silently shattered. It left me with nothing better to look forward to than even more violent beatings, wood-chopping, shopping and tedious floor scrubbing. Beatty was fanatically old-fashioned and ridiculously strict about it, and dragged me back into her time warp in every way that she could, including forcing me to dress in her adult brother's old woollen hand-me-downs that I hated. Not only did they make me itch all day because of my allergy to wool, but they also didn't fit properly, making me the laughing stock of the school. Beatty was a cold-hearted perpetual bully and excessively unkind to me. It was even worse after the Lovelace family had left, especially when Dad wasn't around. As part of my revenge to get back at Beatty, I'd tell her lies that would usually send her into a spin of worry and unease. During my many moments of provoked madness, I stumbled across a particular strategy that never failed to serve my needs, which not only ruined Beatty's day but allowed me to steal a few hours of peace for myself when Beatty was having a nap due to one of her every-other-day migraines. I'd wake her up with a tall tale that I'd just spotted Mum creeping around in the backyard, and that would have Beatty jumping up in a panic and racing around the house to make sure that all the doors and windows were locked, as she was scared stiff of Mum. After that, we'd wait in silence for a knock on the door, and even though one never came, Beatty would remain nice to me throughout the rest of the day, in case Mum was listening in on her. The only other times that Beatty ever acted nicely towards me were on the rare occasions that any of my siblings or relatives visited the house. Whenever that happened, she'd go overboard to create the false impression that I was being well-treated, and tricking them into thinking that any problems were my fault alone, which worked, as none of them once bothered to ask me why I was so unhappy. I was no little angel, but I was nowhere near as bad as Beatty deliberately made me out to be. Sadly my siblings and other relatives lacked the sensitivity, awareness and empathy to detect what was really going on. Either that or they didn't care, but to give them the benefit of the doubt, back then people weren't as aware of what is considered today to be child abuse.

As the years went by and my segregation from other kids continued, I started inventing much wilder stories about being shot at by men in passing cars. By then I was starving for attention and recognition, and willing to do just about anything to achieve it. Sometimes the pressure from my solitude would reach a desperation point, and without any thought or consideration of the outcome or consequences, I'd snap up just about any opportunity that presented itself. For example, when two hardened criminals named Simmonds and Newcombe escaped from prison and were believed to be hiding in our neighbourhood, I wasted no time in seizing my chance to rouse the rabble. Everyone in the area was fearful and paranoid, so, using a public phone booth near my school to call the police, I made up a story that I'd just seen the escapees dragging a woman into the bushland close to my house. Within minutes, an army of police and reporters were on my street, and the thought of Beatty being alone in the house and scared out of her wits gave me such a buzz that I was almost levitating from the excitement and joy. However, there was always a price to pay for my disruptive, troublesome antics, without exception, and whenever anything I did upset Beatty or Dad or I showed any sign of defiance, Dad would take me into a spare room and hold me down while Beatty whipped me with a thick willow branch. This time I'd upset them so much that I almost got beaten into a state of unconsciousness. It sickens me now to even think about it, and I'll never understand how they got away with it. I'm sure the neighbours would have heard my howling screams but they did nothing. There were also plenty of other times when Dad would lose his temper and beat me around the floor all over the house, as I tried desperately to escape from him. Like Beatty, he was a cruel and heartless bully and a dangerously violent man, especially with me, the seriously confused, out-of-control kid on a hell-bent mission to reunite his parents. Unlike what I'd witnessed many times with Mum, I never even once heard Dad raise his voice to Beatty, let alone his hand. If any so-called 'happy' moments for me had ever included Beatty, they must have been so few and minimal that they're not even memorable. Praise or encouragement from her to me was non-existent unless it was to show herself off in good light for the benefit of a visiting relative. For most of the time, I felt so nervous and on edge that I was too afraid to open my mouth in fear of saying something wrong and having to pay for it with another ferocious back-hander or beating from Dad. Beatty never failed to report every single thing to him, and always added more to it to make it sound worse.

I'd not seen Mum for almost two years, and I was constantly fretting and worrying about her. Beatty must have sensed it one night while I was drying the dishes, and repeatedly kept trying to force me into agreeing with her that Mum was no good. Her nagging words felt like a knife twisting into a wound, and when I stood my ground and argued in defense of my mother, berating Beatty rigorously, Dad overheard the racket and came rushing into the kitchen, abruptly demanding to know what was going on. Before I could open my mouth to say a word, Beatty cut in and lied through her teeth that I was throwing a tantrum about my mother.

**"BANG!!!!!"**

Without any warning, Dad's fist pounded my head into the internal weatherboard wall and sent me crashing to the floor. The last thing that I can remember seeing is stars, and I think I must have passed out after that. Sometimes, during the school holidays, Dad would take me with him to his furniture factory in Artarmon for the day to give Beatty a break, but as dull as it always was at his workplace, I regarded it as me getting some much needed and welcomed relief. My two elder brothers, Fred and George, worked at Dad's company, and one day I overheard Fred telling Dad that Mum had gone on a holiday with my sister, Flo, and her husband to The Entrance, a popular beach resort on the NSW Central Coast. Instead of doing the shopping for Beatty the next day, I used the shopping money to catch a bus and train to The Entrance and took my dog, *Tinka,* with me. It was a harrowing journey, and many daunting thoughts filled my head, creating painful waves of fear of what my father would do when he eventually caught up and got his hands on me. By the time I arrived at The Entrance, I was shaking in my shoes, but the excitement and expectation of seeing Mum again after such a long time soon outshone my fears. I expected to find Mum straight away, but that didn't happen. After roaming the streets with Tinka trailing behind me for two long days, I ran out of money to buy food and was feeling miserable, disappointed, alone and very hungry. Before every corner that I turned, I'd imagine that Mum and Flo would be waiting to welcome me with wide-open arms. There aren't any words to describe the sadness that I felt each time it didn't eventuate. Seeing and listening to other 'normal', happy families enjoying each other's company, made me feel even worse. I was a prisoner of my own dismal circumstances, looking out from my cage of fear at a freer and far happier world that I so desperately wanted to join. While I continued searching the beach-front, a circus couple noticed me and took pity on me, inviting me to join them in their caravan for a meal, and allowing me to sleep on their couch for a couple of nights. Unbeknownst to me, a missing person's alert had been sent out, asking the police around Australia to keep a lookout for me. I was absolutely horrified early one morning when I opened my eyes to the sight of Dad and Beatty staring down at me, so much so that I lost control and wet myself. They'd come up from Sydney to collect me, and the furious and hateful anger glaring out from Dad's eyes said it all. How they discovered where I was is still a mystery. Beatty was more concerned and upset about Tinka than she was about me, even though he was my dog that I'd brought with me from Riverstone. She'd since claimed him as hers, and I despised her for that as well. She and Dad spent that night in a comfortable motel, while I was spent the night next door to several foul-mouthed drunkards and criminals in a police station cell after dad had asked the officer on duty to lock me up for the night. It was a disgusting and irresponsible thing for any cop to agree to, let alone for a parent to request. I'd run away many times and had always been found, dragged back home and beaten senseless. One of those horrific outcomes happened on a bitterly cold winter's night after I'd hidden between some rocks in the bushes for several hours, begging God to let me die. By the time that I'd come to terms with my prayer going unanswered, it was pitch-black dark, the middle of the night and so cold that my teeth were aching from chattering. The police eventually found me wandering along a dirt track and took me home, and as soon as they left, I got one of the worst thrashings ever, but it was nothing compared with the walloping I copped when Beatty and Dad got me back home from to Sydney. It was years later, that I finally found out why I hadn't been able to find Mum and Flo at the Entrance – the holiday that Fred mentioned to dad had taken place three months earlier.

The laundry and toilet were in a separate weatherboard shed behind the house, and just across from where I chopped all the wood. The bathroom was opposite and up higher than the laundry at the far end of the back veranda. Some of the wood that I cut was for heating the wood-burning copper that Beatty used for doing the washing. One day, I became so frustrated, bored and fed up with my monotonous daily routine, that I used some of the wood to set fire to the laundry and toilet. Once I had the wall alight, I raced upstairs to the bathroom and locked myself inside, then waited for the larger flames to appear. It was an act of insanity, I admit, but even though I'd always end up paying a severely painful price for any of my antics, I still couldn't resist a chance to retaliate for my miserable existence. By then, I'd developed a mental state that was almost completely out of my control, and my state of mind was similar to how an animal mind must be locked inside a box for an extended period of time and regularly tortured and beaten until eventually it goes nuts and retaliates. As I was watching through the frosted glass window, large orange and red flames flared up and began reaching across to the back wall of the house. Before I could think anymore about it, Beatty arrived outside the bathroom, and started banging on the bathroom door, ordering me to unlock it and to let her in, as she screamed and panicked about losing the house, I stood my ground and refused to budge. Fortunately, the fire brigade arrived in time to extinguish the fire before it could spread beyond the laundry.

After the fury within me had subsided enough, I suddenly thought about what would happen to me when Dad got home, and a massive surge of fear caused me to throw up. Minutes later, I heard Dad's voice, and almost fainted. Beatty remained adamant that I'd deliberately started the fire and repeatedly blamed me for it, but Dad refused to believe it. It was the only time that I can recall him ever standing up for me against Beatty, but even so, the battle was far from over – more evil ideas fuelled by fear, vengeance and frustration were already brewing in the back of my mind...

## Chapter 6

# INTO AN EVEN BIGGER FIRE

Mum had barely enough money to get by on, while Dad had plenty, and he used it along with his influence to gain full custody of my younger brother, Billy, who was only six years old at the time. I can still remember how sad I felt on that dreadful day when Billy arrived at the Frenchs Forest house. Mum had made me one of my favourites, an apple pie, but before Billy could hand it to me, Beatty snatched the bag from him and threw it in the bin, and if I'd been big enough to do it, I'm sure that would have slapped her down. On the weekend before the court hearing, Dad ordered me to pack my few belongings into a box and to wait for him in the car. His plan was to give me back to Mum's so that I'd be out of the house by the time that Billy arrived. I was ecstatic, 'soon I'll be free', I kept thinking to myself, but as we neared Mum's place, Dad had a sudden change of heart and stopped the car. He then started yelling at me aggressively, and warning me that he wasn't going to let me ruin his chances. Before I knew it, I was back at Frenchs Forest! He must have realised that by giving me back to Mum it wouldn't look too good in the eyes of the judge. A few days later, when Mum phoned me at my school to see how I was going, I relayed to her what had happened. Her solicitor then reported what I'd told her during the hearing, but Dad adamantly denied every word of it. That night when Dad and Beatty returned home, they thrashed me to within an inch of my life, and the next day Dad instructed the school that under no circumstances was I to be allowed to accept another phone call from anyone.

The court decision a week later to grant Dad and Beatty custody of Billy broke Mum's and Billy's heart. Billy was happy living with Mum and didn't want to leave her, and if the court had been aware of the bullying and violent abuse that I was being subjected to on a daily basis under Dad and Beatty's care, Dad would have lost the custody case. After Billy came to live with us, Dad and Beatty kept us apart and soon turned Billy against me by telling him lies and making me out to be someone to fear. Before that, Billy and I had been closer than any other two other siblings in our family. Billy was around the same age as Beatty's daughter, Glynis, and much easier to control than I was, and having my little brother's love and affection stolen from me was more painful than all of the thrashings that I'd endured put together. The Frenchs Forest house had five large bedrooms, and to keep me permanently away from Billy as much as possible, I was forced to sleep out on the open back veranda where the cold winter frosts would settle on my blankets On the terrible nights when the wind-driven heavy rain would lash across onto the veranda and soak through my bedding, I'd wake up drenched, cold and shivering. On good nights, I spent many lonely hours in that bed, drifting off to sleep on a sea of fantasies about Ian, an older boy at my school that I was in awe of. I'd usually follow him around the playground during the lunch hour, and keep just close enough to see what he got up to at all times. I didn't understand what I was feeling then, but it's clear to me now that I was physically attracted to him. Sometimes my fantasies about him at night were so hot, that it's a wonder my bed didn't go up in flames. On other nights, while most of my male school friends were going off to sleep fantasising about members of the girls in the TV show, *The Mickey Mouse Club*, particularly Annette Funicello, my bedtime fantasies were about a Mouseketeer by the name of Tommy. I'd be naked, defenceless and in some sort of trouble and Tommy would become my hero by rescuing me. He'd usually wrap me in a blanket, shower me with tenderness and affection and then whisk me away to a safer and much happier place. There was never any imaginary sex involved, as I still didn't know what that was, just some happy, romantic and sensual love thoughts. I think that my nakedness was more symbolic of my defencelessness and vulnerability at the time. Those beautiful, uplifting bedtime fantasies were my only source of love and affection and the attention that I was so desperately yearning for in my life. I spent most of my days looking forward to going to bed at night.

AS THE MONTHS dragged past, Beatty and Dad's relentless bullying, torture and cruelty escalated me to such a state of hatred and desire for revenge that I was cursing them in my mind almost every other minute of the day. I had random thoughts of killing them – it seemed to be my only means of escape. On one rainy night when they were out, I got so fired up that I put rat poison in the tea caddy and then waited in terror for their return and their usual tea ritual. The moment that I heard the car doors slam shut and realised that there was no turning back, my legs almost gave way beneath me, and my heart was almost beating in my throat. Lucky for all of us, they noticed the bits in the tea leaves before spooning it into the teapot, and after a lot of hemming and hawing about what the bits could be, they eventually concluded that the tea leaves had gone mouldy and threw it in the bin. By then, I was a lump of jelly and drenched from head to toe with sweat. When things got even worse a few weeks later, and I grew even more enraged than ever, I made a second attempt to eliminate Beatty from my life and to punish her for all her beatings and for stealing my father, my little brother and my dog from me. Shortly after arriving home from school, I stood on our back veranda holding a huge knife in my hand and waiting to stick into Beatty. I had my mouth gaping wide open ready to let out a fake scream that would bring Beatty rushing out onto the veranda when Dad unexpectedly arrived home hours earlier than he should have. It was the loud ritualistic barking routine of my dog, Tinka, when Dad's car pulled up that brought me out of my intense moments of madness. I suddenly came to my senses and realised what I was about to do, and jumped from the veranda to quickly buried the knife in a pile of sand. Rethinking all of this now is sending shivers up my spine. I don't believe in 'coincidence', so whatever the 'forces' were that stopped me from succeeding in harming Beatty and Dad during those dark, turbulent times, I will always feel deeply grateful to. I now believe that all human beings, children included, have the potential of reaching their own personal 'breaking point' if they get pushed hard enough and for long enough. Even domesticated pets have been known to retaliate with savage, violent rage if their owners cruelly mistreat them. As a child, I probably couldn't have done too much damage with that knife, and just as well, it would have irreparably wrecked not only other lives but also my own. It still upsets me when I think about a cat that I accidentally ran over shortly after I got my driver's licence 50 years ago. Thanks to those forces that intervened, I haven't had to live my life with murder on my conscious.

DETERMINED TO GET my revenge on my father for what he'd done to Billy, Mum and myself, in 1959, at the age of twelve, I made another serious attempt to escape. This time I took Billy with me and ran off to the Queensland outback where my eldest sister, June, and her husband, Herb, were living. I'd been there once before when I was seven, and when Mum and Dad were still together, so I had a clear recollection of the place. Their homesteader stood isolated many miles from their nearest neighbour, and their only contact with the outside world was via a crackly radio and an old-style crank-up phone. I'm still mystified by how June managed to cope with being left all alone in such isolation with their two little children, which happened several days at a time while Herb was off mustering cattle and mending fences. I certainly couldn't have coped with it, and I suspect that it was Herb's prolonged bouts of absence that made June so perpetually neurotic, as she was forever screaming at me and calling me a 'stupid bloody imbecile'. Even though I had no idea what the word meant back then, I still didn't sound like something nice. But to be fair, it was probably as much my fault, as I was such a mixed-up mess that it's a wonder I didn't drive myself nuts. Herb taught me to ride a horse so that I could help him to bring in the cattle and move the bullocks around, which was a lot of good fun until the day that I walked behind one of the horses and got kicked in the chest – a very painful lesson learned that I'm still reminded of to this day, especially whenever I'm around horses or anything else that kicks. There was also a lovely old placid horse named *Beetlebomb* that I used to ride by myself at dusk to round up the few cows that were kept separate for milking. Everywhere I looked was red and barren, and the weather was stinking hot, but it was paradise compared to living in the Frenchs Forest house. I was only there for six weeks before it was time for June and her family to set off to Sydney on their annual holiday at Mum's.

The torturous two-day trip felt like a journey to my demise, and because I'd taken Billy with me, I was expecting a worse severe punishment than ever before. The constant thought of it had my head spinning and painful waves of fear repeatedly racing throughout my body, and the closer that we got to Sydney, the worse it all became. We arrived at Frenchs Forest just after lunch on Christmas Eve, and because Dad was so thrilled to see Billy and June again, the thrashing that I was expecting didn't eventuate. Beatty certainly had her revenge, though. She'd thrown my few belongings out into the backyard weeks earlier, and everything was faded, damp and mouldy, including the modern clothes that I'd never been allowed to wear which Mum had sent to me. I didn't get a chance to go inside the house, Dad instructed me to wait in his car, and as soon as June and Herb were gone, he drove me straight to my brother, George's house. George was in his mid-thirties, and having spent a lot of his life incarcerated in 'correctional facilities' for various crimes that he'd committed, he was considered to be the black sheep of the family. Even so, George's wife, Hazel, had stuck by him devotedly. At a cost to our father, in order to 'straighten me out', George's plan was to apply the disciplinary lessons that he'd learnt while being incarcerated. I'd only seen George a few times while I was living with Dad and Beatty, when he popped in with his eldest son, *Little George,* who was about two years younger than me, and whom I considered to be one of my very best mates. His visits with his dad were always like a breath of fresh air, and a ray of sunshine all rolled into one, and the thought that I'd soon be living in the same house had my heart almost dancing with excitement and delight. During the short drive to their house in Brookvale, Dad remained rigid and didn't speak a single word to me. It didn't bother me at all, because I felt confident that I was about to start a new and carefree life away from him, and a future beyond all of my wildest hopes and dreams. My sister June had managed to talk Dad into letting Billy and I spend a couple of days with Mum between Boxing Day and New Year's Eve, which was a wonderful surprise. Mum fussed over us the whole time that we were there, and made me a delicious chocolate cake to celebrate my 13th birthday – it was the best birthday that I'd ever had.

I arrived back at George's, continuing to feel confident that my life had changed for the better, but when the hidden truth eventually unfolded I couldn't have been more wrong if I'd tried. George and Hazel had seven sons and another baby on the way, and living with them was like living in a madhouse. The first couple of weeks that I was there were full of fun and games, but once the festive season was over so too was George's good mood. In next to no time, my life became an even worse horror situation than it was living with Dad and Beatty. George made fun of me day and night and found faults in almost everything that I said or did. He forced me to wear boxing gloves and to spar with a willow tree trunk for up to five hours every day before and after school, including during a record-breaking heatwave. George soon had me fighting up to fifteen kids every Saturday afternoon, and one was six years older than me. He also forced me to drink beer with tranquillisers, which would have me falling all over the place and terrified that I was going to die, while George and his x-con drinking buddies stood over me laughing down at me and making cruel, perverted remarks about me. This abusive torment occurred each weekend, and George justified his cruelty by telling anyone who dared to question it that he was making a real man out of me. Watching me get ridiculed, knocked to the ground and generally violated must have given George a tremendous feeling of power, and his wife, Hazel, my apparent godmother, loved every bit of it and eagerly looked forward to each new bout. She'd usually lean out of the house windows with her younger teenage sisters, and yell cruel and degrading remarks about me while laughing hysterically and cheering loudly each time that I got thumped to the ground. Sometimes Little George would join in with them, and that would hurt me as much as the beatings. Even though living with my older brother, George, gave me better opportunities to mix with other kids, he'd incessantly put me down and ridicule me in front of them, calling me names such as 'a dirty little poofter', 'a fairy', 'a fuckwit' or any other disgusting term that he could come up with, and believe me he had plenty. As a result, some of the neighbourhood kids treated me as though I was a pervert or the local village idiot. George's sickening abuse was unrelenting, and he even told me one night that our mother only wanted me back to get me into her bed and have sex with me. His descriptive words in-between, which I prefer not to repeat, were far more shocking and disgusting.

Sometimes when the weather was hot George would prance around the house in his budgie-smugglers, and if I happened to glance in his direction, he'd grab hold of his dick and balls and snarl at me, "Ya fuckin' little queer, ya fuckin' like this don't ya?" Whenever that happened, my head would spin with a cocktail of shock, fear, guilt, confusion, embarrassment and excitement, all rolled into one. He was a good-looking man, and although I was far too terrified ever to admit it, I enjoyed what I saw, regardless of his abusive name-calling. I guess it was a bit like sweet and sour torture. George and Hazel were already married by the time that I was born, and from what I've been told, they doted on me until their first child, Little George, came along. That's when everything changed and they completely abandoned me. Because George had spent his younger years in and out of boys' homes, I didn't get to see much of him at all during my earliest years of growing up, in many ways, he was a brother only by bloodline and almost a stranger to me in every other way.

After I commenced school at Manly Boys High, it wasn't unusual for me to turn up on a Monday with a split lip, bruises or other facial and body injuries, all thanks to George's weekend sparring sessions – why no one ever questioned it, I will never understand. Throughout the previous year at Frenchs Forest Primary, I'd constantly daydreamed about seeing Ian again, and had kept count of the days until my time for high school arrived. I spent every school lunch break in search of Ian, but there was never any sign of him anywhere, which soon had me feeling disappointed, sad and distressed. Then early one morning after I'd all but given up hope of ever seeing Ian again, I spotted him running up some stairs, dressed in a military uniform and carrying a musical instrument under his arm. I followed him down to the far end of the school grounds, where to my surprise, I discovered that he was a member of the school's army cadet band, and spent all of his lunch breaks practising – no wonder I hadn't been able to find him! In a strategic attempt to get closer to Ian, I talked my father into allowing me to join the school cadets, and then spent several weeks cleaning guns and marching around the school's assembly area after school each day. I didn't think that anything could be more tedious and annoying than chopping wood or sparing with the willow tree every day, but boy, was I wrong about that! And to make matters worse, I was still no nearer to Ian. One day I saw a message on the notice board saying auditions were being held to find new members for the cadet band and that any cadet interested was invited to try out, and I couldn't get my name down on the registrar quickly enough. I had no front teeth at the time so just blowing into a trumpet was a futile challenge, as the noise that I produced sounded like an animal in its death throes. My drumming was much worse – it was like a car crashing and made everyone there cringe, including me. In the end, I failed miserably on every instrument, but the worst of it was when I overheard Ian and his fellow band members laughing and making fun of me. I just wanted to go somewhere and die. To add insult to injury, Dad refused to let me leave the cadets, so I was stuck taking orders, cleaning guns and marching around the playground for the remainder of that year.

A lot of the older boys at school were forever talking about shagging girls and often loudly debated with each other about which ones had the biggest tits. Females and their parts didn't interest me at all, and I just couldn't relate to any of it. But the one thing that always made my ears prick up was anything that they had to say about their penises. As fascinated and excited as I was to listen to them boasting, I was never game enough to ask any questions or get involved in their 'highly arousing' dick talk. George and his abuse had left me feeling so guilty and ashamed of myself and my body that it was even a painful embarrassment to undress and shower in front of other boys during the school sports and swimming days. For that reason, I absolutely dreaded even going, as it was always such an awkward and terrifying ordeal for me. George's cruelty and cold-hearted bullying had me so scared and confused that I'd sometimes crawl underneath the foundation of his house and hide like a wounded dog, weeping and begging God to put a stop to it all. It was a ritual that I'd repeated many times while I was living with Dad and Beatty, especially when I was gathering wood to chop from the surrounding bushland. Out of desperation, I'd often cry out to Jesus at the top of my voice and beg him to send some of his angels to help me, but help never seemed to come. One day, a member of the local Gospel Church who gave religious lessons at my school talked Dad into allowing her to take me to see the Reverend Doctor Billy Graham at the Sydney Show-grounds. On that incredible night, as I stood alongside thousands of others, who'd believed Billy's promise of a happier future life, I too was convinced that my prayers were about to be answered. I'd even gone forward and given myself to Jesus, but my miserable and unhappy life still didn't change.

ONE OF THE VERY rare occasions that I can remember ever enjoying any real happiness while living under George's care was the day that his first daughter, Belinda, was born. After fathering seven sons in a row, George was ecstatic about it, and celebrations extended throughout the entire night. It was such an uplifting change, while it lasted. Unfortunately for me, his unusual good mood was gone by dinnertime the next night. It wasn't long after that when George forced me into lying about my brother, Denis, sexually molesting me. I was terrified to refuse his demands, and then by pretending to be kind to me, he tricked me into lying about it to our father as well. When Denis caught wind of the lies, he became so enraged that he brought a gun to shoot us all – or at least that's what everybody thought. George eventually defused the situation by declaring that I'd admitted to lying. Following that, Dad thrashed and beat me until I couldn't stand up. Then, later the same night when George returned from the pub and found Dad still there, he got stuck into me as well, by dragging me out of my bed and thumping the living daylights out of me all over again. He did this to impress Dad, his cash cow, and by the end of it all, I was in so much pain that I could hardly move for days. Then just when I thought that things couldn't get any worse – they did...

*A human heart acts like water that alters in*
*shape to whatever it may occupy and the*
*nature of beings is like the reflection of the*
*moon*
*undulating on the waves.*
*...Nichiren.*

# Chapter 7

# INCARCERATED

Dad and Beatty sold the Frenchs Forest house and bought a more updated one at Narrabeen Lakes – close to Sydney's northern beaches. While they were waiting to move in, they stayed at George and Hazel's place for a week, which almost turned out to be my demise. Beatty's young daughter, Glynis, was used to seeing me get whipped with willow branches and thought that she'd have a go herself one afternoon while we were all playing a chasing game around the yard. She deliberately whacked me across the shoulder with a branch, and it hurt like hell, so I snatched the branch from her and whacked her straight back with it, just as hard. The shock sent her running into the house, crying hysterically to her mother. I expected Beatty to come marching out of the house with fury and vengeance glowing from her face, and I was right! She appeared almost instantaneously, screaming at me and ordering me to hand over the branch. The other kids tried telling her that it wasn't my fault, but she refused to listen. Thanks to my boxing training, I was no wimp, and when Beatty attempted to tug the branch from me, I shoved her away, and she fell backwards onto the grass. As Hazel was helping Beatty up onto her feet, she warned me that I was going to be in big trouble when Dad got home, and her words left me feeling petrified and motionless with fear, and she was right! When Dad came home from work that night, Beatty put on a performance that could have won her an Oscar. Soon after, the repercussions that I was expecting took place while I was eating my dinner and least prepared for it. Dad came marching into the kitchen as though he was going past me, then suddenly spun around and punched me clean off my chair, sending my head crashing into the wall behind me and almost driving my fork down my throat. The heavy blow left me semi-conscious and lying under the table, which he violently dragged out of the way before repeatedly stomping on my head. I don't think I'll ever forget the horrific sight from the corner of my eye, as his hard leather shoe came down again and again. By the time Hazel climbed on top of him and was able to drag him away, so much blood was pouring from my face, that I could barely see my hand in front of me. Later that night, when George returned home and heard about what I'd done, he dragged me out of bed and gave me another violent beating.

George couldn't have cared less about Beatty, and his insane actions were about getting on Dad's good side so that he could hit him up for more cash in the future. As the next few weeks went by, it became clear that George wasn't getting a big enough kick out of watching me get bashed by the other kids, so he started joining in punching and kicking me himself. Then, one night while I was sparing with the willow tree and George came home drunk, he ordered me to punch him in the face, I was almost legless with fear. Terrified of making him any madder, I took a half-hearted swipe at him...

"Hit me like a fuckin' man and not like a fuckin' little fairy, ya fuckin' poofta idiot!" He screamed.

As I mentioned earlier, I'd acquired a pretty decent punch by then, so I let rip with my best shot full force into his snarling face, and it must have hurt a lot more than he'd bargained for because he went berserk, picked me up and shoved me up against a shed, smashing my head clean through its fibro wall. Another of George's brutal assaults came a week later when he dragged me down to the bottom of his yard and threatened to kill me if I didn't beat every kid the following Saturday...

"If ya don't think ya can do it, ya'd betta piss off outa here quick an' smart, ya fuckin' little cunt!"

His hateful words were like jagged knives coming at me, and I knew that he meant every word of it, and I also knew that I could never live up to his expectations. I was on a good behaviour bond for running away to Queensland with Billy, so whether I stayed or ran, I was doomed. George was probably looking for a quick and easy way to get rid of me before he did end up killing me. Even now, sixty years later, I can still hear his voice screaming abuse at me, and just thinking about it can still make me shudder.

BY THE TIME THAT Friday arrived, I was so panic-stricken that I couldn't think straight. I struggling to get dressed in my cadet uniform and instead of going to school, I made another run for it. I took a bus to Manly, a ferry across the harbour to Circular Quay and then a train out to Liverpool in the outer west where Mum was living, hidden behind an acre of thick, long grass, in a silver tin shanty. Mum's shack was a far cry from Dad and Beatty's homesteader or George's modest council house, but for me, it was like arriving at a majestic royal palace in a different universe. I could sense Mum's presence radiating around me the moment that I entered her long, winding dirt path that leads to her door. After Mum greeted me with a big, long hug and then made me something to eat, she left on a forty-minute walk to her local corner shop to buy extra food, and before leaving, she instructed me to stay inside, to keep perfectly quiet and not to answer the door to anyone. She wasn't gone long before there was a barrage of loud crashing knocks on her corrugated iron door, and I almost jumped out of my skin. In a panic, I climbed into Mum's bed and hid under the blankets. I then heard a man's voice calling my name and telling me that he knew that I was in there, and waves of terror raced throughout my body like a massive earthquake – I could hardly even breathe. While all the loud banging and yelling continued on and off for several minutes, I remained curled up under the blankets in a foetal position, until he finally gave up and left. Early the next morning, he was back again and caught me coming from the outdoor toilet. Mum tried her best to keep me with her, but because Dad had sole custody, the officer had no other choice than to take me away from her forcefully, and then to deliver me to the Yasmar Children's Shelter in Ashfield, close to the CBD. I remained there captive behind its huge surrounding brick wall until it was time to appear before the adjoining Children's Court and face the consequences for breaking my bond. Because kids back then had little or no say in what happened to them, I doubt that anyone would have listened to my story of the abuse even if I'd been brave enough to tell it. When my day in court finally arrived, the elderly magistrate didn't bother consulting me or even trying to get my side of the story. Instead, he interviewed Dad and Beatty privately, then arbitrarily made his decision that I should go back and live with them. My stomach turned, my heart sank, and I fell into an instant state of despair – I was screaming on the inside, trying to make sense of it all...

"How can these grown-ups be so cruel? How can this magistrate make me go back for more pain 'n' suffering? Why didn't he try ta find out tha truth?" These thoughts racing around in my head felt like a barrage of giant needles attacking me..

THE NEW HOUSE at Narrabeen was smaller than the Frenchs Forest house and a lot more modern and closer to the beach, but even before I arrived, my mind was already made up to make another run for it. I'd changed a great deal since I'd last lived with Dad and Beatty, and I knew that it could never work. I'd turned thirteen, I'd reached puberty, and I was seeing life in a very different light. Dad and Beatty seemed happier with themselves and made a conscious effort to try to get along with me under their terms, but it was too little too late. I didn't trust them, not for a minute, and I had no intention of letting down my guard to risk staying around for any more of their abuse, which, as far as I was concerned, was inevitable. The next morning, instead of going to school, I headed straight back out to Mum's place. I was only there for a day before I was yet again hauled off to Yasmar, where I remained until my second hearing. Considering what Billy and Glynis have told me since about their sufferings of similar abuse with Dad and Beatty after I'd left, I know that I did the right thing by leaving. On the evening before my second appearance in court, this time to receive a sentence of possible incarceration, I was rushed to Lewisham Hospital to have my appendix removed. Dad arrived just as I was being wheeled into the theatre, and he cold-heartedly accused me of putting on an act. The underlying truth was, he was correct but neither he nor anyone else, except perhaps the surgeon, ever found out. Being locked behind four brick walls for over two months had almost driven me nuts, and I was ready and willing to do just about anything to join the outside world again. Be that as it may, my crazy plan to escape didn't go anywhere near as smooth and straightforward as I'd hoped – it almost turned out to be a tragedy. On my first night out of the hospital and back at Yasmar, my wound split open during the early hours, spurting blood everywhere. It scared not only the officer in charge but all the other kids and me, half to death, and I had to be rushed back to the hospital for restitching. Some of the nuns at the hospital were concerned for my wellbeing and didn't want me to be locked up again. So, on the day that I was due to be officially discharged, two of them secretly gave me my cab fare to Mum's place. I was that excited about a chance to be with Mum again that I didn't even consider the consequences, and the nuns' kind-hearted act of sympathy ended up being all in vain. A couple of hours after arriving at Mum's place, a welfare officer collected me and I was escorted back behind the walls of Yasmar again. The officer in charge at Yasmar demanded to know how I got the money for my cab fare but my lips remained sealed. Two months later, when I appeared before the Yasmar Children's Court for my hearing, the magistrate asked Dad what he wanted the court to do with me, and without a moment's hesitation, Dad told the magistrate assertively that he wanted me committed to an institution for juvenile delinquents. The magistrate looked across at me and asked if I had anything to say for myself, and all that I could do was hold my head down in shame and say nothing. I was still too frightened to defend myself, and to reveal the hidden truth about why I kept running away from home. Just like last time, I didn't think that he'd believe me anyway.

Before sentencing me, the magistrate gave me a stern lecture on how Dad, Beatty and George had done everything that they possibly could for me and how I'd repaid them by being uncontrollable and disgustingly unappreciative. I just stood there, kept quiet and took it all on the chin. He then reprimanded me again for my past bad behaviour, sternly reminded me of all the trouble that I'd caused the welfare department and the court and then sentenced me to twelve months incarceration at Mittagong's training school for wayward Boys. As the magistrate was reading out the conditions of my sentence, Mum intervened by calling Dad a barrage of nasty names and threatening to take the magistrate to court. I felt my body go numb from disbelief and horror, and there was no time to think much about it before I was whisked from the courtroom and back behind the walls of Yasmar again, where I could still hear

Mum on the other side of the wall, screaming abuse at Dad on the courthouse front steps.

IT WAS A FREEZING mid-winter afternoon when I stepped off an old steam train at Mittagong Station, accompanied by a welfare officer. My legs were weak from the fear of the unknown and what might lie ahead, and my heart skipped beats. The institution where I was to spend the next twelve months of my life, consisted of several large old mansions that were spread out across the fertile green Southern Highlands, just inland from the coast in southern New South Wales, and ironically, close to where the highly successful TV series 'A Place to Call Home' would be filmed several decades later. Some of the older inmates were almost as rough and violent as George was, and I suffered a bloody nose and a black eye even before the first week was out. Each day after breakfast, we'd dress in our pale blue shirts, woollen shorts and long grey socks, form rank outside the tired, old mansion for an inspection, and then march the long trek to school and back to the annoying sound of someone repeatedly shouting...

"Left! Right! Left! Right!"

By then, I'd lost so much weight since the appendix saga that I almost resembled a survivor from a concentration camp. Still very sore and fragile, it was a painful ordeal trying to keep up with everyone. At lunchtime, we were given a plain Vegemite or peanut butter sandwich and a piece of fruit, later on back at the house, dinner would be an 'every man for himself' kind of situation where all sorts of trickery were used to steal your plate – if you weren't sharp or quick enough to figure this out, you'd simply go hungry. The most popular method of all was someone calling out your name from behind with great urgency, and when you quickly turned around to see who it was like I did several times at first, then before you had time to turn back around your full plate would have been replaced by an empty one. If you didn't want to get your head bashed in, there was nothing that you could say or do about it. Late at night, there'd be a lot of bed-hopping going on among the older boys in the dormitory. I still knew nothing about sex, but going by what I can recall hearing and seeing, it's clear to me now that there was plenty of sexual activity taking place both beneath the sheets and down at the toilet block, where there'd usually be four or five boys on guard duty outside and letting those inside the toilets know who was coming, pardon the pun. I wouldn't say that those involved were all gay, many of them were merely young males dealing with their puberty, hormonal changes and sexual tension, and releasing it by experimenting with the limited availability under the circumstances. Some of the teachers at the school were spitefully cruel and violent, including the man in charge of the house where I stayed. He'd regularly verbally abuse and whack into some of us with a horsewhip while treating his favourites as though they were little angels who could do no wrong, but even so, he was nowhere near as terrifyingly cruel as George had been. Once a month, and only if you could present the man in charge with the two pairs of socks and other clothing you were given to wear upon your arrival, were you permitted to go out on a day trip with your family. When my family came to take me out for the day, someone had stolen my socks to stop me from going. I was beside myself with worry until one of the other boys came to my rescue and handed me his socks. He had an intellectual disability and copped continuous crap from most of the older boys for it, who seemed to thrive on teasing him and make fun of him. He was a gentle soul, so I don't know what he could have done to be in there. His kindness that day meant the world to me, and I've never forgotten him for it. I still often send a prayer to him in the hope that he went on to have a much happier and fulfilling life.

MY DAY OUT with my family was like a dream come true until I had to go back again. The following week, Mum appealed and filed for my custody, and I was returned by train to Sydney to be locked back behind the walls of Yasmar, where I remained for a further six months until my case went before the Appeals Court. One night while I was there, I experienced my first wet dream, and it frightened the life out of me! My head spun in circles, I had no idea what had happened, and I was convinced that something was seriously wrong with my body. In a confused state of panic mixed with lingering feelings leftover from an incredible few moments of phenomenal pleasure, I woke the kid in the next bed and anxiously told him about what had happened. He just laughed and told me to stop worrying about it and to go back to sleep but I couldn't, and laid awake worrying all night. Then early the next morning, one of the older boys who'd heard about my overnight erotic few moments of ecstasy pulled me aside and told me all about masturbation and ejaculation. As he was speaking, his words almost blew my mind away, particularly when he told me about how he and some of the other boys his age masturbated and ejaculated several times a day in the toilets. Until then, no one had ever explained a single thing to me about the facts of life or such bodily functions before, and I now finally understood what George had repeatedly accused me in detail of doing. The boy's erotic explanation had me so aroused that my body throbbed with excitement and expectation. That amazing day a door was opened by Nature to a whole new and wondrous world for me, which had also added a very different and exciting meaning to my growing attraction towards other males. Not even George had admitted that masturbation and wet dreams are a normal part of life that most people begin to experience and participate in during their early adolescence and periodically during their lives. All George had ever done was poison my mind by making homosexuality out to be shameful, evil and disgusting, and to this day his cruel and degrading words still sometimes echo in the back of my mind.

"I wonder what else's waiting ta be discovered 'n' experienced." I asked myself as all this new, exciting and overwhelming information began sinking in...

*Baby turtles are many but only a few of them survive to become adults.*

*Many blossoms appear on fruit trees, but only a few of them survive to become fruit.*

*Many people set a goal to reach their enlightenment, but only a few continue steadfastly to attain it.*

*...Nichiren.*

# Chapter 8

# DIFFICULT READJUSTMENTS

The year 1960 started with a whopping big bang when France tested its first Atomic Bomb. A few weeks later, the USSR agreed to stop their nuclear testing and shortly after that, became the first to touch the moon when one of their craft, Lunik 11, crashed onto the lunar surface. It was also the year that Britain's revolutionary Mini-Minor was first released, but more importantly, to Mum and me, it was the year of my appeal. The court hearing took place in November – a few weeks prior to my fourteenth birthday. During the proceedings, Dad interrupted and told the judge in no uncertain terms that Mum wasn't to have custody of me under any circumstances. The judge quickly responded by informing Dad that he no longer had a right to give any instructions or make any decisions regarding my future – then ordered him to either remain silent or to leave the courtroom. The judge asked the two members of the Yasmar staff, who'd appeared voluntarily at the hearing as character witnesses, to give him an accurate assessment of my general conduct and attitude. They both told him that I wasn't a bad boy and that all I needed was some love, compassion and understanding. Moments later, Mum was awarded full custody of me, but as we were leaving the courthouse, Dad aggressively grabbed hold of my arm, and with a snarling face, warned me that I'd soon be back inside Yasmar. His angry words echoed in my mind for weeks, and I was too afraid to go anywhere on my own in case he showed up somewhere and dragged me into his car. Once I became more accustomed to my freedom, the first people that I visited were my brother, Denis, and his new wife, Gay, at their modest, one-bedroom flat in Croydon – near Ashfield, on the outskirts of the city. It was a special and exciting time to visit them as their son, 'Denny Junior', had only just been born. During the years that I'd lived with Dad and Beatty, and then George and Hazel, Denis and I had hardly seen each other. In the meantime, we'd both changed a lot, and I was unsure what to expect. At the moment I knocked on the door, the lie that George had forced me to tell about Denis sexually molesting me suddenly sprung into my mind – I felt sick to the stomach and turned to make a run for it just when Denis opened his door and greeted me with a loud, warm and cordial welcome that almost made my bones jump out and run. For the next few hours, we talked about everything except 'that' incident, and it ended up being a wonderful and joyous reunion. After that, Denis and I became very close, but even so, I never felt trusting, relaxed or confident enough to discuss my sexuality with him. Denis was a ladies' man to the core, and it soon became perfectly clear to me that he expected me to be just like him.

THE 1950s FOR gays were a scary decade of bigotry, ignorance and repression. Most males were too afraid to express or admit that they were homosexual for fear of being arrested and hauled off to a hospital to be force-fed drugs, subjected to barbaric 'electric-shock therapy' – or to get thrown into prison. Superstitious, dogmatic and rigid religions that thrive on preaching prejudice and hatred have always been a powerful force, and in many places, they are still the main force behind the sufferings endured by members of the lesbian, gay, bisexual, transgender and queer community (now known as the LGBTQ+). At my young, impressionable age back then, there was no one that I could trust enough to talk to about my sexual feelings and nothing to read, except harsh warnings about how 'homosexuality is a sin and a certain way to end up in Hell' – for many, just surviving another day without being exposed was an ongoing distressful and ever-threatening ordeal. Thank goodness for the wonderful, brave people and their supporters who've since faced the homophobic armies and never given up the fight to have these archaic laws changed. It's also thanks to them that there are now laws that allow gays the freedom to be themselves – to protect gays from illegal homophobic abuse, and to allow gays equal rights in marriage. However, there's still a lot more to be done, including laws to stop God-botherers from knocking on people's doors and instilling their hateful and dangerous homophobic beliefs. I believe that these sort of people who create contempt, despair, isolation and feelings of hopelessness among gays – especially the young and vulnerable, are responsible for helping to prompt thousands of gay people to resort to suicide. In my opinion, what they do should be an illegal and punishable crime – the 'Hell' that these religious fanatics so often speak of is nothing more than the hellish conditions and outcomes that they and their distorted, illogical beliefs are creating. How sad that they're far too obsessed with ignorance and hatred to even realise it. To see an explicit example of this, I highly recommend that you watch the true-to-life movie *Prayers for Bobby*, starring Sigourney Weaver and Ryan Kelly; also available on YouTube...

https://www.youtube.com/watch?v=sqIF50lSNVo&t=2078s

AFTER COMMENCING school at Liverpool Boys High, as it was at Manly Boys High, I soon discovered that the most popular topic for conversation between many of the boys was sex – especially their graphic descriptions of, and desires for, the large-breasted girls in the adjoining girls' school. Once again I had to be on my guard at all times – cautiously selecting everything that I said, disagreed with or agreed to. I also had to be careful to hide any arousals brought on by what the boys had to say, particularly about their dicks. I sometimes felt resentful and envious of the girls for the attention that they were getting, while people like me were considered to be the lowest scum of the earth – 'Filthy poofters' was one of the most common terms used by the boys around me. These hurtful 'names' never failed to reignite painful memories of George and his foul mouth, and what I'd gone through while living under his care.

MUM HAD BEEN in a relationship with a man named Eric for some time, he'd helped her to get suitable accommodation to improve her chances of gaining custody of me in the appeals court. Eric did his best to support us and tried to reach out to me, but when I should have been grateful and appreciative towards him, I rejected him relentlessly, and instead, I went out of my way to defy and upset the poor man. In my young mind, I think that I may have been unwittingly taking out my anger and distrust for Beatty on him. Something else that had me walking on eggshells was how Denis and nearly everyone else was pressuring me about getting a girlfriend. One day, after hearing it mentioned by some of the older boys that a girl at school by the name of Helen had a reputation for being 'easy', to satisfy my curiosity about girls once and for all, I pursued her, until she led me behind some bushes after school, pulled down her knickers and then showed me what to do. Being inside of her felt phenomenal, I had to admit, and I could hardly wait to do it again and again. Although she was a sweet enough girl, other than for her vagina, I had no romantic feelings for her at all. The one thing that never failed to turn me on in a perverted sort of way whenever we had sex was perverse thoughts about the other boys that had been inside her before me. I started having sex with Helen two or three times a week, but it was never anything more than pure lust, fuelled by the usual fantasies – no kissing or cuddling was ever involved. Looking back now, I think Helen may have picked up on my attraction towards other males. Her older sister had a handsome boyfriend and one day when we were about to get into it, Helen whispered in my ear that she'd secretly had sex with her sisters' boyfriend twenty minutes before meeting up with me – hearing about it made me so rampant that I had multiple climaxes, as most males can, especially at such a young age. Later, when Denis found out about my erotic adventures with Helen, he reacted as though it was a miracle and made me out to be a Don Juan. Fooling Denis into thinking that I was a ladies' man like him may have helped me to camouflage my hidden attraction towards other males, but living up to it was bloody exhausting. When he introduced his mate, Arnold, to Helen, and she decided that she didn't want to be with me anymore, it came as an enormous relief. When Denis later tried to convince me that she was too mature for me and needed a real man, his words cut like a knife, and any desires for women or confidence that I may have developed were immediately shot down in flames and extinguished – which, in the end, turned out to be a blessing in disguise. I continued to dabble and experiment sexually with a couple of other girls from school, but it was never anything more than a quick few moments of physical relief for me – usually over and done in a flash! Then, one day, I went into a toilet at a railway station, and a middle-aged man popped his head out of the cubicle and invited me to join him – from then on, most of my sexual encounters took place with older men, or other boys around my age, in public toilets. It was potentially very dangerous, and often left me feeling low and ashamed, but even so, I'd always go back for seconds and thirds. As time went on, I took far more dangerous risks by getting into cars with older men, who'd take me to remote and secluded spots. It had never occurred to me that I could have been hurt or even murdered, but there wasn't much of that going on back then, and those were my only options. This sort of thing still goes on today with those kids who are afraid to admit their sexual feelings to their parents and siblings more openly – who are forced to share them in secret with strangers instead.

DURING 1962-63, we moved house more times than I care to remember. While Mum worked hard in a shoe factory, like a lot of other teenagers back then, I became a lazy, irresponsible and unreliable lay-about, foolishly chain-smoking Marlboro cigarettes and believing that I'd end up looking like the 'Marlboro Man', who many years later died of lung cancer. My other main interest in life was sketching ladies' stiletto shoes and female faces – I had drawings scattered from one end of the house to the other. My biggest joy of all was babysitting Denis and Gay's children – they were the light of my life back then, and I'd babysit them every chance that I got. Although I'd been molested and abused as a child, it hadn't affected my relationship with children in any sort of negative way – on the contrary, I was always overprotective towards them, especially those of my siblings. In my opinion, there are no excuses for violation towards children, even if the perpetrators were unfortunate enough to have been molested or abused themselves.

SHORTLY AFTER we moved to the outer-western suburb of Kingswood, I got involved in an erotic and kinky sexual relationship with an older girl named Janice, who lived a kilometre or so down the road past the local cemetery. At night, I'd be too scared to pass it on my own, so she'd have to walk me home first and then go back to her place alone. Janice was no beauty queen, her face was quite masculine, but she was naughty, uninhibited and always ready and willing to accommodate any of my wishes. She had two handsome older brothers that she strongly resembled and in a twisted way, that's what turned me on while having sex with her. One afternoon, during a heat-wave, I was overcome by a strong urge to do something with her hair. I suggested it to her and she just laughed and told me that I knew nothing about doing hair – she was right, even though I refused to admit it! After some friendly persuasion on my part, she eventually gave in and agreed to at least let me give it a go. My next challenge was not having any hairspray or rollers – I told her that I could make my own, and determined to prove that I could do it, I raced down the backyard and grabbed some of Mum's round wooden pegs from the clothesline to use as makeshift hair rollers – I then warmed some honey and sugar with water in a pot on the stove. When the gooey mixture was ready, I poured it into an old hand-pump fly sprayer and then proceeded to set Janice's hair...

"Gee whiz Tommy, I'd never've thought o' doing all o' that," she told me in amazement – utterly impressed with how well the clothes pegs had served as rollers.

I then sprayed her hair all over with my makeshift 'lacquer' and sent her out to sit in the sun to let it set. About twenty minutes later, she came back inside with goo running down her face, neck and back...

"Do ya reckon you're doin' it right, Tommy?" She asked me anxiously, looking a bit like a melted toffee apple.

I quickly wiped her down before she attracted any ants, and then got her to stand with her head in the fridge freezer for a while. When she pulled out her head several minutes later, her teeth were chattering, and she was going blue in the face – her hair had glued solidly to the pegs, and it took me the best part of an hour to get them all out. During the process, Janice pulled some of the scariest and hideous faces that I'd ever seen on a woman in my life and vowed never to let me touch her hair again. A few weeks later, I accompanied Mum to a hair salon and watched her having her hair styled and set into one of the fashionable, puffy hairstyles that were all the rage in the 1960s. It was also then that the idea of me becoming a hairstylist got etched in stone. My photographic memory aided me with creating the very same hairdo for Mum a week later at home. Word soon got around after Mum told others who'd asked where she was getting her hair done and almost immediately several of the neighbourhood women were asking me to style their hair and paying me good money for doing it. The money that I made illegally each Friday and Saturday came in very handy indeed. From then on, to improve my technical skills and to learn how to create other styles, I'd stand outside hair salons and watch, while making mental notes, then I'd go home and practise on Denis's wife, Gay's, long black hair. Although she and Denis didn't have much money back then, their neighbours must have thought that they were swimming in it because of Gay's continuing up-to-the-minute, latest hair creations – and then came Rock 'n' Roll…

*With my niece Christine.*

*From left:* *Little George, me, Darrell, Glynis, Billy and Danny.*

*My brother George.*

*Australia's F.J.Holden.*

*America's Ford Customline.*

*Tinka.*

*Mum with Billy, Flo and me at our house in Greenacare.*

*Riverstone residence.*

*Frenches Forest house.*

*Mittagong Boy's Home (marching to school with our lunches).*

*Sweet 16.*

*The Bushy Walkabout.*

*Twisting the night away.*

*My first band.*

*My second band.*

*Singing with The Gallaxties.*

*Surfy days.*

*Hippie days.*

*The New Gunyah Hotel.*

*Mum and me at my 21st.*

*UFO patch Bankstown 1966.*

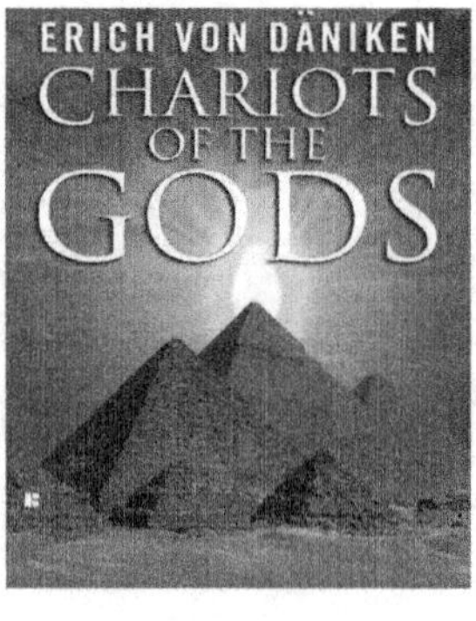

# Chapter 9

# CLIMBING THE ROCK 'N' ROLL LADDER

The idea of becoming a Rock 'n' Roll singer had first dawned on me when I was an eleven-year-old student at Frenchs Forest Primary School. Once a week our teacher, Mr Dimmock, allowed us to hold a concert in the classroom, which was always a perfect opportunity for me to escape from the prison that Beatty and Dad had built by banning any modern music at home on the radio. Whenever I got to perform in front of the class, I'd usually sing *The Witchdoctor* or *The Purple People Eater* – both novelty hits at the time that I loved. I dread to think what I must have sounded like, but along with anyone else who was game enough to get up and give it a go, I always received a big round of applause, accompanied by a loud eruption of laughter. Those sporadic, exciting and happy moments during that dark and miserable period in my life meant the world to me. One of the few happy memories that I have from when I was living in George's house was being able to watch Australia's King of Rock 'n' Roll, Johnny O'Keefe, rocking up a storm on his popular nation-wide show *Six O'clock Rock*. Most Saturdays, while George was away running his illegal bookmaking business, along with his wife, Hazel, and their army of kids, I'd be glued to the television, watching JOK and other new up-and-coming stars singing their hearts out. The show added more and more fuel to the fire of my ambition to become a Rock 'n' Roll star myself one day.

My dream began to become a reality shortly after I left school in 1962, at the age of fifteen. There were heaps of new popular dances being invented at the time, including the *Watusi*, the *Stroll*, the *Mashed Potato*, the *Bird*, the *Madison*, the *Dog*, the *Frug*, the *Hully-Gully*, the *Swim*, the *Hitch-Hike*, the *Limbo*, the *Pony* and the biggest one of them all, the *Twist*! I'd often spend my Saturday afternoons at Sydney's Channel 9 TV studios in Willoughby as part of the audience for a pop show called *Saturday Date*. It was also there that I discovered that I could dance, and each week my hips would gyrate almost endlessly either doing the *Twist* or another new Surfy dance called the *Surfy Stomp*. One Saturday Australia's hottest new teenage heartthrobs, 'Little Pattie', sang her big hit *He's My Blonde-Headed, Stompy-Wompy, Real Gone Surfer Boy,* and a whole new level of expectations came into my mind. While most of the starry-eyed surfy boys in the studio audience were fantasising that she was singing about them, I was busy fantasising that one day I'd be on 'Saturday Date' singing my new hit record and some of them would be fantasising about me. I became so good at doing the Twist that I was asked to demonstrate it in venues around the city. One night, when I was performing at a popular south Sydney venue called the Riverwood Hotel, the highly intoxicated audience became overly excited and pushed me onto the stage, shouting out loud requests for me to sing as well. The only appropriate song that I knew the words to was Chubby Checker's *Let's Twist Again*. As they all twisted, screamed and shouted for more, I must have sung the same verses over and over again for at least a half an hour. This encouraging experience gave even greater credence to my dream of one day becoming a singing sensation, and I felt more determined than ever to do all that I could to achieve it. During my initial stages of practising to become a singer, some of the neighbours must have been wishing that I'd chosen to become a coal miner instead. I made noises that even made my own hairs stand upright, let alone my poor cat's, who'd usually reach a certain breaking point, before letting out a loud snarl and running for her life. The person who persevered regardless of how bad I sounded and never once wavered in his support and encouragement was my brother Denis. I was living with him and his family when the Beatles first took the world by storm, and when I joined my first band, 'The Expressmen'. I didn't have a clue about the technicalities of the Beatles' vocal harmonies and was constantly confused between what was the lead melody and the harmony notes in their songs. After repeatedly jumping from one vocal line to another and making a distorted mess of things, I eventually gave up trying in frustration and sang Cliff Richard, Elvis Presley and The Rolling Stones songs instead. While I was the lead singer with The Expressmen, I also created a new dance step that I called the *Bushy Walkabout*. After giving the other band members a demonstration and having them all agree that it could catch on, we hired a small church hall in Liverpool, west of Sydney, and started promoting it. On the first week, only a handful of people came to see us, but word spread, and the hall was soon full of local 'Bushy Walkabouters'. Everything was going great guns until the promoters of another dance further down the street got seriously jealous when most of their patrons started defecting and coming to see us instead, they sent along a mob of louts to cause trouble and cause us to lose the venue. Even though their nasty little scheme worked, it wasn't the end of the 'Bushy Walkabout', not by a long shot. As time passed and the dance became fine-tuned by others, it continued to gain popularity, albeit with different names, including the 'Madison' and what is now called 'line dancing'. A disco version of it was done in the movie *Saturday Night Fever*, and although I've never received any recognition for it and probably never will, I still get a thrill knowing that it was me who'd initially set the wheel rolling.

BY LATE 1963, surfing music had completely taken over and become all the rage, and the venue in Sydney to be seen in was a big old converted cinema in Kings Cross called *Surf City*. Every night it would be jam-packed with *blond-headed, stompy-wompy, surfies,* all going for their lives stomping away to the latest surf music that blared out from a large sound system. It was at Surf City, around the same time, that a female dancer-friend and I competed in the Australian Stomp Championships and came second to Jack Thompson and his partner – Jack later became a very successful actor known internationally for his movies and deep voice. Throughout the 1960s, it was illegal for adult males to go inside female hairdressing salons, and because barbers would only cut hair, and not colour it, we 'surfies' were forced to spend long hot days baking in the sun with lemon juice and peroxide in our hair. I personally spent many hours frying on Cronulla and Bondi beaches trying to lighten my hair, often returning home looking like a sun-burnt, bleach-blonde lobster. It didn't seem to matter how outrageously I chose to dress, my brother, Denis, never complained about it or wavered in his full-hearted support and encouragement to help me to reach my dream of becoming a pop star. He'd build me up and make me feel like I was destined to become Australia's version of Elvis Presley one minute and then pull me to pieces until I felt like I was a complete failure the next. It was like being stuck on a roller coaster and would get me so pissed off that I'd feel like throwing in the towel and giving up. Denis seemed to know what he was doing and always ended up making me try even harder to get it right the next time. In so many other ways, Denis was my rock, and I dread to think what my life in those days would have been like without him.

NOT LONG AFTER I'd begun using Toddy Bird as my stage name, I scored my first gig as a solo artist by passing an audition to perform as a sideshow act during the 1964 World Fair that was held in Wellington, New Zealand. Each very afternoon and night I performed in a big white tent, competing against other stars such as 'Bimbo the baby elephant' and 'The half-man-half-woman' – very exciting stuff indeed for a beginner. One night a local TV producer who was in the audience invited me to appear on a show called *Let's Go,* hosted by Peter Sinclair, and two weeks later, there I was singing away on NZ national television, and loving every minute of it. I visited a local barbershop for a trim and he deliberately cut a big chunk out of the back of my hair, leaving me with no other option than to have the rest of it cut short as well. Unbeknown to me at the time, that barbers were protesting against long hair on men and were deliberately doing this. When I got back to the showground, and the show's manager spotted me, she was instantly enraged and fired me on the spot. 'Beatlemania' was raging, and Long hair was an essential part of the image of the show – my hair had helped get me the gig in the first place. I appeared on the 'Lets' Go' show a second time and I met a young guy my own age named Phillip, with whom I experienced my first 'romantic' gay relationship – albeit a short one. Phillip had angelic looks, and I soon fell head over heels for him. We were awkward and very inexperienced when it came to the physical side of our relationship, but there were genuine feelings between us that went far beyond just a quick fix in a men's toilet. Phillip had just finished having a casual fling with the show's handsome host, Peter Sinclair, when I met him. They'd met while Phillip was doing some modelling on the show. During the short time that we were together, Phillip proved to me that two males could feel real love and affection for one another that went far beyond just mere lust and a quick-relief session in a toilet cubicle. It was all going beautifully between us until I needed to travel down to Oamaru on the South Island to do gigs, which turned out to be the beginning of a prolonged, ongoing nightmare. The worst of it took place on the flight back to Wellington when the plane got caught in a turbulent storm, and we were hurled around from pillar to post for nearly two hours. After the pilot had made several unsuccessful attempts to land the plane, and we were each given a pillow and told to assume the crash position with our heads in our laps – I could hardly believe what was happening! I was horror-stricken and convinced that we were all about to die when the plane went into a virtual dive, and I ignored the instructions given by the pilot, and instead sat up to see what was going on, and I was almost concertinaed when the plane suddenly bellied out and hit the tarmac. The violent and frightening landing left me unable to get up and walk at first, and I needed help to exit from the plane. Along the way, someone told me that I looked green, which made me feel even worse. I was still struggling to recover later on at home when Phillip dropped a massive bomb on me that he was leaving me to go and live with New Zealand's number one pop idol, Lue Prime. Phillip's news hit me like a sledgehammer and I soon fell into a state of depression. Refusing to give up and accept it, I followed them to Auckland a few days later, but it was all in vain. Unbeknownst to me, Phillip had been madly in love with Lue ever since before I'd even met him, and I didn't even stand a chance. The moment I found all this out, my feelings of depression turned into anger and disgust, and I furiously accused Phillip of using me as a means to make Lue jealous and to get him to commit to a relationship. Weeks later, I was still hurting inside when I met and became friends with a nineteen-year-old sailor from Scotland named Jimmy. He was also very handsome, but in a different way to Phillip. We were two lonely strangers in Auckland, and soon became emotionally attached. Jimmy told me that he wanted to take care of me, but on the day that we rented a flat on Auckland's Waterloo Quadrant and were about to move in together, another dream came to a hasty ending. On Jimmy's way back from the shop, he got picked up by the police and arrested for jumping ship and incarcerated – lover number two gone in a flash! Because Jimmy and I had been spending a lot of time together, I was taken into custody for questioning on suspicion of harbouring naval deserters. During a prolonged and lengthy interrogation that followed, I was asked to look at hundreds of photographs of other deserters that were said to be hiding out in New Zealand, and although I'd never seen any of them, there were certainly some that I wished I had. I was terrified that the police were going to contact my family in Australia and let them know what I'd been up to, and it was a huge relief when they finally released me with a warning to steer clear of sailors. Sadly, Jimmy was sent back to Scotland by ship, and I never heard from him again. Spending time with Phillip and being away from my family had allowed me to let my guard down about being gay, but after the arrest, I jumped straight back into the closet, locked the door and was more afraid and secretive about my sexuality than ever.

A few months later, after returning home to Australia, Denis arranged for me to audition for the Johnny Chester Show at Melbourne's ABC TV Studios. I passed the audition and was then invited back onto the show to sing the Rolling Stones' version of *Route 66*. In a last-ditch effort to prevent me from singing too close to the mic, the producer piled sandbags up at my feet to help me maintain a correct distance, but it failed dismally! By then I'd learnt to do the *Mod's Nod*, a new dance craze that was created by the famous New Zealand group, 'Ray Columbus and the Invaders'. It was almost like doing the Limbo Rock in reverse, and I'd become quite an expert at bending as far forward as I possibly could while I continued to sing. Back in those days, many of the locally-made TV shows were pre-recorded onto tapes and then broadcast at different times around the country. I managed to make it back home to Sydney just in time to watch my very first Australian TV performance in the company of my family, and what a thrill it was for us all to see me singing on the TV to viewers all over the country. Things had been shaping up for me incredibly, but as much as I was enjoying being a part of the glamorous entertainment world, I wasn't making enough money to live on, and I needed to find a day job to supplement my earnings so that I could at least pay for my stage gear. In the past, I'd lost several jobs dealing with the public as a shop assistant, because of my outbursts of uncontrollable laughter, so my chances of holding onto a job in a shop longer than a week or two were minimal. The problem was, I was easily amused by the facial expressions and accents of the elderly, especially the British, which is also why most of my favourite comedians have been British. I get a kick out of seeing the funny faces that they often pull and the camp way that they react to and speak about things. One thing that always got me in strife at work was when a customer would wander into the shop, usually with a walking stick, line their eyes up with the displayed goods and then move towards them with the precision of a soldier carefully advancing through enemy lines. Sometimes they'd stand and thoroughly study the merchandise while making facial expressions that were worthy of a comedy act. Then, after taking several minutes of dead-serious decision making, they'd often only end up buying a slice of chicken or ham for a sandwich for lunch. By the time that they'd decided and were ready to order, I'd be on my knees curled up in a bundle behind the counter, laughing myself stupid – my head spinning so much that I'd be unable to get back up and face them. Eventually, the customer would either leave or get fed up with waiting and start shouting to be served, and that's when the boss would rush out from the back of the shop, and I'd be in the firing line again. I lost count of how many times that happened. In an attempt to try something different, I took an exam for a clerical position with The Public Services and to my utter amazement, I passed. A few days later, I commenced working at the Australian Taxation Office as a clerk in the annexe department. I'd only been there for a fortnight before Mum arranged for me to have lessons with a singing teacher two evenings a week after work, which was Mum's way of helping me to continue to fulfil my dreams of becoming a pop star. The elderly singing teacher's living room was cluttered from floor to ceiling with collectables and piles of musical manuscripts and books. It gave me a dose of the creeps, and I felt a bit like I'd gone back through a time warp. He was a short little man in his late 60s, extremely rotund, quite eccentric and he closely resembled film director Alfred Hitchcock in both his looks and how he spoke...

"First," he announced, with a pretentious smile. "I want you to do some simple voice exercises so that we can determine what your capabilities are."

The wobbling of his multiple chins as he spoke soon had me fighting back laughter. Following that, he burst into a weird array of loud noises, as his face became distorted, and his arms flapped like a wounded bird...

"Me me me me me me me me me me me me!" He wailed loudly.

I thought that he was stuttering at first and was never going to stop. He then looked me straight in the eye and started singing several other meaningless words in an even higher-pitched voice. As his chins danced and wobbled more vibrantly than ever, and I was unable to bear another moment of watching him, I spun around and pretended to have a sudden coughing fit, releasing some of the pent-up, uncontrollable laughter at the same time...

"Why aren't you paying attention?" He shouted in anger as I stood with my face stuck in a bookshelf, desperately trying to contain myself and hide my laughter, as tears streamed down my face, and my sides felt like they were about to split open...

"Here, now!" He yelled, "Let me hear you do some!" He ordered.

As he stared up at me with a look of the utmost seriousness, I tried with everything in me to obey him, but it was impossible. The laughter I was trying to contain felt like a giant balloon inside of me about to burst, and all I could do was to make a dreadful grunting noise...

"That sounds absolutely appalling!" He snapped. "Not a scrap of tone in your voice at all! Here, watch me again and do it with me!"

"Ah... No!" I thought before he quickly restarted with his 'me me meing'.

By then I was doubled over with pain from suppressing an even greater build-up of laughter...

"Come on, lad!" He cried out, "What are you doing for goodness sake?"

"Toilet! Toilet! I need tha toilet!" I gasped, sprinting across the room without daring to look back at him.

I slammed the door behind me and kept flushing the toilet to try to hide the noise of my loud hysterical laughter, and at one point, I became so lightheaded that I almost fainted and fell headfirst into the bowl. I must have been there for about twenty minutes before I could gain enough control of my laughter and summon up the courage to venture back out. With my hands clasped around my throbbing head, and cringing from the torture of my aching limbs, I rejoined the strange little man, who was now sitting impatiently at his piano and looking thoroughly aggravated...

"Good Lord, lad! Did you come here to spend the lesson in my toilet? Here, I want you to sing *la* to each note that I play. Do you understand?"

"Yes," I muttered, trying my best to think horrible thoughts to help me maintain a straight face...

"What did you say? Speak up! Speak up, boy! That will never do!"

"YES!" I shouted, feeling a bit pissed-off as well, but the laughter won out and as much as I tried to obey his instructions, I just couldn't. Looking at him from behind was even funnier than face to face, and I wasn't able to get those dancing chins out of my mind. As he hit a note and I attempted to sing out a *la*, I lost control and let out a loud fart instead...

"Great Scot!" He yelped, almost jumping up from his seat and licking his lips as he quickly closed his piano...

"You're completely tone-deaf boy. How the devil they ever put you on television is beyond me! I honestly don't believe that I've ever heard anybody sing and sound more atrocious!"

As he strutted across the room and opened the front door to let some air in and show me out, he warned me that he'd be phoning Mum and telling her not to waste any more of her good money. As I was exiting his front gate, I could still hear him yelling and advising me to choose another career...

"Perhaps you could try joining the army!" He finally shouted.

I got around the corner as fast as I could and then let go with a humongous roar of hysterical laughter that was probably heard a block away. If anyone had been listening or watching they probably would have thought that I'd gone nuts or I was high on drugs. No matter how hard I tried to think of horrible things, I repeatedly made an utter fool of myself with periodic fits of loud laughter all the way home on the bus – when I finally arrived home and told Mum what had happened, we were both rolling about in hysterics – such fond and happy memories...

# Chapter 10

# SURF CITY - MYSTERY LIGHTS - BEE GEES

Along with other artists, during the late 1960s, I performed in Australia's outback country towns, where some of the shows that we put on created quite a few eye-popping, shocked looks on the locals' faces. Long before *Priscilla Queen of the Desert*, it was the 1960s Rock 'n' Roll artists who were the first to dress up in all the 'way-out' colourful gaiety, fancy flares and glittery gear. I was one of them, and so proud to be part of that fantastic psychedelic generation of *flower children* – the first pioneers of the new outrageous, flamboyant, Australia to ever hit the outback. When it came to the latest fashions, I always did my best to go a step or three further than the rest to stand out more – judging by most people's reactions back then, it worked! Many of the promoters that we worked for were con artists and rip-off merchants, and all too often we never got paid. I was taken for a ride time and time again by them, but even so, I wouldn't have missed it for anything. I don't think my Mum felt the same way though – always having to bail me out of the crazy predicaments that I regularly got myself into. From one day to the next, Mum never knew what to expect. One memorable tour that we were unexpectedly unable to finish took us through several country towns along the far-northern NSW coastline – travelling like 'superstars' in two brand-spanking-new VW Kombie wagons and a couple of late-model Aussie Holden sedans. We felt utterly prestigious until we were pulled over by the police, and our promoters were taken into custody for stealing all the vehicles on the day that we left for the tour. The situation left us stranded with our instruments on the roadside near a one-horse town named Gloucester – and once again Mum had to wire me the money for my fare back home. Between tours, along with several other Sydney up and coming artists, I regularly auditioned and competed for gigs in venues all over the city. It would usually be the same crowd of hopefuls turning up each time, so the auditions also served as little reunions to catch up on the latest gossip. In the mid-1960s, when Surf City began featuring live bands and performers, the popular venue soon became *the place* where you needed to be if you wanted to get a break in the Sydney music scene. Anyone who was anyone either performed at Surf City or spent their evenings on the dance-floor there – grooving for hours on end to the sounds of the nation's top groups, including 'Billy Thorpe and the Aztecs', 'Ray Brown and the Whispers', and an up and coming band known as 'The Roadrunners' – that usually backed the solo artists. I managed to push my way in and was invited to perform at Surf City regularly three nights per week – sharing the stage with two or three other solo artists. I loved every minute of it, and even created a dance there that I called the *Mip-Mip* – it only took off with the regular crowd, but it was still well-received and a lot of great fun. The manageress of Surf City, Mrs Harrigan, ran the venue like a school headmistress for her well-known promoter son, John Harrigan. She had her favourites and could be very uninterested or even quite rude at times towards others – boy, did she keep us all on our toes. Performing each week alongside such big stars was like being in Rock 'n' Roll Heaven for me. I wasn't very well known myself but just being in their presence made me feel like I was up there with them.

IN FEBRUARY 1966, I was on my way to Surf City with some friends one night, when we were confronted by an aluminous bright glow that resembled a giant pear-shaped light bulb in the sky. It remained stationary for a few seconds, and then quickly disappeared behind the dark silhouettes of some houses in the distance. The sudden sight of it took my breath away, and I became so mesmerised by its presence that I momentarily lost control of where I was going and almost drove my car into a nearby schoolyard fence. I'd heard somewhere that during the 1950s, when Britain was testing atomic bombs in the outback of South Australia, the sky had lit up so brightly that the glow could be seen from almost a thousand miles away. That was the first thing to enter my mind the moment that I saw the strange glow. Because Australia was in the midst of a war with Vietnam, I initially thought that Australia was under a nuclear attack – by the time that we reached Surf City, we were in quite a fluster about it. I mentioned to a couple of friends what we'd seen and one of them suggested that it might have been a UFO from another planet – I felt my hair stand on end. My Catholic upbringing had brainwashed me into believing that God only made one world – Earth. I'd seen a few scary movies about aliens and 'flying saucers', but I'd never taken them seriously enough to believe for a minute that they were for real. A few days later, I was even more unnerved when Sydney's Channel 9 News reported that a lot of other people in the Bankstown area also witnessed a strange glow in the sky on the same night. The TV coverage showed a circular patch of tall reeds that had been depressed into the mud in a perfect clockwise formation – as if by some tremendous force, the reeds were bent at the base, but not broken. The 'nest', as they termed it, was hidden in bushland next to Bankstown Airport, and two school kids had discovered it on their shortcut home – close to where we'd seen the glow disappear. The report also stated that the area had a particular pungent-chemical smell that hung in the air and that the area had been cordoned off by police to allow scientists to analyse. No further reports were aired, but there was still a lot of talk among the locals, especially when more similar lights and glows were seen in the sky during the weeks that followed – two of which, a friend and I saw while chatting one night as we were staring southward across the Royal National Park, spread out beyond Sydney's Lucas Heights Nuclear Reactor. The tiny pale-blue dots of light that we saw followed each other at an astronomical speed across the sky from east to west – just above the horizon. They stopped abruptly one after another at around the halfway point, did a quick little zigzag and then continued across the horizon at the same indescribable speed – completely disappearing out of sight, almost instantly. In hindsight, it was as though they knew that we were watching and they'd zigzagged on purpose. We wondered if it might have been car lights flickering across overhead wires, but no cars had passed behind us and on the following day, there weren't any wires either. After discussing it further, we agreeably concluded that no known human-made craft could have moved at such speed or stopped so abruptly – let alone zigzagged the way that they did. The idea of them being alien crafts sent more chills up and down my spine, as well as spiked my curiosity – I yearned to know what they were and what they might be doing here.

A note: Many years later in the early two-thousands, I would learn that, during the same year as our sightings, another unexplained UFO incident involving two craft – witnessed by 200 school children and their teachers – took place at a school in Westall Victoria. Just as the Sydney sightings were, the incident was abruptly covered up by the government. Many of the students who are now in their 50s and 60s are presently demanding that the truth be told.

https://topdocumentaryfilms.com/westall-66-suburban-ufo-mystery/

https://www.pedestrian.tv/news/westall-ufo-incident-aamh/?fbclid=IwAR20zpaNsvuhiqS_MV0aKWHgwraPAce_bFXSk3-80Rzs2V0PJap57ug4L0A

Not long after that mysterious and eerie night, a Sunday newspaper started publishing segments from a new book written by Erich Von Daniken entitled *Chariots of the Gods*. I soon became so deeply engrossed with what he suggested that I could hardly wait to read each new episode – it left me feeling more and more determined to find an explanation for the events that I'd been witnessing. Putting it down to the 'Devil's doing' or an over-active imagination, as some that I told had insisted, did nothing to quell my curiosity. Erich's book presented and re-evaluated an abundance of new and intriguing interpretations, regarding several well-known historical paintings and photographs in the light of extraterrestrial visitations. It soon had me racing back and forth to the local library checking out pictures in the books that he'd referred to and rummaging through the Bible left, right and centre – while I tried my best to prove Von Daniken's interpretations wrong. But in nearly every account, what Von Daniken suggested appeared to be correct, or at least make sense – that left me feeling more confused, insecure and disillusioned than ever, and also had me seriously questioning my Catholic faith and many other things that I'd been led to believe throughout my life. Although Von Daniken's suggestions had sent me climbing out on a limb, I still couldn't get my head around the 'not of this world' interpretations – nor some of the other concepts presented in his book, especially where the Bible was concerned. I tried to discuss some of what I'd read with my brother, Denis, to hear what he thought, but I'd have been better off consulting his cat about it. He went straight into denial and blatantly refused to even listen, which is often typical of how people deal with a situation that threatens to take them out of their comfort zone. As a Catholic, when I was young, I'd lived most of my life in fear and guilt where 'God' was concerned – I'd always been made to feel spiritually contaminated, or a 'mortal sinner' carrying the heavy burden of, and responsibility for the crucifixion of a man who'd lived nearly 2000 years before I was born. None of that made sense or seemed fair or right to me anymore – especially what the Bible has to say about homosexuality. From then on, I questioned or reconsidered everything spiritual that I'd ever been taught, heard or had read.

Point of interest: I couldn't have even guessed back then, that by the dawning of the 21st Century, the Vatican would build a dish and employ scientists to search for extraterrestrial life – declare that God may have made other worlds inhabited by non-sinners. (You can find this statement on Google.)

IT WAS DURING my 'Surf City' days, at age nineteen, that I missed out on an opportunity that potentially could have boosted my singing career significantly. It happened while I was doing some recordings at 'St. Clair Studios' in Hurstville – an inner south-western suburb of Sydney. The studio was nothing elaborate, just an old converted ex-grocery shop, and the soundproofing was egg cartons glued to the walls, but even so, it had some fascinating history – it was where The Bee Gees recorded their first big hit single *Spicks and Specks,* and where they spent a lot of their time most days, just prior to leaving Australia. One day, while Barry Gibb and I were having a friendly chat, he offered to write me a love song to record. Barry lived up to his word – a few days later there he was, sitting beside me, playing and singing a beautiful song that he'd written especially for me to record. Barry promised to leave me a demo tape copy of the song at the studio, but when I went to collect it, his managers, Nat Kipner and Ossie Byrne, refused to give it to me. The Bee Gees had already left on a ship bound for the UK by then, and there was no way of contacting Barry before their managers followed them a couple of weeks later, taking the tape of my song with them. Like so many of the young artists that had tasted fame, Barry and his younger brothers, Robin and Maurice, could all occasionally be a bit conceited, but most of the time, they were genuine, down-to-earth friendly guys who were more than happy to help other artists who were associated with the studio whenever they could. I found them very uplifting to be around, and I enjoyed their company immensely, but losing that song left me feeling deflated and depressed – particularly later when the Bee Gees hit the big time in the UK. I believe Barry's song could have given my career a substantial push forward, but I guess it just wasn't meant to be.

IN THE SAME way that I kept my sexuality a secret from my family, I was also afraid of anyone in the music business finding out the truth – I did everything that I could to keep it locked tightly in the closet. To try to camouflage my true identity, I deliberately mislead and misused girls, and one weekend, I unintentionally and very unexpectedly began a relationship with a woman named Bernice who was more than twice my age. It happened around the same time that the controversial movie *The Graduate* and the hit song *Mrs Robinson* were epitomising the 'older woman' seduction scene. I didn't plan or initiate the relationship, but I was happy to be in it – even though I now deeply regret it. Bernice served a purpose that helped protect me from anyone finding out about my true sexuality – especially anyone from my family. No one ever directly confronted me about it, but I knew that people were gossiping about my affair with Bernice behind my back, which was still far less of a burden to carry than anyone knowing that I was gay. Bernice didn't expect too much from me – I was just her toy-boy to have fun with, and we certainly did have a lot of good fun together. However, pretending to enjoy myself when it came to intimacy was always a challenging situation. As I'd always done with my other sexual encounters with the opposite sex, I'd close my eyes and think about the men that I fancied or had previously had sex with. Be that as it may, in time, I grew to love Bernice in every other way, she not only became the best friend that I'd ever had but a wonderful mentor. Her husband would have known what was going on, or at least to some degree. He loved Bernice very much, so I suspect that he deliberately turned a blind eye for fear of losing her altogether. Although he could be very moody at times, which is understandable under the circumstances, he was also very kind and good to me. Whenever I think about my 'relationship' with Bernice now I feel inundated with regret and deeply ashamed and saddened for him. If I'd known then what I've learned about life since, especially about karma, this, and many other things that I've since come to regret, never would have happened in the first place.

DAD AND BEATTY sold their Narrabeen house and bought a small grocery business near Sydney's Manly Beach – Glynis and Billy helped out in the shop after school and at weekends. When Dad later began to suffer from high blood pressure and his doctor advised him to get away from the stress of city life, he and Beatty sold the shop and bought the managing rights to a hotel called *The New Gunya*, in the southern New South Wales town of Lockhart. A week before they left for Lockhart, I saw Dad briefly for the first time in seven years and asked him for an advance on my money that he'd invested in his business for when I turned 21, which was only a few months away. His answer was that it wasn't possible as all of his funds were tied up in the hotel.

# Chapter 11

# TURBULENCE!

In December 1967, Mum won some money at the races and was able to afford to hire the Bankstown City Capital Hall for my 21st birthday party. She sent Dad and Billy an invitation, but there was no reply. Dad staying away was probably a good idea, but what upset me most was Dad's refusal to allow Billy to attend. Since investing my money in his business, Dad had owned two houses, plus two businesses, so the original amount of my money that he'd invested should have increased significantly. A week after my twenty-first, I received a birthday card from Dad containing a cheque for the same amount that I was awarded for my injuries fifteen years earlier. I was stunned, shocked, hurt and f---n angry! After enduring a childhood of suffering and abuse, I'd had enough, and decided that this day would be the turning point, as the last straw had finally broken the camel's back. Encouraged by Bernice and my brother, Denis, I began legal action against my father to recover the money that I believed he owed me – Mum did her best to talk me out of it, but my mind was made up. I was hoping that a subpoena to appear in court would provoke my father to do the right thing by negotiating with me and offering a more realistic settlement, but no such chance! Instead, he and Beatty flew up to Sydney a few weeks later to fight the case, and although Dad looked frail, he also looked like he was determined to beat me at any cost. Denis and his wife hadn't expected Dad to come to Sydney, and while he and Beatty stayed at their house, Denis chose to say nothing about agreeing that I should take Dad to court, and left me looking like the lone villain. During the hearing, the magistrate instructed a clerk to retrieve the records of my legal settlement fifteen years earlier, but they'd been destroyed in a fire that had gutted Bankstown Council's records department. Taking full advantage of this, Dad told the court the lie that he didn't promise to invest my money, but he'd only looked after it for me. He also claimed under oath that he'd given me every cent that I was entitled to receive. It suddenly looked like Dad was about to be victorious until I remembered that Mum had brought the issue up during their divorce hearing a couple of years earlier. When asked about it, Dad assured the divorce court that he'd invested my money in his company for when I turned twenty-one. As soon as I whispered this into my solicitor's ear, he informed the magistrate. The case was then adjourned and rescheduled for a hearing by a judge in the Sydney Supreme Court. I could tell by the angry look of frustration on my father's face that he wasn't only furious about it but very worried as well. If he was found guilty of perjury, he could have ended up spending time in prison. As much as I believed he deserved it after everything that he'd put me through, revenge and punishment was never my desire – neither was his money nor his hotel. I was fighting for my dignity and a chance to show Dad that I was no longer willing to accept being treated like the dirt beneath his and Beatty's feet. My solicitor assured me that if the divorce court records verified that Dad did indeed say that he'd invested the money, I stood a 99.9 % chance of being awarded a substantial amount of money as well as part-ownership of the New Gunya Hotel. He then asked me to sign some forms, but much to his disapproval, I declined and advised him not to take the case any further. I may not have received the money that I should have, but by standing up for myself, I achieved my objective, but it's not something that I'm proud of having done today.

IT CAME AS a huge disappointment when I heard that Surf City was about to close down and would soon be demolished to make way for the Kings Cross Crest Hotel. The famous old venue had been a significant part of mine and many other people's lives and it almost felt like someone was about to die. As a farewell to an era, Mrs Harrigan invited many of the artists that had ever performed at Surf City to appear on stage one last time on the final closing night. When it was my turn to perform, and I raced out in all my sparkling, glittery glory, my denture flew straight out of my mouth and into the audience below at the moment I started singing, and I exited the stage so fast that the band didn't even notice me go past. Like most Rock 'n' Roll artists back then, I was overly vain and concerned about my image and appearance, and while others laughed hysterically about it, I hid in the back of the stage area almost crying from embarrassment. To retrieve my precious chompers, I had to pay two of the go-go girls' cigarette money to go down and find them for me. It was dreadfully humiliation at the time, but I've sure shared a lot of good laughs about it since. Putting that unfortunate incident behind me, I continued my struggle to stardom by appearing on various national TV shows and performing in clubs and pubs. It was also during this period that I met and became friends with Australia's number one disc jockey, Donny Sutherland. As he did with many other up-and-coming artists, Donny gave me his encouragement and support to help me with my career and invited me to some of his private parties to meet and mingle with his influential guests. It was a lovely gesture, but I always felt awkwardly out of place, introverted and paranoid about doing or saying the wrong thing and blowing my cover. Donny lived his life to the fullest, he was constantly surrounded by beautiful women who doted on him, left, right and centre, and boy, didn't he love every minute of it. I, on the other hand, felt constantly uncomfortable about being in the company of so many intoxicated, 'oversexed' heterosexuals, all wanting to pop their corks with a member of the opposite sex. It would often have me in a state of disarray, and I'd be difficult to have a conversation with. I'd freeze up and end up speaking a load of crap, and then afterwards, I'd return home feeling alienated, frustrated, an idiot and basically a total failure – it was like an endless grind.

BY 1969, most of the artists that I associated with had ventured off to try their luck in the UK, and nothing was ever the same anymore. I did my usual gigs, appeared on TV shows, had articles written about me here and there, even did a bit of modelling on the catwalk, but none of it made me feel happy. Memories of George's insults and abusive words would constantly spring up in my mind like strings of firecrackers suddenly going off. If it wasn't enough that I had to hide my homosexuality from people in the music industry, I also had to keep my relationship with Bernice a secret. On top of all that, I also had to live the lie of pretending to be what I wasn't to hide the truth about my homosexuality from Bernice. Since the early 1960s, the narrow-minded attitude of many Australians towards various issues had come a long way from the dangerous and cruel ages of the '40s and '50s, but it was still a very serious risk for a gay male to express himself openly. While living out of wedlock for men and women had become much more common and acceptable, sex between two males remained a criminal offence and gay men were being imprisoned and medically experimented on for it. Queen Victoria had apparently created the law against gay men in the first place but had refused to believe in lesbianism, allowing gay women to be free to be themselves without fear of being arrested. It's always amazed me how so many straight men can be easily turned on by the thought or sight of two women in a sexual encounter with each other, yet hatefully despise the idea of two males together. Some psychiatrists and doctors have claimed that straight men who are not bothered or threatened by being in the company of gay men are more likely to be secure and relaxed with their heterosexuality. On the other hand, those who feel threatened, uncomfortable, insecure, or who go out of their way to condemn and despise gay men, are likely to have latent homosexual tendencies that they're suppressing. At least there was a ray of hope on the horizon for change – the social revolution of the 1960s had opened the door to 'gay liberation' which was well and truly on the way. The YouTube video below as an example of what some young gay people are forced to endure...

*https://www.youtube.com/watch?v=EPth8o-6dVE*

SATURDAY DATE was coming to an end and I was invited onto the final show to sing Nancy Sinatra's, *These Boots Are Made For Walking,* and Scott McKenzie's big hit at the time, *San Francisco (Be Sure To Wear Flowers in Your Hair).* I was in my element in my skin-tight pants, knee-high boots and a couple of flowers stuck in my hair, but looking back now, I must have seemed completely off the planet to a lot of the viewers. It mystifies me that I was able to dress and act so flamboyantly on stage and still remain paranoid about concealing my sexuality at the same time – who the hell was I trying to kid? It wasn't until later in the 70s and 80s when artists such as Boy George and David Bowie made glitter and makeup fashionable, even for straight men. Maybe I'd been a 'glitter' pioneer without even knowing it. Standing in the studio green room that day ready to go on and reminiscing how I'd dreamed years earlier of one day appearing on the show, was such an exciting experience. Although it wasn't my own songs and records that I was performing, it still felt like a tremendous achievement to be fulfilling such a huge part of what once was only a dream.

WHILE THINGS WERE looking prosperous for me career-wise, my moods were continuing to jump up and down, and it was a bit like being on an out of control pogo stick. I'd already reached my early twenties and was still struggling to find my true self, and despising my brother George more and more each passing day. In some of my worst moments of self-loathing and despair, I thought seriously about getting a gun and shooting him – Dad and Beatty were close seconds on my list. It's a terrible thing to desire, but during those low moments of depression, I wanted them all dead, and I'd be lying if I didn't admit it. To me, they'd been cruel, evil bastards and had wrecked my life, and I inwardly vowed to pay them back for every rotten thing that they'd ever said and done to me. Thankfully, the universe intervened in 1969, when George's name was splashed all over the front pages of the Sydney newspapers, and he was on the run after being involved in a spate of armed bank robberies. My initial reaction was to hide my connection to him, so I changed my stage name from Toddy Bird to Tommy Beaumont. It may have been an odd career move since I'd already become known as Toddy Bird, but it was better than taking on the added stress of being associated with an armed criminal for a brother – not to mention, becoming a potential target for his enemies. At any rate, it wasn't all that uncommon for solo performers and bands to change their name back then, in fact, there were so many changes that it was often hard to keep up with who was who. On the funnier side of it all, some viewers were probably surprised or confused by how much Tommy Beaumont looked like Toddy Bird. Apart from anything else, it was a blessing for us both that George was arrested and locked away, as even if I'd wanted to, I could no longer get near him, especially with a gun.

IN MARCH 1969, my brother Billy turned 16 and was finally free to leave Lockhardt and return to Sydney to live with Mum. A few weeks later, when Dad took ill, Billy returned to Dad's hotel and was there at Dad's side when he succumbed to a stroke. Strangely enough, I'd had a very significant dream about Dad only a few weeks before his death, and in the dream, Mum and I were in a field surrounded by dry, yellow grass, and she was wearing a black dress. An aircraft with chains of flowers wrapped around it flew overhead and some family members were hanging out of its windows waving and looking down at us, and Mum and I seemed to be outcasts in some way. At the time of Dad's death, he was still living in the The New Gunyah Hotel that he and Beatty were leasing in the Riverina area of southern New South Wales, and some of my family flew down from Sydney for his funeral. During the same week, Mum had made herself a new black dress, and because there was a severe drought, the grass had turned yellow – since Mum and I had severed our relationship with Dad, we were more or less on the outside looking in.

On July 20th, 1969, the same night that Neil Armstrong and Buzz Aldrin first stepped onto the moon, I awoke from a nightmare, where I'd been floating above the moon-landing module, looking across to my right. Hovering just above a row of small grey hills in the background towards the horizon, were three white discs, and I got the impression that the discs were somehow 'observing' what was going on. I suffer severely from arachnophobia, fear of spiders, and even the little ones can scare the crap out of me. These discs freaked me out as much as if I'd looked up and spotted a cluster of deadly funnel-web spiders. Since then I've heard rumours that objects were seen in a similar location by the astronauts. How true that is or not, I don't know. In the latter half of 1969, I performed in a lot of New South Wales country-town clubs, pubs and dance halls, and then I spent Christmas and New Year's Eve back home with my family in Sydney.

On January 26th 1970, the Australia Day Long Weekend, I was fortunate enough to be invited to perform in front of 11,000 people at the 'Pilgrimage for Pop' – Australia's first large-scale outdoor rock festival. It was a sort of 'Mini Woodstock', held at a large farm owned by Lt. Colonel Henry Nicholls in Ourimbah, up north from Sydney. All around, the sound of '60s music, mingled with the sweet smell of incense and marijuana that wafted through the air, and in between performances, the chanting of Hare Krishna mantras could be heard taking over as the shaven-headed followers moved through the crowd shaking and banging their tambourines. British pop group, 'Reverend Black and the Rocking Vicars' backed me and most of the other solo vocalists – what a great band they were to work with. Among some of the well-known artists that performed with us over the three-day event were; Tamam Shud; Doug Parkinson in Focus; Jeff St John and Copperwine; Stevie Wright and his new band Rachette (making his first public appearance since the breakup of the Easybeats); Chain; Max Merrit & The Meteors; Ray Columbus & The Invaders; The Nutwood Rug Band; Billy Thorpe (also making a 'comeback' appearance after two years of absence); The Aztecs and 'wild lady', Wendy Saddington. For me, it felt like I'd entered into an other-worldly rock'n'roll dimension.

WORKING WITH a different backing band almost every time I did a gig could often be a nerve-wracking and stressful experience, especially if they played a song in a different key to what I usually sang it and I fell flat on a high note. The audience wouldn't know that it wasn't my key, and it always made me look and feel like an amateur, but even so, I still had to perform as best I could and face the criticism regardless. The obvious solution was to put a band of my own together, so I started searching through the 'musicians wanted' ads, and a week later, joined up with a bass player, guitarist and drummer. A keyboard player that joined the band later came with a Hammond organ, which enormously improved our sound. We rehearsed four nights a week, and after throwing around some ideas for a band name, unanimously chose to call ourselves 'Port Jackson'. After I'd arranged some spots on a couple of TV shows, we found ourselves gigging several nights a week, and also secured management with a young guy named Sebastian Chase, who years later founded MGM Distributions and managed bands such as The Whitlams and Dragon. I first met Sebastian at a Catholic Church gig that we did, he was still very young at the time, as we all were, and doing some volunteer work, while he was putting together his career. We may have even been the first band that he ever managed. Sebastian was a trustworthy guy who believed in us and was always supportive, encouraging, honest, and reliable. The problem was, success had happened so quickly and easily, way before some of the band members were ready to deal with it. Heads soon began to swell from the praise that we were receiving, and a state of disharmony arose. It also eventually became apparent to me that the rest of the band knew that I was gay, and I began to feel increasingly alienated. I always did my best to avoid talking to the girls that gathered around the group during breaks and after performances, and maybe that's what let the cat out the bag. Either that or the other band members had put two and two together and got the proverbial three. They never directly mentioned anything about my sexuality to my face, but whenever we gigged out of town and stayed overnight, I was invariably allotted the single room, which always made me feel unjustly ostracised, as I'd never shown the slightest sign of interest towards any of them. When Sebastian organised an open-air rock concert to be held at the Liverpool Showground, under the banner of 'Black Friday', as things turned out for Port Jackson on the night, it couldn't have been a more appropriate name. We were placed at the top of the bill and Sebastian had arranged for a

TV network to film the show, to help propel Port Jackson to loftier heights. Fashionable, colourful clothing in those days was as scarce as chicken's teeth, exorbitantly expensive and exclusive to shops such as the 'In Shop' and 'Mr. John'. Luckily, my mother had taught me to sew and make my own stage wear, based on photographs of what British and American styles were dictating. During the week leading up to our 'Black Friday' show, I worked my fingers to the bone making red velvet flared pants and matching tops for each member of the band to wear on stage and for the TV cameras. When I arrived at the venue, I was shocked to find them all dressed in ragged jeans and faded T-shirts and to make matters worse, two of them were drunk. We got into a verbal altercation about it, and then, in front of onlookers and fans, one member of the band screamed...

"We're not a fuckin' poofta like you, ya bloody fairy!"

He sounded just like my brother, George, and it was more than I could possibly bear, so I jumped straight into my car, zoomed off and left them to eat the dust. As tears streamed down my face and I struggled to keep focused on the road ahead, I swore to myself that I'd never return, and I didn't. That night I hardly slept a wink, wondering and imagining what might or might not have happened after I'd left. There'd always been other singers hanging around and acting like hungry piranhas hoping to take my place and join the band, so it was no surprise when I later learnt that one of them did...

"What's Sebastian, gonna think?" I kept asking myself repeatedly. "Is this tha end? Is my future in music stuffed?"

I didn't have the nerve to admit that I was gay to Sebastian openly, and the best that I could hope for was that he'd accept my resignation from the band without delving too deeply into the reason for my leaving. The following night, Port Jackson was obligated to work together for one last time, on channel 10's 'Late Night Show'. Luckily we only had to mime to two of our pre-recorded songs, and there was no need for us to speak to each other, and we didn't. It was an extreme case of *the show must go on*, though miserable and torturous it was. When the show's hostess and her big smiling boobs (she was wearing a see-through top and no bra) interviewed me on-air and asked why I hadn't shown up for the 'Black Friday' concert, I obediently followed Sebastian's instructions and lied through my teeth, telling her that I'd lost my voice shortly before we were about to hit the stage, and saying nothing at all about leaving the band. In so many ways, I was relieved about the breakup, as it meant that I'd no longer have to lug my two six-feet-high speaker columns in and out of gigs or help with the Hammond organ up and down the stairs. As much as I loved having it as part of our powerful sound, it was so fricken heavy! Not one to sit around and procrastinate, I picked myself up and was soon back on the circuit again as a solo artist. Writing about this now has me wondering how successful Port Jackson could have become had we kept it all together. Sebastian was a fantastic force, as history shows, destined for incredible success. Perhaps if I'd been out of the closet and able to confront Sebastian with the truth beforehand, he may have been able to sort things out with the other band members and still take us to the top. I guess some things in life are just not meant to happen, this being one of them.

EVEN THOUGH LIFE had blessed me with so much creative potential, during my unstable and precarious teenage years, I hadn't been able to hold down even a simple factory job for more than a few weeks, or at best, months, or sometimes only a few days. I'd be stable for a while, and then I'd start imagining that my fellow workers had noticed that I was gay – that's when the lie that I was living would rise up and become like a heavy load on my shoulders, or a gun pointing at my head. It would weigh me down to the point where despair and a severe lack of self-worth would become so overwhelmingly powerful that I'd barely be able to think, let alone function. Sometimes I'd reach a point where I could not see any future. I'd feel as though my spirit was getting devoured, and that the only way out would be to end it all by taking my own life. Even when things were going well for me, I was still never able to experience complete happiness within, as constant thoughts of what George had drummed into my mind, along with Denis's habit of labelling everyone that he didn't like or agree with as being a *fuckin' poofta,* would re-emerge and feel like darts going into me. Some members of my family regarded me as being a no-hoper, and that only added more pain to my suffering, because in so many ways, they were right! I'd prayed to God with all my heart in more churches than I care to remember, I'd attended huge gatherings with ministers such as Dr Billy Graham, I'd sworn my life to Jesus several times over and even tried to become heterosexual, and yet nothing had ever worked, and nothing could as long as I continued living my lie. Little did I know at the time that, like me, millions of other gay men around the world were suffering from the same cruel, tormenting injustices.

FROM A CHILD, I've always been what is often termed 'psychic' – 'a knower of things' – and I'd sometimes innocently predict that someone was coming to visit the house and sure enough they'd turn up unannounced and unexpected. I also sometimes heard voices in my head that would upset me and cause me to break out into a cold sweat, especially when they were telling me to do things against my will. Sometimes the voices would become so loud, intense and frightening that they'd almost drive me to the edge of my sanity. On one occasion, shortly after Mum had gained custody of me in 1960, there was a particular incident when the voices became 'super-intense'. I was ironing a shirt for school, and Mum was outside watering her garden when the voices started off in their usual distant manner, and then quickly became so much closer and louder, eventually reaching a point where I could hardly keep breathing. It sounded like an enormous crowd of people all talking to me at once from every direction. I sprinted across the room and turned the radio up full blast to try to block them out, but the voices rose even higher. I turned the TV up to its full volume as well, and that's when Mum came rushing into the house, wanting to know what on earth was going on. The moment that she started shouting to get above the noise of the radio and TV, the voices instantly stopped. I was afraid of being considered a loony, so I didn't tell Mum or anyone else anything about the voices. After that, I lived on a knife's edge, expecting them to return at any time and catch me off guard – thankfully nothing as severe has ever happened again. Over the years since, I've searched my mind to find logical explanations for my many unusual experiences in life. In more recent years I've heard about *DID* (Dissociative Identity Disorder), which has made me wonder if I'd suffered from this condition, where two or several more distinct identities or personality states are present that can alternately take control of an individual – or was it something else entirely?

*While no one living in this world is exempt from suffering, everyone born in this world has got the hidden potential within them to become exempt from contributing to suffering.*

*...Nichiren.*

# Chapter 12

# AFTER THE '*LIGHT*'

My blast into the stars and back in 1970, was an experience that I'll never forget. The lightning strike that had instigated it couldn't have come at a worse possible time for me career-wise, as I was in the midst of a significant challenge regarding my future as a solo artist. My manager, Sebastian Chase, had been doing his best to get me re-established, and I'd also just signed a three-year contract with EMI. I was preparing to record my first single on HMV for British producer Michael Barclay, who'd been sent to Australia by EMI Headquarters in the UK to help run their Sydney office. He was also in search of new and potential talent to record for the international market. After seeing me perform on a popular TV breakfast program one morning, and tracking me down, he offered me a contract. Of course, there were many others just as or far more worthy, but Michael chose me as one of three acts that he wanted to produce and promote internationally – it was an opportunity of a lifetime that went aeons beyond even my wildest dreams, and I'd been waiting for the studio schedule to arrive when the lightning struck. Michael was a lovely man, but he was also very strict about the way that I was to handle my private life. Back then, even celebrities such as Elton John, Rock Hudson and others like them were reluctant to come out and admit that they were gay, for fear of having their careers ruined. For anyone like me, who was gay and just starting out in the music industry, it would have been suicidal career-wise. As much as I'd fought to hide it, Michael soon figured out the truth about my sexuality and gave me strict instructions to keep it under covers. I'd been doing my best to try to live up to his demands, but adding to the aftermath of my messy departure from Port Jackson, the remaining turmoil in my mind from the lightning strike had left me feeling more confused and vulnerable than ever. I felt as though I'd been living my entire life confined to a small room, and then the lightning had suddenly torn down the walls to reveal a vastness beyond anything that I'd ever known or had even begun to imagine. I felt exposed to the wilderness and lost without a clue as to which way to go or what to do next. Whether I wanted to or not, I was being forced outwards into a great unknown – there seemed to be nothing that I could do to resist it or stop it.

Several months before the band split, Port Jackson had been contracted to perform over the Christmas holidays on an Italian luxury liner called the *Castel Felice*. When I informed the shipping company that we'd broken up, and they still wanted me to perform as a solo artist, I was over the moon. I certainly needed space and time to sort things out and to try to clear my head, and the cruise was a perfect opportunity to get away from everything and think. As 1970 was drawing to a close, I could hardly wait to get on board the ship and leave some of my worries and confusion behind – not a chance! I spent that Christmas, my twenty-fourth birthday and New Year's Eve merrily singing my way around the sunny South Pacific and becoming more disillusioned by the day. However, it wasn't all doom and gloom, there were also some funny moments, including a few very embarrassing ones, particularly one night when a violent storm threw the ship around like a toy floating upon giant waves. It became so bad that dinner was cancelled and many of the passengers suffered severe seasickness. The all-male Italian band and I spent most of the evening hanging out together in their cabin, waiting for things to settle down enough for us to perform. By midnight, we'd given up hope, and we were all feeling famished. I offered the guys some peanuts that I had stashed upstairs in my cabin, and they all reacted anxiously with shocked looks on their faces, waving their hands around and telling me no thank you – I couldn't make head nor tail of it, they looked like they were about to make a run for it. It wasn't until the next day that I found out that they'd thought I'd been offering them some 'penis' – how embarrassed I was! I must have offered them peanuts a dozen times, at one point, I was almost begging them to have some – repeatedly assuring the guys in broken English that it would make them feel so much better!

On the surface of things, it turned out to be a magnificent trip – I saw some of the most exotic places on Earth. However, no matter how bright, sunny and pleasant it was on the outside, I still couldn't escape the storm that was waging a war inside of my head. Seeing openly-gay males aboard the ship and witnessing how free some of them were to be themselves made me want to break out of my cage and be like them – the person that I truly was – if only I could have figured out how? By the journey's end, my feelings of security with Bernice had all but diminished – I could no longer play the role of her secret lover or use her as camouflage. I needed to be honest and face the truth once and for all, and to do that, I needed to get as far away from Bernice, my family and Sydney as I possibly could for more time and pace to sort myself out. I'd made a lot of new friends among the passengers on board the ship, and some of them had invited me to visit them in Melbourne – it seemed a perfect solution for my dilemma. On the night before I left for Melbourne, I took Bernice for a drive and told her the truth about my sexuality – that I could no longer continue the toy-boy charade. She was devastated and didn't want to accept it – with tears flowing from her eyes, she begged me to see a doctor and offered to pay whatever it cost – I kept telling her that nothing was going to change the way that I was and that I was sorry, but no doctors. In the end, we fell helplessly into each other's arms and sobbed. Bernice had been the most precious friend that I'd ever known – the way that my admission caused her so much pain and suffering tore me to pieces inside, and that night, I vowed I'd never misuse or deceive a woman to hide my sexuality again. Choosing not to tell anyone other than my immediate family where I was going, I packed some clothes, jumped into my car and drove to Melbourne.

One of the passengers that I'd made friends with on the ship was a youthful seventy-five-year-old millionairess named Elizabeth. She'd phoned me to ask how I was getting along the morning following my confession to Bernice, and I'd happily accepted her invitation to come and stay with her in her luxury villa in Toorak. Elizabeth lived the superficial lifestyle of a city socialite and, as I quickly found out, was a person that always liked to get her way, no matter what. While I was staying at her house, she insisted on bringing me breakfast in bed every morning, and each time that she did so, she wore less and less clothing. I just thought that it was because she knew that I was gay and felt free to dress as she pleased. Elizabeth also insisted that I join her and her associates at the various social functions that she attended, which always made me feel awkwardly out of place. What I wanted most was to get away to some of the gay bars and hopefully meet the man of my dreams, but Elizabeth wouldn't let me out of her sight. During the cruises, I'd also become close friends with Mario – a very sensual, young Italian singer that was also performing on the ship, but I wanted much more if I could get it. Mario had promised to visit Elizabeth and me when the ship made its final stopover in Melbourne before returning to Europe – as that day approached, I tried to work out a way to spend some time with him alone, but Elizabeth had other plans of her own. In preparation for the occasion, she'd bought a set of vinyl records to learn to speak Italian and asked me to test her. Each afternoon, we'd sit together in her luxurious living room, sipping expensive champagne and listening to the records, until one day, after she'd downed one too many drinks, I was shocked to discover that she too had a crush on Mario. She would have thrown a massive fit if she'd known that by helping her, I was learning to speak Italian myself, and for the same reason. One evening while we were coaching each other and I'd drunk more than I should have, Elizabeth led me into her dimly-lit bedroom, unzipped my fly and before I knew it, she was on top of me – we were having sex. When I woke up the following morning and vaguely remembered what had happened, I went into shock. I was hoping and praying with everything in me that it had just been a dream, but with my nakedness beneath the sheets, I soon realised that it hadn't. I felt disgusted, ashamed and suddenly sick to the stomach – I just wanted to hide somewhere and never have to face Elizabeth again. In the meantime, Elizabeth carried on around the house as though nothing had happened. Fearing that it could happen again, and much to Elizabeth's discontent, I packed my things and went to stay with a gay biochemist friend that I'd also met on the ship and who also knew Elizabeth. When I told him what had happened, he refused to believe a word of it and insisted that I'd been hallucinating because I'd drunk too much champagne. In the end, Mario never visited anyway, and neither Elizabeth nor I got a chance to say anything, let alone try our luck at getting him into bed – but we'd certainly come a long way with our Italian.

I RENTED A ROOM in a South Yarra share-flat and soon started frequenting a gay pub around the corner on Toorak Road where I had the misfortune of meeting some of the roughest gay people that I'd ever met. From then on, things went from bad to worse, and my earliest impressions of the gay scene became as dismal as everything else in my life. I began drinking excessively to try to help deaden my dreary disappointments. Like a lot of other up-and-coming hopefuls from around the country, I'd previously made regular trips to Melbourne to appear and sing on Australia's top TV pop shows *Uptight, Happening70* and *Happening71* – performing alongside big stars such as Johnny Farnham, Normie Rowe and the show's host, Molly Meldrum. It was a huge privilege and I always tried my best to give the impression that I was having fun, but behind all the limelight, I was as lonely, miserable and unhappy as hell. It got even worse after I overheard Molly and a couple of his associates exchanging sleazy homophobic remarks about me. As Molly did with other interstate guests on the show, he interviewed me one day, and because of what I'd overheard him saying about me, I was a fumbling mess. It was almost as though my brother George was interviewing me – if only I'd known at the time that Molly was as gay as a row of camp tents – I can't stand hypocrites and would definitely have outed him. Johnny Farnham was an individual and a lovely one at that. Usually, when we appeared on the show together, he'd always go out of his way to come up and greet me, have a friendly chat, wish me all the best and make me feel welcome. Whenever I had to talk to any girls from the audience after a performance, as per usual, it would be a nerve-wracking experience and I'd become close to panic-stricken. I'd feel like I was about to faint, and I wouldn't know what to say or how to respond to them. If any male fans approached me, my reaction was much worse – I'd have a barrage of mental flashbacks of things that George had said and done to me – my lips would quiver, my eye would twitch and then I'd get my words all mixed up worrying about it. I can only imagine that many of the guys that I spoke to would have thought that I was either high on drugs or nuts. I'd get so angry with myself afterwards, that I'd feel like bashing my head up against a wall – there was never anything that I could do about it except to dread the next time and the times following that...

EVAN JONES, who co-wrote the big hit *The Push Bike Song* for the Mixtures, came to my flat one day to discuss ideas for a song that EMI had commissioned him to write for me – I was thrilled to the bone! Evan spent around an hour or so recording my thoughts on current world events and life in general, and then jotted down the lyrics to a song that he titled, *You Can't Take It With You To Your Grave.* I liked the words, but the melody wasn't suitable for my style of singing, and because Evan was a highly successful songwriter, I refrained from mentioning my discontent in fear of offending him. The second song, *Too Bad You Don't Want Me*, written and recorded by Chris Andrews in the UK and used as the B-side for his big hit *Yesterday Man,* had been chosen for me by Michael Barclay and was far more suitable. Sandy Shaw, among others, also recorded and released the same song. A few weeks later, Michael sneaked me into Sydney on a late-night flight from Melbourne to record in secret during the early hours of the morning. I thought that it was a strange time to be doing it but didn't dare question him about it. Waiting for me in the studio when I arrived was a full orchestra of some of the best musicians in Australia. Just as I was about to begin singing, as a gesture of good luck, Michael covered my microphone with a handkerchief that he'd used similarly for Mick Jagger's earliest recordings. (It has recently occurred to me that the Rolling Stone's song *Route 66* I'd sung five years earlier on my first Australian TV appearance may have been one of the songs that Michael produced – using that same handkerchief.) Michael wasn't always credited on the records that he produced, so I guess I'll never know. After that incredible night, I felt confident that my dreams of achieving international stardom could be about to become a reality – the single was finally released in the second half of 1971.

At the time, I was sharing a luxury home with a couple of guys that worked at Melbourne's ABC TV studios. One of them, Nick, was affectionately kind-hearted, not to mention, knock-dead gorgeous. I was desperate to have someone special in my life that I could love and be loved by, and I soon fell for him hook, line and sinker – foolishly misinterpreting his kindness and acceptance as a 'come on'. When Nick figured out that I had the wrong kind of feelings for him and then let me down gently by telling me that he liked me very much and that if he'd been gay, he'd have definitely been interested in pursuing that sort of a relationship with me, although it was better than how most other straight guys would have reacted, it still caused me immense pain, breaking my heart and leaving me feeling more miserable and pissed off with my non-existent love life than ever. A local entrepreneur, who'd taken a keen interest in my singing career, threw a party in a popular downtown Melbourne restaurant to assist in promoting my record and invited several of his influential acquaintances from the music industry. My life as an EMI recording artist seemed to be going great guns, but little did I know that hidden behind all the expectations and celebrations, a secret plan in Sydney was in progress to sabotage my record as part of a plot to destroy Michael Barclay and any of his other projects.

At a local nearby coffee shop one day, I ran into an attractive nineteen-year-old woman, who introduced herself as Alice. She'd just broken up with her boyfriend and had nowhere to stay, so I offered to put her up in my part of the house, just for a couple of weeks while she sorted herself out. I told Alice that I was gay, but during her first night there, and after I'd had too much to drink, she crept into my bed naked, mounted me and raped me. The next morning, I told her that I could no longer trust her and asked her to find somewhere else to stay ASAP. While I was out, Alice got to know Nick intimately and moved in with him – although I'd accepted that there could never be anything other than just friendship between Nick and me, it still cut my feelings to ribbons knowing that Alice was in bed with him, and there were moments that night when I could have easily ripped her hair out. A few days later, I left Melbourne to do a radio station tour in Sydney and to meet the city's DJ's – it had been arranged by EMI to promote my newly-released record. I still felt as angry as a wounded bull about Alice and Nick, but somehow managed to keep it undercover and put it at the back of my mind. It was such a relief to be getting away from Melbourne, even if only for a few days – the timing was perfect. I didn't think that I'd have a chance to change my clothes upon my arrival in Sydney, so I got dressed up for the tour before leaving. Ever since the lightning incident, I'd been losing my hair, and it was starting to show. Men's wigs were becoming increasingly popular, so I bought one that was streaked at Myer after yet another barber did a crappy job of cutting my hair – I'd been wearing the wig as a substitute. For the first part of the promotional tour, I was scheduled to stop off at Canberra and pop into a couple of radio stations there first. In a mad rush to catch my plane, I completely forgot that Melbourne's new Tullamarine Airport had opened and went to the old airport at Essendon by mistake, missing my scheduled flight by over half an hour. My only hope of making it to Sydney that morning was to take an alternative flight with another airline, and after a nerve-racking, bumpy flight in an old DC3 I was transferred onto, we eventually landed at an airport that was completely unfamiliar to me. All the other passengers looked happy enough to be there, so I just assumed that it was a different airstrip on the outskirts of Canberra used for smaller aircraft, similar to the one that I'd flown in on. I asked the hostess where we were, and when she told me that we were in Albury, I was gobsmacked. No one mentioned that the plane would be making a stopover there, let alone for three hours. Adding to my disorientation, I was as hungry as a horse in a drought, and I'd left my wallet at home on my bed. The tiny airport consisted of a small shed-like building, surrounded by cattle and sheep, and the only people there were a couple of airport staff and the odd farmer or two collecting deliveries. While I waited impatiently to re-board the plane, I was ridiculed left, right and centre. Although I can laugh about it now, it certainly wasn't funny at the time. I was dressed up in a trendy, flaming-red safari suit with the trousers tucked into knee-high black leather boots, and a matching bag over my shoulder – I stood out like a bush-fire, with my new silver-streaked wig. By today's standards, it was nothing out of the ordinary, but back then it was a major shock, especially for those living in country towns. My luggage was stuck on the plane, so I couldn't even get to it to change my clothes, and there was nowhere to hide. The expressions on the faces of some of the local farmers when they spotted me made me feel like I was an alien from another planet, they were saying things to each other like...

"What tha bloody 'ell d'ya reck'n it is mate?"

"Stuffed if I know, Charlie, I've neva seen nothin' flamin'-well like it!"

With the three-hour stopover finally behind me and a new lot of happy passengers queuing up in front of me, I finally boarded the aircraft, and we were airborne. Sometime later, as we were nearing Canberra Airport, the hostess tapped me on the shoulder and asked me if I could go with her and identify my luggage – she explained that the pilot had radioed ahead and that there was a connecting jet standing by and waiting to take me and several of the other passengers straight on to Sydney. As the little plane began losing altitude rapidly, I hurried along the aisle behind the hostess to a cordoned-off area at the back of the cabin where everyone's luggage was piled high – my case was nowhere in sight. The pretty, little hostess had a small, shapely, tight build and was wearing a micro-mini skirt – if I'd been straight, I'd have been in seventh heaven watching her climbing through the cases looking for mine. I could see that she was having a difficult time, so I suggested that she come out and let me take over, which she did. I had everything stacked up, including three big movie film canisters, and finally spotted my case right at the bottom. I bent down to retrieve it at the same moment the plane hit the tarmac – there was a sudden big jolt and the whole bloody lot tumbled down on top of me...

"Mr Beaumont! Mr Beaumont!" Cried the hostess in an anxious voice as the plane kept bouncing and more things fell.

After I'd eventually fought my way out from beneath everything, I swung around to face the hostess, and the poor girl turned an instant shade of ghostly white. Fashionable wigs for men were still very new – she must have thought that I'd suffered a severe head injury, as my wig had been twisted around in all the commotion, and one of its side-burns was hanging across my nose. Minutes later, I raced like a maniac through the terminal from one plane to another, which was full of what appeared to be businessmen and politicians dressed in suits – I was still trying to straighten up my wig as I raced right by them – some of the surprised expressions on their faces seemed to say it all – 'The youth of today are stuffed!' When I finally arrived in Sydney, the EMI reps had given up waiting for me and had long left. With no money, I then had to beg a bus driver to take me into the city free of charge, where I managed to borrow a few dollars from a friend to see me over. The day had been, long, crazy and exhausting, and if that wasn't enough, upon my return to Melbourne, I was greeted with yet another unexpected surprise. Alice had run off with most of my belongings, including my wallet and a brand-new stereo record player that I'd only just purchased before I'd left. I can only assume that she used my money to leave town because she was never seen or heard from again. This disruptive stream of events had me feeling shattered, but there was no time to sit around and feel sorry for myself, I had to get straight on with promoting my new record and do it with a smile. In those days radio stations usually played a new release for about a week or so and then checked around the leading record shops to see if the record was selling. Some of the top stations, including 3UZ, were playing my song but nobody could buy it! It turned out that the B-side was listed on the order sheets instead of the A-side, making my song appear to be nonexistent. By the time that I eventually discovered this, and contacted 3UZ to let them know what had happened, they'd already taken my song off their playlist. Later that week, the manager of 3UZ phoned me back and explained that he was fed up with EMI for messing the station around with their release details – he apologised for what had happened with my record and promised that if I let him know in advance the next time I had a single coming out, he'd make sure that it didn't happen again. I was still trying to get my head around the awkwardness of performing the 'A' side, so when I presented my new record for the first time a few weeks later on national television, I performed the 'B' side instead...

https://youtu.be/xBiKWUiZgss

MEANWHILE, unbeknownst to me, Michael Barclay was having some serious issues with his fellow workers at EMI. From what Michael later told me, they considered him to be an intruder sent from the UK to take over in Australia – he'd been receiving resistance from them ever since the week he'd first arrived. Michael had a drinking problem, and taking advantage of it, some staff members had been secretly messing things up for him. Sadly, an opportunity to make that call to 3UZ never eventuated, as my two-year contract with EMI guaranteed that I could record two singles within that time frame, but didn't ensure their release. A couple of months later, I received two songs to learn from EMI and a date to record a second single. Upon my arrival at the studio, I was told that Michael was ill and that someone else would be producing me. Although the recording went down without a hitch, and the songs suited me perfectly, the single was shelved and never released. Amid my growing despair, two members of the Italian orchestra from the ship returned to Australia with some fabulous and uplifting news. They'd taken my first single and some tapes of other cover songs that I'd previously recorded for TV appearances to Europe, which had been very well received. The guys wanted to take me back to Rome with them, groom me and then launch me onto the European market – I was ecstatic, especially knowing that I'd be working alongside my spunky Italian singer friend, Mario. I also thought about how pissed off Elizabeth would be if she heard about it. The main sponsor of the deal was RCA Records in Rome, but only if I could get out of my contract with EMI. It was a fabulous second chance, and I could hardly wait to get on board the plane with them and fly off to Italy, but when my manager, Sebastian, asked EMI-HMV to release me from my contract, his request was refused, and the RCA deal eventually fell through. I couldn't have been more bitterly frustrated and pissed-off with EMI if I'd tried. Michael Barclay later explained that EMI-HMV were afraid to risk giving me a chance to succeed elsewhere, as it would have given him too much credit, and made them look bad instead – I felt like I was falling from a great height with hands reaching out to rescue me that I couldn't reach. I've since come to believe that it would have been evident to EMI that the type of songs Evan Jones wrote wouldn't suit me, and that their ridiculous decision to ask him to write the A-side was a part of their planned sabotage. Years later, a new CEO at EMI, told me in no uncertain terms that Evan's song was the biggest load of rubbish that he'd ever heard and that it should never have been recorded in the first place.

After being told that I was to remain stuck on a shelf until the duration of my contract, I fell into a worsening state of misery and began drinking heavily to try to drown my sorrows. By then, my memories of the beautiful Light had been obscured by the monstrosities that were eating away at my life, and things became so bad that I could no longer fulfil most of my singing commitments. Consequently, I ended up with no bookings to earn enough money to pay my rent and to buy food to eat.

OVER THE YEARS that I'd been struggling to become a successful singer, I'd tried my hand at all sorts of jobs. I'd built car batteries in a factory where fireworks were let off during the night-shift hours to keep the workers alert and awake, I'd pulled apart and assembled refrigerators, stoves, washing machines and record players, I'd dug ditches for the Department of Main Roads, I'd done some spot-welding, I'd worked as a clerk and had even made money from doing illegal hair styling without a licence. On top of all that, I'd also volunteered to have my tonsils and adenoids removed unnecessarily, under the false impression that it would improve my voice. However, all of the disappointments and hardships that I'd endured along the way combined didn't come near the disillusionment, frustration and anger that I was now feeling.

I took a day job as an outpatients' clerk in the emergency department at Melbourne's Alfred Hospital, and while the doctors and nurses fought tirelessly to try to mend wounds and save lives, an essential part of my job was to go through accident victims' pockets to establish their identity, which included facing some of the most horrific sights that I'd ever witnessed. It turned out to be the worst job choice that I could have made. Seeing and listening to other human beings suffering agonising pain, and watching some of them die, became more than I could bear. Each night, after work, I was anaesthetising myself with excessive amounts of alcohol, and when the hospital staff noticed that I was failing to do my work correctly because of it, and reported it, the admin had no other alternative than to let me go. Unemployed and without money coming in to pay the rent, I was forced to give up my flat and move into the home of a lesbian friend named Eva, a kind-hearted, bubbly character, who soon had me feeling a little bit happier with myself. Eva belonged to a lesbian soccer team that played against other lesbian teams every Sunday. After each game, the teams took turns in hosting an afternoon tea party at one of their homes where they'd sip wine and munch on sandwiches and cakes – or sometimes each other. ;o)

One Sunday after a match and when everyone was relaxing at Eva's place, I got up to some childish mischief. Whenever a team member popped down the hall to use the bathroom, I whispered a little fib in her ear that another team member in the room had the 'hots' for her. At the beginning of their gathering, it was difficult to hear yourself think over the noise of chatter and laughter, but by the time that I'd finished with them, you could have heard a pin drop. In the end, I got busted when I told one of the girls that her long-term partner fancied her. One afternoon when Eva was out, I had a terrible row with one of her other less friendly lesbian acquaintances who'd been trying to force me into having a sexual relationship with her fourteen-year-old brother. This woman was a practising witch who was said to have the power to put terrible curses on people – she certainly looked like a witch! A few days later, someone who knew her told me that she'd performed a ceremony to put an evil curse on me because I'd refused her demands. Hearing that was the final straw. I decided that my move to Melbourne, like so many of my other decisions, had been a huge mistake, so I packed my bags and arranged to return to Sydney on the first available flight.

*Regardless of the evils and obstacles that may confront us or attack us during our journey into the center of our life, we must have no fer and always continue to move forward without ever retrieving even an inch.*

*If we do not harbour uncertainties within our hearts, we will as a matter of course attain our enlightenment and successfully achieve a state of interdimensional peace .*

*Do not doubt this, not even for a moment.*

*...Nichiren.i*

# Chapter 13

# HORROR WEEKEND!

Most years, during the marking of the end-of-term School Certificate exam, I'd work part-time for the Education Department in Sydney as a clerk. The job always paid well, and the people that I worked with were usually a lot of good fun to be around. On the day that I was leaving Melbourne, I called the Education Department to let them know that I'd be available in Sydney the following week and to please let me know if there were any vacancies. Just as I was about to walk out the door, on my way to the airport, a recruitment officer phoned me back and offered me a job to start immediately. The timing couldn't have been more perfect! It meant that I'd be able to afford to move into a shared flat soon after I arrived. Most of my family lived in the western suburbs of Sydney, where people back then were often unworldly and narrow-minded. I didn't only not want any of my family to discover that I had a drinking problem, I also didn't want my drinking problem to uncover the truth about my sexuality. A couple of days after returning, I found a room to rent in a shared flat on the east side of the city, overlooking Waverley Beach – a very trendy and open-minded area to live, especially if you were gay. On the same day that I moved in, I crossed paths with Colin Stead, a competent guitarist who'd been a member of a well-known 60s band called Lloyd's World. Colin lived just across the park from me and was on a break between bands. When I suggested that we team up and do some gigs together over the festive season, he happily agreed to do it. We started rehearsing right away, and when an agent that I knew heard about it, she offered us some gigs during the approaching Christmas and New Year's period. It didn't seem to faze Colin in the least that I was gay. His girlfriend, Kate Green, shared a flat with her mother at their Belleview Hill apartment block. After Kate's father died, it had hit her mother so hard that she needed to move in with Kate to try to cope with it. In mo time at all, Mrs Green and I hit it off and soon became good friends. She was a beautiful and fashionable woman who exuded a charisma that made everything seem okay, even when it wasn't, and she always went out of her way to make people feel welcome, I just adored being in her company. As usual, there were a few hiccups in my planning, as I'd mistakenly double-booked myself for New Year's Eve.

One show was with Colin in the Blue Mountains and another as a solo act at a Sydney gay dance two hours later. My biggest problem was that the gigs were about a two hours drive apart and I couldn't get out of doing either of them. Worrying about this as we sped through the drizzling rain along the wet and slippery Great Western Highway to Katoomba in the middle of the night, I took a wrong turn, and we got lost for about an hour. To this day, I have no idea where we ended up or what happened during the hour that went 'missing'. By the time that we eventually found our way back to the highway, it was almost midnight, and as everyone at the Carrington Hotel customers was cheering in the start of 1972, I was stuck halfway up the hotel's front steps being severely dressed down by the angry manager for not arriving on time to do a show before the clock struck twelve. While I was collecting our room keys, an elegantly-dressed, middle-aged woman, wearing clothes that resembled the 1940s era, wandered across from the other side of the hallway and then moved up very close to me, stopped and then stared at me for a few seconds, her heavily made-up eyes seemed to pierce right through me...

"Excuse me, young man," she said in a forceful but softly spoken and controlled voice, "I've just been informed that you're our entertainment for the weekend, would that be correct?"

Her voice matched her haunting eyes perfectly, and after I affirmed that I was, she let me know that she and her husband were at the hotel celebrating their thirty-fifth wedding anniversary. Then, continuing to stare straight into my eyes, she requested that I make a special announcement and dedicate a song to him. Her stiff, wide smile that followed gave me a dose of the creeps. I politely agreed that I would and then quickly looked away, hoping that she'd just go off and leave me alone...

"Any song will do," she called out, as she slowly slithered back across the plush carpet with her black-beaded dress trailing along behind her.

The century-old hotel had two separate entertainment areas – one was for the overnight residents and the other was for the locals and the general public. While the general public sector was decorated appropriately for the festive season with balloons and streamers, the resident-guests' lounge was void of any indication of what time of year it was and had only long wooden tables and plastic-covered chairs. The dull, middle-aged jazz trio playing on an unkempt wooden stage only added to the weird and eerie atmosphere. Our first show for the public audience was a huge success, and they kept shouting and screaming for more. Our second show for the hotel guests was almost as disconcerting as performing to a row of headstones in a cemetery. We were dressed up to the nines in our outrageously colourful gear, and when we raced into the room and onto the stage, some members of the audience let out a loud gasp that sounded like they were witnessing a disaster of some kind.

We pulled out all the stops to try to get them going, but it was impossible. They looked like they'd all taken sleeping pills, and apart from their scary, prolonged stiff smiles and empty, lifeless stares from their glassy, soulless eyes, they showed no emotion or response whatsoever. I left the lady's request and dedication until last, waiting for her husband to join her. His drink was sitting on the table, and there was an empty chair beside her, but he never showed up. I'd find out later that he'd been dead for several years. By the time that we'd finished for the night, I felt as lifeless as our audience had looked. I took a final check around the stage area to make sure that we hadn't left anything behind and quickly made my way upstairs to our room where Colin and Kate were busy unpacking...

"It's a bit too late for you to go back down to Sydney now!" Colin declared as I entered the room...

"Yeah, I know," I replied, inwardly dreading the consequences.

None of us wore a watch, so I ran back downstairs to check the time on the old grandfather clock that stood in the hotel's foyer – what a surprise I got when I discovered that it was only just after 1.00am...

"You little beauty!" I thought to myself, as I raced back to grab my gear for the Sydney gig. "I'll be late, but with less traffic on the roads, I should be able to make it there by around 2.30."

Moments later, I returned to the foyer to find it full of the resident-guests, who were all standing around and staring up at me in silence...

"Why are you in such an almighty rush lad?" Asked a middle-aged man inquisitively – breaking the silence just as I reached the bottom of the stairs.

"I'm trying ta get to show that I'm meant ta do in tha city at two o'clock," I answered, anxiously searching for a place to push my way through.

The small crowd of guests then broke out into strange little laughs that sounded a bit like chickens cackling...

"You'd better have another good look at that clock, young man!" The same middle-aged gentleman exclaimed – staring me straight in the face.

I did, and it was almost 2.30am – I was bewildered! Where had the time gone? We'd begun at 12.15am and had done a 20-minute set in each of the two rooms, and at the very latest, it shouldn't have been more than just after 1.00am. It left me with no choice but to abandon any plans of getting back to Sydney that night for my other gig, and the very thought of it made me cringe. There were no mobile phones back then, so I couldn't even call anyone to let them know. Shortly after I returned to our room, there was a sudden loud knock on the door by one of the hotel staff wanting us to move our car. Because of our rushed arrival, I'd left the car parked randomly in the middle of the horseshoe driveway, making it difficult for traffic to enter and exit.

When I reached the car, I was again surprised to find the same small group of guests that I'd seen at the bottom of the stairs, all gathered around the car and silently staring at it. Not sure what to make of it, I got in and tried to move the car forward, but each time I attempted to do so, it kept on stalling. While I was out checking to see if anything was jammed beneath one of the wheels, a member of the group climbed into the car and moved it effortlessly...

"How'd ya do that?" I asked, in disbelief.

"It was the handbrake," he replied, smugly smirking as he climbed out and followed the others back inside.

I'd checked the handbrake each time that the engine had stopped and it was definitely *not* on, and none of it was making any sense! The hotel's toilets and bathrooms were in a large communal room at the end of the first-floor hallway, and before going to bed, I popped in to freshen up. It was a hot summer night, but the bathroom felt as cold as a freezer, and I had the strangest feeling that someone was watching me. I took a good look all around but there wasn't a soul in sight, so I just put it down to my imagination playing games, and by the time that I got back to our room, Colin and Kate were fast asleep.

ON NEW YEAR'S DAY we kept ourselves amused by strolling around the town and sampling some of the local coffee shops and restaurants. The day had been pleasant enough, but the evening that followed was a total contrast. That night's audiences were almost a repeat of the night before, empty chair included. After we'd finished and stored away our gear, Kate and Colin hurried off to bed while I remained in the bar to allow them some privacy. The interior of the century-old hotel had been kept looking close to its original state, and it gave me the feeling of stepping back in time. The bartender and I shared a drink or two and chatted, and what he told me only added more strength to the already eerie and haunting atmosphere. He swore that he'd seen numerous bizarre occurrences in the old hotel, which usually took place late at night after everyone had gone home or to their rooms. He claimed to have witnessed curtains moving apart of their own accord, doors opening and closing by themselves, and glasses moving about on the tables. I think I was more intrigued than spooked, and happy just to sit there and listen. Then he took me into a small, dusty storeroom filled with memorabilia that was covered in cobwebs. Hanging on the wall was a picture of King George, whom the bartender said had visited the hotel in 1927 with his wife when they were Duke and Duchess of York. As the bartender rummaged around and continued explaining these things, I must have become unwittingly entranced or something, as I have no recollection of what happened next other than getting a glass of milk from the kitchen, placing it on a small table in the hallway, and popping into the bathroom on my way to bed. By then, I'd already been in the bathroom several times – I'd even had a long, hot bath and a couple of showers in there. Yet, even though I knew that I was alone, I always felt like I was being spied on. That night, the feeling was stronger than ever, and the chill that came with it made my bones shudder. Just as I was leaving, I suddenly felt compelled to search the entire bathroom again. While doing so, I came across a large opening about the size of a doorway that I'd overlooked the previous day, and which was hidden behind a partition wall. I poked my head through to have a quick sticky-beak, but it was too dark to see anything, so I entered the hole and begun wandering along what seemed to be a corridor. In the distance, I could see a faint fine line of iridescent-blue light that seemed to be coming from beneath a door. At the same time, I felt as though something was taking control of my body, my arm suddenly seemed to have a mind of its own and started reaching out for the doorknob. Simultaneously, a screaming voice, from somewhere deep within me, ordered me to turn around and to run for my life. Following that came a diabolical few moments of struggle, and it was as though two forces were in conflict within and around me, and tugging me in different directions. Then everything changed to slow motion, similar to a dream when you're running and getting nowhere. I managed to turn around, and just when I'd almost reached the entrance back out into the bathroom, another more powerful battle erupted. This time it was like standing on slippery ice and trying to push against an oncoming invisible force, and it took every bit of strength that I could muster to keep from being slid backwards. When I finally reached the opening of the hole and was about to step through, I felt something suddenly wrap itself around my waist and try to tug me back in. I felt like I was fighting for my life, and at the moment that I was able to break free, numerous needles of light sprang out all around me into the surrounding darkness. It was similar to an experience that I'd had a week earlier in my room in Waverly, when I'd woken up in a pool of sweat, believing that it was only a nightmare. Something had a hold of me then too that was trying to stop me from reaching the light switch, and just as it was with the mystery corridor, when it broke apart, many small wriggly streaks of bright light were released into the darkness, instantly disappearing the moment that I switched on the light. The streaks of light in the corridor were swirling all around me too, but they were more like car lights at night photographed using time exposure. The moment that I finally burst out into the brightly-lit bathroom, the voice from within screamed again...

"GET OUT! QUICKLY! GET OUT!"

My heart was beating so hard that I thought it was going to jump out my chest and beat me to my room. As soon as I was back in the hallway, without any further ado, the negative feelings and my fears just disappeared. I walked nonchalantly along the hallway with a sense of peacefulness and calmness – it was as though none of it had even happened. I collected my milk and then quietly opened the door to enter our room...

"Is that you, Tommy?" Colin called out anxiously. He looked flustered as he sat up in bed, peering straight at me, as the light from the hallway shone directly upon him...

"Yes, it's me," I answered softly, gently closing the door behind me – I turned back around and, Colin was asleep again.

Very early the next morning, the continuous, irritating barking of a dog, that sounded like it was coming from right outside of our window, woke us up. It was driving me nuts, so I got up to yell at it and shoo it off, but when I looked out of the window, I couldn't see or hear a dog anywhere. The rooftop of the lower floor below made it seem even more mysterious. Brushing it from my mind, I went back to bed and never thought any more of it. Not long after, when we all entered the breakfast room, the guests appeared to be dressed in their clothing from the day before. I just assumed that they'd been celebrating all night and hadn't gone to their rooms first to shower and change. On top of that, none of them seemed to be saying anything, not even to each other, and the only acknowledgement we got was their usual long, penetrating stares. That Sunday, Colin, Kate and I spent most of our time taking in some of the spectacular cliff-top views of the beautiful scenery around Katoomba. It was to be our last performance that night for hotel guests only, and we were eagerly looking forward to getting it over and done with and back home. In those days, hotels were closed to the general public on Sundays unless you could produce evidence that you'd travelled a far enough distance to get to one. It was close to dinner time when we returned to the hotel, and because it was such a lovely warm evening and the fresh mountain air smelt so good, instead of going up to our room, we remained on the patio chatting for a while, swaying back and forth on a long swinging sofa. We weren't there long before one of the middle-aged female hotel guests approached us. She looked robotic as she marched directly up to where we were sitting, wearing a look on her face that made us think she was about to hurl a mouthful of abuse at us. She immediately proceeded to recite a repertoire of her crudest jokes – we were absolutely astounded! They were some of the filthiest, most perverted yarns that we'd ever heard, and on top of that, the woman was a total stranger to us. She was on a roll, and it seemed that nothing could stop her. Then, just as suddenly as she'd started, she stopped talking, quickly turned around and marched straight back inside the hotel, leaving us open-mouthed and lost for words. Soon after, another guest approached us and invited us to join him and some of his fellow guests for a pre-dinner afternoon cup of tea. We'd been employed by the hotel to entertain their guests, so we felt obliged to accept his invitation. He led us into a large room that we hadn't seen before, where a lot of the other guests were in groups at small tables, sitting quietly and staring at us in silence in their usual scary manner. Before we had time to think much about it, we were swiftly ushered around the room and placed us at various selected tables. I was seated with a doctor and another guest, who immediately wanted to know my entire life story, even before had time to take a sip of my tea. It's not unusual for performers to be asked questions by a curious public, but this was bordering on interrogation – these people were probing us with questions that went far beyond anything to do with our music.

Most of the hotel-guests appeared to be professional people and far more intellectually-minded than any of us were, and their overzealous questioning made little sense to us. The third degree abruptly ended, and we were quickly gathered together and led back out of the room, in a manner that made us feel like we'd offended them in some way. Returning to the swinging sofa, feeling a bit bedazzled and bewildered by the strange episode, we'd only just settled back down before one of the hotel staff came along and informed us that our services were no longer required. After he'd politely thanked us, he handed us a cheque for all three nights and asked us to leave the premises immediately. A few minutes later, driving around the curved driveway as we were leaving, we could see the hotel-guests peering at us through windows. They looked like caged monkeys at the zoo, and we couldn't make head nor tail of it.

Some people that I've since told about what happened on that mysterious Sunday have suggested that the guests could have been members of a religious cult who'd gathered at the hotel to perform séances. Others have suggested that our modern look may have ruined the vibes for them, and a few have said that they'd heard or read stories about the same hotel, concerning ghosts and such. On a more practical level, it's since occurred to me that Colin or Kate may have mentioned that I was gay and unwittingly set the usual wheels of disapproval and bigotry in motion – or was it something else entirely...?

*When a tree has been transplanted, though fierce winds may blow, it will not topple if it has a firm stake to hold it up.*

*But even a tree that's grown up in place may fall over if its roots are weak.*

*Even a feeble person will not stumble if those supporting him or her are strong, but a person of considerable strength when alone may fall down on an uneven path.*

*...Nichiren*

## Chapter 14

# THE BLACK-EYED MAN!

Kate drove the car home from Katoomba, which was roomy enough for the three of us to share the front bench seat. During most of the journey, hardly a single word was spoken between us, and for some unknown reason, I kept peering over at the back seat, as though I was expecting to see someone there. Mrs Green had mentioned that she'd be going to a *hippy* party in Paddington that Sunday night, so we popped in there on the way, arriving around 9.00pm. As we entered the long hallway of a dimly-lit, bohemian-style terraced house, we were met by a strong smell of incense and marijuana in the air, and the atmosphere in the place felt eerily negative. A woman rushing past in the opposite direction spat something out about everything going wrong but she didn't stop to elaborate. Kate's mum had already left and gone home, so we didn't stay – our own beds beckoned. When we arrived at Kate's apartment, we found Mrs Green sitting on the sofa enjoying a belated New Year drink with a couple of her local girlfriends, who both got up and left the moment that we walked through the door. Mrs Green asked Kate how our weekend had gone, but before Kate could answer, Colin let out a sudden alarming shriek from the bathroom. Immediately following it there was an even louder scream from Kate, and then it was my turn to start freaking out. We'd all begun remembering the weird, frightening and obscene things that had happened to us during our grotesque weekend away at the Carrington Hotel. It was as though we'd all been simultaneously released from some sort of hideous spell. At first, Mrs Green thought that we were playing a silly joke on her and was soon telling us that we'd already gone too far and that she'd already heard enough – her words had no effect whatsoever. In between sobs, Colin told me about how he'd seen a figure standing at the foot of his hotel bed that instantly disappeared through the wall, the moment that I opened the door to enter the room, following my scary ordeal in the bathroom. He kept shaking his head in disbelief at what he was saying, and then Kate broke down in tears again, causing her poor mum to become frantically concerned. While I was explaining my strange visit to a dusty room full of cobwebs and my journey along the dark corridor in the toilets, Kate let out another spine-chilling scream, when she remembered going into the same room, or one very similar. Kate was almost hysterical, and in between her loud sobs of horror, kept yelling out something about someone stopping her from going along one of the hotel's corridors, in a threatening way. It was then that I also remembered seeing an old cradle, but like Kate, I couldn't recall when and where I'd seen it. With all of these terrifying memories of the weekend resurfacing, everyone in the apartment became a blubbering mess. Kate's mum was in tatters. She'd begun losing control the moment that Kate first screamed, and it didn't matter what logical explanations she came up with, nothing Mrs Green said could ease the tension. My head was throbbing so badly by then that I could barely keep my eyes focused or even open. I felt like I was going insane, and it wasn't until Kate's mum handed me her car keys to drive home, that I suddenly remembered the worst of my gruesome experience...

"Oh, no! Oh, shit, no!" I gasped, backing away and throwing the keys down hard onto the floor in front of Mrs Green...

"What on the earth's the matter with you, Tommy? For goodness sake, pull yourself together!" Mrs Green shouted as she bent down and picked up her car keys.

I'd suddenly remembered turning around in the car on our way home and seeing a man with huge black eyes and a big, swollen bald head staring straight at me from the backseat. By then, I was no longer sure if I was alive or dead, and to make sure one way or another, I wanted to get home to my own flat as fast as I could so that I could talk to someone who wasn't involved. I phoned for a cab, and while I was waiting for it to arrive, I kept searching my mind for a logical explanation to it all. I'd experienced a lot of crazy and unexplainable things, but this was the weirdest of them all. Boy, did I need a drink...

"Gawd almighty mate, ya look like ya've seen a flamin' ghost mate!" The cab driver declared as I was climbing into the front seat next to him – his spooky greeting made me feel suddenly worse...

"Wadda ya mean by that... WADDA YA MEAN?" I almost screamed.

The driver just chuckled and then insisted on telling me that he'd just finished reading a story about a film commercial made in an old disused church somewhere in Europe, and how when the film got edited, several elderly monks appeared who hadn't been there at the time of filming. The moon was bright that night, and his unwelcome creepy story had me so on edge that I almost told him to stop the cab and let me out. Moments later, I entered my flat to find everyone dead to the world, including some of my flatmate's friends who'd crashed out on the living-room floor. I quickly woke them all up and told them about what had happened, and their initial response was to look at each other with expressions of disbelief and just smirk. They must have thought that I was high on drugs, and who could blame them? Had I been in their shoes, or socks, I would have thought so too. After we'd had a cup of tea, and they'd given up trying to convince me to go to sleep and stop worrying about it, they all called it a night and went back to sleep themselves. I had as much chance of relaxing or sleeping that night as winning a lottery without a ticket, and I spent the remaining hours of the night sitting in my room with the light on, feeling far too afraid to nod off in case something else happened and hoping with all my heart that it would all turn out to be something silly that would make us feel like idiots and have us in fits of laughter. Among other things, I recalled how, when I was a teenager, I'd been spiked with LSD at a gay party held atop a Sydney high-rise, and how, when the drug kicked in, my senses had gone haywire. I was stopped just in time from climbing over a tenth-floor balcony to reach a shop below that had a large 'Bushels Tea' sign painted on its sidewall that seemed like it was right there in front of me, and if someone hadn't noticed what was happening and dragged me away just in time, it would have been certain death...

"That's it!" I blurted out loudly to the walls, the bed and the curtains. "Our food's been spiked with LSD!" I could hardly wait to get over to Kate's place to let everyone know.

Mrs Green was out shopping when I arrived, and Kate and Colin were still half asleep and feeling as miserable and confused as ever. I told them about my theory, but after we'd discussed it at length and given it a lot of serious consideration and thought, none of us were convinced that I'd found the answer after all. Kate felt certain that if she'd been hallucinating on LSD, she'd have never been able to drive the car home safely down the winding mountainside roads. After breakfast, I accompanied Colin across the park to his home in Bondi. Along the way, we crossed paths with the two girls that had been at Kate and her mum's place the night before, and they looked as miserable as we felt, and it soon became apparent that they were deliberately trying to avoid us. After we started following them to ask if anything was wrong, they suddenly stopped and looked back at us with expressionless stares, saying absolutely nothing, and then they spun back around and hurried on their ways. Determined to get some answers, Colin and I continued following them, until we got too close and one of them swung around with a face full of anger and said...

"We don't wanna talk about it to yas, alright? Its nunna yer fuckin' bizness, so just piss off an' leave us alone, will yas?"

Their foul-mouthed outburst made Colin and I wonder if their problem may have had something to do with ours. Unwilling to give up, and determined to find out, we continued following them all the way home until they eventually stopped at their front gate and agreed to talk. When we explained some of what had happened to us after they'd left to go home, the dam was broken and they finally opened up and told us their intriguing story, which had taken place after they'd left Kate's flat. They'd gone straight home to bed because it had been a hectic week and they were feeling worn out. Then, in the darkness of their shared bedroom, they were startled by a strange cross-shaped misty glow on the wall that danced and swayed around their room, and they were too petrified even to move. Before the apparition left through a window, several items of clothing were dragged from their chest of drawers and tossed all over the floor. When one of the girls showed us her black, crinkled, 1940s-style top that was thrown directly at her, it gave me quite a start, and it looked like it was from the same era as what some of the hotel guests in Katoomba had worn. By the time they'd finished telling it, Colin and I found their story to be just as ridiculous, outrageous and scary as our own.

I WAS AFRAID to drive Mrs Green's car at night, in fear of seeing the black-eyed man in the back seat again and potentially having an accident, except on one occasion when I drove it during the day to visit Mum. Whenever I felt unwell, confused about anything or was in trouble, talking to Mum about it always helped. She had varied experiences in her own life and would never make light of or dismiss even the strangest of my tales. That day I needed her love, support, wisdom and security more than anything else in the world. I arrived to find my sister Flo and her son, Rodney, visiting Mum, and they were just about to leave and go home. I thought of giving them a lift, but that would mean being in Mrs Green's car after dark, and there was no way that I was willing to risk that. We saw them off in a cab instead, and then Mum prepared dinner. I was so tired and exhausted that I could barely keep my eyes open even to eat. Before hitting the sack, I looked through Mum's front window to check on the car, I could have sworn that someone was sitting in it! Many years later, Mum would tell me that she'd seen the figure in the car that night too, and that it had unnerved her so much that she'd spent over an hour saying her rosary afterwards. Mum also told me that my nephew had kept Flo awake with his strange behaviour for most of the same night.

INSTEAD OF simmering down, our mysterious and ridiculous ordeal grew worse by the day. Returning home from the corner shop where I lived some of the neighbourhood dogs started barking savagely at me. I was shocked as I was familiar to them and they'd never acted aggressively towards me before. I've since learnt that animals can sense people's fear and anxiety by way of electromagnetic fields. My vibes must have been like a red flag to a bull that day, which would explain their out-of-character hostility towards me. After we'd reached a mutual conclusion that there was something beyond our understanding, trying to manipulate us adversely, we unanimously decided to keep it between ourselves to avoid being laughed at or ridiculed. During the week following the incident, when Kate's grandmother visited from the country, Mrs Green instructed us not to mention anything about what was going on under any circumstances in her mother-in-law's presence. She was concerned that the elderly lady wouldn't be able to understand and that it would only aggravate the situation more for everyone involved. To avoid risking a slip-of-the-tongue, we all did our best to stay out of the poor old dear's way, but sadly, she must have felt completely left out, unwanted and alone. The final straw came when her handbag was snatched from her in the street, after which she'd had enough and decided to return home immediately. As she was saying her sad goodbyes to us all, tears were running down her cheeks, and she looked broken-hearted – it's upsetting me now just thinking about it. Later that night, Kate's mum endured a dreadful nightmare and woke everyone up with her loud moans. Kate rushed to her mother's aid and was horrified to find her sweating profusely and gasping for air. Later, when Mrs Green was consciously awake and had settled down enough, she explained how her nightmare had been big black square things trying to suffocate her and felt almost certain that it had something to do with our bizarre ordeal. From that day on, we all made a conscious effort to stay as close to one another as we possibly could.

Ever since Mrs Green had been living in Sydney, she'd been visiting various psychics to try to make contact with her husband, whom she still loved dearly and missed immensely. Just prior to Christmas, she'd made an appointment with a former Catholic priest in Kings Cross who read Tarot cards, and her reading was scheduled to take place on the second weekend following our Katoomba ordeal. Mrs Green was afraid to go alone and pleaded with us to accompany her, which, in the end, we all reluctantly agreed to do. After we'd been waiting impatiently for what seemed like hours while Kate's mum was having her reading done, we were suddenly jolted out of our chairs when she burst through the door, shaking and sobbing hysterically. My first thought was that the ex-priest had approached her inappropriately, but that wasn't the case at all. Through the Tarot, he'd seen that an evil force had entered her home and warned her that unless something was done about it immediately, it could lead to a disaster of some kind. As Mrs Green was relaying all this to us in between her lingering sobs, the ex-priest noticed how scared we all were and offered to come to Mrs Green's apartment to perform an exorcism on us all that very afternoon. Ready and willing to try anything that could bring an end to our crazy predicament, we all nervously accepted his offer. Before we left his office, he instructed us to gather together every person that had been affected, stressing assertively the importance of us all being present for the exorcism. As the ex-priest spoke with life-and-death urgency in his voice, all I could think of was how stupid I'd feel if anyone else found out about it, especially the media, or even worse, my brother, Denis! But there was more – the Tarot cards also revealed that Mrs Green had performed an occult ceremony using a wine glass at her home on the same weekend that we'd been going through our weekend of horror in the Blue Mountains. Mrs Green swore black and blue that she'd never dabbled in the occult before and that she hadn't thought anything more about the wine glass ceremony until the ex-priest revealed it to her in her Tarot reading. She was petrified, and after hearing about it, so too were we! When the ex-priest arrived at the apartment an hour or so later, I suddenly felt extremely nauseous...

"No need to worry, lad! It'll all be taken care of, you'll see!" He assured me – smiling and gently patting my shoulder as he passed by on his way through to the living room.

His kind and reassuring words were sorely appreciated, but only briefly comforting. A few moments later, I was trembling from my head to my toes. The man wasted no time in getting things started by quickly placing some candles in various positions around the living room, and then ushering us into a circle around him. When he asked us to hold hands, to keep our eyes shut and to hold our heads down, I felt eerily uncomfortable about being involved in such a ritual. Not fully convinced that I could trust the man, I did as he asked, and inwardly hoped with all my heart and soul for the best. The man stood more than six feet tall and was built like a tank, and when he started loudly invoking words that included some familiar Christian prayers, it felt like a series of electric shocks was zapping me. A sudden thought that he could be a maniac and that we could all be about to die shot across my mind, forcing my eyes open just when he was wielding a huge knife and slicing through the air between us – my bones almost leapt from my body! By the time that we were asked to recite the Lord's Prayer together, I'd already inwardly recited both it and several other prayers that I knew several times over at break-neck speed...

"You can let go of each other's hands, open your eyes and walk around the room now," he told us cheerfully, as he was extinguishing the candles. "But there's still one more thing that needs to be done..."

"What tha bloody' hell could that be?" I asked myself in a panic, as the others were busily telling each other how much better they were feeling.

Mrs Green felt so good that I thought she was about to start singing and dancing. The ex-priest instantly caught all of our attention when he announced that the glass which Mrs Green had used for her ritual needed to be identified and destroyed by one of us. No one spoke a single word until Mrs Green broke the silence, by declaring in a whimper that she wasn't sure which glass it was that she'd used. Luckily, the ex-priest managed to take a look around and identify it for her...

"Yes! Yes! That's it! I remember that pretty flowery pattern!" Mrs Green confirmed with a sudden, loud sigh of relief.

Nobody wanted to touch it, let alone smash it. Then I piped up...

"Here! Give me tha bloody thing 'n' I'll do it!" I snapped, feeling like I'd agreed to take hold of a deadly spider. I was terrified to the core when I flung the glass as hard as I could across the room – smashing it to smithereens against the wall. While it may have been the end of the glass, by no means was it the end of the atrocious nightmare, certainly not for me anyway...

*Regardless of the evils and obstacles that may*
*confront or attack us during our journey into*
*the centre of our life, we must have no fear and*
*always continue to move forward without*
*ever retreating even an inch.*
*If we do not harbour uncertainties within our*
*hearts, we will as a matter of course attain our*
*enlightenment and successfully achieve a state of*
*Interdimensional Peace.*
*Do not doubt this, not even for a moment.*
*...Nichiren.*

# Chapter 15

# RUNNING FOR MY LIFE!

The Katoomba incident and what followed had left me feeling jittery, insecure and depressed. In a futile attempt to escape from it, I drank myself into an alcohol-induced stupor. At the same time, I went on a crazy spending spree without the funds to cover the cheques that I was writing out all over the place. My record producer, Michael Barclay, had quit EMI and returned to England, and before leaving, had somehow managed to free me from my contract. To help make up for lost opportunities, he'd invited me to join him in the UK, where he promised to record me for Decca Records. His final request was not to mention anything about it to anyone, especially the media. With my life in a shambles with conflicts of confusion raging in my head, Michael's offer seemed like the perfect escape from my messy predicament, and the chance of making a fresh start in the UK sounded very appealing indeed. If I didn't make it there and things got any worse, I'd already had thoughts about taking a hand full of pills and just ending it all. With nothing to lose by giving it a go and just enough money to buy a ticket to London, I went for it! Just prior to leaving Australia in March 1972, I visited my friend Mrs Daisley – an accurate psychic and reader of tea leaves. She'd often offered to read mine, but after some of what I'd already been through in life, I'd always been afraid of what she might tell me was coming up next and had repeatedly declined. However, none of that mattered anymore, so I drained my cup and handed it over to her...

"You'll be going up north alright, Tommy," she affirmed, "But you won't be going to England – not yet, anyway!"

"I don't mean ta be rude Mrs Daisley, but I think ya may have a few fake leaves in yer teapot." I answered, bemused and a little aggravated, "Cuz I'm def'nitely gonna be in London in two weeks time."

"No – no you won't!" Mrs Daisley insisted. "You're going to continue further up north with a male that you'll meet along the way, and he'll have tan skin and very dark hair. You'll come in touch with the Crown, too, before you leave, and there'll be a great deal of confusion. You'll think that you're not going, but you will go 'though," she reassured me after a short pause. "You'll travel up north with this male to where you'll meet another male with the initial 'A'. He'll be very influential and a good friend who'll help you a lot."

She paused again and screwed her face up as though something was wrong, and I felt a sudden sense of alarm...

"What the hell's she gonna tell me now?" I wondered anxiously.

"No, you're definitely not going to England yet – not even then, she insisted as she continued to study my cup more carefully. "You're going to go even further north, and then something wonderful is going to happen to you! Yes! There it is! It's something really, really wonderful!"

Mrs Daisley became so excited that I felt like someone hearing that they'd just won a new house, and I was amazed that so much information could come forth from a few left-over tea leaves. I humoured Mrs Daisley by giving her the false impression that I was convinced, but in reality, I didn't believe a single thing that she told me. I was off to London, and that was that! The next day I popped in to say goodbye to my friend John Forrest, who was a well-known singing teacher in Kings Cross. John was an outrageously eccentric middle-aged man who, among other weird and wonderful things, always kept some spare cash handy to bail out any friends that got caught with LSD or marijuana in their possession. He'd been a good friend to me and had given me a lot of valuable support and encouragement with my singing career. After I explained about the mess that I was in, he insisted on giving me a couple of hundred dollars out of his 'spare cash' tin to help keep me going along the way. On the same day, just after I got back home, I received a phone call from Mrs Green offering to set me up with my own fashion label and boutique in the city. She'd taken a keen interest in some of my stage-wear designs, and believed that with her financial help, I could be very successful. Her wonderful offer would have been a fantastic dream-come-true once, but sadly, it was too late. I was in no fit state to run anything, and my life and moods were about as stable as a three-legged table in an earthquake. I sincerely thanked her, declined her incredible offer and proceed with my plans.

I WAS SCHEDULED to fly to Brisbane the following Friday night to connect with an international flight to Singapore early the next morning. However, because I was in such a tizzy, I left my passport at home and ended up missing the plane. In order to still catch the connecting flight to Singapore, I needed to be on the very first flight out of Sydney to Brisbane. With Denis doing the driving, after we returned to Mum's to pick up my passport, we decided to stay in the city for a night out on the town, which seemed a far better choice than going home and putting Mum through all the painful 'goodbyes' for a third time. As Denis was reverse parking the car, I came straight out of the closet to him and announced point blank that I was gay. At first, he didn't say a word and kept his eyes focussed on the car in front. From the corner of my eye, I saw Denis's Adam's apple moving up and down as he gulped...

"I thought you might have been," he eventually admitted in a faltering voice. Then after another short pause, he added, "you're still my brother though, no matter what."

It was as if a massive weight had suddenly been lifted off me – true to my namesake, I felt as free as a bird! I asked Denis if he'd ever been to a gay bar, and when he said that hadn't, I invited him along to one. For the following few seconds, Denis hesitated to answer and then finally agreed to come. I'm sure it was only to prove that he meant what he said about still being my brother, and I couldn't help feeling sorry for him, and so frustratingly sad and sorry for myself...

"Why couldn't this've happened years ago," I asked myself, in frustration. "Having Denis accept me for who I truly am would've made everything in my life a million times better and easier, and I could've done so much more."

We weren't far from one of Sydney's trendiest gay venues, the *Purple Onion* became our first port of call. Entering the dimly-lit bar section, I could sense that Denis wasn't comfortable about being there. Some of the guys were sizing him up and giving him the eye, which must have been pissing him off big time, but somehow he managed to persevere and get through it. I introduced him to a couple of my gay mates, and then I took him to another more popular gay dance club that I often frequented. There were only two other family members aware that I was gay, Denis's wife, Gay, who'd sworn to secrecy, and my brother, Billy, who'd found out from Lisa, his girlfriend. She often went to the same gay dance clubs as I did, because she felt safer in the company of gays. Lisa was on the dance floor when Denis and I walked in, and before we had a chance to reach her, she was nowhere in sight. She told us later that when she spotted Denis, she quickly hid behind a stack of chairs because she thought he was a 'closet gay' and felt too embarrassed to risk letting him know that she'd seen him there. Being a friend of Denis's wife, Lisa also didn't want to have to deal with her about Denis's wrongly-presumed 'secret'. Once the cat got let out the bag, we all had a darn good laugh about it and then hung around together until it was time for me to head for the airport.

I landed in Brisbane with about two hours to spare before my connecting flight to Singapore. Waiting at the airport to meet me, was a local gay medical student that I'd met in Sydney over the Christmas weekend, and as a going-away present, he insisted on taking me for a drive to the Gold Coast in his brand new convertible sports car. I'd never been to the Gold Coast, and believed him when he said that it was 'just down the road'. Back then, there was no superhighway, and it took us well over an hour just to get there. I ended up missing my plane and then found out that there were no more flights out of Brisbane to Singapore for five days. After spending that night in a hotel near the airport, I reluctantly flew back to Sydney early the next morning and caught a connecting plane to Perth where a Qantas flight was leaving for Singapore later the same afternoon – my situation then went from bad to worse. At Perth Airport, I attempted to pay for my ticket with a Sydney bank cashier's cheque, and it was deemed unacceptable because banks weren't open on Sundays to verify its authenticity. It was over 100% Fahrenheit outside and to say that I was a little 'hot under the collar' would be an understatement. As a goodwill gesture and to calm me down, the Qantas ground staff offered to waive any excess baggage charges on the next day's flight. I then spent that night at the Perth YMCA, where much to my dismay, there wasn't a single *macho man* in sight. Before checking out the following morning, I took advantage of the ground staff's offer of free excess baggage by transferring all the heavy stuff from my huge carry-on bag into my cases. Feeling confident that things would go more smoothly this time, I arrived back to the airport to find a completely different ground crew behind the check-in desk, who knew nothing about the promise and refused to honour it. To avoid missing another flight, I had to quickly pull everything out onto the floor in front of everyone and separate what I needed to take with me from what could come on a later flight as unaccompanied baggage. By the time I got all that sorted and entered the departure lounge, I felt like screaming my lungs out in sheer frustration, and the journey had barely even begun. A little while later and close to boarding time, the departure lounge was suddenly swarming with police, and we were all told to get out. The first thing that I thought of was what Mrs Daisley had said to me about coming into contact with the 'Crown' as I was leaving. She'd been 100% correct, and just as she'd predicted, there I was standing scared, trying not to think of what could go wrong next and asking myself if I was ever going to leave. It was a bomb scare that turned out to be a false alarm...

"Thank goodness for that!" I sighed, as the massive waves of fear within me began diminishing to smaller ripples.

Soon afterwards, as we were taxiing along the runway to take off, a man in front of me screamed out for the plane to stop immediately, and I almost let out an accompanying scream from the fright that he gave me! He was a doctor, and because of the upheaval and long delay, he'd absentmindedly left his briefcase in the airport bar. Thoughts were racing through my mind to shove a sick bag over his head to shut him up until the flight attendant told him that it was too late to abort the takeoff and that his briefcase would be retrieved and forwarded on to him at his destination. Moments later, watching the Western Australian coastlines sink into the distance, I wondered if I'd ever set foot on Australian soil again, it was such a sad and disconcerting thought. I'd long dreamed of flying off to see the world but not like this. My mother, in tears, had begged me not to go – a war was raging in Vietnam, Irish terrorists were blowing people up on the streets of London, planes were getting hijacked around the world, and there was me running away from everything that I loved to escape from an imaginary black-eyed man and a potentially adverse outcome due to my irresponsible shopping sprees.

IN SINGAPORE, I performed some live shows and also appeared on a local TV pop show. The country had strict laws against men wearing their hair long at the time, and I had to wear my hair pinned up at the back to meet the country's archaic fashion regulations. One of my most unexpected highlights during the short stay in Singapore happened at the TV studio, and while I was waiting in the shadows for my turn to go on. I received a very painful slap across the face from the female singer of an Asian band after I asked her softly if she 'played'. I was referring to an instrument but she'd thought that I was asking her to have sex. At my hotel, I became friends with an Australian singer from Perth named Jenny Marshall, who'd regularly been performing throughout the region and gave me some advice on how to make the most of Asia. She also introduced me to some of her artist friends from various parts of the world that performed on the same circuit, and one of them was a young guy named Eddie, who had tan skin, black hair and even more remarkably, was a Singaporean recording artist, signed to EMI. Eddie fitted Mrs Daisley's description in her prediction to a 'T'.

Eddie hadn't long returned from abroad, and after we became lovers, he convinced me to scrap my plans to go on to England and to accompany him to Hong Kong instead. Enraptured by his amazing good looks and egged on by a growing desire to pursue a long-term relationship with him, I approached some of the shipping companies and lied through my teeth to eventually gain free passage. After I'd convinced them that I was a top Australian pop star and that I could get their company promotion and media exposure in Hong Kong in return for granting Eddie and me a free first-class cabin, I was successful in getting us aboard the good ship *Taipooshei* to Hong Kong, which had a swimming pool but was by no means a luxury liner. I can't describe how shocked I was when I went up on deck one day to discover that we were only half a mile off the coast of North Vietnam. A female dancer and I were the only Aussies on board, and although the Chinese weren't at war with North Vietnam, Australia was! Throughout the entire day, she and I waited in fear of the Viet Cong coming on board to inspect the ship and the possibility of being taken away as war prisoners. While we waited, several American bombers flew overhead, and two of their battleships appeared on the horizon. Then, Just before dusk, I heard and saw an explosion in the jungle close to our ship that made my legs almost turn to jelly. We'd find out later that a European cargo ship had been blown up in the same vicinity by a mine only a week earlier. During the voyage, Eddie would often disappear for hours on end, and I could never find him. What a disappointing shock I got when I discovered that he'd been sneaking off to have sex with some of the other passengers. Eddie couldn't get why it upset me so much, or that there was anything wrong with his self-indulgent trysts, and I still had a lot to learn about the facets of gay life – especially where Asia was concerned.

Hong Kong's number-one disc jockey at the time was an Australian named Ashton Farley. I'd been listening to him on the ship's radio during the final day of the voyage, and as soon as we'd finished checking into our room at a cheap hotel in the 'famous' Chunking Mansions on Nathan Road, prompted by Mrs Daisley's prediction regarding my meeting a man with the initial, 'A', I caught a taxi to Radio Hong Kong and introduced myself to Ashton. We hit it off instantly and soon became good friends, and Ashton and his lovely wife were a fantastic support to me. In a very short while they promoted me into local stardom, after which hardly a day went by without my picture or a story about me appearing in one or more of the local newspapers. I also kept my word to the shipping company and was able to give the Taipooshei a couple of really good plugs. My record *You Can't Take It With You To Your Grave* had never been played or performed outside of Australia, but thanks to Ashton, I got to perform it on both the British and Chinese TV networks several times, including the famous number-one Chinese variety show *Enjoy Yourself Tonight*. My first appearance on EYT was outrageous. Six single beds were placed side-by-side behind me, and as I performed my record, dancers dressed in pyjamas pretended to sleepwalk, with their arms stretched out in front of them, around the beds. I can only assume that the director/producer was as puzzled about how to present the song as I was. The B-side *Too Bad You Don't Want Me* was a catchier tune and received regular airplay on Radio Hong Kong every day until it eventually became one of the top 20 most played songs. After each play, Ashton Farley would usually say complimentary things such as...

"Oh I don't know about that, Tommy, I think pretty soon the whole world's gonna be wanting you!"

His comments always put a rose in my cheeks, a smile on my face and a lot of hope in my heart. Ashton approached EMI locally to have the record released in Hong Kong and other parts of the Far East, but the Sydney branch refused. I'd learn later that if it had sold well in the Far East, it still would have weakened their efforts to discredit its producer, Michael Barclay, so they didn't even consider it.

I ACCEPTED an invitation to appear as an extra in a Chinese movie but forgot to ask what it was about or its title. Nobody spoke any English, so I needed to be told, via hand gestures, to sit at a bar in a film-set basement nightclub and take sips of cold, disgustingly-sour herbal tea, which was meant to be beer. Then I was instructed to dance with a beautiful Chinese girl, which was all going fine until a guy burst through a door, whizzed past us and got into a violent Kung-Fu fight with another guy who was standing near the bar. It all happened so quickly and seemed so real that I thought I was going to be next. What a relief it was when everyone started laughing, and the lead actor explained in broken English that it was just a scene for a Kung-Fu movie. Reporters were often present wherever I went, and one of them, Terry Geary, invited me to the Shaw Brothers Studio, where Hong Kong film star Lily Ho was working on her new movie *Of Wives and Lovers*. On the following day, our photo and story featured in the Hong Kong Standard and was also printed in Chinese characters in another newspaper – it was quite a thrill to see.

ONE AFTERNOON while I was resting on my bed, I fell into what I can only describe as being a strange hypnotic state. I was neither asleep nor awake, and I could hear everything that was going on around me, such as people walking past in the hallway and the heavy traffic and tooting of horns outside on Nathan Road. As I lay on my bed, unable to move at all, I began receiving intriguing information and images in a sort of knowingness – like experiencing something, as opposed to just seeing it or hearing about it. Although I couldn't respond or change anything, I was free to analyse and make judgements. I'd had similar experiences in the past, but none had ever been quite as vivid or extraordinary as this one. At first, I found myself floating in what appeared to be a giant cone of whirling energy. It was neither day nor night, and as everything swirled around me, it felt similar to what it might feel like being caught in the eye of a hurricane. The communication was telepathic, and I was informed that I'd soon end my association with Eddie and travel to somewhere further afield. Hearing this upset me, but I didn't have any say in the matter, and there was nothing that I could say or do about it except pay attention. I understood that there was going to be even greater turmoil in my life, and knowing it made me feel anxiously depressed. The whirlpool that was gushing around me closed in, and then hunks of debris spinning around in it started belting into me. It wouldn't be until years later that I'd interpret them as being representations of the disappointments and sufferings that I was about to endure. It was a terrifying and upsetting experience, but it wasn't all doom and gloom. There were a few pleasant moments too, such as a calm period when I saw myself making new friends somewhere, but those moments were on 'fast forward' and came and went in a flash, and I understood that the friends that I'd lost weren't right for me, which may have explained some things but did little to console. Then everything became peaceful and calm, and I suddenly found myself floating in silence above fluffy white clouds. I felt so comfortable and relaxed until the clouds split apart and left me levitating high above a vast sea. The various shades and hues of the beautiful blue ocean beneath me crowned with two large green gem-like islands, surrounded by smaller islands was a magnificent picturesque sight to behold...

"It's New Zealand," I thought, exhilarated by the beauty of it all.

Before I could think any more about it, I was down hovering above the ground, surrounded by what appeared to be large pastel-coloured blocks, which soon transformed into skyscrapers. That was when I understood that I was in the middle of the city of Tokyo, a place I'd never been before nor had I ever wished to visit. Being a post-war child who'd grown up hearing about the Japanese atrocities, I was terrified of the Japanese people. After all, 'we' Westerners had dropped atom bombs on top of them. Next, I witnessed several more vivid flashes, one of which was a tall snow-capped, mountain draped in the soft moonlight, and as I gently floated forward through the pitch-black darkness towards it, I felt no fear at all. Rather, I felt happily contented and at peace with everything, and it was somehow reminiscent of the feelings that I'd experienced with the beautiful Light. While I was lingering in the darkness, another telepathic message came through explaining that I'd soon go to Japan and meet a young Japanese male who'd become the best friend that I'd ever known. I tried to imagine who he might be or what he might look like, and then another message overrode those thoughts instructing me not to attempt to 'make it happen', and to just let things unfold naturally. It felt like it was destined to be. While the exciting news gave me an uplifting feeling of optimism, I also felt confused and mystified, especially after I was told that my new found friend would help turn this dreamlike glimpse of the future into reality by leading me to the truth of mine and all other life, after which, I'd be able to change my circumstances for the better. I awoke, feeling momentarily uncertain about who or where I was. The dreamlike fantasy world had felt so much more enjoyable to me than the real world, and I initially resented having to leave it and come back. Jenny Marshall had arrived in Hong Kong the previous day, so the first thing that I did was contact her to give her a hearty welcome and to let her know all about my latest 'far out' adventure. While I'd been in Singapore, I'd told her about Mrs Daisley's predictions and some of the other supernatural experiences that I'd had.

"Oh, Tommy. You and your funny, strange dreams and happenings! Whatever will we do with you?" She responded with a friendly giggle...

Oh, Jenny, how little did either of us know back then...

*When condemning others, even if it is justified, one should always include a positive alternative o act as an encouragement for improvement at the same time. Otherwise the outcome can end up being a futile cause and a lost opportunity.*
*It is easy to condemn, but it takes a great deal of compassion, wisdom and understanding to turn something that is bad into something that is good*
*...me..*

# Chapter 16

# MULTIPLE CATASTROPHES

There were offers of gigs and television appearances coming at me from left, right and centre, but I couldn't accept most of them or live up to what was expected of me. I was in a deteriorating mental state, regularly showing up at venues and TV studios drunk and incapable of performing. Sometimes when I should have been performing, I'd instead be roaming aimlessly around the streets of Kowloon day or night, desperately hoping to spot Eddie, who'd gone missing for several days. It seemed that the very success that I'd fought so hard to achieve was crumbling all around me, and there was nothing that I could do to stop it. When I eventually discovered that Eddie had an 'elderly man' fetish and that he couldn't control his desire for them, it shook my spirit to the core. I was only twenty-five – how could I possibly have competed? Unable to accept his sneaking around to satisfy his older men activities, I argued with him about it day in and day out, until late one evening, after I'd downed one too many gin and tonics, we had a massive heated row about it, and Eddie packed his few things and walked out. It all happened so fast that my head was still spinning weeks later. I was intensely infatuated with Eddie, both emotionally and physically, and having him in my life had been some of the most magical moments of my existence, and just knowing that he was there for me had not only kept my spirits up and motivated me to try harder but also prevented me from tumbling further down into a very dark place. I'd learn later that the success I'd been enjoying in my singing career had deeply frustrated Eddie because he wasn't doing as well with his. It had particularly upset him when we both appeared on the same bill at a rock concert in Macao, and only I got featured in the newspaper. Apparently my success had been damaging his self-esteem, and I'd been far too self-absorbed in my own life even to notice it. I wanted so much to apologise and make it up to him, but this time he'd gone for good.

Being a young, Caucasian, gay TV pop celebrity in Hong Kong gave me plenty of opportunities to indulge in casual sex with other young men. Had I been bisexual, there was no shortage of willing, sexy females that I could have bedded as well, but up until the night that Eddie walked out on me, I'd only been interested in him, which is also why his gallivanting about had hurt me so much. With Eddie no longer around, my fear of seeing the imaginary black-eyed man in my mind's eye soon re-emerged, and my anxiety levels escalated. Although my mental images of the man were vague and undefined, I still felt tortured and haunted by the memories of him staring at me from the back seat of Mrs Green's car with those scary, big, black eyes. No matter how hard I tried, I couldn't get the fear of seeing him again out of my thoughts. I'd heard rumours that a husband-and-wife 'erotic dance' duo, living a couple of floors above me in Chungking Mansions, were Satanists. The idea of asking them for help had my stomach turning, but I was desperate, and as a last resort, I went ahead and did it. I felt certain that my hideous experiences were somehow connected to the Devil and as deluded and crazy as it may sound, I was hoping that these people would be able to make a deal with him to set me free, and what a ridiculous mistake that turned out to be! I pleaded with them to help me and offered to give them whatever I possessed, promising that I'd do anything that they asked. The husband took full advantage of my fear and foolish vulnerability, and almost pushed me completely over the edge. Speaking in Australian slang, this is what he told me...

"Ain't nothin' we're gonna be able ta do fer ya matey! Pretty soon ya'll see tha bloke face ta face 'n' ya'll drop dead right there on tha spot mate!"

He was stunningly handsome, with the body of Adonis and the sexiest, deep, penetrating blue eyes, but his voice was colder than a block of solid ice, and his scary words left me feeling even more afraid and confused than ever

WHILE I'D BEEN in Hong Kong, I'd made a lot of friends and acquaintances, and among them were musicians, dancers, drag queens and lots of male and female prostitutes, who were all great friends to me and deeply concerned about my declining condition. Some tried their best to help me, but their efforts had been in vain. I was a lost cause and nothing that they did or said seemed to make much difference. I'd already tried an exorcism, prayers, I'd even fled my homeland, and now I was trying to do a deal with the Devil! What the hell was I thinking? Night after miserable night I'd spend hours roaming around the streets of Kowloon until dawn broke, too afraid to sleep in fear of waking up and finding the black-eyed imaginary man staring down at me. Adding to my despair, the Satanist's warning, and although Eddie had been gone for months, his memory still remained steadfast in my heart. In between all my ups and downs, I'd been making up for lost time in the fun and games department, but it was only ever physical sex. I yearned for was someone like Eddie who'd be more meaningful and without the hang-ups and complications – someone who would reciprocate my feelings honestly.

A ballet-dancer friend that I often shared a coffee with became overly concerned about my lack of proper rest, and insisted on coming to my room in Chungking Mansions to keep me company for a night while I tried to get a proper night's sleep. There wasn't any sex involved, he was far too feminine and not my type, but he was a lovely friend with a gentle and caring nature. Just having him there gave me an enormous sense of peace and security, until the early hours of the morning when I opened up my eyes to see a giant, black, hairy spider crawling slowly across the pillow toward my face. I've always suffered from arachnophobia, so I was terror-stricken as I stared helplessly across the pillow at the spider, paralysed with fear and unable to move. Then a beautiful white butterfly appeared, fluttering its delicate wings and hovering just above the spider. Suddenly, the butterfly got too close for its own good, allowing the spider spring up and dig its ugly fangs into it, quickly seizing it and devouring it. Still unable to move, my mind was racing around in circles trying to escape from itself. Then the spider resumed its trek across the pillow towards my face, raising its fangs and ready to strike, and just as it was about to bury its ugly fangs into my nose, I snapped out of the trance-like state and screamed hysterically. I jumped up out of my bed, and frantically fought my way around the room in the darkness, bashing against the walls while trying to find the doorknob to get out. My loud commotion woke most of the other hotel guests, and some of them raced out from their rooms to see what was going on. As my fellow hotel guests were doing their best to try to calm me down, the hotel manager and his staff searched my room from top to bottom for the spider and butterfly, but no trace of either could be found. I'd suffered from a hallucination caused by a combination of excessive alcohol, stress, lack of sleep and exhaustion. My poor ballet-dancer friend was left traumatised by what had happened and needed to take a tranquilliser to settle his nerves. Understandably, he never offered to keep me company again. My outrageous reaction wasn't entirely unfounded, as Chunking Mansions was a magnet for some of the oddest and weirdest entertainers on Earth, and one never knew what to expect next. Some performers used snakes, weapons and even giant spiders in their acts, which is why I'd always check to make sure that no one was carrying a basket or a large bag before entering a lift with them.

Shortly after then, I moved from Chungking Mansions to an apartment on Hong Kong Island, belonging to an older gay friend named Fred. The other tenants at Chungking Mansions must have been jumping for joy to see the back of me. Fred's apartment was large and presented a breath-taking, million-dollar view of the city, the entire harbour and Kowloon, as well as the New Territories and beyond. It was everyone's dream view, but sadly I was unable to fully appreciate it because of the miserable state that my mind was in. Fred, a dedicated Brit to his core, was in his fifties, held a high position in Hong Kong's Department of Immigration and was attracted to young men between the ages of 18 and 25. Each weekend he made sure that there was a supply of them available to entertain the guests at his popular sex parties. He was a kind and caring friend to me, but that's as far as it went between us. At weekends there'd be naked men mingling around all over the apartment, who were ready, willing and available for anyone who wanted to have sex with them. I certainly had plenty of sensual moments with my fair share of what was on offer, but try as I may, I still couldn't get Eddie out of my mind. Another high profile gay person living in Hong Kong who I became close friends with was Ralph Pixton MBE, who presented *Open Line*, a public access programme, on Radio 3, and also liked younger men. Ralph would sometimes invite me to his home for drinks and to discuss my singing career. His close friend, Wilfrid Brambell, of the television series *Steptoe and Son,* would visit Hong Kong and stay with Ralph at his apartment during filming breaks. Even in real life, Wilfrid was outrageously eccentric and one of the strangest little men that I'd ever met. Whenever he was visiting, there'd be young Chinese boys running around half-naked all over the flat, and Ralph would be happily watching Wilfred as he chased after them taking their pictures. I was only attracted to men around my age or a few years older, so neither the boys, Ralph or Wilfred ever interested me sexually. But even so, Wilfred still took pictures of me. Every time that I asked him why he wanted them, the only response that I ever got was a giggle, as he carried on clicking away regardless. Looking back on it now, I think he was either out of his head on drugs or partially insane because it was never possible to get any sense out of him at all – I actually felt quite sorry for him.

I HADN'T BEEN living at Fred's for long before a dreadful tragedy struck the Hong Kong Island, Kowloon and the outer New Territories. The continuous heavy rains caused record-breaking floods and mudslides that killed hundreds of people, and an old house sitting halfway up between Fred's apartment block and the Hong Kong Peak suddenly lost its gripping and slid down the mountainside, knocking over a twelve-storey apartment building, which in turn, tore the top five floors off of another building below it, as it fell – all in very close proximity to us. A few days later, while I was all alone in the apartment, the putrid stench of decaying corpses trapped in the rubble below wafted through Fred's living room and sent me racing for my life from the building. I didn't stop running until I reached the city square, where I booked myself on the first available flight out of Hong Kong, which happened to be to Manila that night. Later that evening, while I was waiting to board my plane, the female dancer that I'd met on-board the ship to Hong Kong showed up out of the blue. I hadn't had any contact with her for months, and my first thought was that she'd heard that I was leaving and had come to see me off. When she suddenly realised that we were on the same flight, she became panic-stricken and wept out loud. Thanks to the Satanists, rumours were rife around Hong Kong that I was cursed and she'd believed them. With the way that things were going wrong all around me, I'd even begun to think that the rumours were true myself! Her visa had expired that day, and she'd forgotten to renew it in time. It was the last flight out of Hong Kong, and she had no other choice but to get on the plane with me and leave. Between her tears and my fearful thoughts and doubts, I soon became as scared about being on the plane as she was. As our 727 was roaring down the wet runway, I felt her hand tightly gripping the armrest and heard her nervously mumble a prayer...

"Please, God, if anything's gonna happen, please, God, let it happen now before we leave the ground."

Although we made it down to Manila and down to the ground safely, her terrified reaction made it one of the scariest flights that I'd ever been on. As we were deplaning, it started to rain and didn't stop for weeks, creating the worst flood in the history of The Philippines. Just across the park from where I stayed in Manila stood a giant hangar that was jam-packed with thousands of men every night, and many of them were good-looking and available for sex for as little as two US dollars. At the far end of the hangar, a band would play hard rock music while, one after another, hot naked men would come out from behind the curtains and dance, exhibiting what they had to offer and sometimes masturbating under an array of colourful, flashing lights. I found out later that most of these male prostitutes weren't gay, but unemployed men who couldn't find any other sort of work. With their wives' consent, they were selling themselves to gay men and older sugar daddy's, to earn enough money to pay for their rent and to provide food for their kids. I was also taken to restaurants where live gay and straight sex shows were presented on the dance-floor while you wined and dined. All in all, my six weeks stay in the city of Manila was another mind-blowing-eye-opener, and like nothing that I'd ever experienced before. Travelling around the provinces, each week, performing in nightclubs and making television appearances also presented me with other exciting and unique moments of opportunity. One of which happened when Manila's number one TV show, hosted by female celebrity Filipino singer Carmen Soriano was dedicated almost entirely to me – if only there'd been iPhones and video cameras back then. Another popular programme that I appeared on regularly was *Seeing Stars with Joe Quirino.* After I heard rumours that Joe was a leading gangster boss in the Philippines and not one to be messed with, I was always on my very best behaviour around him. Thank goodness that I never had to find out if the rumours were true or not. I was on Joe's show one night with fellow Australian Belinda Green, (soon to become *Miss World 1972.*) She was on a promotional visit to Manila and what an awkward situation it turned out to be for both of us. While I was performing, *I'm Leaving on a Jet Plane,* Belinda had been asked to stand still beside me and just look sexy and pretty while staring into the cameras. It was live-to-air, and when the band mistakenly stopped playing in the middle of the last verse, and I kept singing and hoping for the best until they started up again, all I wanted to do was run away and hide my face, and I'm sure that Belinda would have been feeling the same.

AS THE RAIN continued to pour down and the floods rapidly worsened, there was an outbreak of cholera and diphtheria. With nowhere else to go, hundreds of flood refugees, including little children and their mothers, were living and begging for food on the dirty, smelly, wet city streets, and their clothing was damp and putrid. It was such a horrifying ordeal to witness and I desperately wanted to help some of them, if only I'd been in a position to do something that would make any difference. Hearing and reading about poverty and suffering is one thing, but seeing, smelling and experiencing its vibe first-hand every day is quite another. I appreciated more than ever how fortunate I'd been to be born and raised in Australia where, for me, food, clothing and shelter had always been plentiful. Regardless of how horrible my childhood had been, in my mind, these poor people had it so much worse. For many of them, there was no escape, and the future held only more of the same sort of suffering. As the days crawled by, and Manila grew dangerously closer to a full-scale revolution, gunfights, robberies, looting and violent street crimes became a common occurrence. With little law and order available, murders were also commonplace, which is why I spent most of my time hiding away in a gin bottle.

WHETHER BEING struck by lightning had caused it or not, I'm not sure, but ever since the encounter, I'd been losing my hair rapidly. In today's music world, a shaved head is considered to be cool and trendy, but back then it wasn't and losing my hair had me feeling inadequate and insecure. While I'd been in the Far East, I'd worn a wig at all times, but keeping it dry in Manila was turning out to be unattainable. As the tension grew, amid all the continuous rain and upheaval, and along with US jazz legend LaVerne Baker and a British songstress Alison Burns, I was sent to do shows at the US Air Force Base at Subic Bay, which is located on the coast near the city of Olongapo, and close to Mt. Pinatubo, an active volcano that years later erupted and buried most of the nearby area in hot ash. LaVerne had a lot of big hits during the 1950s, including *Tweedlee Dee*, *Jim Dandy*, and *I cried A River*, and I'd heard rumours that she was refusing to leave the Philippines until her little adopted Filipino baby was granted a visa to live with her in the United States. We left Manila in a reasonably comfortable coach after our booking agent faithfully promised us that it was safe to travel to Olongapo, but along the way, the coach was stopped in its tracks by a flash flood that not only cut off the road ahead but also behind us, making it impossible to turn back. After enduring a bumpy ride on the back of a banana truck, we continued the nerve-wracking trek to the base in a dug-out canoe, which had a small motor and a guy with a long pole standing at one end skillfully dodging the tree-tops that were poking up all around us, as he steered us along. As a child, I was a devoted fan of the *Jungle Jim* TV series, but not even in my wildest dreams had I ever expected to experience such a scary situation first hand. As we slowly made our way across the snake-and-crocodile-infested flood waters, I had to anxiously hold on to my case full of glittery jackets with one hand and my water-logged wig with the other to prevent it from slipping off. A Filipino fling had chosen to come with me, and he and the girls were sitting right behind, and they didn't stop cursing until we reached solid land. From there we had a very uncomfortable and bumpy ride further through the jungle in a jeep with severely worn-out suspension. The final spine-tingling leg of the journey was down a steep, muddy mountainside, aboard a huge truck that could barely fit on the road at the cliff edge. My Filipino fling sat on my lap for most of the journey, and by the time we arrived, I felt like I'd lost both my legs. A few days later, part of the road that we were on gave way and collapsed down the cliff-side. We arrived too late to go to our hotel and clean up before performing, so we had to use the toilet cubicles at the gig as dressing rooms. When I strutted out onto the stage in my waterlogged outfit and matted wig, I felt like a zombie in drag and judging by the facial expressions on some of the audience, I must have also resembled one. It really was like living a waking nightmare, then just when everybody thought that things couldn't get any worse, they did...

Alison Burns went on straight after me and made noises that sounded like a woman having an agonising time giving birth. When she'd finished, she had the audience looking even more shocked, stunned and horrified than I had. In contrast, LaVerne, who performed at another club on the base, did a three-hour show and brought the house down. She was a first-class act, one of those unique entertainers who can withstand just about anything and still perform at their best, and she gave a perfect example of 'the show must go on'. By the time LaVerne had finished singing her last song, her crocheted dress was stretched to its limits from the weight of the water, and the bulk of it resembled a pile of seaweed gathered around her feet. Arriving at our hotel to be told that our rooms were rented out to someone else because they thought we weren't coming became the final straw, and LaVerne's angry outburst left my ears ringing for hours. With no alternative accommodation available, we were eventually forced to stay in one of the city's brothels. Olongapo's water pumps had broken down and stopped working, so to wash and use the toilets, we had to collect rainwater in plastic buckets and then carry them all the way up several flights of stairs, and if that wasn't enough to deal with, my

'Filipino fling' was so pissed off about everything that he refused to even speak to me the whole time that we were there. Meanwhile, our four-day stay at the brothel became yet another incredible eye-opener for me, and I saw just about everything but a giraffe show up. I have to say, those Filipino hookers can sure make some hair-raising and hideous noises when they're busy at work pretending to enjoy themselves – a decent night's sleep was out of the question. Perhaps I may have enjoyed listening if I'd only known what they were screaming. On my way to the Subic Bay Airbase for a rehearsal one afternoon, I was kidnapped in a jeepney by its handsome, young driver and taken into the jungle. I thought he was going to invite me to join him in some rough 'n' ready afternoon delight in the jungle, and I was feeling optimistic and excited until he stopped the jeepney and pulled out a knife. He'd noticed my diamond ring and ordered me to give it to him. I was nervously trying to get it off to hand it over when two American GIs happened by chance to pull up beside us. Believing the driver's lie that he was lost, they escorted us back to the base. The would-be thief had already warned me that he also had a gun, so I was too terrified to let the GIs know the true story. Arriving safely at the base entrance, I jumped out the Jeepney, thanked the soldiers and then ran through the gates like a scared puppy.

BY THE TIME that we'd finished all our shows and were ready to return to Manila, all roads out of Olongapo were underwater. Accompanied by my fling, who was still refusing to speak to me, I spent three long days stuck in a massive hangar, waiting impatiently for a seat on a flight back to the capital on a military plane. My waking nightmare grew progressively worse, when the hangar resembled a slaughterhouse, after the arrival of dozens of wounded young soldiers, airlifted from the fighting fields of Vietnam. They were awaiting further transportation to Guam, Hawaii or the US mainland. It was a terrifying sight to behold, as some of them had missing limbs and mangled bodies, and the smell of blood and sweat mixed with an antiseptic that was strengthened by the high humidity permeated the air. The sickening display of pain and suffering reminded me of how fortunate I'd been not to have had my number come up in the *lottery* back home during my country's draft for National Service, and the moans, groans and expressions of agony on many of their disillusioned faces shook me to the core. Yet, even though their nightmare was so much worse than mine, I still couldn't help feeling sad and sorry for myself for just being there. I should have felt shameful for being so selfish, but, by then, I'd become numb and desensitised, and all I could do was ask myself why anyone in their right mind would choose to travel halfway around the world in the prime of their life to risk being mutilated or killed. I'd failed to realise that many of the young men had been conscripted into the armed forces and were there against their will...

"How can a lovin' God let this evil shit happen?" I asked myself in frustration.

The old wreck of a plane that we eventually flew to Manila on had no interior lining, and I could see the ground below through cracks in the floor. The only two passenger seats on the plane faced the back of the cabin and were located directly behind where the pilot sat. Net hammocks hung all the way along each side of the cabin walls for the soldiers on board to sit on, and everyone, except my pissed-off fling and I, seemed to be wearing a parachute. When their commanding officer warned them to be ready to jump at a moment's notice, my heart almost made the initial jump then and there! I felt even more terrified when the officer in charge explained that the plane was malfunctioning and might not make it – if it was all just a joke to scare the living crap out of me, it worked big time! The first thing that I heard as we entered the streets of Manila was loud gunshots. During our absence, the dire situation had grown significantly worse, and the constant sound of gunshots echoing through the air day and night made it almost impossible to get any sleep, and I wished that I'd remained under the protection of the US Navy. Before leaving Manila to go to Olongapo, I was introduced to Rudy Fuentes, a famous Filipino fashion designer, and for fear of catching a stray bullet, I accepted his invitation to stay at his heavily-guarded home. Rudy was 'high-camp', and enjoyed spending most of his evenings at the big hangar where the *two-dollar men* were. Along with his entourage, we'd travel there and back most nights with armed bodyguards, in his bullet-proof car. I wasn't aware that he was a keen political supporter, and because I didn't understand or speak Tagalog, I never knew what was going on from one minute to the next, nor the extent of the risk to my life that I was taking each night. Shortly after I'd moved in, I was forewarned by one of Rudy's staff members that it was rude and insulting to refuse a gift from Rudy. On one of our outings, Rudy invited two stunningly handsome young men to come back home with us, and I just assumed that they were his friends or more members of his entourage. As soon as we arrived back at the house, Rudy told me that he'd paid for them and that one was a gift for me – I was gobsmacked! Remembering what I'd been warned, I thanked Rudy awkwardly, and then before I could say anything else, Rudy's gift grabbed my hand and led me into a room. Back then, I was very superficial and usually only attracted to young guys my age with long hair. The guy Rudy took into his bedroom had hair cascading halfway down his back and the looks of a macho fashion model, and although my 'gift' was every bit as handsome, his hair was cut very short. Rudy caught me sneaking a peep at his guy a few minutes later when I popped into the toilet and asked me if I preferred him. I admitted that I did, and then without a moment's hesitation Rudy said something to them both in Tagalog, and an instant swap was done. I felt deeply embarrassed and sad for the guy that had been with me, but it didn't take long to get over it all once I hit the sack with the new guy – it turned out to be quite a night to remember, and then some.

WHEN RUDY'S LIFE became seriously threatened by the political uprising that was gaining strength by the hour, my agent suggested that it would be safer for me to stay at a new hotel, where I was scheduled to perform. The nightclub was due to open a few weeks later, and the hotel manager agreed to deduct my discounted hotel bill from my future earnings. When I first set eyes on the beautiful state-of-the-art nightclub, I was spellbound. I was to perform in the beautiful club each night for six months, but after only living in the hotel for two weeks, a full-scale revolution broke out and the streets of Manila become bathed in blood. Everyone that I spoke to kept telling me that Martial Law was about to be declared at any moment, and they were right! My agent upped and disappeared, the opening of the club was cancelled, and to top that off, I received a non-discounted hotel bill that I couldn't afford to pay. Overnight my circumstances became a life-and-death situation, especially after I was warned that if I didn't come up with the money within two days, my life would be in grave danger. My friend Jenny Marshall, was also performing in Manila at the time. She'd been a hairdresser before taking up singing, and on the morning before the revolution had started, she'd taken my wig to her hotel room to shampoo and blow wave it for me. When her contract was also cancelled, and she too was presented with a whopping hotel bill that she couldn't pay, her belongings were taken from her and kept as collateral, and my precious wig went with them. I was beside myself with frustration as I stood arguing with Jenny's hotel manager in the foyer of her hotel, demanding my wig back, but it was useless, and I never saw my wig again. On the following day, along with a lot of other non-residents and tourists, I had to flee the country in what I was wearing and leave everything else behind, including my stage gear and most of my sheet music charts. I also had to leave without saying goodbye to any of my new friends. The hardest thing of all was parting with Diego, the new guy in my life that I'd only just begun to get to know – without his kindness and help, I never could have escaped safely. Sadly, it would be the last time that I ever saw him. It would be years later before I came to realise that the heartbreaking ordeal of having to leave him and the others behind had been the first part of the dream that I'd had in Hong Kong, becoming a reality. I had no other choice than to leave the Philippines wearing an old half-melted cheap plastic wig that I'd kept as a spare for when I was having my good human hair wig shampooed and styled. There had been a cyclone approaching, and because I'd guzzled down far too many of the on-board complimentary gin and tonics, trying to keep myself calm, I had to be half-carried from the plane through the Customs area. Fred and some other friends were waiting outside to pick me up. Later, they jokingly told me with a giggle that I was a chaotic and dishevelled mess.

WHILE I WAS performing in Olongapo with LaVerne Baker, she'd invited me to be part of her package show entertaining the US troops in Vietnam. Due to all the upheaval, I didn't see or hear from her again, but I often wondered afterwards if she'd succeeded getting her adopted baby out in time. On the day after I returned to Hong Kong, I scored a gig performing in an underground basement nightclub that mainly catered to older Chinese businessmen. Its dull atmosphere and its audience's equally dull response, brought back memories of how it was at the hotel in Katoomba – bloody creepy! I only got to perform for one night, as upon my arrival at the club on the second night there was a large hose pumping out water after a downpour of rain earlier in the day had caused a flash flood. Unable to see any future for myself and fed up to my back teeth with things continuously going wrong, I fell into a state of despair. Standing on Fred's eighth-floor balcony a few days later, while staring blankly out across the busy harbour below, I almost ended it all. I was reminiscing about my teens and how I'd been expecting something extraordinary to happen in my life when I reached the age of 25. My 26th birthday was just around the corner, and by the way that things were going, it looked like it might never happen. Feeling miserable and cursing God for being so cruel and spiteful to me, tears welled up in my eyes, and I began seeing little imaginary animals dancing all around me in the air. It was like a scene from a fairytale, and they all seemed to be having the time of their lives. I was yearning to be with them, but I didn't know how, until one of them joyfully invited me to join in...

"All you have to do is come down through here," a cute little rabbit dressed in denim overalls said to me ever so sweetly.

He was swinging on the balcony railing and pointing to the car park below, and the pebbled concrete seemed to be swirling around like sugar going down a sinkhole. As I was bending over the railing and looking down, all the little animals became overly excited and egged me on to make the jump and to come and join them. I was about to let go of the railings and dive when the entrance door to the flat behind me suddenly slammed shut...

"Hey Tommy boy, I've got us some Aussie beer to have with our lunch!"

It was Fred, and my head was suddenly spinning like a top – I felt as though I was stuck in between two realities. Fred had never come home during the day before, and his unexpected arrival completely threw me. It wouldn't until a year that I finally confessed to Fred what I was contemplating that day and thanked him for arriving just in time to stop me. Thinking about this now has me questioning whether it could have been the tears in my eyes blurring my vision that created the images that I saw. It was very realistic and convincing, and it concerns me that other people may be getting tricked into taking their lives owing to similar kinds of distorted hallucinations.

A FEW DAYS later, I heard on the evening news that there was a severe outbreak of Cholera throughout the city of Manila. I tried to contact Diego, desperate to know that he was okay, and also to get his postal address so that I could send him a ticket to join me in Hong Kong, but it was impossible to get through. Marshall Law had been declared in the Philippines shortly after I'd left, and that would have prevented him from leaving the country anyway. Sadly, I never heard from him again, but I still think of him and pray that he survived and has gone on to do well in life.

I received an offer from my friend Ralph Pixton of Radio 3 to fly me to London, where he'd arranged for me to record a single. I was eagerly looking forward to it and believed that things were finally on the up again. Well, they were, until he caught sight of my drinking problem first hand and withdrew the offer. It was also around then that a Japanese agent by the name of Kashiwagi came to Hong Kong in search of new acts and just about every artist in town was phoning him for gigs. He urgently needed a replacement lead singer for an American band that was playing at a Roppongi nightclub in Tokyo, and during his discussions with Jenny Marshall, he asked her if she knew of any young male Caucasian Rock 'n' Roll singers that might be available – without a moments hesitation, Jenny recommended me.

*Denis, Flo and Billy.*

*When I was the date*
*on The Blind Date Show–poor girl.*

*Rehearsing.*

*Late Night Show Channel 10 Sydney.*

**Port Jackson**

My group to watch this week are Port Jackson who've been together for six months. Since winning a New Faces heat, they've worked a couple of months on the Millers Circuit and are now working the local dance scene. Recently they managed to gain a recording contract with John Crossland for International Polydor. Recording plans are to release an album in a couple of weeks' time and a single will come off this L.P. The guys have written a lot of their own material which should hold them in good stead.

**If the album takes off it is being released world-wide.**

*Hit Scene TV Channel 2 Melbourne.*

*'Surfside Ten'*
*Channel 10 Sydney.*

*Doing some casual modelling in Melbourne.*

*The Carrington Hotel Katoomba.*

*Hong Kong Shaw Brothers Studio with famous film star Lily Ho.*

*'Enjoy Yourself Tonight' Hong Kong Chinese TV 2*

# Tommy's doing okay...

WHILE Hongkong singers are going abroad in the hope of making a name for themselves, quite a number of singers from abroad have been making a name for themselves here.

There is good ol' Tommy Baumont (pictured) who is already getting to be quite well-known in Hongkong in spite of being here for only two months.

He is going to appear on RTV's "Weekend Spectacular" next Saturday and will be featured on The Joe Chen Show on Commercial Radio as well.

**Invited**

In the short time he has been here, Tommy has been invited to appear in a Macau pop show and also the Jay and Bee Special.

His single "Too Bad You Don't Want Me", recorded for E M I in Australia is already getting good air play in the local stations.

When he is not busy with shows, he is busy with a new record which he hopes to make here. It will be a ballad about the Orient.

Meanwhile, Eddy Montana from Singapore, who has also been here for about two months, is planning a recording also.

He has been singing in Macau and is planning to leave soon for Europe.

# New faces on Hongkong's pop scene

THE Hongkong pop scene is certainly brightening up these days.

Every other week finds singers from overseas making their way to Hongkong hoping to get in on the local music scene.

The latest is Jenny Marshall (left), from Australia, who arrived this week and hopes to be able sing professionally here until November when she is due for performances in Korea.

Also in Hongkong this week is Australian singer Tommy Beaumont (right) who just finished a stint in the Philippines.

When Tommy arrived in Hongkong a few months ago, he was virtually unknown in this part of the world, but now he has made a name for himself in Hongkong, Manila and Singapore.

# Pop goes Macao today

MACAO goes pop at 4.30 this afternoon with its first rock concert in almost five years.

Topping the bill is Anders Nelsson and his group, Gingerbread with Australian globe-trotter Tommy Beaumont, Singaporean Eddie Montana and a Macao group in support.

Compering will be leading Hongkong disc-jockey Ashton Farley.

Tickets for the show, ranging in price from $2 to $10, are obtainable from the theatre from 4pm this afternoon.

Tommy Beaumont

# ROTTING BODIES HEALTH THREAT

**SQUADS of Medical and Health Department workers today will start disinfecting the two Black Sunday disaster areas.**

The move follows an announcement by Director of Medical and Health, Dr Gerald Choa, that the areas pose a growing health hazard.

**HAZARD**

**SAFE**

**ADVICE**

# Landslide death toll may reach 172

HONG KONG, Monday. — The death toll from a three-day rainstorm which set off two disastrous landslides may reach 172, officials said today.

Route of the landslide: three buildings have disappeared in the swathe cut by a fall of mud and rubble.

*The View from Fred's apartment.*

*In Hong Kong when I was best man at my friend Geraldine's wedding.*

*At the Manila home of fashion designer Rudy Fuentes.*

*Truck to Olongapo Philippines.*

*La Vern Baker and Alison Burns and me in the background caught up in the flash-flood.*

*Manila Jeepney*

*'Seeing Stars with Joe Quirino' alongside future Miss World .*

# Floods a problem for touring singer

TOURING the Philippines during a flood is not the best way to see the country, a fact that Tommy Beaumont recently found out.

Tommy, a plumpish Australian entertainer, is back in Hongkong as exhuberant as ever following two months performing in the Philippines.

He said that the disastrous flooding caused many nightclubs in Manila to close down temporarily and this meant that entertainers had to move out into the provinces to keep in work.

Along with Alison Burns and LaVerne Baker (both familiar names to Hongkong night owls), Tommy did a tour of American Service bases in Subic Bay.

"I don't want to talk about it. No I don't want to talk about it," he repeated burying his head deep into his hands. But with a little cajoling, Tommy told all.

"It was the most hair-raising adventure of my life," Then more dramatically; "I thought the end of the world was coming.

"When a bus, Alison and LaVerne and I were taking broke down we ended up in the back of a fruit-truck and when the flooding became too deep we found ourselves in the hold of a dug-out canoe until it toppled over."

Tommy said that the three of them did eventually reach Subic Bay, albeit wet and bedraggled – their costumes ruined but their morale buoyant.

But Tommy's trip to the Philippines was not all unpleasant. While in Manila the Australian appeared on the Joe Quirino television show three times and on various other music programmes.

Tommy will be in Hongkong until around the end of the month and will then go to either South Vietnam with LaVerne Baker or Singapore for cabaret work there.

# Marcos puts nation under martial law

TA 25 SEP 1972

## 'Only way to save Philippines'

From LEE LESCAZE: MANILA, SUNDAY

PRESIDENT Marcos last night declared martial law in the Philippines and announced the mass arrest of communist conspirators and a number of leading Opposition MPs.

The President told his people that he imposed martial law to save the republic and to reform its society.

Speaking on national radio and television, President Marcos said he had no alternative in the face of growing armed rebellion and imminent economic collapse.

But he stressed that martial law did not mean a military takeover of civilian functions.

President Marcos spelled out details of what martial law does mean, many of which had become apparent earlier yesterday as police throughout the nation arrested men whose names appear on previously prepared government lists.

All schools and universities will be closed indefinitely. Newspapers, radio and television stations will be controlled by the Government.

No overseas telephone calls or cables can be transmitted without government clearance. Carrying a firearm in public places without authorisation from the armed forces is punishable by death.

A midnight to 4 am curfew is in effect. No Philippine citizen can travel abroad without special clearance from the Defence Department.

Strikes, demonstrations and public rallies are banned and the arrests of those directly involved in the conspiracy to overthrow the Government has been ordered, President Marcos said.

All foreign news agencies and correspondents of foreign publications and networks must clear their dispatches with the Press office before they will be transmitted.

President Marcos made his martial law proclamation a combination of authoritarian steps and promises of quick reforms.

Starting tomorrow, he said, the Government would begin sweeping changes of the social, economic and political institutions of the nation.

*Enjoying a coffee with Jenny Mashall.*

*Asaka White House with some fans.*

*With Masami in his Tokyo apartment.*

*Mr. Causton giving a lecture.*

*Shohondo Head Temple Taisekiji.*

*A day out in my Panda Bear coat.*

*Giant pillars at Shohondo.*

*Inside Shohondo to see Dai Gohonzon.*

*Nichiren's exile on Sado Island.*

# Chapter 17

# NAM-MYOHO-RENGE-KYO

When Jenny was seeing me off at the airport, she pulled me aside to whisper something in my ear...

"Remember that dream you told me about that you had, Tommy? Didn't it predict you'd be going to Japan?"

With everything that had been going on in my life since the dream, I'd completely forgotten all about it. It was to be my first-ever flight on a Jumbo-747, and the plane was packed full of noisy Texan tourists, who all seemed to know each other and were talking at once. Their strong southern accents reminded me of fireworks exploding throughout the cabin in slow motion. When the plane later landed and everyone clapped and cheered for the pilot, I thought they'd sent each other nuts. I asked a passing hostess if she knew what was going on, and was told that the plane had been malfunctioning throughout most of the flight. Was I ever grateful for being one of the lucky ones on-board not to have known about it, especially with my track record of things going wrong, I'd have been beside myself with worry the entire journey. Unlike the warm Hong Kong evening at the time of my departure, Japan was bitterly cold, and Tokyo was the largest city that I'd ever laid eyes on. A little while later, as I was waiting to check-in and collect my room key in the foyer of my hotel in Roppongi, I became engrossed in a chat show on the hotel's TV, and I couldn't understand why everyone on the show, as well as people in the foyer around me, kept bowing repeatedly and saying what sounded like *hi* to each other, and one Japanese lady must have said hi to the hotel's receptionist at least a dozen times. I'd later learn that they were saying *hai,* which means *'yes'* in Japanese and that they'd merely been agreeing with each other, so 'hai' became the first Japanese word that I learned. My next lesson in Japanese took place the following day when someone answered the phone by saying *moshi-moshi.* This phrase translates into English as 'hey you' to get someone's attention or 'hello' when answering a telephone, which is the most common usage. To me, it sounded comical and almost child-like, and to this day, for some whacko reason, hearing it always makes me think of marshmallows. As per usual, nothing worked out the way that it should have. Firstly, the agent turned out to be a liar and a jerk, and not only was my accommodation to be unexpectedly deducted from my pay, but I was left with practically nothing to survive on in a city where the cost of living was through the roof. Before I'd left Hong Kong, the agent told me that I'd be working with a cabaret-style band, and that became the second big lie, as they were a hard-core rock group with torn jeans and guitars hanging down near their knees. Their matted hair looked like their heads had exploded, which is nothing unusual by today's standards, I know, but quite a shocking sight back then. In contrast, I arrived in bell-bottoms, high-heeled boots and a frilly-lace, satin PJ Proby-style shirt. When the band got their first glimpse of me, their faces almost fell off the stage and to make things even more difficult and awkward – they didn't play a single song that I knew. I was given a tape of their songs on the night that I arrived, I had less than twenty-four hours to familiarise myself with them. Over the years, I'd worked with many kinds of bands, but this was a first. Unable to learn the words to their songs in such a short time, and adhering to the adage that 'the show must go on', I improvised by singing about doorknobs and anything else that came into my head that would fit the melody. I also let out howling screams at what I thought were the appropriate moments, and it was about as close to singing the telephone book as you could get. If I couldn't think of what to sing next quickly enough, as a last resort to protect my pride, I'd tap or shake the microphone as though it wasn't working while I mouthed the words in silence. Lucky for me, very few Japanese spoke or understood English back then, so I managed to get away with most of it, but even so, I still felt guilty about the mic's continuously being unnecessarily pulled apart between breaks. After a few drinks and a couple of songs, the audience seemed to get into the groove and were loving every minute of it, after a couple more 'songs', the band looked like they desperately needed a drink or three themselves! After only a week, we were transferred from the Italia Nightclub in Roppongi to the Whitehouse Nightclub in Akasaka, which was a lot further away from where I was staying. With no spare cash to afford cabs, I needed to walk the long trek to and from the club each night.

During the first couple of days I performed at the Whitehouse, I met and made friends with a young Japanese man named Masami, who'd only been working there for a week or two himself as the club's receptionist. Masami could barely speak a word of English, but when he noticed me hiding in dark corners getting drunk during my breaks, he made it known that he was concerned for me. Free drinks came with the job, and the club also supplied me with the only decent meal that I got to eat each day. Other times, when I wasn't at the club, I'd spend long and lonely hours sitting in my hotel room suffering from severe hunger pangs while listening to American FEN Radio, torturous thoughts about Mum's home-cooked meals that I'd always taken for granted only added to my despair. On the second weekend, after I'd arrived,

Jenny Marshall landed in Tokyo to perform and invited me to her hotel for lunch. I'd already been lost in Tokyo several times by then, which had freaked me out big time, as coming across someone who spoke English or a sign that was written in English was a very difficult accomplishment. As hungry as I was, and as much as I wanted to see Jenny, I politely and reluctantly declined. As soon as I put the phone down, I suddenly remembered that I'd agreed to go sightseeing with Masami the next day anyway, so it was good that I'd turned down Jenny's invite. It was a chilly autumn morning when Masami arrived at the hotel to collect me – the first place he took me was up to the top of the Tokyo Tower, where the view of the city was sensational, and skyscrapers reached out as far as the eye could see. There were also lots of overseas tourists around, and when I loudly voiced my fears of a potential earthquake occurring, there was a sudden rush to the elevators by people who'd overheard me, and their anxious reaction soon had me rushing right behind them. Japan had recently been given a gift of two Panda bears from China, so wearing a black and white Panda bear fake-fur maxi coat, I was right in fashion. I'd made the coat before leaving Australia, to combat the cold weather in the UK. It was the only thing that I had with me to keep me warm, and by then I'd become a familiar sight in it around the streets of Tokyo. Masami took me into the nearby Imperial Park, which was a hive of activity with little kids running around all over the place. Although I couldn't understand a single word that any of them was saying, it was clear that my coat was a huge hit. Amid all the noise and excitement, I glanced across the park at the huge Imperial Hotel, and could hardly believe my eyes. I quickly coaxed Masami to follow me inside and went straight up to Jenny's room...

"Maybe this is the bloke that your dream told you about," said Jenny, ever so subtly – smiling at Masami and taking a quick sip of her tea.

"Nah, it wouldn't be him," I whispered back, subtly letting Jenny know that Masami was merely a club receptionist. "Tha person mentioned in my dream was s'posed to show me tha way to change my whole life," I concluded softly as Masami starred across at us with a smile and in silence.

I had it in my head that the *person* predicted in my trance-like dream experience would be a big-time producer or someone with power...

"Well, you just never know," Jenny cheerfully concluded, pouring us all a second cup of tea.

By the time that we got around to leaving Jenny's hotel room, it was already pitch-black dark. I followed Masami to a nearby railway station, and as we walked, I felt as light as a feather. It had been the happiest day that I'd had in a very long time, and I felt so fulfilled and uplifted by Masami's compassionate nature and kindness. We went through one tunnel after another and changed trains almost as many times, and I began to wonder if we'd soon end up in China. Finally arriving at a station called Shinanamachi, and as I was following Masami along a lot of dark and narrow streets, my paranoia started running wild, and it suddenly occurred to me that it might all be a trap and that Masami could be part of a group that went around Japan taking revenge on Westerners in retaliation for the atomic bomb. Around the next corner, I spotted a well-lit building and made a flying dash for it – Masami keeping up the pace right behind me. The moment we entered the building's foyer area, I breathed a huge sigh of relief and Masami started speaking in Japanese with the middle-aged man sitting behind the reception desk. As they chatted, I could hear the sound of heavy machinery in the background, which, to me, seemed very odd for a Sunday evening...

"Would you rike to go wid Masami to tha meeting for worda pissa?" The receptionist asked.

His unexpected outburst of broken English took me by complete surprise, and it was a few seconds before I realised that he was talking about world peace and not a pizza, and what a massive disappointment that was – I almost had my mouth open ready to take a bite...

"It's with students and other peoplu who rike to discuss worda pissa." He continued explaining in a soft voice and with a warm and persuasive smile.

The man's friendly and polite manner made it impossible to refuse, and I could see by the look of anticipation on Masami's face that my willingness to accept the invitation was of great importance to him. Having enjoyed such a wonderful day out thanks to Masami, I saw it as a perfect opportunity to do something for him in return, so I happily agreed to go...

"Yeah, okey-dokey, then," I chirped, thinking that it was to be some other time in the future. Before I could get another word out, Masami was already leaving the building and beckoning me with hand gestures to follow him.

We went down another little road, then an even smaller laneway, until we finally arrived at a large house that was surrounded by a tall fence. I followed Masami through the gate and into a courtyard and then heard a strange humming noise that grew louder as we neared the house...

"Holy shit! It's a bloody beehive!" I gasped in horror. "Don't tell me I'm gonna get stung by a pack o' bloody bees!"

The fearful thought of it sent me charging for my life along the path and into the house, slamming the door behind me in Masami's face. Standing nervously in the foyer, my legs feeling so weak that I thought I was going to drop, and my heart pounding like a bass drum, the strange humming noise was louder than ever, and then I suddenly realised that it was people's voices...

"What tha fuck's goin' on? What is this place?" I asked myself in a panic.

My first thought was to race straight out of the door and not look back, but I was too shocked to even move. When Masami entered the house, he gave me the oddest look and then quickly passed me by, beckoning me to follow him up the stairs to where all the noise was coming from. A huge part of me was refusing to go, but because I had no idea how to get back to my hotel and didn't want to stay in the foyer alone, I took my chances and followed Masami up the wooden staircase that was leading up to a room that occupied half of the upper level of the house. In it were a large group of people down on their knees and chanting the same Japanese-sounding words repeatedly in unison. Masami got down on his knees and joined in, and when I glanced across the room towards where they were all facing, I got another massive shock! The focal point was a small black box with a scroll hanging inside...

"Holy fuckaroo no! This's black magic!" I whispered frantically under my breath. "It's more o' them weirdos from tha Carrington Hotel in Katoomba! What tha fuck am I gonna do now? I gotta get outta here!"

The last thing that I wanted to do was give anyone the impression that I was against their 'ritual'. Continuous horrifying thoughts were racing around in my mind that reminded me of the Hong Kong dream, and the debris caught up in the whirlwind that I'd experienced. Masami gave me a sudden tug on my pants to indicate that I should sit down, and I almost let out a scream! The black box had me convinced that they were a group of Satanists and that the chanting was possibly a prelude to a sacrifice of some sort, and I shuddered at the thought of it. Desperately trying to ignore what they were chanting, I anxiously scanned the room for an escape route. Expecting the black-eyed man to appear at any moment, the moment he appeared, my plan was to jump from a nearby window, even if it meant not reaching the ground safely...

**"CLANG!!!!!!!"**

The terrifyingly loud, ear-piercing, high-pitched ringing noise instantly ended the chanting and sent me leaping up from the floor like a frog. I didn't know for sure if I was dead or alive – my eyes twitched, my lips quivered, and my body trembled all over from head to toe. Several of the chanters quickly gathered around me and did their best to comfort me, letting me know that the nerve-shattering noise was from a large bell that they used to signal the end of their chanting sessions. I was certainly relieved to hear it, but it still took me a long time to settle back down...

"Nam-Myoho-Renge-Kyo! That's how I did it!" One lady shouted, who was sitting on her knees at the other end of the room.

She looked like she was Japanese, but her accent was clearly American. She explained to everyone in the room how she'd successfully helped herself conquer a severe illness through chanting Nam-Myoho-Renge-Kyo. After the others were all clapped and cheered for her, a young man quickly stood up and told us how he'd received a fabulous promotion at his job, then someone else in the room told us about how she'd received an unexpected cheque in the mail, just when she desperately needed the money. As all these highly enthusiastic people seemed to be competing with each other to praise this seemingly magic combination of strange-sounding words, I was equating them to *open sesame* and *abracadabra*. The whole thing was so outrageous and surreal that I began questioning whether I'd lost my mind...

"Maybe I'm in a mental asylum 'n' this's just my mind playin' tricks," I thought anxiously. "Just like it did with all o' them little rabbits I imagined seein' on Fred's balcony 'n' tha spider I saw comin' at me on the pillow."

The people in the room varied in age, gender, nationality and status, and it was difficult to conceive that these grown adults, who all appeared to be well-educated, believed in and were promoting such childish things. The man leading the meeting was a well-spoken Englishman and the owner of the house. He told everyone present that his name was Dick Causton, and his mere presence exhumed importance, but with great warmth and friendliness. Dick termed the scroll hanging inside the black box as being a *Gohonzon,* and then further explained that it represented a mirror-reflection of the three fundamental laws of all life throughout the universe. He also promised us that by focussing on it while chanting the words Nam-Myoho-Renge-Kyo repeatedly each day, we could bring forth our Buddha-nature and that if enough people in the world were to chant the words Nam-Myoho-Renge-Kyo, a true and lasting state of world peace could one day be achieved – he termed that time as being *Kosen-rufu.* Another person in the room then cut in and explained that the True Buddha of the Latter Day had left the Dai Gohonzon for all of humankind to use in order to reach that goal. I was still none the wiser about what any of it meant and I'd never heard of a Gohonzon before in my life. All I knew about Buddhism was that Buddhist monks in Vietnam were setting fire to themselves in protests over the war. The stories that some of these people told were almost as difficult to believe as many of my own...

"Try it and find out for yourself," one man declared to those of us who were attending a meeting that night for the very first time. "All you need to do is face east, the same direction that the planet's turning, and chant Nam-Myoho-Renge-Kyo repeatedly for five minutes or more a day. Do that and I guarantee you'll receive some actual proof in your life in no time at all! This isn't blind faith, we do it because it really works!"

I'd never come across an absurdity quite like it before, and was I in need of a good stiff drink! Long after most of the others had gone home, a Korean girl who spoke very good English, refused to give up trying to convince me to chant...

"What do you have to lose? Just try saying Nam-Myoho-Renge-Kyo a few times with Masami and me, and I promise you that you won't regret it!" She cheerfully insisted. "After all, what's the point in me spending so much of my own time telling you that it works if it doesn't?"

What she said made sense, and I was certainly in need of some help in my life, but I still felt wary of her and suspiciously scared about the whole chanting deal in general. Ever since my experience with the lightning and the living nightmare that followed it in Katoomba, plus the warning from the Satanist in Hong Kong, I felt convinced that I was in deep trouble with God. It took the young woman at least another half an hour to wear me down and get me to agree to chant with them, but not before I'd inwardly made a silent pact with what I then believed to be God, promising that I was only doing it to get out of there and back to my hotel. I also assured God that I didn't believe in any of it and had no intention of coming to another meeting or chanting the words again. Then, with the girl to the left of Masami and me to his right, I cautiously joined in facing Dick Causton's Gohonzon and chanted Nam-Myoho-Renge-Kyo slowly three times.

*Just as we believe*
*exquisite gems are hidden beneath the ground*
*or expect lotus flowers to bloom from muddy ponds,*
*we need to believe that enlightenment exists deep within*
*our own life before we can awaken and develop it.*
*...Nichiren.*

# Chapter 18

# G'DAY HIROSHIMA

"ANNE! ANNE! YA'VE GOTTA HELP ME! THESE PEOPLE'VE DONE SOMETHIN' WEIRD TA ME!" I yelled– giving Anne and the other guests in the dining room a dreadful scare...

"What? Who? Done what?" Anne asked anxiously, jumping up to look. "What people? What are you talking about, Tommy?"

Constantly being woken up by shocks in my sleep, I'd usually be up by around 5.00am, puffing on cigarettes and pacing the floor for the best part of an hour to try to settle down. My hands would be trembling, and I'd be full of anxiety, but on the morning after I'd first chanted Nam-Myoho-Renge-Kyo, I didn't wake up until 11.00am, feeling calm and relaxed, and the sudden and unexpected change freaked me out. Anne Young, a black American jazz and blues singer, was staying at my hotel and had been a bit like a big sister to me. When I charged into the breakfast room shouting at her, she almost choked on her coffee. Unable to remember the words of the chant, I searched my pockets for the piece of paper that the Korean girl had given me with the words written on it, and then I handed it to Anne...

"Wait just a minute," she mumbled assertively – looking at the words more closely, as I anxiously followed her into her room.

Anne opened a drawer and retrieved a letter that she'd recently received from her mother. The letter said that a couple of Anne's best girlfriends in Los Angeles had been chanting Nam-Myoho-Renge-Kyo, and according to Anne's mum, it was doing them a world of good. Anne's mum had encouraged her to find out more about it while in Japan and to try it out for herself. Anne was busy doing three shows seven nights a week and was unable to get to any of the Buddhist discussion meetings to find out more for herself, so she asked me if I'd attend on her behalf, as she wanted to know everything that I could tell her about it. Feeling somewhat relieved by her unexpected response, I agreed to go along to the meetings and fulfil Anne's wishes, but because of my confused state of mind, I failed dismally to comprehend much of what was being said accurately. By the time that I got back to the hotel and relayed what little I could remember to Anne, it was so distorted that she changed her mind and warned me to stay well away from the meetings instead.

WITHIN THE space of two short weeks, I'd experienced my first earthquake, a street demonstration, an introduction to Nam-Myoho-Renge-Kyo and my very last performance as a makeshift Hard Rock singer. Because the apartment supplied for the band was in a putrid state, I'd refused to live there. After a heated argument with the agency about it, and when they refused to accommodate me elsewhere, I told them to shove it and walked out on my contract. The agent later came to my hotel and demanded the return portion of my air ticket back to Hong Kong, but I adamantly refused to give it to him. I was then left stranded, with only 500 yen to my name – just enough to buy a cup of coffee and a small snack. I was about to get stuck into a half bottle of gin that I'd kept stashed away in my room for a rainy day when out of the blue, Masami turned up. After another hotel guest who spoke Japanese and English explained to Masami what had happened, Masami invited me to come and stay with him in his tiny apartment at Nakano Shimbashi, a couple of railway stations away from Shinjuku and Tokyo's sex-club district. I gratefully accepted his offer, and for the next few weeks, I lived my life in the typical Japanese tradition, eating my food with chopsticks, switching trains left, right and centre to go anywhere and relying on a miserly few words of Japanese that I'd learnt, in a desperate effort to try to communicate with the locals about almost everything and anything. I also pulled my bedding out from a closet each night to sleep and then put it back each morning. Masami treated me with delicate care and compassion, using a Japanese/English translation book to communicate, he later explained that he was concerned that I was going to have a mental breakdown – or even worse! Masami only asked one thing of me, and that was to do some chanting with him each night after he returned home from work, and he promised me sincerely that it would help me to grow stronger and overcome my problems. Masami had a personal Gohonzon scroll of his own hanging in a little walnut altar that was surrounded by delicate ornaments and other paraphernalia. It was similar to the Gohonzon scroll I'd seen hanging in the small black teak box at the meetings, and at first, I was afraid to touch anything, for fear of accidentally damaging it. An even scarier concern that emerged while I was chanting was that God would get mad and retaliate. For this reason, I'd always draw the blinds before I started and check to make sure that there wasn't any lightning around. These concerns were eventually overcome by a deep desire to be happy, as no matter how down-in-the-dumps I was feeling, I always felt so much better after a session of chanting.

Not everyone that I met at the meetings was at peace with themselves. Some were from war-torn environments where they'd suffered childhoods that made mine seem like a candy picnic. There was also a bit of thoughtlessness, egotism, a little nastiness and even moments of downright rudeness, but more noticeable than anything else were people who just oozed with compassion and sincere friendliness, such lovely, warm-hearted human beings, who were always happy to offer their time and help. Dick Causton, the English leader in charge, seemed to have a logical and convincing answer or a solution to just about every question and problem. Among other things, he assured us that by consistently chanting Nam-Myoho-Renge-Kyo each day, we could tap into our Buddha Nature, our Enlightenment, and bring forth our hidden potential. He also said that we could bring forth the wisdom that we needed to conquer and overcome our problems and succeed to change our destiny for the better. Dick often referred to it as changing misfortune into fortune or turning poison into medicine. I told him one day that I was finding it difficult to accept the concept of reincarnation, after which, he assured me that once I'd been chanting consistently for a while, I'd come to understand and accept reincarnation as a natural flow of all life. He also said that I'd awaken to many other things about myself and life in general, including things that I may never have before considered possible – not even in my wildest dreams. As he was telling me all this, I couldn't help chuckling inwardly about the outcome of a few wild dreams that I'd already had, and jokingly debated with myself, whether I should cut my losses and make a run for it while the going was still good. Even though I understood very little about the practise, the one thing that I knew for certain was that ever since I'd been chanting Nam-Myoho-Renge-Kyo, something significant had been happening within me that felt so good, I never wanted it to stop.

FROM THE FIRST few minutes of 1972, on the steps of the Carrington Hotel, it had been the most extraordinary year of my life. In so many ways I felt as though I'd been through the pits of Hell and back again. Now that the year was coming to an end, and my visa was about to expire just before Christmas, dark clouds were again gathering in my mind. I'd not only begun to learn how to live a much happier life, but I'd also stopped drinking, not consciously, I'd naturally lost a desire for alcohol, and the last thing that I felt like doing was returning to Hong Kong. Somewhere along the grapevine, I'd heard that my friend, Rosita Argentina, was performing in Japan and had been asking about me. I decided to track her down before I left and hopefully share a coffee and a chat with her. Rosita was an all-around performer and had been touring the Far East for several years, where the audiences young and old adored her. I'd first met her when she was doing some shows in Hong Kong and had since lost contact with her. I eventually tracked Rosita down and was surprised to discover that she was doing a resident gig in a nightclub called Golden Hong Kong in Hiroshima, of all places. I phoned her for a chat one day, and when I told her that I was about to return to Hong Kong, she insisted that I stop off at Hiroshima along the way to spend a couple of days with her before Christmas...

"Hiroshima?!" I gasped. "Oh, I dunno about that, Rosie, are ya sure it's all okay 'n' safe down there?"

It took her a lot of reassuring and persuasion to eventually convince me that the city was safe and to finally encourage me to make the stopover. On the following night, as the small, prop-engine DC3 was taking off from Tokyo en route to the historical city, I thought about Masami and all the other new friends that I'd made and were leaving behind. I'd never felt so settled or secure, and it was torturing me to the core that a lousy visa was forcing me to abandon them all and my new and much happier life to return to the lonely, miserable existence that I'd thought I'd escaped. The pilot interrupted my thoughts by announcing that we were passing Mount Fuji to the right of the plane, and with little interest and tears welling up in my eyes, I glanced casually out of the window and what I saw took my breath away. Blue moonlight was shining down one side of the mountain, looking exactly as it had done in the dreamlike premonition that I'd had six months earlier in Hong Kong. I stared at it, dumbfounded, and that's when I heard a voice in my head tell me that I wouldn't be leaving Japan yet and that everything was going to be alright. I leaned up and glanced around the cabin to see if the voice had come from another passenger, but everyone appeared to be sitting quietly and keeping to themselves. In the end, I concluded that it must have just been wishful thinking or my mind playing tricks on me. Rosita shared an apartment with a glamorous American stripper named Angelique, right above the nightclub where they performed, and from the moment that I arrived, they didn't stop fussing over me...

"Hey Rosita, I have a great idea! Angelique shouted from the shower room down the hall, excitedly. "Maybe we can get Tommy a gig here with us!"

Many of the club's customers and staff members, including the owner, had a mad crush on Angelique, but he was away and wasn't due back until the following afternoon. My visa was to expire the next day, and the flight to Hong Kong was scheduled to leave early that morning. After discussing it further, we all decided that it was too risky to gamble on being hired, so to make up for me not being able to stay for Christmas Day, Rosita and Angelique planned to give me a big night out as a going-away present. A few hours later, after they'd finished their shows, and we were leaving the apartment for our night out on the town, I heard the same mysterious, disembodied voice that I'd heard on the plane. This time it warned me that I was about to fall ill, but not to worry about it. Again, I looked around to see where the voice could have come from, but just like before, there was no apparent source. I brushed it aside as another silly thought and pushed it to the back of my mind. Halfway down the stairs to our waiting taxi, Rosita suddenly felt too sick to go on, and we all had to return to the apartment. Some time afterwards, when Rosita said that she was still feeling too ill to go anywhere, we decided against going out and ordered some sushi and sake to be delivered instead. By 2.00am, Rosie had turned ghostly-white and was repeatedly throwing up. Then Angelique and I started throwing up as well! By 5.00am, I became so ill that I had to be rushed half-conscious to Hiroshima Hospital, where I was admitted after being diagnosed with severe food poisoning. The cause turned out to be a chicken that I'd baked for dinner. In the early hours of the previous morning, I'd found the freezer door open on my way to the bathroom and had closed it. Unbeknown to me, the chicken had defrosted and then refrozen after being contaminated. We'd eaten it for dinner just prior to when the girls went off to do their shows. At the Hiroshima Hospital, the doctors and nurses had to struggle to hold me down – I'd never felt such excruciating pain in my life. While I was there, the club owner returned, and Angelique succeeded in talking him into hiring me. I was ecstatic when she told me the good news and that he'd also offered to arrange to have my visa extended. My gig was to fill the gaps between the main acts, but after only two nights, I became the most popular singer there. This, in turn, brought out the worst in some of the other Asian singers, who did their best to make things difficult for me, by lying to the band and telling them that I'd been saying nasty things about them, including that their playing was atrocious. To get revenge, the band had been deliberately playing some of my songs off-key. Having been backed by some pretty lousy bands in my time, I'd learned how to bluff my way through just about anything, and their nasty little plan ended up failing miserably.

To say that living with the girls was bizarre at times is an understatement. Among many other crazy things that went on, we all had boyfriends and other friends coming and going 24/7, and it was a bit like living in a whorehouse with a revolving door. Rosita made up a roster for the general upkeep of the flat, and my main job was to do all the shopping. One shopping day, when it was snowing heavily, I wore whatever I could find in the flat, whether it fitted or not, to try to keep myself warm. I must have looked a frightful sight, but I couldn't have cared less. Rosita asked me to buy her some lipstick and nail polish at a sale that was taking place on the top floor of a department store, which stood high above Hiroshima railway station. From the moment that I walked into the store, I started getting a lot of strange looks, and some of the people appeared to be rushing away. I felt sure that it couldn't have been because of what I was wearing, as many of them were dressed just as ridiculously, if not more so. I couldn't figure it out at all, but when some of the grannies in kimonos started hurriedly gathering and ushering the little children out of my way, I mistakenly concluded that they were racists. Moments later, while I was paying for the lipstick, the girl serving me began blushing and then looked as though she was about to burst into tears. As a small audience of customers was watching me from a distance, I bent down to put the lipstick into the side-pocket of the shopping stroller, and suddenly discovered the reason for everyone's strange behaviour. Hanging like a string of sausages from the stroller's side pouch, was a long row of padded tampons that I'd dragged from home through the dirt and snow, and they were a ghastly, soiled, sodden mess, and I could hardly believe my eyes. In an all-out panic, I stuffed the wet tampons back into the pouch, fled from the store as fast as my legs would carry me, and then raced all the way home with my head down in shame and the shopping stroller virtually flying behind me. We always kept the stroller stored in the bathroom, and Rosita had pushed the tampons into its pouch and forgotten all about them. The girls were rolling on the floor with hysterical laughter when I told them in a fluster what had happened.

I SPENT MOST of that Christmas Eve waiting impatiently between spots to get a call through to my family in Sydney. While I waited, a group of customers arrived and kept sending me requests to join them for a Christmas drink. When the floor manager noticed and sent me a message, via one of the hostesses, to accept their invitation, I had no other choice but to give in and sit with them. One of them was an American named Suzie, and the first thing that she wanted to know was what I thought of Japan. Far more interested in getting through to my family than chatting to anyone, I told her flippantly that it had its good and bad points – and left it at that...

"Perhaps you're not in rhythm with the universe," Suzie loudly proclaimed above the music, which instantly caught my undivided attention. I'd heard the same thing mentioned several times at the Buddhist meetings in Tokyo.

The group all turned out to be happy Nam-Myoho-Renge-Kyo chanters, and after that night, Suzie kept phoning me with invitations to their meetings. I never did get my phone call through to Australia, as back then it was still very difficult to phone overseas, especially during the festive season, so it ended up being a sad disappointment to me. I wasn't game enough to tell Rosita or Angelique about my chanting, for fear of being ridiculed. I didn't think they'd be open-minded enough to understand, but after I kept disappearing for hours at a time, Angie got suspicious and sent someone to follow me. When she found out that Buddhism was involved, she almost hit the roof...

"Don't go gettin' sucked in, Tommy!" She almost ordered. "I know about those people! They'll brainwash ya and then get ya to set yerself on fire!"

Her angry warning frightened the life out of me – if I *were* ever going to commit suicide, it wouldn't be that way.

Public streaking had become a new trend around the world, and I think that I may have been the first streaker in Hiroshima. To challenge a dare on New Year's Day 1973, dressed only in my birthday suit and displaying my wares, there was I parading through thick snow along the main street outside the club. I'd been up celebrating and drinking all night with several of the bar staff, totally unaware that sake contained alcohol, and I was on another planet. Luckily, before I could get too far away and possibly arrested, or even deported, Rosita raced out into the street in her pyjamas and dragged me back inside and upstairs to my bed. During the next few days, the club manager noticed that I was repeatedly being asked by customers to join them at their tables and turning them down. He called me aside one night and offered to pay me a commission of fifty yen for every drink that a customer bought for me, but only if I'd be willing to do some male hosting between my sets. I accepted his offer, believing that if I just took little sips, I'd be in control – wrong! In a short while, I was back on the booze again. Not only that, I also found out that being a male host came with more than its fair share of obscene and outlandish moments. Sometimes a husband and wife team – or at least that's what they'd tell me they were, would sit me between them and take turns with their hands under the table to check out my credentials. I was too afraid to say or do anything about it because most of the regular customers were hard-line members of the Yakuza – the Japanese Mafia. Most of them, both women and men, were tough-looking hombres who usually refused to take no for an answer about anything. I just wore a smile, tried to enjoy their enthusiasm, took a lot more than just a few sips of my drink to cope, and hoped with all my heart for a good outcome. When the ringleader of a gang of butch lesbians that frequented the club, and who was also obsessed with Rosita, discovered that Rosita and I shared an apartment, she almost went insane with jealousy and became dangerously hostile towards me. Rosita did her best to convince her that I was gay, but the woman wouldn't have a bar of it, and to make sure that Rosita was telling her the truth, she turned up at the club one night with a group of gay men of various shapes, sizes, ages and styles for me to choose from, and then she watched and studied my reaction. Not all of the guys were my type, and I'm sure that for some of them, I wasn't theirs, but the ones that I fancied kept me happily entertained and contented for weeks. Angelique also had a female admirer by the name of Yoko – a cute little thing that owned a trendy fashion boutique in downtown Hiroshima. To avoid things getting out of hand and going too far, whenever Angelique went out with Yoko, she'd always drag me along with her as a chaperone. One night, when we were all having coffee and chatting in a restaurant, I noticed a stunningly handsome man sitting just a couple of tables across from us and made a passing remark about how good looking I thought he was. In the next instant, Yoko was up and over at his table inviting him to come back with us to her apartment for cocktails. When she returned to our table and told me that he thought that I was a sexy man, my lustful expectations suddenly ran wild. Although it was evident that she planned to have him spend the night in the spare room with me so that she could finally seduce Angie, lust and temptation won me over, and I chose to just ignore it. The guy couldn't speak a single word of English, but he looked so good that it didn't matter. After he'd guzzled down a few drinks back at Yoko's flat, and started loudly mumbling things in Japanese, I just kept smiling in sheer bliss, kidding myself that he was letting everyone know how much he liked me. However, when he started shouting aggressively, and Yoko's face turned a lighter shade of pale, I soon realised that he wasn't saying anything romantic...

"Quickry! Quickry! Herpa me to get him downstair' into taxi!" Yoko whispered assertively in broken English as she held one of his arms over her shoulder.

I demanded to know what was going on and when she told me in a loud whisper that he was a hit-man for the Yakuza and that she'd put sleeping pills in his drink, I quickly grabbed hold of his other arm and almost carried him down the stairs singlehandedly. What Yoko did went entirely against my values, and I was bloody furious with her. I later found out that she'd drugged him so that he wouldn't be worried about what I did to him once we got undressed and under the sheets. She'd also lied when she told me that he found me attractive, as it was she that he was interested in, not me. All the young barmen at the club knew that I was gay, and each of them would act embarrassed whenever I talked to them individually or got too close to them in the presence of the others. They'd also secretly make fun of me between themselves in Japanese behind my back, which amused me more than it did them, considering that I'd already been intimate with most of them at some stage, unbeknownst to the others, of course. Then there were the frisky older customers who tried to become more intimately acquainted with me than I wanted, including an elderly Japanese businessman that came to the club one night and after seeing my show told one of the hostesses that he'd fallen in love with me. He was on his way around Japan visiting his many chain stores, and he flew back to Hiroshima every evening for almost a week, just to hear me sing again and to try to win me over. Rosita spoke fluent Japanese, and when she told me that he was offering to supply me with a generous allowance, a large apartment in Tokyo and a brand-new car if I'd agree to be his part-time lover permanently, I was gob-smacked. I may have jumped at the opportunity if he'd been younger and my type, but he wasn't, and I had to graciously decline. The girls' and I had a casual assortment of lovers who'd randomly turn up on our doorstep at all hours of the day and night, usually after playing on gaming machines in one of the many surrounding Pachinko Bars. It was illegal in Japan at the time to win money on them, so the prizes were chocolates and cigarettes. Needless to say, our flat looked like a chocolate shop, with chocolates stacked up everywhere. Occasionally, and whenever it was appropriate, we'd all cross the line and have secret trysts with each other's boyfriends, and things would get so hot and steamy that it's a wonder the chocolates didn't all melt in their boxes. Often when there was a knock at the door, we'd all scatter and rush and hide, afraid of opening the door in case more than one of the boyfriends showed up at the same time and discovered that we'd been cheating on them. I'm not proud of our behaviour now, but that's how we were back then, young, shameless and disgusting, but we certainly had a lot of good fun in the process. I had some cassette tapes of the top forty songs that I'd recorded from American FEN radio while I was living in Tokyo. The recordings also had announcements in between songs of the time of the day and various news items. Sometimes I'd play the tapes in the background and forget that they were old tapes, which would usually confuse all of us as to what day or time it was. One day Rosita rushed like a crazy woman to get to an appointment, only to show up four hours too early. I laughed myself half silly when she came back 30 minutes later, wearing a very confused and pissed-off face. There were also news reports of events that had happened weeks earlier, and we'd all be thinking that they were happening again and again – it was almost as crazy as living in a certified nuthouse.

Masami flew in from Tokyo one day for a visit and discovered that I'd reverted to my old ways. He was deeply disappointed in me, and using his Japanese/English translation book, told me that if I wanted to go on living my life the way that I was, there couldn't be any future friendship between us – his warning hit me like a brick! Masami was straight, but I'd grown to love him anyway, and after everything that he'd done to help get me up out of the gutter and on to the right track, my ungrateful behaviour was unforgivable. He'd been by far one of the most compassionate, sincere and supportive people that I'd ever known, and he was right to tell me to compare myself now with when I was back in Tokyo chanting regularly. The risk of losing his precious friendship forever became too much of a burden to bear, and I was determined to win back his support and friendship, no matter what it took or what Angie, Rosita or anyone else had to say about it. I immediately began the difficult task of getting myself back into a more positive rhythm by fervently chanting at every opportunity I got. Each night, during breaks, I'd race up to the flat and chant as though my life was depending on it – then I'd race back down to sing some more songs. It got to the point on stage sometimes where I had to think first for a moment whether to sing or to chant. The teachings of Nichiren were proving to be very different from anything that I'd ever known. At one of the meetings, someone had explained that there was no point in brushing things under the carpet or expecting God's forgiveness if we remain 'repeat offenders', as God only helps those who help themselves. Another member added that everything that we think say and do is being constantly recorded by the almighty computer called 'Life's Mystic Law', and that everything will surely have an equal effect either in this life or at some point during a future existence. At another meeting, I learnt that the only way that we can lessen, or alter the timing of the effects manifesting from our past bad causes is to make enough good causes in the present to override them, which reminded me a lot of the saying *We reap what we sow.* It was also explained to me that, instead of asking God for help and forgiveness, Buddhism teaches that we must summon forth the wisdom and good fortune from within ourselves to expiate and neutralise our negative karma, in other words, to eventually forgive ourselves. At times when I was chanting furiously for my wisdom and good fortune to manifest so that I could succeed in altering the effects of my past causes and self-inflicted bad karma, I'd find myself recalling something that another older member had once said...

"Just as it takes a lot of hard work to clean up a dirty mess so too does it take a lot of serious effort to clean up one's dirty karma. Filth can never be cleaned up with more filth, and neither can bad karma be cleaned up by making more bad karma. In other words, there's no magic wand to do the job for us."

Although what she said didn't quite register at the time, it still must have had a subliminal influence on me because I'd often feel compelled to clean up the whole flat whenever I'd finished chanting, and it seemed that the cleaner that I kept it, the better I'd feel inside.

What a fantastic surprise it was when Masami phoned out of the blue one morning and invited me to return to Tokyo and stay with him again. For the remainder of that day, I was buzzing with so much happiness and gratitude that I just about could have flown back to Tokyo under my own steam and with on my own wings.

# Chapter 19

# NICHIREN

Before leaving to return to Tokyo, I visited Hiroshima Memorial Museum Hall in Peace Park, which was a very shocking and emotional experience that I'll never forget. Although the Atomic Bomb had been dropped on the city a year before I was born, I still felt intimately connected to it, especially to its aftermath and how we've been destroying the very essence of life ever since. I left the hall that day with tears to my eyes, and with my head hung in shame, and chanted under my breath for the people who'd died to be at peace, and for those left behind to overcome and rise above their suffering. I could almost sense the unfortunate victim's presence and feel the trauma of their horrific pains and sufferings. It broke my heart, even more, when I thought about the lovely people in Hiroshima that I'd met and befriended, especially those who were still suffering from severe adverse health effects from the bomb, and some of them weren't expecting to live beyond the age of thirty. By the time that I got back to the club, I'd developed a throbbing headache felt extremely nauseous. Later that night, I chanted some more about what I'd seen and felt that day, it was so upsetting that I found it difficult to sleep. I also thought long and hard about some of the weapons developed since 1945 and prayed from the depths of my heart that this chant was the key that would bring forth the wisdom in people's minds to prevent anything like what happened in Hiroshima from ever happening again.

I ARRIVED BACK at Masami's Tokyo apartment, just after lunch the next day, and from the moment that I walked through his front door and saw his little altar, my weary state of mind began to dissipate. After a few days of sincerely chanting in front of Masami's Gohonzon, my self-confidence and optimistic outlook on life were beginning to reemerge. I also attended an NS/SGI weekly meeting, to find out everything that I could about Nichiren's teachings, and also signed up to become an official member of the organisation. At the meetings that followed, I was told that NS/SGI was the most legitimate and significant of the lay organisations propagating Nichiren's teachings throughout the world and that the reason Nichiren Buddhism is termed 'the true Buddhism for the Latter Day of the Law' is that it's centred entirely on the Mystic Law 'Myoho-Renge-Kyo' and not on any 'person', including a particular Buddha. On another occasion, I was also told that the first recorded Buddha, *Gautama,* or *Shakyamuni* as he's known, lived in India almost three thousand years earlier and that he'd offered only the provisional teachings, until the last eight years of his life, when he discarded all of his previous sutras and declared the *Lotus Sutra* as the highest of all his sutras. Someone else had mentioned that he'd also proclaimed that the identity and crystallisation of the Law Itself wouldn't be revealed to humankind until a future Buddha appeared at the beginning of the *Latter Day* of the *Law* (estimated to have been some 2000 years after Shakyamuni's death). At following meetings, I was told that Shakyamuni had been born a prince and that he'd prophesied that, in contrast to himself, the Buddha of the *Latter Day* would be born of the lowest status and in very difficult and challenging circumstances, and that owing to interferences and misinterpretations by Shakyamuni's descendants, the teachings by then would be twisted and have lost their true meaning. When I asked to know more about this, I was told that the descendant monks claiming to follow Shakyamuni's teachings at the time of Nichiren's advent were so off-track with their understanding of Shakyamuni's Buddhism that, rather than being Nichiren's supporters, they were his staunch enemies. A lady with a strong British accent concluded the meeting by explaining that all these things eventuated after Shakyamuni's death because various scholars who claimed to be his followers had taken sections of his teachings and integrated them with stories of their own that were irrelevant to Buddhism. She also said that they did this to suit their own purposes or cultural beliefs. Eventually, over hundreds of years, one branch spread across China and into Japan, and the other found its way down through Malaysia and into Indonesia. It was also said that a similar situation had occurred with Christianity and other various beliefs throughout history. At other meetings I attended, someone explained how Nichiren had been born in the thirteenth century to a fishing family in Japan and that while he was growing up, he became extremely interested in religious affairs and joined a temple, hoping to one day become a priest. Then, after he'd studied everything available, he found himself at a dead-end, and while everyone else was content to accept things as they were, Nichiren couldn't, as he knew in his heart that things weren't right and that there was still much more to be understood. In an unwavering quest to find the 'missing link' that he believed existed, he backtracked through almost 2000 years' history of Buddhist teachings. Being the enlightened being that he was, he eventually discovered and gathered together the hidden fragments that represent the deep underlying force of The Great Mystic Law of all Life, namely – Myoho-Renge-Kyo. It was also told about how Buddhism's earliest development in Japan was extraordinarily self-centred and one-sided. For example, people who were born into less fortunate circumstances were thought to have done something evil in a past life to deserve it. Contrary to that, people born into more fortunate circumstances were believed to have done a great deal of good in their previous lives and therefore were considered to be worthy of utmost respect. Under the Law of Cause and Effect, taught by both Shakyamuni and Nichiren, this was fundamentally correct, but only to a certain degree. In other words, it wasn't as 'clean-cut' or 'black and white' as all that. For example, being wealthy or of high status is no guarantee that anyone will have a life of true happiness or be exempt from suffering. This seemed to make little or no difference as far as the mentality of the thirteenth-century Japanese hierarchy was concerned – a system of segregation ruled the roost, as the saying goes. Consequently, those considered to be of lower status were forced to give to those of higher status, even if it meant giving up their lives in the process. The priesthood was regarded as one of the most senior positions in the land and did very well from these poor, unfortunate, misinformed people – who were taught to believe that by dying for, or dying at the hands of someone of higher status, they'd automatically be reborn into a higher status themselves.

On April 28$^{th}$, 1253, at the age of 31, Nichiren Daishonin stood upon Japan's Mount Minobu and chanted Nam-Myoho-Renge-Kyo for the first time in this world, and then explained to those around him that the words Myoho-Renge-Kyo were the *title* of the *Lotus Sutra.* Nichiren had also made it clear that he'd only 'discovered' Myoho-Renge-Kyo, and that it wasn't his invention or idea, as it represented the sound vibration and identity of the eternal 'Supreme Mystic Law of Life'. Nichiren also predicted that, in the future, many people throughout the world would chant Nam-Myoho-Renge-Kyo, and gave strict instructions for his followers, present and future, to put their faith firmly in the *Law* and not in any *person* – including himself, adding that the more people who sincerely and correctly chant Nam-Myoho-Renge-Kyo, the higher the chances are of achieving world peace in the most realistic sense, and he termed that time *Kosen-rufu.* (Peace and harmony between all humans and the entire environment).When Nichiren's publicly stated later that women are equal to men and also equally capable of achieving Buddhahood, it didn't go down well and created a lot of anger. Especially when he further added that the only difference between an ordinary mortal and a Buddha is that one has attained his or her enlightenment, which only created more anger within the heretical priesthood and triggered off a response of immense hatred toward Nichiren. From then on, as he struggled to repair the immense damage that had been done to Shakyamuni's teachings and to propagate and teach the Law to as many people as he could, Nichiren was repeatedly attacked by the authorities and opposing heretical priests, and on one occasion, he was almost beheaded. It happened in 1271, shortly after he'd warned the people of Japan that if they didn't change their wicked ways towards each other and stop their practice of heretical teachings, they'd bring terrible misfortune upon themselves. They'd not only suffer from horrific internal strife but similarly to how rotting meat attracts flies from afar, they'd invite enemies from ten thousand miles away. Nichiren also gave the same warning to the Shogunate in a letter, and that resulted in him being arrested and exiled to a tiny island called *Sado* – a very harsh and inhospitable environment. He was delivered and dumped there by the heretical priests to perish, and for the first six months of his exile, his shelter was a small wooden dilapidated shrine with open gaps that let the wind and snow blow through. The crumbling structure stood alone in a small cemetery that was used only for criminals and surrounded by dozens of frozen corpses and abandoned skeletons, which no one had ever bothered to bury. Fearing that he could die there too, Nichiren knuckled down and wrote some of his most important teachings. At other meetings, I heard that Nichiren was vegan and only wore ragged clothing and furs from animals that had died naturally and that he depended solely on the handouts and the kindness of the few people who helped and fed him. Spending much of his life walking along dirt tracks from village to village, and teaching as many people as he could to chant Nam-Myoho-Renge-Kyo, Nichiren never once wavered in his mission. As I was listening to all of this, I found myself thinking, what a cruel and unjust way to treat a person who'd chosen to devote their entire life helping to bring about a happier existence for others, including their enemies – it reminded me a lot of the story of Jesus.

In the year 1274, when the Mongols began attacking Japan from the west with gunpowder (a weapon that Japan hadn't known existed until then), Nichiren's prediction came true. The main attack came via the sea, and during the conflict, many lives were lost. Fortunately for Japan, nature intervened just in time to save it, when a severe typhoon sank most of the enemy's ships. Soon afterwards, Hei no Saemon, the Hojo regent of the Kamakura Prefecture (Japan's capital at the time), defied the hostile objections of the existing heretical priesthood and pardoned Nichiren. He also gave out strict orders for him to be released immediately and to be returned safely to the Japanese mainland. By then, many of the island's residents had already converted to Nichiren's teachings. One of the main things that Nichiren didn't want his followers to do was build statues of him to worship. So, to prevent this from happening, on October 12$^{th}$, 1279 – two years before his death, Nichiren inscribed his enlightened life-state in *Sumi-ink* upon a mandala, and titled it *Dai Gohonzon* (Great Object of the Embodiment of the Law). Down the centre of the Dai Gohonzon, in Chinese characters, he wrote Nam-Myoho-Renge-Kyo and signed his name *Nichiren*. Someone else at the meeting explained that Nichiren described the Dai Gohonzon as being a *Mirror of Life* and that he'd left it as a gift to humankind so that everyone could have an opportunity to focus on It to tap into the depths of their subconscious and manifest their true enlightenment. On another occasion, Nichiren had warned that in the future, Japan would suffer a dreadful defeat. Then, just as the Lotus flower comes forth and blooms more beautifully from the muddiest pond, his teachings would also spring forth from the 'muddiest pond' of society, and enable awareness of Nam-Myoho-Renge-Kyo to not only flourish, but spread throughout the world. Nichiren also warned that the only people capable of destroying his teachings were those claiming to be his followers, but who twist and distort the true meanings. He'd also explained that, without faith in Myoho-Renge-Kyo and respect for all that it represents, future generations would fail to awaken the crucial wisdom and good fortune that they will desperately need to be able to challenge, survive and overcome the worst aspects of Mappo (A future time when the Buddha's Law will degenerate and humankind will manifest its most evil potential), and when the true faith will again *flower*, after being ushered in by a future enlightened being. The age of Mappo commenced about 2000 years after Shakyamuni's death, and at around the same time that Nichiren was alive and walked the earth. There was always such a lot to take in, but even so, at every meeting I attended, I eagerly soaked up the information about Nichiren Daishonin's Buddhism like a dry sponge. Sometimes, while listening intently to people's intriguing explanations of Nichiren's life and prophecies, I'd find myself thinking about my own dreams and the messages that had often accompanied them, particularly the messages that I'd received in Hong Kong telling me that I'd be going to Japan and that I'd discover the truth that I'd been searching for at the foot of a steep mountain. Watching it all unfold and become a reality in my life was such an extraordinary mind-blowing experience. However, I still remained puzzled as to why Japan was chosen to be the place where the birth of the worst evil and the highest good was destined to manifest during the same periods...

"There's turning out ta be a whole lot more ta life than I've ever been taught ta believe, that's for sure," I told myself as another meeting came to a close.

## ABOUT NAM-MYOHO-RENGE-KYO

Before continuing, I'd like to jump a few decades ahead and explain how I now understand and describe the fundamental and underlying meaning of the words Nam-Myoho-Renge-Kyo, and what they represent to me today...

Throughout the 1970s and 80s, I was led to believe that, in order to practice Nichiren's Buddhism correctly and to receive benefits, one needed to attend meetings and belong to an organisation. I've since discovered through experience that this isn't the truth, as anyone, regardless of whether they're a 'member' of a group or not, can benefit from their own personal and individual practice. That's because Myoho-Renge-Kyo represents the identity of what some scientists are now referring to as the *unified field of consciousnesses*. In other words, it's the essence of all existence and non-existence, and the ultimate creative force behind planets, stars, nebulae, people, animals, trees, fish, birds, and all phenomena, manifest or latent. All matter and intelligence are simply waves or ripples manifesting to and from this core source. Consciousness (enlightenment) is itself the actual creator of everything that exists now, ever existed in the past, or will exist in the future, right down to the minutest particles of dust – each being an individual ripple or wave. The big difference between chanting Nam-Myoho-Renge-Kyo and most other conventional prayers is that instead of depending on a 'middleman' to connect us to our state of inner enlightenment, we're able to do it ourselves. That's because chanting Nam-Myoho-Renge-Kyo allows us to tap directly into our enlightened state by way of this self-produced sound vibration.

'Who or What Is God?' If we compare the concept of God being a separate entity that is forever watching down on us, to the teachings of Nichiren, it makes more sense to me that the true omnipotence, omniscience and omnipresence of what most people perceive to be God, is the fantastic state of enlightenment that exists within each of us. Some say that God is an entity that's beyond physical matter. I think that the vast amount of information continuously being conveyed via electromagnetic waves in today's world gives us proof of how an invisible state of God could indeed exist. For example, it's now widely known that specific data relayed by way of electromagnetic waves has the potential to help bring about extraordinary and powerful effects, including an instant global awareness of something or a mass emotional reaction. It's also common knowledge that these invisible waves can easily be used to detonate a bomb or to enable *NASA* to control the movements of a robot as far away as the Moon or Mars – none of which is possible without a receiver to decode the information that's being transmitted. Without the receiver, the data would remain impotent. In a very similar way, we need to have our own 'receiver' switched on so that we can activate a clear and precise understanding of our own life, all other life and what everything else in existence is. Chanting Nam-Myoho-Renge-Kyo each day helps us to achieve this because it allows us to reach into the core of our enlightenment and keep it switched on. That's because Myoho-Renge-Kyo represents the identity of what scientists now refer to as the unified field of consciousnesses.

To break it down – *Myoho* represents the Law of manifestation and latency (Nature) and consists of two alternating states. For example, the state of *Myo* is where everything in life that's not obvious to us exists, including our stored memories when we're not thinking about them, our hidden potential and inner emotions whenever they're dormant, our desires, our fears, our wisdom, happiness, karma, and more importantly, our enlightenment. The other state, *ho,* is where everything in Life exists whenever it becomes evident to us, such as when a thought pops up from within our memory, or whenever we experience or express our emotions, or whenever a good or bad cause manifests as an effect from our karma. When anything becomes apparent, it merely means that it's come out of the state of *Myo* (dormancy/latency) and into a state of *ho* (manifestation). It's the difference between consciousness and unconsciousness, being awake or asleep, or knowing and not knowing.

The second law – *Renge* – *Ren* meaning cause and *ge* meaning effect, governs and controls the functions of *Myoho.* These two laws of *Myoho* and *Renge,* not only function together simultaneously but also underlie all spiritual and physical existence.

The final and third part of the tri-combination – *Kyo,* is the Law which allows *Myoho* to integrate with *Renge,* or vice verse. It's the great, invisible thread of energy that fuses and connects all Life and matter, as well as the past, present and future. It's also sometimes termed the Universal Law of Communication, and perhaps it could even be compared with the *string theory* that many scientists now suspect exists.

Just as the cells in our body, our thoughts, feelings and everything else is continually fluctuating within us – all that exists in the world around us and beyond is also in a constant state of flux, constantly controlled by these three fundamental laws. In fact, more things are going back and forth between the two states of *Myo* and *ho* in a single moment of time than it would ever be possible to calculate or describe. And it doesn't matter how big or small, famous or trivial anything or anyone may appear to be, everything that's ever existed in the past, exists now or will exist in the future, exists only because of the workings of the Laws 'Myoho-Renge-Kyo', the basis of the four fundamental forces, and if they didn't function, neither we nor anything else could go on existing. That's because all forms of existence, including the seasons, day, night, birth, death and so on, are moving forward in an ongoing flow of continuation, rhythmically reverting back and forth between the two fundamental states of *Myo* and *ho* in absolute accordance with *Renge* – and by way of *Kyo.* Even stars are dying and being reborn under the workings of what the combination 'Myoho-Renge-Kyo' represents.

*Nam,* or *Namu* – which mean the same thing, are vibrational passwords or keys that allow us to reach deep into our life and fuse with or become one with 'Myoho-Renge-Kyo'. On a more personal level, nothing ever happens by chance or coincidence, it's the causes that we've made in our past, or are presently making, that determine how these laws function uniquely in each of our lives, as well as the environment from moment to moment. By facing east, in harmony with the direction that the Earth is spinning, and chanting

Nam-Myoho-Renge-Kyo for a minimum of, let's say, ten minutes daily to start with, any of us can experience actual proof of its positive effects in our lives, even if it only makes us feel good on the inside, there will be a definite positive effect. That's because we're able to pierce through the thickest layers of our karma and activate our inherent Buddha Nature (our enlightened state). By so doing, we're then able to bring forth the wisdom and good fortune that we need to challenge, overcome and change our adverse circumstances, turn them into positive ones, or manifest and gain even greater fulfilment in our daily lives from our accumulated good karma. This also allows us to bring forth the wisdom that can free us from the ignorance and stupidity that's preventing us from accepting and being proud of the person that we indeed are, regardless of our race, colour, gender or sexuality. We're also able to see and understand our circumstances and the environment far more clearly, as well as attract and connect with any needed external beneficial forces and situations. As I've already mentioned, everything is subject to the law of Cause and Effect, and the 'actual-proof-strength' resulting from chanting Nam-Myoho-Renge-Kyo always depends on our determination, sincerity and dedication. For example, the levels of difference could be compared to between making a sound on a piano, creating a melody, or producing a great song, and so on. Something else that's very important to always to respect and acknowledge is that the Law (or if you prefer God) is in everyone and everything.

NB: There are frightening and disturbing sounds, and there are tranquil and relaxing sounds. It's the emotional result from any noise or sound that can trigger off a mood or even instantly change one. When chanting Nam-Myoho-Renge-Kyo each day, we are producing a sound vibration that's the password to our true inner-self, and this soon becomes apparent when you start reassessing your views on various things, such as your fears and desires etc. The best way to get the desired result when chanting is not to view things in a conventional way, as rather than reaching out to an external source, we need to reach into our own lives and bring our needs and desires to fruition from within, including the good fortune and strength to achieve any help that we may need.

Chanting Nam-Myoho-Renge-Kyo also reaches out externally and draws us towards, or draws towards us, what we need to make us happy from our environment. For example, it helps us to be in the right place at the right time, and to make better choices and decisions and so forth. We need to think of it as a seed within us that we're watering and bringing sunshine to for it to grow, blossom and bring forth fruit or flowers. It's also important to understand that everything we need in life, including the answer to every question and the potential to achieve every dream, which already exists within us.

*When a mother bird gives warmth to its eggs, liquid*
*within the eggs will naturally transform into a*
*beak, two eyes and all the many other parts,*
*including the feathers and wings*
*that will enable it to soar into the heavens.*
*Humans are like the contents of an egg,*
*ignorant of their true selves, but when nurtured*
*by the power of Life's Mystic Law, they are then able to*
*transform their ignorance into wisdom and ascend*
*into the true aspect of all phenomena*
*and Life's deepest realities.*
*...Nichiren.*

# Chapter 20

# FREE AT LAST

I hadn't envisaged the imaginary black-eyed man for quite some time, but still remained stringent about never letting my guard down. I tried to be prepared at all times, just in case he turned up in my mind's eye or in some other way and caught me by surprise. One evening, after a Buddhist meeting at Dick Causton's house, we all went to the local coffee shop near Shinanamachi Railway Station for some coffee and cakes. Willing to risk sounding like a complete loony, I started telling Dick about my weird experiences at the hotel in Katoomba, as I desperately needed to know if Buddhism had any logical answers to what had happened to us. I'd hardly begun explaining before my tongue seized in my mouth, and I couldn't speak. I don't know what caused it, maybe it was just an overwhelming build-up of anxiety, but whatever the reason was, for a couple of moments I genuinely thought that I was going to swallow my tongue and choke. I jumped up in a panic, and so did Dick...

"Don't say another word, Tommy!" He almost yelled, gesturing with his hands for me to stop talking.

His serious facial expression and change of voice tone jolted me. It was as though he already knew what I was about to say...

"Rely on Nam-Myoho-Renge-Kyo, Tommy!" He told me assertively.

Thank goodness that Dick was wise and worldly enough to understand my atrocious predicament, as I dread even to think of what might have happened if it had been otherwise. Most people who've had similarly bizarre experiences would agree that the worst thing to be told is that you've just imagined it all, especially by someone with a limited understanding and no real knowledge or experience themselves. That's like being told by a blind person that what you're wearing doesn't fit you well or look right. After I'd calmed down a bit, Dick explained that my scary vision, whether it be real or a hallucination, was related to my past causes or *karma* and that I needed to use my compassion as a strategy rather than be controlled by fear or hate. As he spoke, the other English-speaking Buddhists that were present listened intently. Dick assured me that by chanting Nam-Myoho-Renge-Kyo about it, I could help set free whoever or whatever it was that had hold of me and allow it to merge with the universe and find its inner peace. I wanted so much to believe him, but it reminded me of what the ex-priest had said after the séance in Sydney – which, for me, hadn't worked at all.

WHILE ATTENDING the meetings at Dick's place, I became close friends with American couple, Kathy and Gene McCaslin, who'd often travel up from Yokohama to Tokyo by car, to attend the Sunday Buddhist lectures. The couple and their two small children lived in a sizeable American-style house on the Atsugi Air Force Base, where Gene held a high-ranking position in the US Navy. Sometimes I'd catch a train down on a Friday afternoon, spend the weekend at their house and then return to Tokyo by car with them on Sunday. Kathy and I got along like a house on fire and would often spend the entire weekend involved in in-depth conversations about the meaning of life. One night, when Gene returned home early and overheard me telling Kathy about the UFOs that I'd seen in Sydney during 1966, he joined in on our discussion and told us about a similar experience that he'd had in 1967. It happened while he was on duty at the Malmstrom Missile Base in Montana, and he'd never even told Kathy about it. Before he started his story, he asked us to swear a solemn oath never to reveal it to anyone, as it could get him into serious trouble. He and his working colleagues had witnessed a UFO, which he described as being a very bright circular bluish-coloured light, hovering above a silo containing a nuclear missile that was aimed towards Russia. The men had watched in awe as the UFO beamed down a ray of light that disabled the missile. The next morning, Gene learned that other similar weapons around the base also got modified in the same manner. Those who'd witnessed the incident, including Gene, were all forced to sign an agreement that they would not reveal what they'd seen, but in recent years, the truth has come out, and the full story is now online at...

*http://www.cufon.org/cufon/malmstrom/malm1.htm*

I visited the McCaslins a week after the coffee shop incident, and things seemed just fine'n'dandy – as Kathy would often say. Then, at about 11.30pm, someone phoned to say that one of the McCaslin's close friends had been in a severe car accident and was fighting for his life. Before I knew what was happening, they were out the door, in their car and off to the hospital, leaving me to care for their children, who were sound asleep upstairs. I was horrified! I'd been following Dick's advice all that week, and it seemed to have been helping to keep me calmer, but nowhere near enough to prepare me for a night on my own in a big house with the responsibility of two little children. My first instinct was to run away and not look back, but my concern for the kids made that idea impossible. I thought of wrapping them up and taking them to where other people might be, but it was snowing outside and I didn't have a car. Struggling to come to terms with my fate, I scuttled across the living room, opened the large alter doors to the McCaslin family Gohonzon, and then got down on my knees and chanted fervently for the wisdom and strength to overcome my fears and to maintain my sanity. The clock on the wall read 11.45pm, and as the following fifteen minutes ticked away, I grew more intense and afraid by the minute that something was going to happen at midnight. The children's little dog was curled up on my feet and would have been picking up my anxious vibes. Just as the clock reached twelve, the ear-piercing scream of the loud door buzzer sent the dog barking-mad and made it dig its claws into my feet, scaring the crap out of me, and sending me diving straight up into the altar. I not only knocked the candles and incense all over the carpet, and crash-landed on top of their beautifully carved antique table that sat in front of their Butsudan, smashing it to smithereens beneath me. I quickly picked myself up, and stumbled nervously across the living room to the door, where I was cheerfully greeted by another Buddhist serviceman and friend of Kathy and Gene. They'd informed him about the accident and had asked him to drop by to keep me company. Still uncertain whether I was coming or going, I invited him in and tried my best to stay composed. I explained a bit about my fear of the black-eyed man to him, and although he listened intently and didn't so much as bat an eyelid, looking back now, I'm sure he would have thought that I was either a nutter or stoned out of my head. He was probably also concerned for the children's wellbeing and safety, which is also probably why he stuck around until the McCaslin's got back home. After the soldier helped me clean up the mess, we indulged in several cups of coffee while we chatted away the early morning hours. It was around 6.00am when Kathy and Gene finally returned home and were shocked to see the pile of damage. I was explaining how it had all happened when Kathy cut in and gave me an amazing example of 'Buddhism in action' that I've never forgotten and have tried to live by ever since...

"Tommy, if a broken table and some stained carpet are the worst of our karma today, compared to what we've just witnessed at the hospital, I'd say that we're very fortunate people."

And for reasons that I still don't fully understand, from that day forward, the image of the black-eyed man never bothered me again. Since then I've jokingly told people that whatever it was that was haunting me, probably got an even bigger shock than I did that night from my erratic behaviour and had shot through for fear of becoming the victim itself. Considering how some scientists now suggest the possibility of other dimensions, and after reading several articles that were written by people claiming to have been abducted by aliens etc., I'm even less sure what to make of some of my off-the-shelf experiences in life. I do, however, feel confident that future scientists are going to discover new waves hidden in the electromagnetic spectrum that will reveal logical answers to everything, including the most absurd. When that happens, it's going to bring a measure of credibility to the many things that we 'weirdo's' experience, which more often than not gets dismissed as being far-fetched, BS or ridiculous, even though it's not that long ago that the ideas of TV, the Internet and Skype would have been considered in the same way.

AT OTHER MEETINGS I continued hearing more about the concept of *karma*. The first time that I'd ever even heard the word karma mentioned was by the *Hare Krishna* movement during the hippie revolution of the 1960s. I was never game enough to delve into it and ask what it meant because I was 'Catholic-controlled' and afraid of offending the Catholic version of God. When it was explained that karma is the accumulation of every good and bad thing that we've ever thought, said or done, it sounded a lot like the 'sinners' brigade' to me. I also learnt later that the contents of my karma extended from beyond this life and would carry through into the next, which was too different and difficult even to begin to get my head around. I'd always believed that we went to Heaven or Hell after we die, and listening to what these people were saying about reincarnation had me feeling like I was being sacrilegious. In the end, I decided that the whole idea of reincarnation was far too weird and challenging to even try to comprehend or accept. When I later gave Dick a more in-depth explanation of how I felt about karma, his response was that in this life, our present circumstances are always the result of our past causes, and that our future circumstances would always be the result of both our past and our current causes, and that even though we can't change what we've *already* done, we can lessen the severity of the *future* results of any past bad causes, just as we can ruin the *future* good effects of any past good causes by the good or bad causes that we make in the *now*, present and onward. (As it was for me back then, you may need to go over this a few more times for it to make sense and sink in.)

Even though this new karmic way of looking at life was proving to be almost impossible for me to accept or understand, it did, however, remind me a lot of what Jesus taught regarding how we will all *reap what we sow.* It also had me wondering about the torments and pain that I'd endured as a child, particularly how I'd always blamed my sufferings on those who'd instigated them, including an uncaring and ruthless God. The Buddhist idea of needing to accept at least some of the responsibility for the actions of others towards me was extremely disturbing and uncomfortable just, even just to hear about, let alone to accept or believe. In the end, I chose to keep chanting and not to over-think it.

I HADN'T DONE A show for months, and Kathy and Gene were egging me on to get back out on stage again. They eventually secured a gig for me at the Atsugi Base Nightclub, and to get me to agree to do it, they told me the lie that it was only for a few of the local servicemen and their wives. When the club manager phoned me a few days prior to the gig to verify that I'd be doing a one-hour show, I almost dropped the phone down! I didn't know what to tell him, as I'd left the bulk of my music charts behind when I fled the Philippines, and only had enough left for three or four songs – I phoned Kathy...

"I'm not gonna be able ta do a one-hour show with what I've got, Kathy, it's impossible!" I told her anxiously.

"Yeah, ya can! Sure ya can! You've got Nam-Myoho-Renge-Kyo and everything's gonna be just fine'n'dandy! You'll see!" Kathy kept assuring me until she finally convinced me to at least give it a go.

I arrived at the base to find my pictures posted up on walls and fences everywhere! Anyone would have thought that I was someone as famous as Tom Jones or Elvis Presley, and it frightened the living daylights out of me! Later, that afternoon, nearly anything that could go wrong did. The Japanese band hired by the club to back me got caught up in a traffic jam and didn't arrive until there was no time left for a rehearsal. I also accidentally sat on an LP containing some old twelve-bar-blues songs that I needed the band to hear and snapped it in half, and my voice was as croaky as a frog with laryngitis. By the day's end, poor Kathy was pacing around in circles frantically chanting for us all to get through it. She had her hair in curlers and was wearing a puffed-up portable hair dryer cap, connected to a power-point by an extra-long extension cord. As Kathy paced the floor chanting Nam-Myoho-Renge-Kyo with one breath and with the next, reassuring me that everything was gonna be fine'n'dandy, and that they were only obstacles. All I wanted to do was make a quick run for it, and if it hadn't have been for Kathy's unbending trust in both me and the power of her chanting, I doubt that I could have gone through with it.

I'd often heard a Gohonzon described as being a *mirror of life.* So, as a substitute, I started chanting to a row of the club's dressing-room mirrors to try to summon up the strength and the courage that I was going to need to go through with it. While I was chanting my head off, the club's manager came downstairs to deliver me a portable microphone, and all I could do was turn around and give him a shocked smile. Peering at me with a very weird look on his face, he shoved the mic' in my hand, quickly spun around, and raced straight back up the stairs. No one had mentioned that the show had been completely sold out in advance, which was hard to believe considering no one there had ever heard of me or seen me sing before. Moments later, I heard myself being introduced, and realising that there was no turning back, I took a huge deep breath, climbed the stairs and then leapt out onto the stage into a flood of bright spotlights appropriately singing *Get Ready, Cuz here I Come*. The crowd gave me such a loud welcome that I could hardly hear the band playing, and from that point on it seemed that I could do no wrong. It felt like a powerful force had come forth from within me and taken over. After I'd sung the few songs that I had charts for, and the band played continuations of twelve-bar-blues riffs, I sang bits and pieces of just about every old Rock 'n' Roll song that I'd ever known, and by the end of an almost two-hour show, some of the members of the audience were standing up on the tables and chairs, cheering their heads off at me. Many of them had bought drinks for me, which were lined up from one end of the big curved stage to the other, and as desperate as I was for a good stiff drink, I ended up not drinking any of them, but I was certainly blown away by everyone's kind generosity and support. Back in the dressing room, while I was sitting for a few minutes, pondering over what had just happened, and how I'd managed to keep going for nearly two hours with only four charts and a stream of endless twelve-bar-blues riffs, I found myself thinking about the story about Jesus and how he'd fed thousands of people with just a few loaves of bread and two fish. I certainly didn't compare myself with Jesus, but I did wonder if it was an inconspicuous benefit from my chanting – something that I often heard mentioned at the meetings.

It was one of the most fantastic experiences of my entire singing career, and although my performance had gone down amazingly well, and I felt deeply grateful for it, beneath all of the excitement and happiness, remained an ocean of hang-ups about my sexuality, and I suddenly felt threatened by the proximity of so many US combat soldiers who'd come to see me perform...

"I've gotta get outa here fast, and before someone wants ta chat with me 'n' figures out I'm gay!" I told myself in a panic.

I cringed from the thought of being 'outed' in front of so many heterosexual macho men, and I saw my brother George in each of them, and it was filling me with electrifying apprehension and fear. I'd already experienced a very upsetting homophobic verbal attack from a fellow Buddhist in Tokyo who was a US soldier, and it wasn't pretty. He was on leave from the Vietnam War, and we'd become good friends, often engaging in lengthy discussions about Life, especially after the meetings. When someone mentioned something that let the cat out of the bag that I was gay, his attitude towards me did an immediate 360-degree turnaround. Jumping to his feet, and in a furious and judgmental outburst, he told me that I was disgusting for choosing to be gay and that he wanted nothing more to do with me – then he just stormed off. His reaction not only gave me an instant sickening shock, but it was also very hurtful. Like me, he was relatively new to the practice and still had a lot to learn about the teachings, not to mention, Life's realities. It wouldn't have helped that we'd spent so much time together chatting, and perhaps a big part of his reaction was his fear of being considered gay himself. With that disturbing memory glowing in my mind and in a futile attempt to avoid mixing with the audience after the show, I made an anxious move towards the back door, and Kathy and Gene's car, but before I could even reach it, the club's manager stopped me in my tracks, and insisted that I go with him back into the club. While I'd been changing out of my sweat-drenched stage gear, he'd taken a plaque from the club's football room to give to me, and as the crowd cheered loudly with approval, he awarded it to me for being the best act of that year...

"Not bad at all, considerin' some of America's top acts have preceded you, eh?!" Kathy shouted proudly with a beaming smile. "Didn't I tell ya that everything'd work out just fine'n'dandy?!"

The most important thing that I learnt that night was that when you chant for the success of anything, it can sometimes come with a price to pay first. A lady had once said at a Buddhist meeting...

"Similarly to how we make a mess in the kitchen to prepare a nice meal, any negative karma has to come out somewhere. Just living's a challenge."

The negative aspects of my karma concerning the show had manifested earlier that day when I broke the record, and the band turned up late. However, because of Kathy's devout faith and trust in the power of Nam-Myoho-Renge-Kyo, her resilient determination and encouragement for me not to give up and to challenge and overcome my obstacles, my *poison* that day had been turned into *medicine*. For me, it presented a lesson of actual proof that the more obstacles we face, challenge and overcome, the higher will be our accomplishments – and to top things off, Kathy's curls turned out perfectly!

*One may have access to every available medicine, but if one never takes the necessary medicine to cure one's illness, one may never be cured.*

*One may have an abundance of wealth, but if one never uses it to buy food, one may starve.*

*Likewise, one may have good fortune hidden within, but unless one is able to tap into it and release it,*

*one can never enjoy the experience of ts beneficial effect.*

*...Nichiren.*

# Chapter 21

# THE GREAT MYSTIC REFLECTION

At the foot of Mount Fuji, on the grounds of *Taisekiji*, stood the Nichiren Shoshu Head Temple – *Sho-Hondo*. It was where Nichiren's handwritten teachings and letters to his followers, collectively termed the *Gosho*, were kept. It was also where the Dai Gohonzon was enshrined for the world to visit (The present replacement Head Temple, *Hoando,* was completed and opened in 2001.) Each week, members from around Japan and the rest of the world would go on a pilgrimage called *Tozan* to visit Sho-Hondo and to chant Nam-Myoho-Renge-Kyo in front of the Dai Gohonzon. My first Tozan was meant to be in March 1973, but I foolishly failed to make it. A couple of days before I was due to go, I flew back to Hiroshima to collect the rest of my belongings, arriving right in the middle of preparations for a party that Angie and Rosie were throwing. My selfish nature, along with the girls' persistent persuasion, soon got the better of me, and I chose to stay for the party instead of going on Tozan. Although I'd been very much looking forward to seeing the Dai Gohonzon, I still didn't fully appreciate the unique opportunity of being one of the few people in the world able to do so. I was also convinced that a lot of what the other members were saying about the Dai Gohonzon was highly exaggerated and that the real reason for all their raving was more to do with the stately building that housed It. I phoned Dick Causton to let him know that I wouldn't be attending because I had a party to go to, and his angry response completely threw me...

"Do you have any idea how many people there are in the world who'd give *anything* for a chance to see the Dai Gohonzon, Tommy?" He shouted.

It was the first time that I'd ever heard him get so upset, but even so, I still didn't get what the big deal was and stayed for the party anyway. It turned out to be as exciting as watching clothes spin around in a dryer. After I returned to Tokyo, nothing seemed to go right for me, and the smooth road that I'd been travelling since returning to Masami's apartment from Hiroshima and chanting with him each day had become more like a rough track. It seemed like a punishment, and I found it difficult to conceive that giving the party priority over a visit to the Dai Gohonzon could have such a profound effect. Of course, it wasn't a punishment at all, it was the subconscious effect of my *cause* in neglecting to nourish my inner-self – an effect similar to when one neglects to water a plant and it withers somewhat. Several weeks later, on May 3rd, I got a second chance to visit the Head Temple and jumped at it. I was flat broke, and during the two-hour coach ride down to Taisekiji, the other members didn't stop talking about a Fuji restaurant where they were planning to have their lunch. Their repeated descriptions of their favourite foods soon had me feeling ravenously hungry, and I spent what little money I had to buy lunch at the first roadside cafe we stopped at. After that, what to do about lunch became for me the most worrisome problem of the day. Too proud to allow anyone else to pay for me, I decided to pretend to be dieting.

Standing beside one of the giant marble pillars that formed part of Sho-Hondo's massive structure, I could see how easy it could be for someone to become awestruck by it all, as it was almost inconceivable. While I was waiting patiently in line with thousands of others, my thoughts switched to Mum and the harsh life she'd endured, and I decided to write and tell her about Nam-Myoho-Renge-Kyo the moment that I got back to Tokyo. Moments later, I was admiring the spectacular beauty of Mount Fuji, when an enlightening realisation regarding reincarnation popped up into my mind, and I suddenly felt subconsciously aware of having lived past lives, and it finally all seemed to make perfect sense to me. Next, I was overcome by a profound desire to take some responsibility for my present life! Rather than the unfortunate victim that I'd always believed I was, I understood that I'd actually been the most fortunate one. Had I been the hateful, deluded person that George was or the cruel and spiteful people that Dad and Beatty had been to me, I'd have been much worse off. It then became crystal-clear to me that the terrible and evil things that had occurred in my life were the *effects* of my own negative karma, which I'd carried through from this and past lives. As crazy as it may sound to some, I also understood that it was my bad karma which had been responsible for drawing on the torment from George, Dad and Beatty. For years I'd been encouraged by Mum to hate Beatty for stealing Dad away. Until that day, I'd never even considered the fact that Dad was just as much to blame, as he'd chosen to leave us and go to be with Beatty of his own volition. Due to my confused state of mind, I'd been at war with Beatty ever since, and she'd retaliated by spending most of her time trying to break me down and overpower me. Yes, her methods were despicable, but at least I was now at last able to accept the fact that I wasn't entirely blameless. In the next few moments that followed, my anger and hatred towards George, Dad and Beatty dribbled away like dirty water trickling down a plughole.

Dad had already died in 1969, so it was too late to reconcile our long-standing differences in person, but there was still time to purge myself of the immense hatred that I'd felt towards George and Beatty. In a letter that I'd received from Billy before converting to Buddhism, he'd mentioned that

George was still in prison and that Beatty was slowly wasting away with cancer. At the time, the news gave me feelings of great joy and satisfaction, and I was even eagerly looking forward to hearing more news in the future of Beatty's demise. Whoever could have guessed that I'd be praying that day for George's happiness, for father, and for Beatty's health to improve for her to survive long enough for she and I to resolve the hatred and differences that we'd held so long for each other? It was time to enter Sho-Hondo, and the sudden movement of the crowd instantly roused me from my deep thoughts. As I was beginning to refocussing on my immediate surroundings, an unexpected state of calmness came over me, and each step that I took felt like I was walking on a gently vibrating carpet. As we entered Sho-Hondo, the incredible atmosphere was electrifying, and the interior looked like the set of a futuristic space movie. Within the next few minutes, six thousand people had taken their seats and were chanting Nam-Myoho-Renge-Kyo in perfect unison all around me, and I can't even begin to describe, with mere words, the mind-blowing feeling that I got from being a part of it all. Several shaven-headed priests wearing white robes entered from a side passage and assembled on the lower part of the large altar bench. Following that, two giant copper-coloured, curved doors moved slowly apart to reveal a breathtaking design of a magnificent sunrise, and what an overwhelmingly impressive sight to behold it was. As much as I felt deeply moved, I still remained as determined as ever not to allow myself to be confused by the glamour and theatrical wonder of it all. Next, the sunrise was slowly drawn upward and into the ceiling, revealing a smaller golden altar which was visible higher up in the background of the dome and surrounded by clusters of golden lotus flowers. For a short period, everything seemed to be at a standstill, then a young priest wearing white socks and gloves climbed up to the smaller altar and opened it to reveal the Dai Gohonzon. At the moment that It came into view, the sound of six thousand voices chanting Nam-Myoho-Renge-Kyo intensified immensely, and it reminded me of a Jumbo jet as it takes off. I think my expectations may have been too high after being told so much about the Dai Gohonzon. Although It was strikingly beautiful, I'd expected so much more from this *Mystic Entity*, and to me, a cluster of ancient Chinese characters embedded with gold in a piece of wood the size of a standard door just didn't warrant getting so excited about the way that so many people that I'd spoken to had done. With my eyes focused intently on the Dai Gohonzon, I joined in the chanting and kept reminding myself not to get tricked into becoming mesmerised. When the Dai Gohonzon suddenly appeared to be pulsating in rhythm with the chanting, I assumed that it was happening mechanically, as nobody had ever mentioned anything about that happening! To test that it wasn't just me, I squeezed my eyes shut and shook my head a few times, but the pulsating effect still continued, and then the Dai Gohonzon appeared to be turning slowly, similarly to how the eyes in a painting seem to follow you as you move, except the Dai Gohonzon appeared to be moving further towards me even though I was sitting perfectly still, and it seemed like It was greeting every individual in the temple, one by one. When it eventually aligned with my eyes and seemingly greeted me, the sudden immense force that I felt coming from It had such an impact that I dived down onto the floor...

"What tha hell's tha matta with me?" I gasped, flustered and embarrassed, as I lay on the floor surrounded by several pairs of agitated feet.

I was expecting that people would be staring and laughing at me, when I built up the courage to climb back onto my seat, but no one had even noticed. They were all too busy looking straight ahead chanting and focusing directly on the Dai Gohonzon. I eventually joined back in with the chanting and soon noticed that the Dai Gohonzon aligning with me again, but this time, instead of feeling fear, I felt an all-encompassing feeling of absolute wonderment. It was like I was floating and at the same time remembering something that went far beyond anything that I'd ever known in this life, and then that now familiar voice inside of me relayed another wordless message as if to say...

"After all of your gallivanting around, you've finally made it home."

The message gave me a sudden feeling of déjà vu, and somewhere deep down, I felt like I knew exactly what it meant, even though on the surface of my mind, I didn't have a clue. It felt like I was reuniting with the Dai Gohonzon rather than seeing it for the first time, and that I'd done it many, many times before. After the incredible spiritual climax had subsided, I settled back into my surroundings and began acknowledging all the other voices around me again. I felt elated with feelings of boundless joy, optimism and expectation, as though I'd finally broken free from something or switched to another level of some kind, and that nothing was ever going to be quite the same again. I began to direct my prayers towards the happiness of my family, and that's when it became even more clear to me that my earlier thoughts about being responsible for my sufferings were correct, and I also understood deep down that those people who desire to bring suffering upon others have a far worse condition of bad karma than those on the receiving end. Through my pain and sufferings, I'd expiated some of my worst negative karma, by their words and actions, George, Beatty and Dad, had instead added more to theirs and had potentially created a much worse future effect for themselves. (Proof of this will become apparent later in the book.) As all this stuff was manifesting from within, it felt like a weight was being lifted from my shoulders, and I was ready to face just about anything. Finally, the brain within my heart took over and then all the years of anger and hatred that I'd held towards George, Beatty and Dad, transformed into love and compassion, and it was as though none of it had never even existed. Next, something which I'd read in Nichiren's teachings popped into my thoughts...

*The people of the world today are like people who are drunk and have injured themselves, and who are not yet aware of their injuries.*

With this statement glowing strongly within my mind, I chanted earnestly for my relatives to realise their mistakes and to manifest the wisdom needed to make any necessary changes before it's too late. After that, I chanted for just about everybody that I knew, especially Mum. I felt confident that had she known what was going on during all those years that I was kept hidden away from her, she'd have moved heaven and earth to rescue me. I also felt sad and disappointed for my older siblings, who'd always taken the easy road and chosen to condemn me, rather than to make an effort to find the underlying truth behind why I was running away from home and creating so much havoc. My emotions were racing all over the place, and I felt like I'd been on a roller coaster ride by the time that I slipped back down into my everyday mundane existence and remembered that I had no money to buy lunch. Needless to say, my final few minutes of chanting on that unforgettable day was to manifest the strength that I'd need to control my hunger pangs during the coming few hours. The profoundly uplifting ceremony concluded with the ringing of a large bell, followed by the closure of the giant nuclear bomb-and-earthquake-proof altar doors, after which, I joined the long line of fellow worshippers leaving Sho-Hondo – yet again feeling like a feather floating on air. It was a perfect spring day outside, and the beautiful blue cloudless sky and fresh-smelling country air, plus the sight of snow-capped Mount Fuji standing above us in the distance, created an idyllic picturesque setting. While we'd been inside Sho-Hondo, thousands of more people had arrived and they were spread out over the temple grounds as far as the eye could see. The two Americans that had been sitting either side of me inside Sho-Hondo were now walking closely behind me and chatting. I overheard one of them mention something about the opening of a new temple museum that day and suggesting that it might be worth having a quick sticky-beak there before meeting up with the others for lunch. Before the other guy had a chance to answer, I rudely interrupted and invited myself to join them. Not surprisingly, they didn't look all that enthusiastic, especially after putting up with me crawling around in between their feet, but that didn't matter. I was so desperate to avoid having to watch everyone eat lunch and felt so ravishingly hungry, that I couldn't have cared less. As far as I was concerned, accompanying the Americans, regardless of what they thought of me, was by far the much better option. Along the way to the museum we were confronted by dozens of Japanese school kids and university students, all wanting to chat and have their photo taken with us at the same time. They were devoted members of the NS/SGI Youth Group, and it was clear to see that they were as happy as mice in a cheese shop to see so many Westerners at the Head Temple. As we entered the new museum foyer, we were politely informed by the receptionist that only guests with invitations were allowed inside that day. The two Americans quickly responded with a polite bow and a smile and then started heading towards the exit door. I, however, wasn't prepared to give up so easily and stubbornly remained where I was standing, determined to escape a confrontation at the restaurant, even if it meant faking a dizzy spell to avoid leaving. As I hung around just inside the doorway, admiring all the lovely pot plants to the Americans, it became apparent to me that they were getting agitated and anxious to go and eat, but I just kept on talking and holding them back regardless. After I eventually ran out of things to say to them about the plants, and as we were walking away from the building's entrance, a tall Japanese man appeared at a window, loudly knocking on it and gesturing for us to come back. He wanted to know if we'd enjoyed seeing the museum and when we explained that we didn't have invitations, he insisted that we follow him inside, and this time as we passed by the receptionist, she gave us a welcoming smile. We were just about to go through a double doorway when the Japanese man leading us spun around and asked us if we'd had lunch. Instantly aware that the two Americans were about to refuse a potential invitation before either of them could open their mouths to decline, I butted in and blurted out...

"No! We haven't!"

With another bow and big inviting smile, the man then insisted on us being his guests and joining him for lunch, and I honestly couldn't believe our luck! I also suspected that the Americans were probably thinking disgusting things about me, which is why I couldn't look either of them in the face. Then, when I suddenly caught sight of the mouth-watering feast that awaited us behind a partition, their judgement of me became the furthest thing from my mind, as it was such an incredible sight to behold! There were delicious-looking cakes, caviar, fish, turkey, chicken, fruit and bottles of champagne by the dozens, and I just didn't know where to start. Gathered all around the huge room were people dressed in tuxedos and formal wear, many of whom were Japanese dignitaries, but once I started tucking into the food, to me it mattered not who they were – I was in gourmet heaven. I didn't get to see the president of SGI, Daisaku Ikeda, myself, but I knew that he was in the crowd somewhere. I must have heard his name mentioned at the meetings more often than Gohonzon and Nam-Myoho-Renge-Kyo put together, as so many of the other NS/SGI members appraised him as if he was a saint, a great mystic leader, or supreme mentor – some even tried to convince me that he was the Buddha reincarnated. Munching away to my heart's content, I couldn't help wondering if Mr Ikeda was enjoying his lunch as much as I was, particularly since he was probably paying for it all.

At the top section at one end of the room were large triangular windows, through which Sho-Hondo was clearly visible in the distance, and it was like looking out at a beautiful and tranquil picture. While I was happily admiring it and merrily masticating, thoughts wandered into my mind about what had happened inside Sho-Hondo that day. I also thought about what Mrs Daisley had told me before I'd left Australia about going even further north and finding something incredibly wonderful. She'd been so excited when she saw it in the tea leaves, and I didn't know what to make of it then. So far, almost everything that she'd predicted had come true.

Meanwhile, the Americans were in deep conversation with our Japanese host in the background. They still hadn't said a single word to me, but going by the way that they were devouring the culinary delights, I didn't think they were likely to make any negative complaints about the food at least...

"Where's in America do you come from?" Asked our Japanese host, as I was helping myself to some more of the delicious banquet...

"Oh, I'm not from America," I answered with a friendly grin – between bites, "I come from Australia."

"Osutoraria!" He almost shouted, suddenly radiating high energy, "I'm the leplesentative in Japan for all the Osutolalian Soka Gakkai members!"

His unexpected declaration gave me such a jolt that I became momentarily riveted. Hardly an hour had gone by since I'd chanted Nam-Myoho-Renge-Kyo in front of the Dai Gohonzon about what to do for lunch, and here I was heartily enjoying a feast fit for a king, queen, or anything in between. Standing motionless, holding a chicken wing in one hand and a glass of coke in the other, I gazed across the room through the window at the magnificent Sho-Hondo in absolute and utter disbelief and sheer amazement. I probably would have been the only Australian there that day, and it became another spectacular and beautiful moment that I will always hold dear to my heart and remember with gratitude.

## MORE ABOUT THE GOHONZON

A Gohonzon is a physical embodiment, configuration and representation of Life's supreme energy, which anyone can align with to awaken the epitome of their inner-wisdom, good fortune and hidden potential, all of which waits within the core of whom each and every one of us is. In other words, it represents a reflection of our all-encompassing universal enlightenment.

A Gohonzon isn't there to be worshipped like an idol or godhead, it's to be cherished, respected and used as a mirror to allow us to reflect and align with our true inner-self. But even so, the two terms of treasure and respect are often mistakenly misinterpreted to mean idolisation or worship.

The Gohonzon that people receive and then enshrine in their homes are smaller reproductions of the original Dai Gohonzon. And although what's written is in Chinese and Sanskrit characters that many of us are unable to read, a Gohonzon, when used correctly, can still bring forth beneficial results, regardless. To give a simple example, the word HATE, written in an appropriate language, or the sight of a negative picture will usually provoke negative feelings, such as fear, discomfort or even anguish. On the other hand, the word LOVE or the sight of a beautiful view can easily activate far more positive feelings from within. Similarly, by focusing on a Gohonzon while chanting Nam-Myoho-Renge-Kyo, and regardless of how happy or sad, one may feel at the time, anyone can align with a Gohonzon and experience both good and bad feelings, sometimes even simultaneously. By awakening our wisdom, compassion and hidden potential all at the same time, we're able to expiate and replace our negative karma with positive karma. We able to do this by becoming wise enough to make better causes in life, and to use a simple example, it's a bit like the outcome of a sink full of dirty dishes, after the water and soap have been added. Along with some added elbow grease and sincere effort, the dirt and grime will dissipate into the water, allowing the dishes to come out almost like new shiny clean, sparkling pieces of crockery. The same kind of outcome takes place within our life when we sincerely chant Nam-Myoho-Renge-Kyo – especially in front of a Gohonzon. However, just as the dishes get dirty again and need a new wash each time they're used, so too does the condition of our karma content each day – the re-cleaning can only successfully be achieved if and when we choose to make an effort to make it happen. It's the mystic effect that we experience within everyday life that gives us proof of this. To elaborate a little more, just as we can see reflections of our physical selves in a mirror, water, glass and many other aspects of Nature, if our faith in the Mystic Law is sincere, we can tune into It anywhere, at any time, even if we haven't got a Gohonzon. For the first two years of my practice, even though I didn't have a Gohonzon, I still received and experienced many extraordinary benefits, changes and improvements in my life.

# Chapter 22

# WISDOM OF THE 'LIGHT'

After I'd written a letter to Mum, letting her know that I'd become a Nichiren Buddhist, she wrote straight back in a fluster...

"Tommy, come home! Your family is all Roman Catholics! That religion is for *those* people! You're not one of *them*! You're an Australian! Come home before you get too deeply involved and something dreadful happens to you!"

It was clear as day for me to see that Mum wasn't the least bit happy with my news, as her writing ran rampant over the page. While I was disappointed in how she reacted, and I didn't like upsetting her or hurting her feelings, nothing that Mum or anyone else could say was going to stop me from chanting. I felt more confident and happier than I'd ever felt in my life, and it seemed to be getting better by the day. Among many other things, after years of failed and frustrating attempts to write songs, I'd begun to compose since I'd been chanting, including several songs for a rock musical that I'd titled *YOU* after a song that came to me during a dream. Based on what I'd learnt so far and what I'd learn in the future about the fundamentals of Buddhism, YOU was the most important new goal of my career.

AS THE FOLLOWING months went by, I continued to experience more outrageous happenings, particularly during some of my taxi rides between the coach terminal and Sho-Hondo. I'd been struggling to remember the faces of my sixth-grade classmates, but with very little success. Then one day, as my taxi was approaching the temple gateway, nearly every face popped up in my mind like a succession of photographs, including those of my teacher and school headmaster. From that day on I was able to remember them all perfectly. During another can journey to the temple, and while we were winding through the same long and narrow road, the houses momentarily disappeared, and the tarred road ahead turned into a dirt track. My vision was so realistic and vivid that it still seems as though it all actually happened. I also saw monks in robes, crouching and tending to small shrubs, and after making inquiries about it later, found out that the road had been dirt track centuries earlier. This, in itself, came as no surprise, but when I also learned that the dirt track had once been surrounded by a tea plantation, which was maintained by local Buddhist monks, I was quite flabbergasted and wondered if, through my chanting, I was activating old memories from previous lives. A few weeks later, things became even more bizarre, when I found myself having what I can only describe as a 'spiritual conversation' with a crowd of people that weren't even there! I felt like I knew them all, but no matter how hard I tried afterwards, I couldn't put a name to a single voice that I'd heard. The crux of the dialogue seemed to be about me choosing to come into this world for a specific purpose, and how I'd made those speaking to me, promise not to interfere and make things easier. As crazy as it may seem, it was as though I'd deliberately created obstacles for myself in this life before I was born, which I needed to challenge and overcome in order to strengthen my determination and accomplish what seemed to be my *mission*, even though I had no idea what my mission was, or if I even had one or not. However, I certainly wished that I'd been less strict about it all. These sorts of experiences are usually only momentary encounters and often don't fully register or make sense until sometime later. After each outrageous experience, all that I could do was ask myself if, at some point in time, some of them might prove to have an essential purpose.

WHILE WAITING for my train at Shinjuku Railway Station one night, I started thinking about some of the amazing things that had happened in my life since I'd been chanting...

"How tha hell can sayin' words in anotha language that I can't understand, in front of a scroll with writing on it that I can't even read, have this sort 'o an effect?" I asked myself. "No one back home'd believe a word of it! I can hardly believe it myself! Am I already dead!?"

As a sudden cold chill raced up and down my spine, and I began plucking frantically at the hairs on my arms to feel pain and to verify that I was still alive and in a physical body. I suddenly noticed that people around me were hurrying away, and quickly stopped plucking and composed myself. A few weeks later, I was walking down one of Tokyo's busiest streets minding my own business and ran into my American jazz-singer friend, Anne Young, whom I hadn't seen or heard from in months. She'd just finished an extensive tour of the US and Japan, and when she shrieked out loud with excitement from within the oncoming crowd of people in front of me, I didn't know who it was, whom it was coming from or what the heck was happening...

"Don't you say a single word," she ordered, skipping and dancing around me like a jumping jack as several passersby stopped to see what was going on.

Anne was absolutely astonished and couldn't believe that she was looking at the same person. Ignoring her demands, I quickly let her know that it was all because of my chanting – with a look of fierce determination, Anne virtually ordered me to teach her how to chant then and there. A week or so later, Anne became an official member of NS/SGI, and a few days after that, I took her to Taisekiji to chant in front of the Dai Gohonzon. Just before entering the Shohondo, I asked Anne if there was anything in particular that she desired in her life, and after taking a few moments to think about it, she explained how, even though she'd been touring Japan sporadically for more than twelve years, she'd never been able to land a Japanese recording contract. The reason being, even though Japanese record companies were more than happy to release records made abroad, they were reluctant to sign up foreign artists. I explained to Anne that, from my experiences and from those that I'd heard about from other Nichiren Buddhists, it seemed to be that just about anything is possible to change or be achieved through chanting. I then encouraged her to chant Nam-Myoho-Renge-Kyo as often as she could about her future dream of gaining a recording contract in Japan, and to use it to challenge and overcome every obstacle that got in her way until she'd either changed her mind about it or succeeded to reach her goal. I was completely blown away six weeks later when Anne was offered a recording contract with a Japanese label after she'd decided to follow my advice.

LATE ONE evening, I was alone at home doing some chanting, when that ever-familiar, disembodied voice inspired me to get a pencil and paper to write some things down. Unlike the trance-like states that I'd experienced in the past when receiving these sorts of messages, I was wide awake and completely alert. As always, I wasn't sure if the voice in my mind wasn't just my subconscious playing games, but whether it was or it wasn't, I'd learned by then not to ignore it – just in case. I grabbed t a pencil and paper and proceeded to write down a list of things that randomly came to me one after the other, while I continued chanting at the same time. Here is the list exactly as I'd written it…

*Another will inform you of right, but his method is wrong.*
*Let my sounds of music dwell freely in your mind.*
*When my land is green there will come a time, achieve it.*
*Advance on your own accord and delight in success.*
*Don't rely on the loves of other lives; create value for your own.*
*Be patient as the stars may shine, the moon is always in your sky.*
*Face the truth and don't lie down backwards. You have a force, use it and go forward.*
*Splendour is a trickle of dust, as is your mind if you maim it.*
*Overcome all hostilities and then benefit from this wisdom.*

*Don't indulge in something of thirst; use your guidance to gain clear water.*

*Hold on to the pressure of the system; it's your only way to gain perfection inscribed within your life.*

*My hand of assistance is always in your hands; all you need do is hold tight and squeeze it.*

*The man who insists among his insisters is a man of methodical mind.*

*The bells of the heavens are ringing, should you hear them within your mind, smile.*

*Dwell on the friendship that unites you with yourself.*

*Bring forth this ripeness within your mind and converse it with your heart and soul.*

*Retrieve from the spills of a dynasty.*

*White is the moon to your eyes, develop it to reach the outer skies.*

*Handsome is the man that smiles.*

*Thrive in the sunshine, which shines to develop your life.*

*The passions of love beam upon you, cherish them with an open mind.*

*Do not hate what is to be hated, accept it and alter it.*

*The spirits of love are, at last, you have cherished them.*

*A snake may enter your mind, but a fly may fly.*

*All options are now yours for the taking.*

*Your life can be as one in the infinite past but dare not to surface it.*

*You are but a moment of a day, my moments are precious.*

*Be free from your evil karma, trusting your heart.*

*Advance to the token of respect and achieve this plight.*

*Friends can be many and foes may be few should you escape any doubt.*

Most of what I wrote down made very little or no sense to me, and after reading it a few more times, I screwed it up, tossed it in the bin, made myself a cup of coffee, switched on the TV and proceeded to try to put the messages out of my mind, but no matter how hard I tried, I couldn't. In the end, I retrieved the list from the bin and took it to a Buddhist meeting the following night. I was hoping that the members would dismiss it as being nonsense, so that I could get on with my life and forget all about it. After the meeting had ended, I showed the crinkled list to a senior member, and his unexpected response after reading it shocked the socks off of me. He advised me to keep what I'd written and guaranteed me that one day it would all make perfect sense, and as things have turned out since so far, he was right...

ON ANOTHER OCCASION, while I was chanting alone in front of Masami's Gohonzon, I found myself reflecting on my first visit to the Dai Gohonzon, and carefully concentrating on what had happened that day, I tried to bring forth a logical answer that would explain what it was that had sent me diving under the seats. I wasn't having much luck with it, and just as I was about to give up trying, a very unexpected answer suddenly became crystal-clear to me. The beautiful Light that I'd visited in 1970 and the Dai Gohonzon were both somehow one of the same, or at least connected in some way. It also soon became apparent to me that the reason I'd dived under the seats wasn't through fear of seeing the Dai Gohonzon but from my underlying memory of being struck by lightning.

At the meetings, I'd often heard people mention a 'Light of Tranquillity', and a beautiful place of perfection and peace called 'Eagle Peak'...

"Was that the colourful Light that I went to?" I asked myself.

*The two treasures of humankind are food and clothing. If they are unavailable then survival is impossible.*
*For sea creatures, water is the greatest treasure and for plants and trees it's the soil from which they grow. The greatest and most precious treasure of all living things, however, is Life itself.*
*Regardless of whether one has wealth and good fortune or not, Life is still the most precious treasure.*
*...Nichiren.*

# Chapter 23

# A MOST SIGNIFICANT LESSON

Rosita, my fire-dancer friend, had left Hiroshima and moved to Tokyo, where she was working on a popular children's TV show, delighting kids all over Japan by turning coloured balloons into various animal shapes. She was still feeling skeptical about Buddhism but, as Anne had been, she too was amazed at the dramatic change in me. She particularly couldn't get over how the dark rings around my eyes had vanished and my previously harsh face was now beaming. With my visa was about to expire again, this time, there didn't seem to be any way that I could avoid leaving, and I just loathed the idea of returning to Hong Kong, and then, out of the blue, came new hope! I managed to reserve the last available cheap seat on a flight to London – I was ecstatic! On the following night, when I eagerly told everyone the good news at the weekly Buddhist meeting, their enthusiastic response was so loud that they almost raised the roof. My next big hurdle was earning enough money in time to pay for my plane ticket...

"Just chant for it!" They all told me – with smiling faces glowing with optimism – so I did!

Low and behold, a couple of days later, Rosita phoned to tell me that an agent that she knew needed a Caucasian singer to do some gigs in Osaka, and she wanted to know if I'd be interested. I instantly said yes, contacted the agent and had sealed the deal by the end of that day. The three-week contract that he offered meant that I'd be able to earn enough money for my plane ticket, as well as to keep a roof over my head in Europe for at least a couple of months. Eager to share my good news, I attended another Buddhist meeting on the night before I left for Osaka, and when I told them all about what had happened since the previous meeting, they almost raised the whole house! A return ticket on a Bullet Train to Osaka came with the deal, but because I didn't like the idea of being on a speeding train if an earthquake struck, I used my own money to pay for an air ticket instead. At Osaka Airport, I was met by the agent who wasted no time informing me that my gigs were between midnight and 5.00am each morning and that I'd be doing a half-hour show in seven different nightclubs each night. The guy was certainly out to get his money's worth, that's for sure, and it looked like I was about to be worked to the bone. The accommodation was a room in an older-style hotel that had people coming and going 24/7. It was the middle of July, stinking hot, and to make things more uncomfortable, the hotel air-conditioning was hardly ever on. I eventually noticed a *pay as you use* unit that looked like an air-conditioner at the head of my bed, so I reluctantly placed the required 100-yen coin in the slot and then sat back, convinced that the cool air would soon be flowing – no such luck! All I got was the sound of people's voices moaning and groaning that grew progressively louder. I sounded like a couple involved in a hot session of intense sex in the adjoining room. As I listened carefully, and my imagination ran wild, I became so hot that it's a wonder I didn't get blisters. It turned out to be a *love hotel* designed for people to get together and have uninhibited sex. The machine at the head of my bed, which I'd mistaken for an air conditioner, was a tape player that played erotic recordings of people having wild, kinky sex – it was to help set the mood. On the following day, I finally discovered where the correct switch for the air-conditioner was, but I'd have been better off not knowing. After I'd finished performing at seven different nightclubs that night, I arrived back at my room at 5.00am with sweat pouring off me. I pressed the air conditioner 'on' button but nothing happened! Feeling far too exhausted to go back down the stairs and report it, I just stripped naked, fell on top of the bed and virtually passed out. After I awoke a few hours later, struggling to breathe, I was shocked to discover that the air-conditioning had automatically come on while I'd been asleep and that I'd left it on its lowest temperature setting. A duct directly above the bed had frozen my chest numb, leaving me with no voice other than a crackling whisper.

After three long days with little improvement in my condition, my agent came to the hotel enraged, blamed me for my ill health, fired me on the spot and then stormed out without paying me a cent. What angered me the most was not having any voice to yell back at him and tell him what an A-class arse-hole I thought that he was. After he'd left, I packed my bag and caught a cab to Osaka Airport, only to learn that all the scheduled flights for the day had already left. Using a lot of scratchy whispering to beg them, the ground staff eventually gave in and put me on an empty Boeing-707 to Tokyo that had just delivered its international passengers and was heading off to refuel and pick up more. Sitting all alone in the cabin of such a large plane, without even a flight attendant to talk to was an extremely peculiar and scary experience, and I could hardly wait for the plane to land and let me off. It was getting late by then, but I still phoned Dick Causton from an airport pay-phone to let him know what had happened – again, with my very scratchy voice. His cheerful response was to tell me that I shouldn't be too bothered by it, so long as I'd regularly been chanting, adding that even though it might seem as though my chanting had failed me, in time it could very well turn out that it was all for the best. His words made about as much sense to me as the events of the previous few days, and instead of feeling any better, I felt pissed-off with him as well...

"So bloody nice 'n' easy for him ta just sit back 'n' say," I growled to nearby signpost, as I was hurrying off to board the monorail.

When I reached Masami's apartment, shortly after midnight, I was dead on my feet and soaked with sweat. I began explaining what had happened, and before I could say much, Masami jabbed his finger into my arm and accused me of not doing enough chanting. His arrogant response was the last thing that I needed or expected to hear, and I completely lost it with him. Refusing to listen to anything else I had to say, Masami stormed out of the flat and left me ranting and raving to the walls and the ceiling. His fanatical response made me so angry and frustrated that I opened his altar and abused his Gohonzon, which only made my throbbing headache feel ten times worse. Following that, I abruptly turned on the gas water heater for the bath and then put the kettle on for a cup of tea. While I was waiting for the kettle to boil and inwardly cursing everything, the door suddenly flew open and in rushed Masami! He was yelling his head off at me in Japanese, and at the same time, everything around me was spinning, and I felt like I was about to drop. The automatic gas lighters on both the bath and stove had failed to ignite, and the apartment was reeking of gas. Due to my state of anger, I hadn't even noticed the smell. Lucky for me, Masami had been standing just outside having a smoke and had smelt the gas coming through the half-open doorway. After Masami had quickly turned everything off, he dragged me outside and started shaking the living daylights out of me to keep me awake. At the same time, he kept accusing me in broken English of attempting to commit suicide in his flat, and I couldn't get my mouth to function well enough to tell him otherwise. Once I'd regained enough strength in my legs to walk safely, I made a beeline across the room to Masami's Gohonzon, and got down on my knees, apologising to the universe profusely for what I'd said. The bizarre and terrifying incident left me in a state of remorse that kept me humble and on my best behaviour for days. Then my worst fears came true, and whether I wanted to or not, I had no other choice but to return to Hong Kong. Feeling desperately in need of some spiritual support and a build-up of self-confidence, on the day before I left Japan, I once again visited the Dai Gohonzon. While I was there, my outlook completely changed, and by the time that I left Taisekiji to head back to Tokyo, I was happily looking forward to returning to Hong Kong. My heart was almost bursting with confidence, and I was filled with determination to tell all of my Hong Kong friends, who'd always done their best to support me, everything that I could about Nichiren's Buddhism and Nam-Myoho-Renge-Kyo. Since being a Buddhist, I'd often heard it mentioned that if you see Mount Fuji clearly when you're about to leave Japan, it means that you'll soon be back again. To add strength to my new wealth of hope and inner happiness, the last thing that I saw from the coach as we headed away, was a magnificent clear view of Mount Fuji. In his Gosho, Nichiren wrote that our negative karma can easily make things appear to be what they're not. I'd only ever seen Hong Kong through drunken, deluded eyes, and in so many ways, I hardly knew the place at all.

IT WAS LATE AT night when I arrived back in the colony with no immediate prospects and just enough money to keep me going for a couple of weeks. I rented a cheap room in Chungking Mansions and fell straight off to sleep. Early the following morning, I took a leisurely stroll along Nathan Road, where I knew a lot of people, but hardly any of them seemed to notice me. Later that day, I visited my close Filipino musician friend, Rudy, who also lived in Chungking Mansions. Rudy was in bed suffering from a thumping migraine when I arrived, and my unexpected appearance gave him an instant uplifting boost. He and his wife, Tammy, a well-known Japanese pop singer, had always seemed like a perfect couple and they'd been a fantastic support to me during my dangerously wild, heavy-drinking days. I couldn't believe it when Rudy told me that his marriage had finished and that Tammy was moving out that day. He was quite hyper and couldn't get his head around how different I looked. After he kept wanting to know how come, I told him about Gohonzon and how chanting Nam-Myoho-Renge-Kyo in front of it had helped me to escape from my hellhole, to overcome my drinking problem and to get my life back on track...

"Where's this Gon'zon thing? Where can I buy one?" He asked, anxiously. "Quickly, there's no time to waste! Tammy's leaving me!"

Before I had time to answer him, he was up off his bed and pushing me out the door and down the corridor towards the lift, en route to my room. Talk about things falling into place, earlier that day I'd met and made friends with another Filipino musician who was also staying in Chungking Mansions. He'd arrived in Hong Kong on the day before I did, and when I mentioned to him that I'd become a member of Nichiren Buddhism while I was in Japan, and when he told me that he'd become a member as well and that he had his own Gohonzon, I thought I was *hearing things.* He was sharing a flat with the other members of his band who knew nothing about his newfound faith and was concerned for the safety of his Gohonzon. He asked me if he could leave it in my room under my care and come to chant in front of it with me each day, and I'd happily agreed to it. In all the time that I'd wandered the streets of Hong Kong and out of all the many people that I'd met there, never once had I heard the words Nam-Myoho-Renge-Kyo even mentioned, let alone the word Gohonzon.

Rudy and I got quite a surprise when the lift doors opened and out stepped Tammy – the timing was excellent. She'd come to collect the rest of her things, and when she saw me, her sad face lit up like a beacon...

"Look! Look at what Tommy's been doing!" Rudy exclaimed, cutting in and anxiously trying to gain his wife's attention as she and I were hugging and greeting one another.

When Rudy showed his wife the card that I'd given him with Nam-Myoho-Renge-Kyo printed on it, her face lit up even more. Minutes later, we arrived at my room, and at the moment Tammy caught sight of my Filipino friend's Gohonzon scroll hanging on the wall, she burst into tears. It turned out that while Tammy had been away living in Hong Kong, back home in Japan, her mother had joined NS/SGI and begun chanting. For almost a year, Tammy's mum had been making efforts to get Tammy to chant, but she was never the least bit interested. As a final gesture, Tammy's mum had promised her that she'd chant each day for Tammy's happiness. Me showing up with a Gohonzon, on what Tammy considered to be the unhappiest day of her life, caused her to suddenly realise that she was still very much in love with her husband and didn't want her marriage to end. She and Rudy both had demanding careers that often forced them to spend long periods of time apart, Rudy had been unfaithful, and Tammy had found out about it, which certainly didn't help. However, after only a few days of chanting together, they were able to rise above Rudy's cheating episode enough to start rekindling their dying relationship. Not long after that, Tammy revisited her mother in Japan and received a Gohonzon of her own. During her absence, Rudy confessed to me that he'd made one last visit to his secret lover and had been incapable of becoming aroused, which had never happened to him before, and had given him quite a scare – he just didn't know what to make of it.

I MADE A FEW phone calls to some people that I knew in the business and soon had enough gigs to keep me going for at least a month, which took a big load off my shoulders. Many of the musicians, strippers, drag queens and prostitutes that I knew wanted to know where I'd been and what I'd been doing to look so good. Until then, I hadn't realised that so many people cared so much about me. I was deeply moved by how they responded and kept telling me how happy they were to see me back again, which had even brought a few tears to my eyes. Now that I was sober, it was like meeting them all for the very first time, and such an astounding experience.

One of Hong Kong's leading newspapers ran a half-page spread that read: **'Tommy Beaumont Back from Japan'**, and the article created so much interest that my phone didn't stop ringing for days. As well as being asked to appear on variety shows by producers at the local Chinese and British TV stations, I was also asked to be the special guest on episode one of a brand new pop show that was due to be launched a week later. During the next few days that followed, I discovered that some of my old friends had problems of their own, which they'd probably always had, but I'd been too 'out of it' with my own issues even to notice. As these old friends came to my room, one by one, revealing their obstacles and challenges, I found myself giving advice and support to people who, less than a year earlier were struggling against impossible odds to help me survive for another day – what an astounding transformation it was! At first, they'd sneak up to my room on their own and chant with me for a few minutes at a time in secret because they didn't want certain other people to know, probably for fear of being ridiculed. Looking back, I think it was probably for the best, as some of them were staunch enemies. Be that as it may, their fears and differences were soon overcome or dissolved by a new wave of excitement and confidence in their lives, especially after they started receiving some actual proof from their chanting. Within weeks, I had up to fifty of these people, enemies and friends alike, jammed into my room and bathroom, chanting together with me in unison for World Peace and happiness. I'm getting emotional now just thinking about it all.

STAYING ALONG the hall from me in Chungking Mansions was an American woman who was said to be a witch. I'd met her younger sister at one of the Buddhist meetings in Japan, and she'd asked me to look in on her older sister and to try to encourage her to chant. When I finally got a chance to knock on her door, she had a room full of visitors, one of whom was an elderly Russian lady doing a tarot card reading, who looked even more like a witch than my friend's sister. I didn't stay long and promised to visit her again some other time. I wasn't back to my room for long, before the old lady came knocking on my door and begging me to let her read my cards – free of charge! I told her that I wasn't interested, but she wouldn't take no for an answer and kept insisting that it was vitally important. It was when she mentioned that she felt something very powerful and good coming from me, that my insatiable curiosity got the better of me, and I gave in to the reading. More than anything else, I was curious to know if she'd picked up something about my new faith...

"You vill meet a man vith dark skin," she mumbled in her strong accent.

"He vill ask you to carry somesink somewhere. I sink it might be jewellery or somesink like dat. He vill offer you money ond ask you to travel to places far avay."

As she spoke, placing her colourful cards down one by one and side by side, my heart went out to her. She had the character of a sweet little old lady, just to keep her happy, I did my best to pretend to be surprised and convinced by each of her strange predictions...

"Dere is anoder man," she explained with a friendly grin on her face, and after a short break of silence while taking a closer look at one of the cards. "He's a bit like you in some vay. A tall man oo is fair hairs ond dere is a contract to be signed ond aeroplanes are involved. You vill do a lot of trafelling ond gain a lot of money from dis man. You vill also lose some moneys – I sink you vill lose it gamblink, but don't vorry, cuz eferysing vill work out okays."

Each time that she reshuffled the cards, she'd pause before speaking again...

"I've nefer seen dis sink appen before," she mumbled, gathering up the cards, reshuffling them and then placing them back down. "Efery time evil appears, goodness also appears to protect you. It appens efery time! My goodness, I aff nefer seen dese sinks before! At the moment, dere is somesink very powerful in your life dat protects you."

She sounded as intrigued by telling me these things as I was in hearing about them. I didn't know a thing at all about tarot cards, but I could see how the same cards were turning up in the same order each time that she re-shuffled and spread them out. When I mentioned that I chanted Nam-Myoho-Renge-Kyo and pointed across to my friend's Gohonzon, she suddenly shrieked with joy and begged me to teach her how to chant – I didn't need to even try to convince her, as she convinced herself by what she saw in the cards. When she left my room that day, she was still mumbling Nam-Myoho-Renge-Kyo to herself all the way down the hallway to the lift.

I WENT TO Macao to perform for a week at the private elite Casino Lisboa Nightclub, which had been built especially for the locals. I'd heard that as part of their deal that went with the land lease, the casino owners were also obliged to supply the nightclub with top-class entertainment each week. The snag being, the only night that anyone came to see the shows were Saturdays when the mayor was present. Six nights of singing to a few staff members gave me next to no incentive and wandering around all day without anything much to do became a source of prolonged boredom. In my struggles to help while away the hours, I gambled and ended up losing all of my earnings. On the night that I got back to Hong Kong from Macao, I crossed paths with Angie, after not seeing or hearing from her since I'd left Hiroshima. Like everyone else that had known me during my darkest days, she too was amazed at how different I looked. I explained to her that Nichiren Buddhism wasn't the same version of Buddhism that the priests who set fire to themselves in Vietnam had practised, after which, she was eager to try chanting herself. A few days later, I also taught an attractive high-class female escort named Jean how to chant. Jean was in trouble with the authorities for prostitution, and desperately willing to try anything that might help her. She chanted furiously with me to avoid jail time or a hefty fine, but not even in her wildest dreams had Jean ever expected her case to be acquitted. The court's decision was published in the newspapers, and nearly everybody who knew Jean was astounded – including me! A reporter phoned me a few days later and asked me if she could do a story about my new-found faith, and I happily obliged. Jean just happened to pop in to see me on the morning of the interview, and the reporter instantly recognised her face from the newspapers. When I mentioned that Jean also chanted, the reporter begged Jean to be part of the interview. The following Saturday morning, I opened up the Hong Kong Standard and nearly spat out my coffee and my denture. Splashed across the page in giant letters was...

**'MAN WITH A MESSAGE. TOMMY BEAUMONT!**
**AND RENGE KYO TO YOU AS WELL!'**

The reporter's story was so distorted and fabricated that, at one point, I found it difficult to carry on reading. She'd written that people who chanted Nam-Myoho-Renge-Kyo could get just about anything that they wanted, that prostitutes could draw in clients and influence the courts, that homosexuals could have potential lovers lining up at their doors, and other equally erroneous exaggerations. The reporter had been blatantly deceptive, but as a friend later pointed out, if the story had been honest and straight, it probably wouldn't have gained as much attention, and as it turned out, she was right! Some acquaintances talked about the article for weeks, which opened a door of opportunity for me to tell more of them the truth about Nam-Myoho-Renge-Kyo and what it had done for me. I still had a lot to learn about the teachings, so I could only answer a few of their very basic questions, but I did correctly explain that the real reason for chanting is to activate our wisdom, hidden potential and good fortune from within, so that we can achieve our own true happiness, and contribute to the happiness of others. I also told them that it was important to teach Nam-Myoho-Renge-Kyo to others to the best of our ability so that they could forward the good fortune on and allow others a chance to achieve their true happiness as well and help make the world a better place for everyone and everything. Once the gossiping and publicity about Jean's case had died down enough, she got straight back to work and would often phone me late at night from the Hyatt Hotel on Nathan Road to invite me to join her for some supper. One night while I was out, she left a message for me to meet her in one of the hotel's suites. My gut feeling told me that there was something special in the air that night, so I did some extra chanting for added confidence. When I arrived at the suite and knocked on the door, a tall, fair-haired, middle-aged man cheerfully greeted me with a big welcoming smile and in a loud Aussie accent. After he invited me to come in, he quickly poured me a cola on ice from his private bar and then, before I could take a sip of it, insisted that I try a putt on his indoor golf set. It was all quite bizarre, but then so was everything else in my life, so I had a go, and to my utter amazement, I miraculously hit the ball straight into the middle of the cup. I'd learn later that he used this method to judge people's character. Jean had offered to pay for the recording of a song that I'd written entitled *An Oriental Love Affair.* Earlier that night, I'd been to see a professional arranger about doing a score for the song and Jean was keen to hear how everything had gone and what it was going to cost. When our host overheard us discussing it, he politely interrupted and asked to see the lyrics...

An Oriental Love Affair

Like an oriental summer wind, you blow into my mind
Bringing back sweet memories of days of better times
I hope someday, I pray somewhere, our paths will cross again
If you're out there, please tell me where and I'll come to you today
Across the China Sea, I hope you'll wait for me
Upon the pearly shore, each day I love you more
And if you call my name, I'll soon be on my way
An oriental love affair – I love you...
The ancients in the Asian lands where we would spend our time
I almost touch with my hands and feel you by my side
Maybe tomorrow dreams come true, they say it can be done
So I'll just sit and wait for you beneath the Asian sun
Across the China Sea, I hope you'll wait for me
Upon the pearly shore, each day I love you more
And if you call my name, I'll soon be on my way
An oriental love affair, I love you...

He was very impressed with what he read, introduced himself as the CEO of Cathay Pacific Airlines, and then offered me a contract that included a $3000 advance to record the song, plus free travel on his airline for a year to any destination of my choice. In return, I was to agree to permit Cathay Pacific the use of my song for promotional purposes. Like most entertainers, I'd met my fair share of bullshit artists who'd promised the world and came up with nothing, and this bloke sounded like another one. Jean's technique was never to reveal that she was a sex worker until she had her client exactly where she wanted him, which was right at the very last minute. I just assumed that the guy still didn't know she was going to charge him for her services and was spewing cheap words to help himself get her into bed. On my way back to my room that night, I popped into the Chungking Mansions restaurant and joined my stripper friend, Angie, for a late-night coffee. I was right in the middle of telling her what had happened with the CEO when two Indian men, sitting on the opposite side of the room, beckoned me to their table...

"How would you like to earn two thousand US dollars and have an all-expenses-paid holiday in Bombay or Beirut?" One of them asked with a cheesy grin.

Back then, two thousand US dollars was a fair whack of money and not to be sneezed at. I'd only ever waved hello to these men as I was leaving or entering the building, where they'd often be hanging around in the foyer, but up until then, I'd never actually met or spoken to either of them...

"What would I have to do?" I asked politely – uncertain if I'd heard them correctly.

They then explained that they wanted me to carry a box of cheap artificial jewellery to Bombay for them, and I nearly fell off the seat! It sounded exactly like what the old Russian tarot-card lady had predicted! In hindsight, I should have been sensible enough to wait until I knew more about what was involved, but because of how accurate Mrs Daisley's predictions had been and now the Russian lady's as well, I agreed to do it without question. Early the following morning, I was awakened by the phone and a lady's voice inviting me to the Cathay Pacific office, located high up in the new Connaught Building on Hong Kong Island's harbour-front. She explained that a cheque was ready for me to collect after I'd signed the contract that I'd been offered the night before. I couldn't get dressed and down to the Star Ferry quickly enough, in case they had second thoughts and changed their minds. When I next saw the Russian lady and told her how her prediction had come true and that I'd agreed to deliver the jewellery, her jaw almost hit the floor...

"No! No! You must not go! Dis is fery dang'rous for you! You cannot do it! It vill ruin you!"

Her scary reaction took me completely by surprise and caused a massive adrenalin rush that filled me with fear and confusion. I asked her to explain why she hadn't warned me when she'd read my cards, but the old dear was too upset to answer, or maybe she'd warned me, and I'd failed to take her seriously enough to fully understand her. When the two Indian men came to my room the following night and handed me my plane tickets, fearing that my life could be in danger if I told them that I'd changed my mind, I reluctantly accepted the tickets. A few days later I crossed paths with another entertainer who'd been performing in the Far East for several years, and who'd also had dealings with these men. She warned me not to ever get involved with them under any circumstances and told me that the jewellery was just a decoy for something far more sinister they were smuggling into India in the trunks. What rattled me, even more, was hearing about people whom she'd known that were serving long-term prison sentences in India for doing the same thing. I went straight to my room and chanted like a man possessed for a solution to my latest predicament to somehow manifest. I couldn't relax day or night, and then on the day before I was due to leave for India, a revolution broke out in Thailand that disrupted all the airlines. I could hardly believe my luck when my scheduled flight was cancelled, which justified my reneging on my commitment. A week later, when the men returned with a new itinerary, I lied through my teeth and told them that my schedule had become far too tight to allow me to go. They weren't a bit happy and didn't want a bar of it, putting kept putting pressure on me to fulfil my commitment, but I refused to give in, repeatedly insisting that it was no longer an option until they gave up, stormed off in a huff and thankfully, never bothered me again. Once all that had blown over and the dust had settled, longing to see the Dai Gohonzon and Masami again, I took advantage of my free air travel with Cathay Pacific and headed off back to Tokyo.

It was the evening of October 28th 1973, when my plane landed at Haneda Airport, and almost exactly a year since I'd first set foot on Japanese soil. It certainly felt good to be back again, and what an amazing big difference that year had made in my life – I was hardly the same person! Masami had never travelled outside of Japan, so, while I was there, I bought him a ticket to join me on my Christmas tour of Taipei, Hong Kong and South Korea. It was such a joy to be able to do something for him for a change and repay him for some of his incredible help and kindness towards me. Masami was over the moon about it and couldn't wait to get on the plane. It was also during this period that an oil embargo in the Middle East was having a devastating effect on the Orient and other parts of the world. Most venues were being forced to close early, which subsequently put a lot of performers out of work. On the contrary, I had the good fortune of being able to work throughout the entire disruption. But it might not have been the case had I gone across to Europe several months earlier on the cheap flight that I ended up not being able to afford. According to some of what I saw on the news and read in the papers, Britain and Europe suffered terribly from the embargo, as it was one of their coldest winters on record.

By following Dick Causton's advice to maintain strong faith in the Law no matter what, and by challenging my obstacles head-on, I'd successfully turned my poisons into medicine yet again, and just as Dick in his wisdom had potentially foreseen, losing my voice in Osaka had been a blessing in disguise, and the chanting hadn't let me down after all. Another beautiful and rewarding memory, which remains strong in my mind and continues to uplift and encourage me...

*A passage from the Lotus Sutra reads that it is 'the most difficult to believe and the most difficult to understand.'*

*Many hear about and accept this sutra, but when great obstacles arise, just as they were told would happen, few remember it and bear it firmly in their mind.*

*To accept is easy – to continue is difficult. But Buddhahood lies in continuing faith.*

*...Nichiren*

# Chapter 24

# KEEPING THE FAITH

While I was performing at the President Hotel in Taipei, I was befriended by a middle-aged American woman named Rita, who taught English at a local language school and came to see my show every night. She always ended up drunk and miserable, and I started to wonder if it was my singing that was making her drink so much! Each night after my show, Rita would follow me to my dressing room to tell me how down in the dumps she was feeling. As I got to learn more about her life, I discovered that her depression was due mainly to being rejected by her only daughter, who lived in Los Angeles. Rita had chosen to leave her family and friends behind, after marrying a high-ranking US military officer and following him to the Far East, and because of this, her daughter had cut off all ties and disowned her. After Rita's husband had been killed in the Vietnam War, rather than returning home to her family in the US, Rita remained in the Far East drowning her sorrows. She'd tell me repeatedly in tears that she hadn't heard from her daughter for more than eight years and had never seen or met her two grandchildren. Watching streams of tears running down Rita's cheeks as she retold her story night after night had me feeling desperate to try to help her, but her heavy drinking problem made it almost impossible to get through to her. Then, on Christmas Eve, I was finally able to win her confidence enough to convince her to try chanting with me. Two days later, Rita phoned me full of excitement and told me that she'd spent all of Boxing Day giving her apartment a much-needed spring clean, even though it was the middle of winter – she said that she'd never felt better. Rita sounded so ecstatically happy and full of enthusiasm that it was hard for me to believe that I was speaking to the same person. After she and I had chanted together on Christmas Eve, I'd told her not to be surprised if she heard from her daughter in the not-too-distant future. When New Year's Eve arrived, and Rita still hadn't heard a word from her daughter, she tossed down her cleaning rags, lost all hope and started hitting the bottle again. Even though her impatient and erratic reaction left me feeling sadly disappointed, I still didn't give up trying to encourage her. Back then, Taiwan was a miserable and suppressed country. From what I could make out the Taiwanese people were continuously being prepared for a war with China, to prevent them from taking over their islands. Upon my arrival in Taipei, a peace ring that I was wearing was confiscated by a customs officer, who'd made it blatantly clear to me that promoting peace in Taiwan was strictly forbidden. The military presence was everywhere, particularly at night during the curfew hours, and people needed to be very selective and careful about whom they spoke to or befriended. I was hauled off to a police station several times during my six-week stay, to be questioned by officials about talking to particular members of the audience during my shows. I didn't come across any gay bars in Taipei, but I'm sure that there were a few hidden undercovers. But it didn't matter, as I was able to enjoy a casual fling with a cute Taiwanese guy that I met through Rita. One night, while travelling across Taipei by taxi, I witnessed two little children get tossed into the air after being hit by a speeding motorbike. The cab driver slammed on the breaks, but when I tried to jump out to go to their aid, he grabbed me by my arm and sternly warned me that foreigners were not allowed to interfere in Taiwanese affairs. Seeing the children curled up and struggling for their lives on the icy road, meters in front of me was absolutely horrendous, and not being allowed to help them was sheer torture. The government seemed to be in control of everything, including what people could see and do on television. I accepted an offer to do a one hour TV special, but before the ink had time to dry on the contract, I was officially warned by the authorities that if I went ahead and did the show, I'd be deported immediately and never allowed back into Taiwan. To this day, I still don't know why, as no one ever gave me a reason. On a lighter note, the 1973 world oil embargo was creating a massive toilet paper shortage in Japan. When the Taiwanese people discovered that the Japanese were sneaking off with all their toilet paper, and leaving them with none for themselves, there were almost riots in the streets. I sure had a good laugh about that one. On the night that Masami arrived in Taiwan to join me, I had another terrifying nightmare. Scattered all around me were blood, carnage, bodies and planes, and all that I could hear was a horrifying commotion that had me waking up in a ball of panic. The dream had upset me so much that I was convinced that something terrible was about to happen somewhere. Later that day, I could hardly believe my eyes when video images of a massacre at Athens airport flashed across the TV screen. The carnage and mayhem looked just like the images in my dream.

A few days later, Masami and I left Taiwan to spend New Year's Eve in Hong Kong and then continued on to Seoul, where I was scheduled to perform, as part of a non-stop stream of variety entertainment at a large beer club called the *World Cup*. Sadly, South Korea turned out to be just as dismal as Taiwan, and even more bitterly cold. Similar to Taiwan, South Korea was very poor back then, and each day, there were stories in the newspapers about families dying in their sleep while trying to avoid freezing to death. The reason being, people who couldn't afford anything safer were forced to burn large blocks of a coal-like substance to try to keep warm. The blocks stood about a meter or so tall, and we always had one burning in the nightclub greenroom. They would become red hot and radiate intense heat, but just before expiring, they'd emit a final puff of poisonous smoke and gas that could kill you in a matter of seconds. Each night we were reminded to open the windows and run for our lives as soon as the block turned white – nice! Watching some of the other performers from behind the stage and up close each night, especially the Chinese acts, was a fascinating experience. They were able to manoeuvre their bodies in ways that I'd never even imagined to be possible. Most of the audience would be highly intoxicated from drinking too much beer and often had no idea what was going on. Before the 11.00pm curfew took effect each night, the local shopkeepers and restaurateurs would quickly mop their floors and then throw their buckets of dirty water out onto the public footpath, causing ice to form instantly and become dangerous for people rushing by, I slipped on my arse several times. To beat the curfew deadline each night, I'd have to race like mad from my warm dressing room out into the bitter cold and then jog up a hill to my hotel. Wrapped in my ever-faithful Panda maxi-coat and wearing several woollen scarves, I'd be hopping over masses of slippery ice like a Jackrabbit on speed. Due to the sudden variation in temperatures night after night, I came down with a dreadful cold that soon turned into the flu. To make matters worse, Masami had already flown back to Japan, and none of the hotel staff could speak a word of English, so I couldn't even ask for any help.

Across the busy highway from my hotel was a dilapidated hospital. In order to reach it, I had to drag myself up and down the stairs of a long footbridge and then pay an entry fee just to get through the hospital gate. Inside the main reception area looked like an abattoir, with bloodstains splattered everywhere across the bare concrete floors and walls and the sight of it made me feel even worse. The moment that I entered the examination area doctors hurried towards me from every direction, some abandoning their patients – I didn't know what to say or think? None of the doctors could speak any English either, but after they ushered me into a cubicle, and using a small translation book, told me that I had severe tonsillitis, I knew that I had to get out of there, and quick! I'd already had my tonsils removed, and when one of the doctors came at me with a huge needle, I panicked, threw a pillow in his face and ran for my life! On my way back to my hotel, I came across what I thought was a chemist shop. After a great deal of effort to make it understood that I was suffering from the flu and that I required some appropriate medicine, the elderly pharmacist disappeared and came back with something wrapped in a sheet of old newspaper that was tied up with a piece of string, and it wasn't cheap. I opened the parcel as soon as I got back to my room, and was disgusted to find a pile of dead leaves and sticks. I was convinced that I'd been taken for a fool and ripped off, but by then, I felt far too sick even to care, let alone do anything about it. In the end, I used what little energy I still had left to chant for the strength and resistance to get myself better, and then dropped off to sleep, and I didn't wake up until lunchtime the next day. Since then I've learnt that the leaves and sticks were Chinese medicinal herbs, and had I known what to do with them, they probably would have been very beneficial. I've also since learnt that the hospital was underfunded and that the doctors probably thought that lavishing me with attention could have resulted in me donating some money as a thank you – if only I'd known this at the time. In such destitute situations, even a few measly dollars could help to make a valuable difference.

APART FROM a few passing opportunities that I was too sick to respond to, my sex life in Korea was virtually non-existent, and I didn't even think about sex, as all I wanted to do was to get out of Korea as soon as I possibly could. When I'd regained enough strength to travel, I booked a seat on a flight to Tokyo, packed my bags and headed straight for the airport, where I received a pleasant surprise when a young Korean guy that I'd met at the World Cup Club, sat down beside me in the departure lounge to keep me company while the graders cleared the runway of snow. Speaking in broken English, he told me that he liked me very much and gave me a ring to remember him by. Until that moment, I hadn't even suspected that he was gay, let alone like me – his gentle romantic approach came as both a beautiful surprise and a sad disappointment. He must have been a government official, or worked at the airport because when it came time for me to leave, he'd arranged for me to be chauffeured to the plane in a black VIP car, and to be the first to board. I felt a bit embarrassed about doing it, and even more so during the flight when everyone on-board kept staring at me and no doubt wondering who the hell I was. I also felt sadly frustrated about missing out on a chance to get to know the Korean guy more intimately. He wasn't only nice to talk to, but also very cute to look at – but in a masculine way. It just wasn't meant to be and I never got to see or hear from him again. When I arrived back in Japan, Tokyo was covered in snow as well and even colder than Seoul was' The air outside was so icy that my face started to go numb from the moment that I stepped off the plane. I was back in Masami's warm apartment soon after and received some fabulous and totally unexpected news that I was finally getting my own Gohonzon and that I was scheduled to take possession of it at a local temple the following day. On the outside, I looked and felt like crap, but after hearing the good news, my bones were almost jumping for joy! The next morning I awoke to suffer from a relapse of the wretched flu and was initially unnerved by the deathly silence due to an unusually heavy layer of snow that had fallen overnight. My appointment to receive my Gohonzon was for 3.00pm, and I could hardly wait! However, when 2.30pm arrived, and Masami was still nowhere in sight, I soon became anxiously concerned about missing the appointment and decided to go it alone. I'd waited for over a year to get my own Gohonzon, and I refused to let anything prevent it from happening if I could possibly help it, including the wretched flu. With only a piece of paper that had Japanese characters written on it, I hurriedly set off on a train and attempted to match the writing at each station that we stopped at in time before the doors closed. When I finally found the right station that matched, the bloody doors shut before I could exit the train and I was forced to go on to the next station and wait in the bitter coldness for another train to take me back. Talk about obstacles, what a frustrating struggle it all was. Be that as it may, the challenges only made me more determined than ever to succeed. After finally arriving at the correct station, and making my way down several soggy snow-covered streets until I could hear faint voices chanting Nam-Myoho-Renge-Kyo in the distance, I was able to finally reach my destination. The source of the chanting was coming from a tiny, wooden, Nichiren Shoshu temple that was hidden in between two large skyscrapers. Sneezing and almost drained of energy, I dragged myself inside, participated in a short Gohonzon receiving ceremony and then struggled back through the icy wind and snow to Masami's apartment. By the time Masami finally showed up, I'd already hung my Gohonzon on a wall clip, chanted in front of it for a few minutes, rolled it up, and then put it back away. As it all turned out, Masami had already returned home when he'd promised, but after finding me not there, he'd gone back out searching for me. On the following night, I had another disturbing nightmare. This time I found myself in an ancient-looking, dilapidated building with a stairway leading up to what appeared to be a very old community hall. Most of the people inside were wearing black cloaks and pointed hats. As I passed through the doorway, the first thing that I noticed was a large pot in the centre of the room with someone standing near it brewing up what appeared to be a potion. The man who seemed to be in charge of things looked to be in his late fifties. He was tall and skinny with a narrow face, slicked-back hair and a big handlebar moustache. Everyone present appeared to be tripping out on something, cavorting around in their own little world. The next thing that I noticed was a heavily wrinkled old lady, sitting in a wheelchair up on the stage. Her chair looked to be hand-made from old, jagged bits of wood, and she was wearing a tattered black witch's hat over her thick, matted, unkempt silver hair. She seemed to be having the time of her life, as she loudly kept cheering everyone on. The dank, dusty room and everyone in it looked as though they were centuries old. I started wandering around the hall, and nobody seemed to notice that I was even there. It gave me quite a shock when I stumbled across a member of the band

April Garden, tied up, naked and about to be spoon-fed a dose of the potion. I tried desperately to convince him to get out of there, but he was already under their spell, and I couldn't even get him even to acknowledge me. Each time someone received a cup of the potion, all of the others became noisily excited, and it sounded like they were reaching orgasm together. Realising that I could be next on the list to be intoxicated, I quickly wriggled sideways out of the door, and hurried down the stairs into a small room, closing the door behind me. As I hid behind some boxes and anxiously searched the room with my eyes, I suddenly noticed that there was only a little wire latch holding the door shut. I quickly looked all around to find something to prop up the door with and came across two American women that I knew, both lying side by side with their heads at opposite ends of a very old fashioned metal-framed bed. I recognised one of them as being the sister of the witch-woman in Hong Kong, and the other was my American friend Lisa. I tried to warn them about what I'd seen upstairs, but they were too intoxicated by the potion to conceive what I was saying. When I moved a bit closer to get a better look at them, they suddenly rose up zombie-like, giving me such a fright that I fell backwards onto the floor and hit my head. Chills were racing up and down my spine when I looked up and seen the girls staring down at me, with their stiff faces and glaring eyes. There was a sudden commotion outside the door, so I jumped up and poked my head out to take a look. It was the mob I'd seen in the hall, all coming down the stairs with the old lady being carried up high in her makeshift wheelchair, and cheering them on. I thought they'd all gone, but I was wrong! The leader of the group had been dragging along behind them, and when he came into view and spotted me, I was utterly terrified! I slammed the door and held it shut, but he was far too powerful and exploded straight into the room. I felt my life force drain from my body and then I collapsed like a puppet with its strings cut, and by the time that it occurred to me to chant, I was down to my very last dregs of energy. My first attempt was so weak that it was almost inaudible, but each successive time that I repeated Nam-Myoho-Renge-Kyo, it felt like I was re-inflating myself from my feet upwards. Next, the two women on the bed let out several high-pitched, angry screams at the man, and ordered him to go away and to leave me alone. At the same time, my chanting gained the force of a gale and blew the man to oblivion. It was such an enormous relief to wake up and discover that it was all just another one of my outrageous dreams. A few days later, I accompanied Lisa to a luxurious Japanese-style holiday resort, that was several hours' train ride out of Tokyo. It sat amid lush greenery, natural hot springs and some of the most beautiful, picturesque volcanic rock formations that I'd ever seen. An American girlfriend of Lisa's was performing as a snake dancer at the resort's plush nightclub, and my mission was to help Lisa convince her to try chanting Nam-Myoho-Renge-Kyo with us. Later, while Lisa was outside admiring the beautiful gardens with the snake-dancer's Indian toy-boy-lover, I remained in the kitchen of their small cabin with the snake-dancer doing my best to explain what I could about the chant. All was fine and dandy until the snake-dancer brought her snakes into the room and started bathing them in the kitchen sink. I thought that I was 'seeing things' or that she was having a laugh, especially when she released one of them onto the floor to slither around and dry off. It became more than I could bear, and I made a flying leap up onto a chair. When the snake-dancer swung around to see what all the noise was about and spotted me cowering on her kitchen table, I thought that she was going to choke herself to death on her laughter...

"HA-HA-HA-HA-HEE-HEE-HEE! Here you are tellin' me how great this chant is an' yer scared outa yer wits over a coupla liddle biddy ol' snakes! HAHAHAHAHAHAHA!"

To end up convincing the snake-dancer of my sincere trust and faith in the Law, and to get her to agree to chant with us, I eventually plucked up the courage from somewhere to climb back down, and let her to put one of her snakes around my neck. My heart was beating like a machine gun, and I was chanting under my breath so fast that the words were shooting out like the bullets. My bravery convinced the snake-dancer that I was for real, and after her show, she, her boyfriend, and Lisa and I chanted together for twenty-minutes.

WHEN I ARRIVED back in Tokyo there was a message waiting for me from my high-class-hooker friend, Jean, who'd just returned to Japan after a short stint in Hong Kong. She needed my help to encourage an American woman named Mary to chant, who was a friend of Stella, one of Jean's best friends, and who was the wife of a military officer stationed at one of the US bases in Japan. Jean had told Stella about some of the benefits that she'd been receiving from the chanting, and Stella thought that it might also help her friend Mary to challenge and overcome some serious family problems that she was having. By the time that Stella and Mary finally arrived at Jean's room, we'd been waiting for well over an hour. Stella apologised for the delay and then explained how Mary had been so upset and nervous about coming that she kept stalling her car. In the end, Stella had to drive it for her and bring her to the hotel. Hearing their story instantly reminded me of my own experience with the car in Katoomba. On a hunch, when I asked Mary if she'd ever had any involvement with the occult, she immediately reacted shocked and defensive, and adamantly denied it. It was obvious to me that she was too afraid to admit or discuss it, and it took a lot of time and gentle persuasion to get Mary to eventually open up, and finally confess that she'd participated in a séance six months earlier and that it had been ever since then that her present troubles had developed, it all fell into place and made a lot more sense to me. Mary swore black and blue that she'd never mentioned the séance to anyone, not even Stella, and she was virtually panic-stricken that I'd even brought it up. For a quick moment, I wondered if I'd unintentionally acquired the ability to sense such things after being in the presence of the ex-priest in Sydney, who'd, similarly 'seen' what Mrs Green had been getting up to, except I hadn't needed Tarot cards to do it. After Mary was calmed down enough, I explained to her that she'd probably brought her present dilemma upon herself by her own self-inflicted actions and choices, and I suggested that it might be a good idea to avoid experimenting with such things in the future. Then, using what limited knowledge that I'd so far acquired, I did my best to explain to her about the Law of Cause and Effect and the meaning of Nam-Myoho-Renge-Kyo. I also shared my own personal experience with the black-eyed man and finally assured her that chanting Nam-Myoho-Renge-Kyo each day would help her to manifest the wisdom and the good fortune that she needed to release herself from her suffering, just as it had done for me. We all then faced east and began chanting in unison. We hadn't been chanting long before Mary started to convulse and splutter, which created a state of confusion and panic among the rest of us. I didn't know whether to stop and help Mary or to continue chanting. Then a feeling from deep within urged me to keep chanting, and after encouraging the others to do likewise, that's what I did. When Mary eventually calmed back down, it was a huge relief to all of us.

Mary's frothing at the mouth and strange noises had resembled a scene from The Exorcist, and it had left us feeling quite drained and confused. Stella suddenly remembered finding a book on devil worship and the occult sticking out from under the driver's seat of Mary's car. I didn't bother to question Mary about it because it was already clearly evident to me that she'd participated in a lot more than just one séance. I saw Mary again a couple of weeks later, and although she was a much-changed person, she still didn't look particularly happy, so I asked her if anything was wrong. She told me that every time she chanted, her attention had been repeatedly been drawn to the top shelf of her bedroom closet, where she kept some savings hidden for a rainy day. Constantly thinking about her savings whenever she chanted had made her feel uncomfortable and guilty, and to get it off her mind once and for all, she went upstairs, counted her money and was shocked to discover that two thousand dollars were missing. A family gathering was called, and the truth had come out that her eldest teenage son had been stealing the money to buy drugs. Consequently, Mary and her husband had since been able to get the professional help that their son urgently needed, hopefully before it was too late. I then explained to Mary that, as well as bringing forth our good fortune, rather than a magic wand that makes the bad stuff disappear or a rug to hide it under, chanting Nam-Myoho-Renge-Kyo is a sound vibration that also exposes the hidden impurities within our lives, so that we can see them for what they are, deal with them and then change our poisons into medicine.

AFTER ENJOYING a tenth visit to the Dai Gohonzon, it was time to get my bag packed and head back to Hong Kong again. On the night before I left, I had another very disturbing dream, and in it, I saw my father dressed in black pants and a white singlet, spinning towards me on a wheel, end over end. Right behind him, were my stepmother, Beatty, and two other people that I didn't recognise. Each successive time that Dad appeared and reappeared, his face grew more filled with stress, and it seemed like he was becoming increasingly upset about something. I suddenly awoke from the dream soaking in sweat and then spent nearly an hour chanting for my father to be set free from his turmoil, not to mention, my own peace of mind. As you'll learn later in the book, this dream was a very significant and relevant prelude of something else that would be revealed in the future – so many hidden pieces of Life's mystical jigsaw...

*The heavenly forces will surely protect one who is unbending before the eight winds." "More valuable than treasures in a storehouse are the treasures of the body. The most valuable of all are the treasures of the heart." "A coward cannot have any prayer answered."*

*...Nichiren*

# Chapter 25

## SNAKES AND WITCHES

The first person that I bumped into after returning to Hong Kong was the snake-dancer, who wasted no time in letting me know that she'd been chanting regularly ever since we'd last met, but I had a sneaking suspicion that she hadn't. She also told me that it was going to take her two weeks for her to get her Japanese visa renewed, and asked me if I could possibly get her some gigs through my contacts. I told her that I was going to be very busy recording 'An Oriental Love Affair', but that I'd see what I could do. Word soon got out that I was back in town, and I was inundated with calls from people that I'd taught to chant during my previous visit, wanting my help to explain Nam-Myoho-Renge-Kyo to their friends. It was such a privilege to be able to spend as much time as I could supporting and encouraging them. As one person left my room, another would arrive. Although I had very limited knowledge and experience in advising other people about what to do with their personal problems, due to being confronted by necessity, I stumbled across a reliable technique that always seemed to work. Each time that someone came to me with a problem or a question that I wasn't sure how to deal with or answer, I'd get them to sit and chant with me in front of my Gohonzon about it. While doing so, I'd intensively focus on the Gohonzon, clear my mind of any thoughts, and then surrender to my deeper-inner-self, from where the answers would come forth naturally. In doing so, I'd more often than not come up with the right solutions to help others, and also often learn about things that had never occurred to me before, or that I'd previously known little or nothing about. It was such a satisfying and fascinating experience, and it's something that I still do to this day with my own problems. I received a call from Angie, my American stripper friend, who assured me that she'd continued to chant each day, which was easy to tell by the excitement in her voice. Among other things, she'd fulfilled her lifelong wish to meet the man of her dreams, and she was not only head over heels in love with him, but several weeks pregnant with his baby. Another Aussie entertainer named Geraldine, that I'd also previously taught to chant, had met the man of her dreams as well, and a few weeks later, I was honoured to be the best man at their flashy and extremely outrageous and colourful wedding. While attending the wedding, I bumped into Jenny Marshall, whom I'd not seen or heard from since the day that Masami and I visited her at the Imperial Hotel in Tokyo – the same day that I'd first chanted Nam-Myoho-Renge-Kyo and seen a Gohonzon. Like Angie, she too was blown away by how much I'd changed, and after hearing how accurately the dream that I'd told her about in Hong Kong had since become a reality, she too was excitedly anxious to try out the chanting, but not everything was a bed of roses. I soon discovered that the witch-woman in Chung King Mansions was angrily pissed-off that I was back in town. While I'd been in Japan, she'd been busy at work taking over from where I'd left off. By pretending to be an expert on the teachings of Nichiren, and adding a lot of erroneous made-up waffle of her own in the process, she'd led several people, including some that I'd previously taught to chant, completely down the wrong path. The moment that I found out about it, I confronted her, hoping to be able to set her straight diplomatically and peacefully – not a chance! She turned on me like a woman possessed and became an embittered enemy! In a hostile attempt to discredit me while I'd been away, she'd spread a lot of nasty lies about me. It soon became blatantly clear to me that she was envious and jealous of the fact that more people had come to see me than to see her during my previous visit, and when her past efforts failed to keep up her desired effect, she became so enraged and hateful towards me, that I felt physically threatened by her and steered clear of her altogether.

I was soon making enough money from gigs to start living the 'good life' again, merrily burning the candle at both ends. My sex life was booming, and amid all the excitement and free-love gaiety, my chanting soon became more like a superstitious good-luck ritual than a sincere effort in self-improvement. Consequently, my life condition declined rapidly, and among other failures and disappointments, the recording of 'An Oriental Love Affair' wasn't progressing well at all. The engineer was high on drugs for most of the time and didn't seem to know what he was doing, the studio equipment kept breaking down and my voice suffered severely from the strain. I'd already prepaid for the recording, so I had to get on with it regardless and just hope for the best. During these problematic ups and downs, I crossed paths with a girl from New Zealand named Nicky, who was almost at death's door. Along with many other westerners, she'd fled to Hong Kong after being kicked out of Bangkok during a 1970s Thai uprising (the same uprising that saved me from delivering fake jewellery to India.) The poor unfortunate girl was so messed up on heroin that she even had to struggle to remember what her own name was. Her hair was matted, her clothes were filthy and stunk to high heaven, and she was paying for her addiction by stripping in front of perverts in a disgustingly filthy sex-dive near the Hong Kong airport. Nearly everyone that I knew, including the snake-dancer, was warning me to stay well away from Nicky, claiming that she was serious trouble, but my heart went out to her, and I desperately wanted to help her if I could. As it all turned out, trying to help Nicky get off heroin became a perfect remedy to help motivate me to get my faith and practise back on track. When I first tried teaching Nicky how to chant, she couldn't even coordinate her mouth enough to say Myoho, let alone the entire chant, and it took a lot of consistent coaxing and gentle encouragement before she was finally able to pronounce the entire chant correctly, but she did eventually get there. From then on, I encouraged Nicky to chant Nam-Myoho-Renge-Kyo as often as she could, promising her that if she did so, it would help her to manifest the wisdom, strength and good fortune that she desperately needed to overcome and escape her misery. A couple of weeks later, Nicky was arrested by customs officers while entering Hong Kong from Macao, and the people who'd warned me against having anything to do with her didn't stop phoning me – all virtually saying the same thing...

"See? I told you so! Your chanting hasn't done much good for her then, has it, eh?"

Nicky's name and photo were splashed all over the front pages of the evening newspapers, accompanied by reports that Heroin and syringes had been found hidden in the side of her handbag. To reiterate; chanting Nam-Myoho-Renge-Kyo doesn't work like a magic wand that makes problems just disappear or go away – even though sometimes the results can seem pretty magical. Judging by my own and other people's situations, things sometimes needed to go 'wrong' before they could go 'right'. Feeling confident that this latest development in Nicky's saga might have been for the best, I sincerely prayed that her predicament would turn out to be a blessing in disguise and a gateway to a new path leading to her recovery. I contacted my friend Fred on Hong Kong Island, who was still an influential member in the Hong Kong Government and asked for his advice and help. Lucky for Nicky, Fred was more than happy to help and was soon able to get Nicky released on condition that she voluntarily admits herself into a drug rehabilitation clinic. All that I could do then was continue to chant for her recovery and future happiness. I also managed to get the snake-dancer a few gigs and a couple of TV appearances, and when I knocked on the door to let her know the good news, she was in the process of familiarising herself with a new snake that she'd only just bought for her act. The new snake much larger than her other snakes and very restless and playful. For some strange reason, it seemed to always calm down whenever I came near it, in fact, I ended up being the only one who could get the snake to settle down...

"Well, at least my karma must be movin' in tha right direction where 'big snakes' are concerned, I told the snake-dancer jokingly, with a cheeky giggle and a wink. As time passed, I became fondly attached to that reptile, in a similar way to how one does with a faithful pet dog.

A TRIO OF performers, consisting of a married couple from Germany and a teenage girl from Thailand, moved into a room in the next corridor that was adjacent to mine. When the group started acting very strangely towards me, the first thing that I thought was that the witch-woman or one of her followers had been in their ear. The windows of the other rooms were a part of the same long, continuous window that ran the entire length of the building. Unbeknownst to me, where each of the internal walls met the window, there were gaps that had been filled in with screwed up newspaper pages. Sometimes I'd hear rustling noises when I was chanting but had thought that it was just birds pocking around outside and ignored it. One afternoon, I delivered a message that had been left with me for the Trio while they were out, and when the older female of the group opened the door and saw me standing there, she let out an almighty scream that scared the hell out of me. Her husband rushed to the door to see what was going on, snatching the message from me. After I demanded to know what the problem was, he explained that ever since the Trio had arrived in Hong Kong, they'd been experiencing a chain of misfortunes, and had believed it all had something to do with me. I asked him to elaborate more, and he confessed to poking a microphone through the gap at the window and taping my chanting, which he'd played to the hotel manager, who'd told him that it was only voice training. The Trio had accepted the manager's explanation, until one night while they were out dining in the Chungking Restaurant and noticed one of my publicity pictures on the wall, an intoxicated, foul-mouthed drag-queen from Sydney overheard them talking about me and rudely interrupted...

"Oooooooooo, stay tha fuck away from her, dearies! She's a black-magic priestess. She'll put one of her nasty, evil fuckin' spells on ya! Nah, don't go anywhere near that bitch dearies!"

Anyone staying in Chungking Mansions that had ever made a name for themselves in Hong Kong, usually had their picture put up on the restaurant's *wall of fame.* The Trio had believed the hateful queen without a doubt and, from that night on, were convinced that I was performing evil rituals and sending them curses through the wall. As a result, they'd been stricken with fear whenever they saw me. Some of my best friends have been outrageous queens, but no matter how friendly, I've never been physically attracted to them sexually – not even when I'd been drunk. I could only assume that the drag-queen in question was someone that I'd refused to go to bed with during my days of overindulging in alcohol. Once I'd finished explaining the truth of the matter to the Trio, including what I'd really been doing, the husband apologised for his wife's screams and invited me in to join them for a coffee.

After I explained more about the chant to them, they accompanied me to the local NS/SGI Centre, where we chanted together for them to bring forth the good fortune that they needed to overcome their difficulties and despair. The worst of their problems related to the young Thai girl in their group, who'd been arrested in Hong Kong for dancing topless underage. The poor kid was devastated by it, which was never more evident than the evening that I returned to the hotel and found her huddled up in the corner of the TV lounge room, quietly sobbing. After we had a short chat, I invited her into my room to do some chanting with me in front of my Gohonzon. We'd only just begun to chant before she broke down and cried her heart out. After she'd stopped weeping and settled down a bit, she told me her amazing story...

During WW2, her grandfather had helped a dying Japanese soldier, and this had resulted in their deep friendship. Before the soldier died, he gave the girl's grandfather his most treasured possessions – a scroll and a string of beads. Her grandfather used the beads whenever he prayed to the scroll, which he'd enshrined in an altar in his room. The girl explained that he was a gentle and caring old soul, and very much loved by his family and the entire village where he lived. Since everyone around him practised traditional Thai Buddhism, nobody understood what he was doing, but even so, they still loved and respected him. As a child, the girl had often gone into her grandfather's room to play with his beads. Sometimes when he was out, she'd open up his altar and just stare at the scroll in wonder, which had always fascinated her and made her feel good. One day, her grandfather asked her mother to fetch him a fresh flower from the marketplace to put in front of his altar, which she happily did. He'd been acting peculiarly for a few days, and his concerned family gathered together and watched him from a distance while he chanted. When he'd finished, he climbed onto his bed and softly remarked on how tired he was feeling. He then gave his family a loving smile and wave, and peacefully closed his eyes and died. Ever since that day, the young girl's mum had kept his room exactly as he'd left it, always placing a fresh flower in front of his altar each week. The girl recognised the words Nam-Myoho-Renge-Kyo as soon as I'd mentioned them on the day that we went to the Buddhist centre, but she wasn't completely sure about it until I opened my little altar and showed her my Gohonzon. She told me that it was a similar type of small scroll that her grandfather had chanted in front of. The reason the girl had broken down in tears was that she believed her grandfather was still protecting her in her hour of need, and that he'd brought her to me to learn about the benefits of chanting Nam-Myoho-Renge-Kyo. This incredible realisation had such a profound effect on the girl that she could hardly wait to get back home to Thailand and let her family know.

During the following weeks, even though I'd been chanting regularly each day and teaching others about Nichiren's Buddhism, I still found myself losing focus and wandering off track again. I'd be preoccupied with random thoughts of what new clothes to buy, which party to go to, or who I'd like to spend that night with. In a similar way to the previous times that I'd allowed my practise to lose direction, certain aspects of my accumulated bad karma seemed to be manifesting and taking over. As a result, there were fewer gigs on offer, my money was beginning to dwindle, and my confidence and self-esteem were waning. From the moment I realised that I was wandering off on the wrong track again, I began chanting more earnestly with fervour to get back on the rails, only this time, instead of feeling more focused and stronger, I felt very little change or improvement. There was an overwhelming presence of pressure in my life that had me feeling like I was fighting against a mighty wind and getting nowhere, and reminiscent of my hallway encounter in the hotel at Katoomba, I began to fear that it was all starting up again. Thinking that someone or something may have been attacking me spiritually, as I'd previously done, I focused all of my attention on a positive outcome and chanted for the inner-strength to come forth and send whatever the force was back to its source. I'd just finished such a vigorous chanting session and was leaving my room to have dinner at the Chungking Restaurant when the witch-woman burst out of her room with sweat pouring from her face, and looking like she'd just seen a ghost. She came up very close to me and then did something completely out of character, by greeting me warmly and telling me how nice it was to see me. Of course, I didn't believe a word of it, and all I felt was an instant cold chill laced with an immense fear racing up and down my spine. A few days later, I learnt that she and some of her 'disciples' had been busy sticking pins into one of my promo photos, which must have had something to do with the pressure that I'd been feeling. After one of her other acquaintances admitted to me that only minutes before I'd met up with the witch-woman that night, an altar she kept next to her bed had fallen off its shelf for no apparent reason and that several items of her clothing had been tossed around her room. The first thing that I thought of was what had happened to Mrs Green's two girlfriends during the Carrington Hotel saga. I've since come to believe that some mysterious occurrences in life that many of us experience from time to time are related to the power of intense concentration and electromagnetic waveforms. It may work similarly to how we can control the movements and functions of things by remote control and using Wi-Fi. Only instead of using technology to do it, it's Nature at work between one human and another. This is also probably the answer to how some animals can predict changes in the weather, impending tsunamis, earthquakes, know what we're sometimes thinking, or how some mothers can tell if her child is in trouble, even from a great distance. Of course, not everyone has this ability manifest in their life, but then not everyone has the incentive to create an artistic masterpiece or the ability to become a brain surgeon, a scientist or an astronaut.

BEFORE THE CATHAY Pacific CEO had left on a business trip to America, he'd asked me to record two more separate edited versions of 'An Oriental Love Affair', which he wanted to use in commercials to promote Cathay Pacific in the United States. One needed to be thirty seconds long and the other sixty seconds. I did as he requested, but when I went to Cathay's office to collect the two thousand dollars needed to pay for the additional studio time, the woman in charge of promotions flatly refused to release the funds until the CEO got back from America and authorised it himself. This not only held up my plans to return to Japan but also left me powerless in retrieving the main master tape of the full version of my song from the studio, which I'd already fully paid for. The woman refusing me was an ex-cop and a Chinese singer who saw me as her rival and had resented me ever since the first day that we met. I kept trying to explain my predicament to her, but she refused to budge and remained adamant about it. After she'd heard along the grapevine what had happened, on the following night, the snake-dancer turned up at my room and offered to loan me the two thousand dollars that I needed to get my master tapes released...

"You can't just sit around here waiting forever," she insisted. "Come on, take this money. You can pay me back when the CEO returns."

I was tempted, by the snake-dancer's offer, but I declined, thanking her anyway and telling her that I was happy to just wait another week until the CEO returned. When the snake-dancer still kept insisting that I take her money and refused to take no for an answer, I ended up giving in and accepting her money, and what a foolish and regrettable mistake that would turn out to be...

*A tiny mistake can induce one into making a bigger one,*
*if one fails to take responsibility to correct it.*
*A tiny needle will sink in water and rain will fall*
*from the sky, but a great weight, when carried by an*
*airship, can fly across the largest of oceans.*
*Fire can be lit or sparked by a flint stone from a river*
*base and a tiny candle can bring light to a place*
*where it has never shone.*
*The most serious of offences can be obliterated*
*through sincere remorse.*
*Although such ordinary things may appear to be*
*wondrous, nothing is as awe–inspiring as the power*
*of Life's Mystic Law.*
*...Nichiren.*

# Chapter 26

## VENOM OF THE SNAKE-DANCER!

On my way to the airport to catch my flight to Japan, I stopped off at the studio to collect the master tape containing the final mix of 'An Oriental Love Affair. I had no time to have a listen, so I just took the studio engineer's word that it was all in perfect order. When I arrived, Tokyo was blanketed with snow, and just like last time, it looked absolutely beautiful. The first thing that I did the next morning was to make myself a coffee and have a listen to the final mix of my song, and what a horrid shock I got! The studio engineer had lied to me and completely ripped me off. The song's lyrics were about a love story, but the mix made the song sound like absolute shit, especially the version that I'd paid to have translated into Japanese. This utter disappointment marked the beginning of another downward spiral in my life, and from then on, things just went from bad to worse. The 1973 oil embargo was over, but there were still a lot of negative after-effects to be sorted and overcome. Because vinyl records were manufactured primarily from oil, the record companies had become over-fastidious about which records they'd release, and my songs wouldn't have stood a chance even if the recording was faultless. Combined with the return of the wretched flu, this news soon had me feeling down in the dumps and depressed, and then it wasn't long after before my money started running out. I was about to become homeless until the band members of 'April Garden' came to my rescue. They were performing in Tokyo at the time, and when they heard about my predicament, invited me to stay with them at their Roppongi apartment. I'd first met, Alan, the band's lead guitarist, several months earlier in Hong Kong, and had taught him to chant. Since then, he'd received his own Gohonzon, and although hearing about it was uplifting, the joy that I felt came and went in a flash, especially once I realised the full extent of my self-inflicted difficulties. I tumbled into such a dark hole, that I even lost my desire to even chant about it. April Garden spent a lot of time away performing and rehearsing, leaving me to spend most of my time alone. In a desperate attempt to claw my way out of my dilemma, I forced myself to attend a Buddhist meeting, hoping that it might give me the leg-up that I so desperately needed. Just as I arrived, Dick Causton was reading out one of Nichiren's promises to everyone...

"As long as we keep chanting and have sincere faith in the Law, winter will never fail to turn into spring."

Whenever I'd been in dire straights in the past, Dick had always given me good advice and guidance, but this time, his words of wisdom only made me feel worse...

"No matter what happens, keep your faith in the Law, and you'll surely be able to overcome or change anything!" Someone else yelled from the back of the room – aggravating me even more.

The idea of returning to Hong Kong as a failure and having to face everyone was unthinkable, especially with how it could affect those who'd trusted and believed in me. I felt so bad about it that I was even having suicidal thoughts again. On the following night, I was chanting in front of Allen's Gohonzon for my *winter* to start showing signs of *spring,* with my eyes became so filled with tears that I could barely see the Gohonzon in front of me, when a sudden barrage of loud crashes on the door shattered the quietness and almost sent me hurtling towards Alan's altar. Quickly rubbing the tears from my eyes, I got up and opened the door to find the snake-dancer and her toy-boy standing on the entry porch, both glaring at me with so much hate in their eyes that it almost stung! Without uttering a single word, the snake-dancer barged in and started bashing into me like a maniac. By the time that I was able to gather my wits enough to grab hold of her arms and shove her away, she'd already dug her long, sharp fingernails into the back of my neck and ripped my hairpiece off. It later emerged that after I'd left Hong Kong, a bizarre series of events had taken place when the snake-dancer and her toy-boy had gone out nightclubbing and crossed paths with the witch-woman, the drag queen who hated me, and a self-opinionated Australian television compare that loathed me because I was more popular in Hong Kong than he was. The witch-woman had recognised the snake-dancer after seeing her visit me in my hotel room. She asked the snake-dancer if she'd seen me lately, and unaware that they were all my staunch enemies, the snake-dancer innocently told them that she'd loaned me the money to get my master tapes from the studio so that I could take them to Japan, all hell broke loose! In the following few moments, the three of them ganged up and lied their arses off, telling the snake-dancer that she'd been taken for a ride and ripped off because I'd told them that I was never coming back to Hong Kong. The snake-dancer had been gullible enough to swallow every bit of it, hook, line and sinker, and without question. After brooding about it overnight, she'd caught an early morning ferry to Hong Kong Island, charged into the Cathay Pacific office and rudely demanded to see the CEO, after which, she ordered him to pay her the two thousand dollars that she'd loaned me. The CEO didn't know who she was from a bar of soap and told her that he'd need to discuss it with me first. The snake-dancer wouldn't have a bar of it and ultimately lost the plot, threatening him with blackmail, after telling him the lie that I'd been spreading malicious rumours all over Hong Kong about him paying for prostitutes. Not surprisingly, the CEO had ordered her out of his office and told her never to come back, but that wasn't the end of it. She then went on a rampage around Kowloon and spread her lies to just about everyone that even remotely knew me, telling them that I'd ripped her off and stolen her money. Still not content, she wrote a letter full of more lies to the Japanese Immigration Department in Japan and told them that I was working on the streets of Tokyo and earning money as a male prostitute. At that point, I'd heard as much as I could take...

"What tha bloody hell did ya go an' do all that for? How could ya be so gullible 'n' stupid ta believe those lying bastards without even asking me if it was true first? For all ya knew, I could've been in a hospital after bein' hit by a bus or somethin'! I told ya I'd be back in about a month 'n' ya couldn't even wait for two bloody weeks! Now, look what ya've gone 'n' done. Ya've stuffed everything up for both of us!"

In a state of numb disbelief, I jumped up and put the kettle on for a cup of coffee, and then nervously sat back down while we went through the whole disgusting mess-up again. I was wracking my brain to come up with a solution, and inwardly hoping that at any moment, she'd burst into laughter and tell me that it was all just a crazy, big joke. But it didn't happen, and the snake-dancer refused to accept even the slightest bit of responsibility for what she' done. She instead blamed it all on me and kept asking me why I hadn't contacted her...

"If you were so desperate ta talk ta me, why didn't ya just pick up tha bloody phone 'n' call me on tha number I sent ya?" I demanded to know in sheer frustration, but she just kept staring up at the ceiling as though she wasn't even listening.

I asked her the same question a second time, and she jumped up in a huff, grabbed her coat, and left with her toy-boy trailing behind her, who'd wisely refrained from getting involved. How I wished that I'd never given in and taken her money. Realising that it had been my own karma to weaken and go against my gut feelings, I could have kicked myself for it. I also wondered if and effect would eventually catch up with her for her part in the blunder. She was nearing fifty years old, and to improve her looks for her stage show and to stay 'attractive' for her young toy-boy, she was scheduled to have a facelift in Tokyo that week. As difficult as this may be to believe, on the following day, and during a pre-op visit to her surgeon, she collapsed. Tests that followed revealed that the snake-dancer had become anaemic and was unfit to go ahead with the procedure. She'd been given a thorough medical examination in Hong Kong only a few days earlier and was given a clean bill of health. The snake-dancer was in a fluster! Because she'd heard me mention cause and effect many times, she was soon convinced of her own volition, that her belligerent behaviour towards me had been the cause of her sudden diagnosis of anaemia. Fearing that there might still be worse still to come, she offered to accompany me to the immigration department immediately to confess to them that her letter had been a pack of lies – that she was just being a jealous lover seeking revenge. Unfortunately, her offer was too little too late, as I'd already been summoned to the Immigration Department on the day that she'd been diagnosed with anaemia, and had been repeatedly interrogated for several hours, before being served with a voluntary deportation order, and a deadline of two weeks to leave Japan. If I failed to exit the country at that time, the Japanese authorities would forcibly deport me and potentially ban me from ever returning. I phoned the CEO of Cathay Pacific in Hong Kong to let him know the truth of the matter, but before I could say more than hello, he angrily cut in and told me that he no longer wanted me associated with the company and that any unused tickets that I had were no longer valid, and then he slammed the phone down. Many of Jean's acquaintances would have known she'd been prostituting herself to the CEO and one of them must have told the snake-dancer. I'd completely kept my mouth shut and felt cheated that the CEO hadn't even let me get a word in to explain that the snake-dancer had owned up to lying. (I'd learn years later that the CEO was directly responsible for the airline reneging on my contract, and had I'd known at the time, I could have taken legal action.)

I was in big trouble, flat broke, and thanks to the snake-dancer's insane, jump-the-gun reaction, I had no money to buy a ticket and less than two weeks to get out of Japan. The threat of never being able to visit my friends there, or to see the Dai Gohonzon again felt like having a gun pointed to my head.

A few nights later, while I was stretched out on April Garden's sofa feeling sad, sick and sorry for myself, I became subconsciously engrossed in a broadcast that was playing on American FEN radio in the background. It was Richard Harris reading the novel *Jonathan Livingston Seagull*, and I soon became completely lost in the story. Its underlying lessons seemed to parallel with some of what I'd learnt from Nichiren's teachings, and by the time the story had ended, I'd left most of my troubled thoughts behind and was floating around in another time and place which existed in a much happier and more in-depth part of my subconscious mind. While there, I heard that disembodied voice from again, encouraging me to write a book about Nam-Myoho-Renge-Kyo, and to use animals to tell the story. My first response after arriving back to my everyday reality was to laugh at myself for even thinking that I could write such a book. Be that as it may, that night, a seed was planted firmly in my mind that would one day blossom and bear fruit.

AT A BUDDHIST meeting a few nights later, a Japanese/Canadian member named Lorraine, tapped me on the shoulder and handed me an article about a British songwriter named Brian Potter, who lived in L.A. In the article, Brian explained that since he'd been chanting Nam-Myoho-Renge-Kyo, he'd been able to transform his career of repeated failures into one of enormous success. Among other hits, he'd co-written, were One Tin Soldier and Rock'n'Roll Heaven, recorded by the Righteous Brothers. Lorraine was aware that I'd been writing a musical about Nam-Myoho-Renge-Kyo and had thought the article could give me some encouragement. After the meeting had finished and while I was walking home from the station, I thought about my rock musical and contemplated how Brian might be able to help me if I could only get over to America and meet him. It was a crazy idea, considering that I was penniless and with no immediate prospects of earning money, but it still didn't stop me from fantasising about it. I hadn't told them about the immigration order to leave Japan or my financial predicament, when I'd let everyone at the meeting know that I only had a few days left before my visa would expire and I'd have to leave, I felt devastated just thinking about it. I suddenly felt compelled to look up to the sky, which was crystal clear, and as I focused on the millions of stars, I somehow understood that the universe was teeming with intelligent life. I'd heard stories at the meetings about people who'd been in serious trouble calling on the Buddhist forces *Bonten* and *Taishaku* – Nichiren himself had done it on the night that he was almost beheaded at Tatsunokuchi. I was desperately in need of any help that I could get, so I softly chanted to the stars, and in thoughts, asked *Bonten* and *Taishaku* to please help me too. Amazingly, at that very moment, I felt a wave of confidence flow through me that I'd be going to America, and the feeling grew so powerful and real that by the time I got home I was ready to pack my bags and get ready to go.

Allen was home on a band break, and the moment that I walked through the door, he greeted me with some fabulous good news. He'd heard that night through the grapevine that the thirty-second and one-minute edits of my song 'An Oriental Love Affair' had been sent to America and re-recorded by a top American singer. Allen didn't know the singer's name, and because of everything that followed during the next few minutes, I never got around to finding out. After I joined Allen for a cuppa and mentioned to him that I'd had one of my strange, mystical experiences on my way home, he was keen to hear all about it until I mentioned the bit about me going to America. His enthusiasm instantly waned, as he couldn't see how I could possibly afford the fare there and he was concerned that I was getting my hopes up over a fantasy that was never going to happen. I couldn't see how I could afford the fare either, but it still didn't take away my strong feelings that I'd definitely be going. Just then, the phone rang and it was Lorraine...

"Hi, Tommy, whatcha ya gonna do about going ta Los Angeles to meet Mister Brian Potter? Are ya goin' or what?" She asked.

Lorraine had a loud Canadian accent, and whenever she had something to say, she'd get straight to the point. I told her that I couldn't afford it and she just laughed...

"Never mind about tha money! Do ya wanna go or don't ya?" She almost demanded to know.

"Yeah, sure, I do!" I told her hesitantly, then before I could say another word, she was telling me to pack my bags and to get ready to leave. Lorraine had read the lyrics to my songs and was very impressed with them. She offered to finance the entire trip! When I told Allen what she'd said, he was utterly gobsmacked! And so was I! The timing couldn't have been more perfect! Since then, I've wondered if I'd picked up what Lorraine was about to do that night before she called, or if she'd been persuaded to make the call after picking up my thoughts, or was it something else entirely? I couldn't get to sleep for thinking about it and I was up at the crack of dawn booking my flight. Straight after breakfast, I headed off to the American Embassy to apply for a visa. For the remainder of that magical day, as I was floating around on cloud nine, the good news just kept on coming. Rita, my American, lady-friend with a drinking problem in Taiwan, got my number off a mutual acquaintance in Hong Kong and phoned to let me know that she'd received an eight-page letter from her daughter in Los Angeles, who she hadn't heard from for over eight years. Rita told me that when her daughter had attended a New Year's Eve party in Los Angeles, she'd crossed paths with a clairvoyant, who'd pulled her aside and told her that there was an older woman across the sea that desperately needed to hear from her. Rita's daughter knew right away who the clairvoyant was referring to and quickly began a search to track her mother down...

"I don't know if it was all o' them Methodists that kept a'knockin' on m'door or if it was yer chantin', Tommy, but somethin's worked, that's fer sure," Rita happily insisted.

Her incredible story and elation lifted my spirit no end. If that wasn't enough good news to receive in one day, later that afternoon, there were two more unexpected and pleasant surprises. Firstly, an agent rang and offered me an extensive tour of venues in northern Japan, then Nicky, the New Zealand girl that I'd helped get off heroin in Hong Kong, turned up out of the blue on April Garden's doorstep. She looked so pretty and radiantly healthy that I didn't recognise her until she told me who she was. Nicky was a brand-new person, her self-esteem had returned, and she was working as a hostess in a classy Tokyo nightclub. She told me that when she appeared in court on theft charges, there'd been a legal discrepancy and the case had been dismissed.

During her second hearing for heroin possession, a senior staff member from the rehab centre had turned up and pleaded with the judge to give Nicky a second chance. After some consideration by the judge, and a lengthy lecture, Nicky received a small fine, after which, all her charges were struck from her passport records, allowing her to walk free and make a brand new start. Nicky told me that she'd sincerely chanted Nam-Myoho-Renge-Kyo virtually non-stop throughout her drug withdrawals and only suffered some minor discomfort. Seeing her looking and doing so well couldn't have been a more magnificent going-away present.

These incredible stories and outcomes gave me even more proof of the incredible life-changing benefits that can be received by using the strategy of Life's Mystic Law.

Teaching others how to chant and then watching their lives grow and improve, for me, has always been a wonderfully fulfilling experience.

*Although one may be able to read music*
*and can understand the fundamentals of*
*singing, unless one can actually sing or play an*
*instrument, one's knowledge alone will not be*
*enough to allow one to produce a song.*
*On the other hand, even if one has little or no*
*knowledge at all about the fundamentals*
*of music, but can sing or play an instrument,*
*one will then be able to produce a song.*
*Likewise, one does not require a conceptual*
*understanding of Life's Mystic Law in order to*
*receive benefit, one only needs to*
*respect it and to believe in it.*
*...Nichiren.*

# Chapter 27

# HONOLALALAND-SAN FRANSYDNEY

The terrifying overnight flight to Honolulu on Air Siam's only 747-Jumbo jet was a near catastrophe, not to mention, a mongrel of a trip that I'll never forget. All hell broke loose when we flew directly into a tremendous storm as everyone was eating. The sudden severe turbulence sent all manner of things hurtling throughout the cabin, and the blood-curdling sounds of women and children screaming like wailing banshees soon had me screaming out Nam-Myoho-Renge-Kyo at the top of my voice. As the pilots struggled like mad to climb above the storm, and the engines of the straining plane roared louder than ever, massive forks of lightning kept flashing all around us. Convinced that we were all about to die, how I wished that I'd never got the plane in the first place. By the time the worst of it was over, my heart was almost sitting in my throat. A few hours later, we landed safely in Hawaii, and I was the first out the door and off the plane. My spirit had already reached the islands long before my body did, and was I relieved to reconnect with it. So much so that I got down on my hands and knees and kissed the tarmac.

During my week-long stopover in Honolulu, I had a casual fling with a native prince of Hawaii, or at least that's who he said he was. He was certainly proud of his title and was forever boasting about it. Otherwise, he was very romantic and classy, plus a lot of good fun to be with. Each day, he'd pick me up at my hotel and take me on a sightseeing tour across different parts of the island. Then, at night, we'd dance the hours away in the trendy gay bars along Waikiki Beach. He got so drunk one night that I had to drive his brand-new Mercedes convertible home for him along the wide footpaths because I didn't know how to drive a left-hand drive car on the right-hand side of the road. The prince lived in a beautiful home and he wanted me to stay in Hawaii and live there with him permanently. I declined and jokingly told him that I just didn't have what it takes to be a princess. I'm not sure if he saw the funny side of what I said because I never saw or heard from him again after that. When I'd arrived, I'd also met another potential lover in a coffee shop, who wanted to take me sightseeing all over America to get to know me better. Before I left Japan, I was warned by some of my American friends to be careful about who I trusted in America. So, although the guy was hot, and his offer was very tempting because I hardly knew him, I decided to heed the advice I was given and play it safe and broke my promise to phone him.

While I was making my way through L.A. International Airport, a few days later, people were rushing, pushing and shoving in such a manner that I thought there'd been a bomb scare. I would learn later that the craziness was the general pace of everyday life in L.A. It was such a different atmosphere to the gentle politeness and courtesy that I'd become accustomed to in Japan. My plan was to surprise an American Buddhist friend by showing up on his doorstep unannounced, but it turned out to be me who got the surprise instead. He was out of town, and that meant I was left with nowhere to stay. I was in an airport phone booth trying to arrange alternative accommodation when a young woman pushed her way in and began rubbing her body up against me. When I asked her what she was doing, she gave me a cheeky grin and told me that she needed a lift into town in my 'taxi', but I got the impression that wasn't all she was after. I had to struggle to squeeze past her and exit the phone box, but she still refused point-blank to accept that I wasn't interested in her physical advances and chased after me, yelling out that I was her husband abandoning her. Boy, did I cop an 'evil eye' from all the surrounding bystanders. I promised her a lift to shut her up, but then decided to catch a bus instead, and hoping that it would make her happy, I bought her a bus ticket. That only made her hurl more abuse at me for being such a cheapskate, and I suddenly wondered if someone from Candid Camera was filming me – no such luck! My outrageous predicament finally came to an end on the bus, after she found another bloke who was far more receptive to her loony advances. As for me, I never felt more relieved to be abandoned in my life. I finally found my way to the Hollywood YMCA, only to learn that it was closed for renovations. One of the renovators redirected me to an old hotel across the street, that reminded me of the Adams Family's house. Upon entering it huge foyer area, I became even more convinced that it was the same house and that I'd walked onto their movie set. Even the clerk on reception looked and sounded like Lurch. Looking up at the chandeliers and intricately carved ceiling and woodwork, it was easy to tell that the hotel had been a very plush and stylish building in its day, but it was certainly in desperate need of refurbishment by the time that I got there. Some of the ladies residing in the hotel would sit around in the foyer each night, acting like they were Hollywood movie stars. They'd usually be dressed in skin-tight skirts or slacks, with long, fancy cigarette holders in their hands that had brightly painted nails and they'd be wearing so much makeup that they looked like they had masks on. Some of them would remain in the foyer until the early hours of the morning, talking shop about the movie industry and their days of glory. To me, they all looked like leftovers from the 1930s, and that's exactly what they were – out-of-work never was or has-been actors in their late sixties and beyond, all stuck in a time warp. Most of the hotel's residents, including the men, were so grotesquely strange and eccentric that it was a struggle to communicate with them without receiving an absurd response. Late one afternoon, a young black woman raced into the foyer, holding up a dead pot plant and screaming hysterically because it had died. It turned out that she hated drinking alone and had been giving it some whiskey whenever she had some! Several of the other women had rushed to her aid and tried to console her, and one of them even broke down crying with her. To me, an air of lunacy permeated the entire place, both inside and out, and my perception was clarified a few weeks later when I found out that the hotel was a halfway house for released mental asylum patients. How sad – if only I'd known.

I also soon discovered that the local NSA/SGI Buddhist meeting held in a house in West Hollywood was almost as bizarre as the hotel was. While in Tokyo, I'd become accustomed to everyone at the meetings chanting, discussing Buddhism for an hour and then finishing off with a friendly chat with a cup of tea or coffee. The Hollywood meetings were run more like a sports competition, at breakneck speed, the members would recite *Gongyo* (part of the Lotus Sutra), chant Nam-Myoho-Renge-Kyo for a few minutes and then race outside to start dragging people from the surrounding streets to bring back to the next meeting. They'd do this several times each night, and I absolutely hated it. Eventually, after being made to feel isolated and guilty for refusing to participate in their campaigns to find new converts, I gave in and went with them. The activity was termed *Street Shakubuku*, (meaning to awaken others to the Mystic Law), and one night we only just narrowly avoided being arrested, while 'fishing' for people going in and coming out of a giant supermarket. When the manager spotted us and chased us away, threatening to call the police, I felt utterly embarrassed and told the others that it was a disrespectful example of Nichiren's Buddhism. When I tried to convince them to adhere to the shop manager's wishes, they just shrugged their shoulders, ignored me and just carried on regardless. They were so determined to *catch a fish* that they began pestering people as they crossed the busy street, and when we eventually caught the attention of a woman with her arms loaded up with shopping and miraculously convinced her to come back to the house with us – I was flabbergasted! For all she knew, we could have been a murderous, psycho cult! Be that as it may, we arrived back at the house just in the nick of time for another high-speed ceremony, followed by to the same lot of people saying the same lot of things. Then when the meeting was over, the same leaders that were always present came down on the guests like members of an investigation team. I could tell by the alarmed look on our guest's face that she was feeling more than just a little bewildered. While I was trying to explain the meaning of the chant to her in more simple terms, a female leader rudely interrupted us, by pushing her way in between us and asking the woman for a $20 subscription fee to cover the costs of a Gohonzon and a monthly newsletter – I could hardly believe what I was witnessing! With a look of panic on her face, the woman picked up her shopping, got up to leave and then told the leader that she'd only come to listen and needed to get home to cook dinner for her family. Still refusing to give up, the leader ignored what our invited guest had said, and continued harassing her for the $20 charges all the way to the door. The unpleasant incident left me feeling numb and heartbroken, not only for the guest but any others like her. I love telling people about Nichiren's teachings, and it shattered me to think of how many others were being discouraged and driven away by this high-pressure sales pitch routine, without ever getting to know what the teachings are really about. Often our actions more than our words can be encouraging or damaging, and I for one, certainly don't exclude myself from either. When I expressed my concern to the leader responsible afterwards, she cut me down by assertively informing me that when an American pays for something, they usually want to get their money's worth. In other words, she believed that if the guest had paid the $20, the guest would have definitely chanted Nam-Myoho-Renge-Kyo. She also assertively reminded that Nichiren had requested his teachings to be taught in accordance with the place and the time, which I knew to be correct. To me, her rude and dogmatic method made no sense at all. However, I wasn't an American, so I couldn't confidently argue with her, and nor could I bear to attend another NSA/SGI meeting in L.A. On a more positive note, I've recently heard that the propagation of Nichiren's teachings is now done differently in the US and that the method of 'street shakubuku' is no longer applicable – thank goodness for that, says I.

WHEN I'D FIRST arrived in Los Angeles, I'd sent the songwriter, Brian Potter, a message to let him know where I was staying. He visited me at the hotel one morning when he was passing through the area, and although he was friendly and polite, he declined to get involved in my project. Brian was a professional of the highest standard, and my songs were nowhere near up to scratch. I'd be lying not to admit that I felt disappointed, but it wasn't as though Brian had asked me to come. His lack of interest certainly didn't hinder me. On the contrary, it made me more determined than ever to one day achieve my goal. Brian mentioned that Tina Turner was chanting Nam-Myoho-Renge-Kyo, and it blew my mind, as I was a big fan of hers and I even sang some of her songs. A few nights later, I was sitting alone in the hotel foyer minding my own business and reading the paper, when a grubby-looking young man wandered in off the street and up to the reception counter. Apart from a brief side-glance, I'd paid him little very attention, until a violent argument broke out between him and 'Lurch' the receptionist. The poor guy was frantically begging for his luggage to get a change of clothing to wear to a job interview, and Lurch was refusing point blank to oblige. When the young man lost control and tried to grab Lurch by the neck, I rushed across to them and tried my best to calm them down. The young man owed the hotel $80, and Lurch had confiscated all of his belongings in place of the debt. The poor guy was homeless, hungry and broke, and had been roaming the streets of Hollywood for days. He may have sounded hostile and looked dishevelled and unkempt, but my heart still went out to him. All that I had left to my name was $120 (2019 equivalent about $570.00), which had to last me until I returned to Japan. Having been in desperate situations myself and knowing too well what he was going through, I felt that it was my turn to be the one to go out on a limb and help someone in need. So, without another moments thought, I paid his bill, took possession of his luggage, let him get a clean shirt and then delivered his bag up to my room. (I can't remember his name, so from here on in I'll refer to him as Brad.)

I'd given Brad a card with Nam-Myoho-Renge-Kyo printed on it and had asked him to wait out the front of the hotel while I'd taken his luggage up to my room, and when I returned, Brad looked anxiously surprised and about something...

"Are you a Soka Gakkai Buddhist?" He asked with urgency in his voice.

"Umm... Yeah, I am," I admitted, expecting him to tell me to get lost.

We strolled across the street to a nearby burger joint, and it was there that he told me his astonishing story. Brad had been introduced to Nam-Myoho-Renge-Kyo in New York City, where he was born and had grown up. Even though he had virtually no knowledge of Nichiren's teachings, he'd been given a Gohonzon anyway. He chanted in front of it each day for a few weeks, but when a lot of astounding things started happening all at once in his life, he freaked out, rolled it up and put it away. Sometime later, Brad hitchhiked across the United States to the West Coast, carrying his Gohonzon with him in his suitcase. His dream was to become an actor, but things hadn't quite worked out the way that he'd hoped. That night when we met, Brad had reached the end of his tether and was contemplating suicide. I filled Brad in on some of what little I'd learnt about Nichiren Buddhism, and what a jolting surprise it was when we returned to the hotel and Brad informed that I'd carried his Gohonzon up to my room in his luggage. I had to struggle to hold back my tears, and here I am doing it again now. I received another unexpected surprise when Brad told me that he was gay – I'd have never guessed it. And the surprises didn't stop there, as after a much-needed shower, shave and a fresh change of clothes, Brad transformed into an amazingly good-looking guy, and I thought I was hallucinating when he sat on the bed beside me and gave me a kiss and a hug. For the next few days, we enjoyed each other's company intimately and everything was going just fine and dandy until I received a note under the door from Lurch, warning me that if Brad hadn't vacated the hotel by noon, I'd be out too. Before I met Brad, I'd been having a casual fling with a Canadian TV producer, who was staying further down the Boulevard at the Hollywood Holiday Inn. I took Brad to meet him and asked him if he could put Brad up in his room for a few days, which he was happy to do. The producer was trying to arrange for a working visa so that I could perform in Canada. He wanted to fly me to Toronto and have me appear on the Alice Cooper show, but my visa didn't come through in time before the producer had to return to Toronto to work on the show. After that, I then got caught up in things and lost contact with both the producer and Brad.

I PHONED LORRAINE, who'd financed my trip to America, to let her know that so far my mission hadn't been the success that we'd both hoped for. Lorraine wasn't at all happy to hear it and reacted very rudely by refusing to give me any more support and slamming down the phone. Later it would become apparent to me that her investment in helping me had been more about helping herself. Loraine was a wealthy woman who enjoyed standing out in the crowd and especially being noticed by the other Buddhist members. Had I been successful in my attempt, I'm sure that she would have delighted in the attention that it brought her. Be that as it may, thanks to the universal forces, she was there in my time of need to save me from the effects of my bad karma, and I'll always be grateful to her for it. The following few chapters will help you to understand more clearly that there was a much deeper underlying purpose to her assistance, which had far less to do with what happened on the surface of things, and much more to do with my future mission. By then I was running out of money to buy food and living on ten-cent cups of hot chocolate or coffee from the hotel's vending machine. I eventually became so desperate for a decent meal that I walked the streets of Hollywood visiting loan shops trying to pawn my old movie camera, which no one was even remotely interested in. One of my childhood dreams had been to one day visit Hollywood, the home of the Mickey Mouse Club, but not even in my worst nightmares had I ever imagined that I'd end up there destitute and on the streets. I was certainly in dire straits, but at least I still had my faith – and that's all that I did have. So, I took yet another 10 cent cup of coffee up to my room, sat on my bed and chanted fervently until I dropped off to sleep. I'd prepaid for my hotel room in advance when I first arrived, but I only had one night left. On the following day, my plan was to surrender to my fate and throw myself on the mercy of the Australian Consulate. Early the next morning, Jessie, the mother of Rita, whom I'd to chant in Taiwan, showed up at the hotel looking for me with a freshly-baked chicken and some tasty homemade cookies. Just as I'd done with Brian Potter, on the day that I arrived in L.A., I'd posted Jessie a letter to let her know where I was staying.

When I didn't hear anything back from her, I just assumed that she may not have been interested in meeting me and forgot all about her. It turned out that she'd had been away interstate and had only just got back the night before. When Jessie heard how broke and hungry I was, she insisted that I come and stay at her house in Glendale for the remainder of my stay – I inwardly expressed my gratitude to the universe for yet another unexpected last-minute reprieve. Jessie and I got along like a house on fire. I helped her with her chores as much as I could and sometimes watched over her disabled husband while she went shopping. The poor man had suffered severe shell-shock in an aircraft during WW2, which had left him mentally impaired. I also accompanied Jessie and her husband to a Veterans hospital in Los Angeles a couple of times for his monthly check-ups, where I was shocked to see lines of young men sitting around in a large waiting room, staring out at the walls like zombies. When Jessie told me they were casualties of the war in Vietnam, I wondered if some of them were the same soldiers that I'd seen while I was stranded in the flood at the Subic Air-force Base, and my heart went out to each and every one of them. Although Jessie was in her late 70s, you'd never have known it. She was amazingly young at heart and a devoted Rock 'n' Roll fan, and while I was staying with her, Jessie took me to rock venues all over Los Angeles in her little white convertible sports car. Jessie was like the grandmother that I'd never had and one that everybody would love to have. Sadly for both of us, it all came to an abrupt and very upsetting ending one night when Jessie's daughter, Rita, phoned from Taipei, stinking drunk. When Jessie mentioned that I was staying with her, Rita went berserk and ordered Jessie to kick me out immediately. It made no sense, as Rita had given me her mother's address and had encouraged me repeatedly to look her up and spend some time with her. I tried to speak to Rita myself, but she was so intoxicated that I couldn't get a word in edgewise until, in the end, I gave up trying. Thanks to the snake-dancer's destructive vendetta, Rita had been sucked in by all the lies that were getting spread about me back in the Orient. By the time that she'd finished talking to Rita, poor Jessie was sobbing her heart out, and under no circumstances did she want me to leave, and she even offered to lie to Rita if I'd choose not to go. As much as I appreciated Jessie's offer and wanted to stay, I didn't want to cause her any more trouble. So, after sleeping on it, I decided that it was time to head to San Francisco. To show her gratitude for the help that I'd given her, Jessie insisted on giving me a small amount before I left to help tide me over.

I HAD A PLACE to stay in San Francisco and was looking forward to visiting the famous Golden Gate Bridge, however, getting there almost didn't happen. The day that I was to fly out from L. A. International Airport, a bomb did go off, and the airport had to be temporarily closed. After a lot of confusion and messing around, I ended up catching an alternative cheap $10 flight from the nearby Hollywood Burbank Airport on a plane that was painted a grotesque shade of purple. The seating arrangement was 'first in first seated' and the walk through the terminal to board the flight was nothing short of harrowing. Small stalls with scary signs that blatantly offered 'air crash insurance' paved the way. During the short, one hour flight, I pondered over the conduct and attitude of some of the Buddhist leaders that I'd met during my stay in Los Angeles, which had often left me feeling sadly disappointed. One of my worst experiences took place at Lurch's hotel in Hollywood after I struck up a friendship with the hotel's two maintenance men (a father-and-son team). Although they were both heavily into drugs and alcohol, they were keen to hear whatever I could tell them about Nichiren's Buddhism. Before I left for 'Frisco, I'd taught them to chant and then had no other choice than to introduce them to the local members in Hollywood for future encouragement and guidance. On the following day, the men were already preparing to receive a Gohonzon! I'd waited over fifteen months for mine, and I didn't think that they were anywhere near ready enough to take on that responsibility. A local member advised the men that a shirt-box would do to enshrine their Gohonzon in, and when I arrived at their room, they had one tacked to the wall in the middle of the room. I was aware that they had a lot of friends coming and going and that most of them were druggies and heavy drinkers, so I moved the shirt-box further down the wall, to try to put it more out of harm's way. When a women's division leader arrived to do the enshrinement, she hit the place like a Nazi, assertively ordering the men to move the shirt box back into the middle of the room. When I'd politely tried to persuade her to leave it where it was, she'd turned on me like a woman obsessed with power and in my face said...

"Don't you dare contradict a leader! You just do as yer told! Do ya hear?"

For the sake of the two men and their ceremony, I miraculously managed to bite my tongue and to refrain from telling this hierarchical, self-absorbed woman precisely what I thought of her. In hindsight, I can see now that back then the members in the USA were trying to spread the word of Nichiren's teachings as fast as they could, with their limited knowledge and experience. The leaders that I met in Los Angeles were very different from the long-term US and Japanese leaders that I'd met in Japan, and I now believe that they were panicking to get the word out, due to the Cold War between the superpowers that seemed to be getting colder by the day. After WW2 ended, and when Nichiren's teachings first begun spreading around the world, few people barely understood even the fundamentals of the practise, not to mention the many differences between the heretical teachings and Nichiren's. Consequently, a lot of mistakes were made. In Japan, to help bring an end to their post-war sufferings, followers did whatever they felt they needed to do to get as many people as possible to join the organisation and to chant for world peace, and in the USA, Gohonzons were given out haphazardly, almost like pamphlets. While most people's intentions were good, sometimes the way that the early SGI pioneer members went about propagating the Law, caused more harm than good. Among other less fortunate things, I heard that some Japanese women even resorted to having sex with foreigners just to get them to chant and help spread the teachings elsewhere. This method of persuasion was nothing new as far as history is concerned, as a small percentage of women around the world have always provided sexual pleasure to men to gain favours and other rewards. There were apparently also some members, including new converts, who went around threatening people and using frightening scare tactics in an attempt to force them to chant and join the organisation. These desperate misunderstandings and incorrect measures had resulted from severe confusion, trauma and the post-war utter devastation that had befallen Japan because of the war. While some of it may have caused damage to the credibility of Nichiren Buddhism, all was certainly not or lost. At one of the Tokyo meetings that I attended, an American GI shared an extremely moving story about what happened in his life after he'd haphazardly been given a Gohonzon, without knowing what it was. He'd left it lying on the ledge under the back window of his sports car, and it wasn't until after he was shipped off to Vietnam two years later that he realised what a careless and foolish mistake he'd made. He ended up in the thick of battle sharing a tent with another soldier, who happened to be a happy chanter and who had his own Gohonzon with him, and thanks to this soldier, he learnt for the first time what the practise and teachings are actually about. Late one night their camp was bombed, and the only tent left standing was theirs. Following that, the soldier telling the story was granted Rest and Recreation leave and instead of indulging in what was on offer in the exotic Far East, like many other soldiers on leave did, he caught a flight straight back to Los Angeles to search for his Gohonzon. Then, after a long and difficult search, he eventually found the person who'd bought his car the previous year, only to be told that it had since been in a collision and sold for spare parts. Still unwilling to give up, he tracked down the remains of the car that was sitting at the edge of a cliff in a wrecking yard, and his Gohonzon was still wedged in the crevice behind the top of the back seat, water-stained but still intact. Everyone in the room could tell by the quiver in the soldier's voice and the tears welling up in his eyes, that just seeing it again had been an incredible and emotional experience for him – just as it was for us hearing his beautiful story.

WHILE IN San Francisco, I stayed with some friends of a friend who were all gay to the extreme, and who took me to gay bars, gay restaurants and shops and even to a gay nude beach. It was an unusual and exciting experience, but it just wasn't me, and the idea of a world that's so segregated didn't appeal to me at all. In fact, other than with those that I met at the Buddhist meetings, I hardly came in contact with any straight people in San Francisco at all. A visiting female journalist wrote in one of the local newspapers while I was there: *You've got to be a goddamn man in this goddamn town to get one!* That tickled me pink, and I certainly understood what she meant. The atmosphere at the meetings in San Francisco, I'm pleased to report, were very different from those that I'd attended in West Hollywood. This time I found the people to be far friendlier, warmer, less rushed and extremely sincere and considerate, and no one participated in street shakubuku. At one of the meetings, I met a booking agent who had a listen to my tapes and later offered to sponsor me for a green card. His plan was to bring me back to the US and promote me, starting out in Las Vegas! I was over the moon! Meanwhile, a gay Chinese friend that I'd known in Hong Kong, had moved to Greenwich Village, New York, and invited me to come and stay with him. I had just enough money for a dirt-cheap return ticket on the overnight *Champagne Flight*, so I decided to go! The Sunday before I was due to fly out, my gay hosts took me to an annual gay street fair in the middle of San Francisco. By then, I'd met and become acquainted with several of their gay friends, so I was eagerly looking forward to it. We arrived amid an array of colourful streamers and balloons, and the weather couldn't have been better. Among other fancy delights on show, there were kinky clowns, spunky cowboys wearing big 'ten-gallon' Texan hats and some of the most outrageous drag queens that I'd ever seen. Also there, were authentic Native Americans, showing off their muscles and dressed in traditional costumes covered all over in glitter. From what I could gather, the main topic of the day was about a gay rights campaigner by the name of Harvey Milk, who may have even had something to do with that year's theme. (Harvey was the first openly gay person to be elected to public office in California when he won a seat on the San Francisco Board of Supervisors). While I stood watching and enjoying all the colourful delights, I suddenly felt an urgent compulsion come over me to get away from it all immediately, which soon brought about a very scary and awkward situation for me. My past experiences with similar underlying 'feelings' had taught me never to ignore them. So, without giving my hosts a reason, I asked them if we could leave right away and go somewhere else. At first, they thought I was cracking one of my silly Aussie jokes and burst into laughter, but when I told them that I was deadly serious and that if they didn't take me, I'd leave alone, with a strange look of disbelief they agreed to go somewhere else. After we'd left the area in their car, I let them know why I'd had no other choice but to leave, after which no further comments were made about it. We spent the rest of that day relaxing in the sun and ogling the talent passing by at a gay nude beach on the outskirts of the city. The uninhibited public sexual activity that was going on between the rocks down below, tempted my enthusiasm no end. As much I yearned to climb down and join in, I didn't have the guts to do it. I still felt uncomfortable about being demonstratively gay in the presence of other western men, and the only time that I felt entirely at ease sexually was in the company of Asian men. In the end, I resisted temptation. After sitting on a rock watching from a distance and frying in the hot sun for almost five hours, I was so burnt that it even hurt to breathe, and the car journey back to San Francisco felt like a fiery nightmare. We arrived at the house just in time to hear the trail end of someone leaving a message on the answering machine, which was to let the guys know how, shortly after we'd left the street fair, someone had gone berserk with a gun randomly shooting at people. The faces of my two hosts turned an instant shade of grey, and when they quickly turned and looked across at me in utter disbelief, I might have looked even greyer, if I hadn't looked so red. None of us slept very much that night, especially me with my painful sunburn. The guys had already made plans to visit some gay friends in the countryside for a few days and had invited me to go along with them, but I'd already booked my flight to New York by then, so they left me in their house to fend for myself until it was time for my flight. When I phoned later in the day for a taxi to take me to the airport and was told that all the city's drivers had gone on a flash strike, I thought that it was a joke!...

"What's all these obstacles? I asked myself after I was told that the strike could last for days. "Don't tell me there's more potential danger waitin' for me in New York?!"

I spent that entire weekend all on my own, glaring at the TV and feeling nothing but self-pity, as I struggled to try to cope with my unbearable sunburn. Late one night, I received a call from someone who said he was phoning from San Diego. Then, before he even told me who he was or who he wanted to talk to, he bombarded me with a barrage of personal and intimate questions, concerning my sexual preferences and what my top ten favourite kinky activities were. He sounded quite young and had a very seductive voice, and the conversation soon became highly arousing, but when he began moaning, groaning and crying out as if he was in agony, any feelings of excitement that I had suddenly died an instant death. At first, I thought that he was seriously ill or that someone was strangling him, then I heard a loud howl that made me almost drop the phone. The guy then thanked me politely, said goodbye and hung up his phone. One of my hosts ran a phone-sex business, and it took me a while to eventually figure out that the stranger on the phone had been a client having phone-sex with me – his loud yell at the end had come when he did – then it was all over in a flash!

In so many ways, the Golden Gate city reminded me of Sydney and had made me feel increasingly homesick for Australia. By the time that the guys arrived back home, I'd already scrapped the idea of going to New York or back to Japan, and had decided to return to Australia instead. My future plan was to spend some quality time with my family while I waited for my green card to return to America and perform in Las Vegas. My host with the phone-sex business made a lot of long-distance calls to clients all over the country. Hoping that my call to Australia wouldn't be noticed on his next bill, I phoned my brother Denis in Sydney and asked him to loan me my fare to come home, and within a few hours, there was a ticket waiting for me at the San Francisco Qantas office.

# Tommy heads for Casa Lisboa

**AUSTRALIAN singer and TV star Tommy Beaumont leaves today for Macau.**

He will appear as the featured attraction at the Casa Lisboa Hotel for one week starting tomorrow night.

After his return from Macau Tommy may head for Taiwan.

"I have an offer to sing in Taiwan followed by performances in Saigon," he said.

"But I'm also waiting for further details of an engagement in Guam and I won't be making a firm decision until next week."

■ *TOMMY Beaumont is off to Macau.*

■ *TOMMY BEAUMONT . he likes Japan.*

# Japan is the scene where it's all happening, says Tommy

**TOMMY Beaumont, the rotund Australian singer who caused a stir at pop shows here last year with his wild stage act, is back from a tour of Japan.**

And Tommy is full of praise for the Japanese pop scene which he says is more exciting than any other in Asia.

"They get all the top international acts playing there with all the superstar trappings such as hoardes of groupies and wild pop parties," he said.

"I'd really like to go back but I've got my sights set on London."

**Mungo Jerry**

Tommy has a friend in Mungo Jerry, the group currently in the British Top 10 with Alright Alright Alright.

Tommy is unlikely to perform here although he would like to do one or two TV shows.

"What I need, basically, is to have a good rest, the tour of Japan was pretty hectic," he says.

"I may do a short tour of the area before I go to London."

*April Garden.*

*Thai girl in trouble with another member of the German group.*

*Publicity picture.*

*Snake Dancer.*

Diamond Head Hawaii in the background.

Sightseing in San Francisco.

Akiko enshrining Mum's Gohonzon.

Beautiful Akiko.

Cyclone Tracy aftermath.

SOMETHING within my subconscious was signalling me that it was time to move on – that there were other challenges to face and other people to meet and introduce to the Law. At the same time, I was also battling on another level with negative karma of my own that was manifesting, and it was a continuous struggle not to come across to others around me as a 'bad example' while I struggled to deal with it. I'd sometimes feel like I was a hypocrite or a drug addict telling people not to do wrong or to use drugs, but even so, I still tried my best to encourage as many others to chant as I could.

*Though worldly troubles may arise, never let them disturb you. No one can avoid problems, not even sages and worthies.*

*Suffer what there is to suffer, enjoy what there is to enjoy. Regard both sufferings and joy as facts of life, and continue chanting Nam-Myoho-Renge-Kyo no matter what.*

*Never conduct yourself in a shameful manner. Be unmoved by greed, by the desire for fame, or by anger.*

*Strengthen your faith day by day and month after month. Should you slacken in your resolve even a bit, your underlying negative karma will take advantage.*

*...Nichiren*

# Chapter 29

## CHANGING POISON INTO MEDICINE

The time had come for me to face and challenge some of my most powerful demons, so I asked Glynis to arrange a meeting between her mother and myself. I'd been procrastinating for far too long, and I needed to do this to be able to dig deep enough into myself to stir up and address some of my worst and most severe underlying and long-standing negative energy. While I'd been in front of the Dai Gohonzon, I'd vowed to visit Beatty and to do my best to encourage her to chant, so that she could have an opportunity to change some of her long-standing poisons into medicine. The journey to Beatty's house was a truly harrowing experience. Along the way there I felt like throwing in the towel and backing out, as images of the first time that I'd ever laid eyes on her raced randomly through my mind, along with other painful memories of my unhappy and deluded childhood, to which she'd contributed so much suffering. Long-forgotten memories of prolonged, agonising hell were resurfacing in my mind one after another like painful explosions. One moment I was reliving the horrible day that I was unfairly expelled from the convent and how Dad had taken me away and hidden me from Mum, the next moment I was reliving when I tried to kill Beatty and Dad with rat poison and how I later almost stabbed Beatty with a knife. Thinking about it all was chilling me to the bone. Glynis noticed the sweat running down my face and interrupting my thoughts by asking if I was okay. No one else had known about any of these things, not even her. As we turned into Beatty's street, I felt so much repulsion for her that a part of me still wanted to hurt her and pay her back with a vengeance. Helping me to keep control throughout it all, much deeper and far more powerful energy was manifesting from within, and provoking me to stay above the massive waves of negativity and to come out the winner. When Glynis pointed out Beatty's house, I felt suddenly nauseous, and I honestly didn't think that I was going to be able to keep my vow and go through with it. Before I had time to think any more about it, we were pulling into Beatty's driveway, and there she stood, waiting on her front porch, looking so frail that she was almost unrecognisable. Seeing her again gave me an enormous jolt, and the electrifying few seconds that it took me to climb out of the car and approach her seemed like hours, and my limbs felt like they were made of lead. A great divide still stood between us, but I was determined to break through it, no matter what it took. Without saying a single word, I reached out and took Beatty in my arms, and as we held each other, it was like two icebreakers smashing through thick layers of ice to finally unite. I could feel her ailing spirit merge with mine, and then came her loud sobs. It was as though a powerful light had suddenly switched on, freeing us both from our prolonged incarceration in a dark, nightmarish self-inflicted prison. The incredible inner-force that had given me the strength and ability to defeat my immense hatred and anger towards Beatty was the power of forgiveness, love, wisdom and compassion that I'd acquired through my chanting. That victory marked the end of one of the greatest battles of my life, melting my pent-up hatred and anger like the sun melts the dew when it rises. Glynis had already told me that, after Dad died, Beatty lost the hotel and ended up almost penniless. At the time, I wondered if it was karma coming home to Beatty relating to the money that I should have received from Dad on my 21st birthday. Since I'd long accepted responsibility for my karmic contribution to that situation and had put it to the back of my mind, I didn't mention anything at all about it. Glynis had also previously told me that while I was overseas, Beatty had almost died twice on the operating table, and how the doctors who'd resuscitated her had told Beatty that she must have something important that she still needed to accomplish in life. That day, after the war between her and I had finally ended, Beatty told Glynis that she now understood what it was that she needed to accomplish...

"Why couldn't it've been like this when I was a kid?" I asked myself, with feelings of sadness and frustration permeating my body. "What tha hell could we have possibly done in our past lives ta end up such bitter 'n' hateful enemies in this one?"

From that day onward, whenever Beatty visited Glynis and her children, it felt like a ray of sunshine had entered the house, especially on the day that Beatty sat down beside me in front of Glynis's Gohonzon and chanted Nam-Myoho-Renge-Kyo. It was the final step of a mission accomplished, or what some would consider as being a miracle taking place, and if ever two people could be used as a perfect example of turning their poison into medicine, we were it! I prayed that day for any future lives that we might be destined to share to be much happier and less violent ones. Something else that Nichiren taught also crossed my mind, regarding the circumstances in which we come into this world, including where we're born, to whom we're born, and our relationships with others around us. Nothing is ever down to random coincidence, it's always controlled by and in accordance with the strict Law of 'Cause and Effect'. As I've mentioned before, everything good or bad that we experience always relates to the good or bad causes that we make now or have made in the recent or distant past, and every little detail gets entered into the eternal universal chronicles of Life. Perhaps that's what Jesus meant when he told his followers...

*For whatever man sows that shall he also reap.*

I clearly remember thinking one day while waving Beatty goodbye...

"If the power of this chant can help Beatty 'n' me rise above 'n' overcome our life-long hatred for each other, as we've done, then I reckon just about anything's possible." And to this day, I still believe this...

Mum knew that I'd been seeing Beatty, but she'd never mentioned it or made any attempt to dissuade me. I brought Beatty's name up one afternoon while Mum and I were doing some chanting together, and suggested that it would be beneficial for her future peace of mind and happiness if she could let go of the past and bury the hatchet where Beatty was concerned. Mum didn't say anything then, but when I went further out on a limb and suggested that she chant for Beatty's health, Mum exploded like a bomb!...

"I'm not chantin' for that mongrel of a woman! Fancy you asking me to do a stupid thing like that! Have you gone out of your mind, boy!?"

Mum was so furious that it was impossible to get a word in edgewise, let alone to try to reason with her. When I finally did try and attempted to explain it from another perspective, she threw down her prayer beads and stormed out of the room...

"If you want to chant for her, then you do it yourself! But don't you dare ever ask me to do anything like that again, do you hear?" She bellowed all the way to the other end of the house.

I was never game enough to mention it again, and then weeks later, Mum caught me picking flowers from her garden to take to Beatty, who'd become gravely ill...

"You can't give anyone a bunch of flowers that look like that!" She barked, snatching them from me. "They're all half dead! What's the matter with you, boy!?"

Watching Mum pick a bunch of the best flowers from her garden was like watching the impossible unfold and become possible before my very eyes. Everyone in my family had always said that nothing could change Mum's deep-rooted, nagging hatred for Beatty. Perhaps if she hadn't learnt to chant Nam-Myoho-Renge-Kyo, they might have all ended up being right. That day I felt deeply confident that Mum had begun to win a battle within her life to finally achieve her mission here on Earth and had taken a significant first step forward that would alter the direction of her future eternal destiny for the better.

ONE SUNDAY afternoon while several of us were chanting in front of Glynis's Gohonzon for unity, world peace and the success of the band, I noticed that Glynis and Billy were absent. As I continued focussing on the Gohonzon, I began to sense a state of darkness closing in on us from either side of the room, which made me feel increasingly unsettled and uncomfortable. Next, I was puzzled by the appearance of several little flickering white squares that appeared to be darting about in front of me. I thought that it was something in my eyes and wiped them with a tissue, but it made no difference and they were still there. I refocused my eyes more intently on the Gohonzon and then noticed handwritten letters of the alphabet whizzing across on some of the tiny squares. At the same time, my mind's eye began darting back and forth between the room that I was in and another room in the house, where I saw quick flashing images of someone asleep on a bed. It was a bit like being in two places at once, and no matter how hard I tried, there was never enough time to make out who it was on the bed. Something red blocking my view, and as I chanted more fervently in unison with the others around me, an intense feeling of doom engulfed me, and my thoughts were suddenly drawn to the dining room at the rear of the house. Adrian was kneeling down and chanting directly behind me, and without consciously knowing what I was doing, I spun around to face him, pointed toward the back wall and shouted...

**"HURRY! QUICK! STOP 'EM!"**

Every bone in my body was telling that something evil was happening on the other side of the wall, and at the same time, I sensed that I needed to keep chanting, no matter what. Adrian jumped up and rushed into the dining room, where he found Glynis, Billy and a couple of their friends holding hands around a small table and performing a séance that had gone seriously wrong. They were all fighting a losing battle to let go of each other's hands when Adrian upturned the table to break the circle to release them finally. When the rest of us heard the loud commotion, we all jumped up at once and rushed into the dining room to see what was going on. The first thing that I noticed were several bits of paper, with alphabetical letters written on them, scattered across the floor. Simultaneously, there was a loud cry from Glynis's husband, John, who'd fallen in the bathroom and hit his head on the concrete floor. I was anxious to find out if there was anyone asleep in any of the bedrooms, so I searched each room and was startled to find a red ball lying next to Glynis's young son, Jason, who he was sound asleep on his bed. I was instantly concerned that whatever it was may have latched onto him and entered his life-force, but chose to keep that to myself. The bizarre incident left me with a massive dose of the creeps that lasted for days, as well as a feeling of profound disappointment and bewilderment. After that dreadful day, nothing was ever quite the same again, especially where the band was concerned. Glynis later admitted that they were curious to know what would happen during a séance with people close by chanting. I wasn't the least bit impressed, as far as I was concerned it was the epitome of stupidity. Sadly, Jason grew up an angry young man, and later contracted Motor Neuron Disease, which took his life during his early thirties. Even if the séance had something to do with Jason's future destiny, it was still his own karma for that to happen and no one else's fault.

IT WAS COMING up to March and we still hadn't heard any more about the release of the single that we'd recorded with John Bromell. Experience had taught me that schedules in the music business seldom go as planned, so I kept encouraging the other band members to be patient, which didn't work and they'd begun to doubt my honesty and integrity. I phoned the publishing company to get an update on our record's progress and was told that John Bromell had taken the master tapes to London with him and that a new release date would be rescheduled as soon as he got back. I relayed this news to the band members, but they refused to accept it and went behind my back, phoning the company themselves. It was Billy who made the call and was put through to the wrong department, to be told that there was no such record listed in their schedule for new releases. Following that, the band held a secret meeting, excluding me, in John's and Glynis's bedroom, where they all came to a mutual conclusion that I'd betrayed them. When they later summoned me to the room and blatantly accused me of lying, I almost lost my balance and fell over from the shock. Broken-hearted, but determined to prove that I was not a liar, I phoned the company back in their presence, asked for the correct department, handed the phone to Billy to make his own inquiries and then left them to it. Although their false accusations had hurt me deeply, I inwardly understood that it was something that needed to go wrong for other things to go right and that it would all turn out for the best. The band apologised to me afterwards, but in reality, an apology wasn't even necessary, as it was the sign that I'd been expecting and watching out for. After considering how rapidly things had deteriorated between myself and the other band members ever since the séance episode, I saw it as an opportunity to cut my losses and to just get out. Unbeknownst to any of the other band members, there was also another more complicated and potentially destructive underlying problem that was eating away at me. I knew that Adrian wasn't gay, but even so, I'd developed strong feelings towards him, which I'd been dealing with successfully until I noticed that he was attracted to Glynis. When that happened, it became too much for me to handle, and I needed to get away from everything as quickly as I could, so I decided to take the demos of YOU to the UK with me to see if I could stir up some interest there. Five years had gone by since I'd last seen or heard from my producer-friend, Michael Barclay, and I was also hoping to track him down and to see if he was still interested in producing me. Most of all, I yearned to see Masami again and felt confident that, as it had done in the past, chanting with him would help me to get myself back in rhythm and on top of my present demons. After I officially quit the band, I started looking for a day job to earn the money that I needed for the airfare. When I told the other band members that I was planning to take the tapes of YOU to the UK with me, they refused to allow it. According to them, they'd put work into the project, so it was jointly theirs, even though they needn't have worried, as I'd already considered them as equal partners. Feeling shattered by their second expression of distrust, I offered to sign the entire musical over to them, but after some thought, they declined the offer and said that it wasn't necessary. A couple of days later, after she heard about what had happened, Akiko stepped in and fully supported my decision, by encouraging me to take the tapes to England and giving me the airfare to get there. Once things had cooled down a bit more, and after the other band-members happily agreed to allow me to take the tapes with me, we all did some chanting together for the wisdom that we needed to resolve our differences, and to get on with our lives.

PRIOR TO THE band breaking up, I'd left a copy of YOU at the Sydney office of WEA/Leeds Music. A couple of days before I was due to fly out, we received an unexpected phone call from them to let us know that they believed YOU had enormous potential, and to ask us if we'd be interested in signing a deal with them, which we signed on the same day. Under the impression that the Shukbuku Band was still together, and that I'd be returning to Australia within three weeks, the company also got the band a deal with Warner Records to release a single from the musical. If all that wasn't enough, I got an even bigger going-away surprise when Mum finally agreed to receive her own Gohonzon. Like so many other 'Baby Boomers', as a child, I'd been led to believe that the Japanese and German people were among the lowest scum of the earth. I can clearly remember with sad regret, how Mum would always check to see what country had made a toy before she'd buy it for me. If it said 'Made in Japan', she'd angrily toss it back and say things to me like...

"I'm not buying you anything from that evil place!"

Watching Akiko's tiny, delicate hands unroll and then enshrine Mum's Gohonzon that day, was an extraordinarily beautiful and moving experience, and another impossible dream becoming a reality. After the ceremony was over, Adrian and I took Mum into the city for lunch to celebrate, but along the way, Mum let out a sudden loud yelp that gave us both quite a shock. After Adrian quickly pulled over to the side of the road to see what was wrong, it turned out that Mum had an out-of-the-blue revelation that had startled her. She told us a story about when I was only a couple of weeks old, and she'd dressed me up in white satin and lace and taken me to *Phyllis's* corner shop to show me off to her neighbourhood lady friends. The shop, that was on the corner of Waterloo Road and Juno Parade, was not only the heart of the community but also the central attraction in the tiny village of East Bankstown. As horse-drawn carts and the odd car and truck or two were passing them by, many of the local women would often gather there to gossip, swap new recipes, or debate about and discuss the latest news. In those days hardly anyone had a phone, so it was also 'communication corner' for most of them. Mum explained to us that when she took me there that day, an elderly man with a bushy white beard had politely interrupted the fuss that they were making and asked Mum if he could take a look at the palms of my hands. Mum had hesitantly agreed, and as everyone watched and listened on in silence, the older man had predicted that I would grow up to have a significant influence on humanity and world peace through an association with a large temple and that I might even become a priest. After he left and was out of sight, Mum and her friends burst into fits of laughter. Mum hadn't thought any more about it, nor had she ever mentioned it to me before. Of all days to do it, I was stunned that she'd remembered it on the same day that she'd received her Gohonzon. In an attempt to lighten the moment, I jokingly remarked with a giggle…

"God help the priesthood if I'm ever a cat amongst their pigeons."

My sister, Flo, was about twelve at the time and has recently told me that she was with Mum that day and had also witnessed what the elderly man predicted. My brother, Fred, and his wife, Edna, visited Mum later that evening, and after I started telling them a bit about my new-found faith, and Edna showed signs of becoming more than just a little bit interested, Fred yanked her by the arm and virtually pulled her out of the house and into their car, yelling back at me…

"You stay away from my family with ya evil devil worshippin' shit, do ya hear me!? We're good Christians, 'n' we believe in Jesus Christ!" Then they were gone.

Considering how many times I'd heard him use the Lord's name in vain, I found his reaction outrageously amusing. Fred must have heard about the other members of our family who were chanting and was probably afraid of having the same *spell* put on him. Just as Flo did several years later, Edna and her daughter, not only chanted Nam-Myoho-Renge-Kyo but also received their own personal Gohonzon.

THE DAY HAD arrived for me to leave for the UK, and I was already feeling homesick. Since my flight wasn't scheduled to depart until 9.pm, I paid a quick visit to Mr and Mrs Daisley to bring them up to date with what I'd been doing, and also play them the songs from YOU. I'd told Adrian about her teacup readings and how accurately she'd predicted what would happen in my life the first time that I attempted to go to the UK, and he'd been looking forward to meeting Mrs Daisley for some time. He'd also been planning a trip to Japan to visit the Dai Gohonzon and was keen to hear what Mrs Daisley might tell him, so he offered to drive me. One of the less personal things that Mrs Daisley told Adrian was that, in his tealeaves, she could see an eternal flame burning on a hilltop. It meant nothing to him nor me, even though she brought it up several times. She also read my cup, and I was thrilled to the hilltops to hear that this time I was going to make it to the UK at last.

After I got back home that day, I phoned Beatty to let her know that I was about to leave for the UK, and she broke down and cried. Sadly, it was the last chance that I ever got to speak to her, as she died shortly after I'd left. Having my family, the band members and many of my Buddhist friends come to the airport to see me off and to give me a beautiful farewell, was an incredible contrast to the last time that I'd left. Until that night, I hadn't realised that so many people cared about and appreciated me, and it was a struggle to tear myself away. I think that if any of them had asked me to stay, I may not have been able to go ahead and board the plane.

Adrian visited the Head Temple a few months later and was astonished to find everyone at a Buddhist meeting that he attended talking about a flame of peace that had only just been lit upon a hill that overlooked the temple. There wouldn't have been any way that Mrs Daisley could have possibly known about this – I hadn't even heard about it.

# Chapter 30

# DESTINATION LONDON

On my way to the UK, I stopped over in Tokyo and stayed for a couple of weeks with Lorraine, who'd sponsored my trip to the USA. She was close friends with one of the Japanese members living in Australia and had heard about how well my musical YOU was being received. Lorraine's interest had been reignited by the news, and she was eager to listen to a sample of what we'd done with the songs, and when I played her the tape, her face lit up like a Christmas tree. The first few days that I spent with Lorraine at her comfortable Japanese-style apartment were full of fun and laughter. My spirits were lifted even higher when Masami popped in one day to let me know that he'd decided to accompany me to the UK. Although he was straight, Masami and I were very close friends and loved spending as much time together as possible. On the following night, I had another unusual dream and found myself floating way out in the universe, where I encountered a group of monks. They all had their heads shaved in the usual tradition, but instead of the usual white or orange robes, they wore bright, multi-coloured clothing, and I somehow understood that they represented *Nembutsu*. When when the leader of the group held out a sparkling blue gem in the palm of his hand and then brought it up close to my face, I didn't know what was going on. Then, with a warm and friendly smile, he assured me that the blue gemstone would always be there to help me if ever I needed it. Simultaneously, a minor earthquake shook Tokyo and woke me up! I told Lorraine about my dream over breakfast, and when I mentioned the word Nembutsu, she immediately responded with a frown and told me that the followers of Nembutsu were Nichiren's staunch enemies. Her negative reaction and description confused me because it had been a very uplifting dream that had left me feeling happy and at ease. Determined to know more about Nembutsu, I did some research of my own and discovered that it had other meanings that were different from the negative interpretation that Lorraine had given me. Originally in Sanskrit, Nembutsu simply means 'mindfulness of the Buddha'.

Bright and early the following morning, I set out on another visit to the Head Temple at Taisekiji, and on my way to the coach terminus, I was stopped in my tracks by a sudden surge of powerful gale-force winds. Debris started hurtling in all directions and I only narrowly avoided being hit by a sheet of corrugated iron. As I fought against the strong wind to stay on my feet, there were moments when I began to fear for my life, and what a relief it was when I found some shelter under an outdoor staircase and was able to remain hidden there until the worst of the storm had passed. Unbeknownst to me, warnings of the approaching typhoon had been broadcast all throughout the night before, but in Japanese, which explained why I was one of the very few people out in it. Luckily, Tokyo had only suffered minor damage caused by the outer edge of the typhoon's might, and that meant I was still able to continue my journey to Taisekiji. It turned out to be the special day of the year set aside for the annual cleansing of the Dai Gohonzon, and there were a massive number of members in attendance. As I sat inside the Sho Hondo waiting excitedly for the giant nuclear-proof doors to open and reveal the awe-inspiring mandala, I sincerely thanked the universe for me having made it there. The site of a young priest, holding a small cloth in his hand, who was waiting at the foot of the stairs that lead up to the Dai Gohonzon, instantly reminded me of my dream about the Nembutsu priest. It was my ninth visit to the Head Temple and the only ever time that I ever got to see SGI President, Daisaku Ikeda, in person. During a brief lecture that he gave, he likened the morning gale to the power derived from chanting Nam-Myoho-Renge-Kyo, in that, it stirs up hidden rubbish in our lives and forces it out into the open so that its existence can be exposed, recognised and cleaned up. Although I found Ikeda to be impressive and encouraging, seeing him that day was an anticlimax, as I didn't get anywhere near the same *buzz* from being in his presence that others had expressed to me so many times. The real buzz, for me, had already taken place when the doors were opened to reveal the Dai Gohonzon, and I'd been able to express my sincere gratitude for the way that things had turned out for me back in Australia, especially for having survived the adversities.

During the remainder of my stay in Tokyo, I spent most of my days recording a single for MCA Music in a high-tech studio that had me feeling like I was on board the 'Starship Enterprise'. A famous Japanese composer had written two songs, especially for me to record, and because the lyrics were in Japanese, I used up most of the studio time just trying to pronounce the words correctly. Thank goodness I wasn't the one paying for it. Early one evening, after I'd finished the day's recording, I called into a nearby gay bar to unwind and struck up a friendly conversation with a trio of gay Russians. They introduced themselves as being staff members at the USSR Embassy and invited me to a private party that they were throwing at the embassy the following night, and I could hardly wait to get there! I had the hots for one of them and was hoping for a chance to blow on his Zhaleika. It was well after midnight by the time that I'd finished recording the next night, and as I was hurrying off to the party, hoping in my heart that it wasn't already too late, a couple of policemen stopped me in my tracks, arrested me for not carrying my passport, and then hauled me off to the police station. After they'd interrogated me for over an hour and treated me like a naughty schoolboy, they made me write out 'I promise never to go out without my passport while in Japan', a hundred times, which took me the rest of the night to finish. They then put me into a cab and ordered me to go straight back to Lorraine's place, or else. Unbeknownst to me, the police had already phoned Lorraine and given her an angry lecture and warning about being more responsible, as well as instructed her to make sure in the future that her guests abide by Japanese law. It was such a crazy night, and while she was angrily telling me this, all that I could see was the funny side, and I burst into laughter. Totally unamused, Lorraine became even more upset, especially about being dragged out of her warm, cosy bed at 5.30am on a bitterly cold wintry morning. I'd not been aware that such a law even existed. I sincerely apologised to Lorraine several times, but she adamantly refused to let it go. In her mind, it was a bad omen and a warning not to have anything more to do with me and my 'negative karma', as she so bluntly put it. Lorraine threatened to cut ties with me as soon as she'd fulfilled her commitment in helping me with my musical YOU. Sadly, for both of us, she'd completely overlooked the fact that it had been her own lousy karma to be awakened and dragged out of bed in the first place. From then on, Lorraine treated me as though I wasn't to be trusted. Having lived in Japan on and off for several years, I'd noticed that some of the older Japanese, including NS/SGI members, lacked a sense of humour, and that they were often inclined to take things far too seriously. Such an outcome was probably due to the horrors and terrible difficulties that they'd endured during and after WW2. Some of the elderly NS/SGI members mixed left-over elements of their previous beliefs and superstitions with Nichiren's teachings, which more often than not confused people and put them off, especially guests and new converts. Lorraine's superstitious overreaction that day was a typical example of this, but fortunately, by then, I'd learned enough about Nichiren's teachings not to be too affected. Reassessing it all philosophically now, and taking into account outcomes of other similar obstacles that I've since experienced, perhaps being arrested and missing out on the party that night was a blessing in disguise or a form of protection. For all I knew, the Russians may not have been who or what they said they were, and my life could have potentially been in peril.

Before leaving Japan, I took the tapes of YOU to the Tokyo Headquarters of SGI and played the songs to some of the senior leaders in charge. Keeping her promise, Lorraine accompanied me to interpret, but much to our surprise, except to say a few quick words to Lorraine in Japanese as we were leaving, the leaders showed very little interest and not even an ounce of support. Once we got outside, Lorraine explained to me that they weren't interested in my songs because they were not owned and controlled by the SGI, which was a big shame because if anyone had the know-how and connections to help make it happen, they certainly did. As we were leaving the headquarters, I spotted a bookshop and quickly popped in to buy some Buddhist literature to take with me to the UK. While I was browsing around to see what was on offer, I was suddenly taken aback when I came across an album with one of my songs on it that had been recorded by the famous SGI Fuji Orchestra and choir. It was a version of a song that I'd written for my musical YOU, and they'd included it on the album without either consulting me or asking for my consent. There were millions of deeply devoted members in Japan and many more members around the world. A large percentage of them full-heartedly supported anything that the organisation presented to them, and that meant the album had the potential of hundreds of thousands of sales. Apart from not receiving a penny in royalties, I hadn't even been credited as the writer or acknowledged in any other way – I was fuming inside, and I considered taking it further. The only thing that stopped me was my underlying feelings of gratitude towards the organisation for having been there when I was at my lowest, and for making it possible for me and so many other people around the world to hear and learn about Nam-Myoho-Renge-Kyo. In the end, I let it go, albeit feeling ripped-off and disrespected. That day I lost a lot of trust and confidence in the SGI hierarchy, and I now believe that it wasn't just by chance that I discovered that shop and had been drawn straight towards the record that contained my song *Sensei.* I'd written the song about Nichiren, but some of the Australian members had taken it upon themselves to send a copy of it to Tokyo SGI Headquarters, claiming that it was an anthem that they sang at their meetings in adoration of Daisaku Ikeda, whom they also referred to as Sensei. By the time that I found all this out, it was too late to do anything about it, so I just had to let that go as well – begrudgingly though it was. A lot of the organisation's leaders were forever reminding us that anything that we did for NS/SGI was not only a great honour but would come back to us threefold. Like the many other vulnerable members whose lives had been changed for the better since they'd been chanting, I was more than happy to do whatever I could to help promote NS/SGI.

ON THE EVENING before I left Japan to continue on with the final leg of my journey to the UK, I crossed paths with a dancer who'd only just arrived in Tokyo from Hong Kong the previous day. I'd never met her before, but she seemed to know most of the people that I knew, and while we chatted over a cup of coffee, I was horrified to learn that one of the women involved in spreading the vicious lies about me had since committed suicide, another was in a mental institution, and the Chung King Mansions witch-woman was in a hospice dying of cancer. The shocking news had left me feeling a mixture of shock, disbelief, regret and deep sadness, I'd never wanted revenge or to see any retribution, I'd only ever tried to encourage these women to heed my advice and to chant Nam-Myoho-Renge-Kyo, so that they could bring forth the wisdom and good fortune that they needed to change their harmful, destructive behaviour. There are so many people in the world who are completely oblivious or ignorant to the fact, that by saying, thinking and doing evil, they're actually deliberately or unwittingly feeding and cultivating the same evil that already exists within their own lives that's motivating them to do it. If the way that these women had treated me was anything to go by, and if that was their way of treating people in general, then they certainly hadn't done themselves, or their future happiness, any favours. To me, hearing this disturbing news was like a lesson displayed on a giant neon sign, depicting that we should always be consciously aware and careful of how we treat our fellow human beings, including what we think and say about them, as well as what we hear others say. Bad causes can quickly accumulate, and other people's karma can be just as infectious as a virus, especially if and when we believe or agree with something, without first verifying whether it's true or not. Such causes can sometimes accumulate and have seriously devastating future effects.

AFTER A short stop-over in Anchorage, a hop across the North Pole on another 747-Jumbo – this time with Zsa Zsa Gabor on board, and a darn good laugh at a new Woody Allen movie, I was finally stepping off the plane at London's Heathrow International Airport. The first thing that I noticed was London's trademark bright-red phone boxes and double-deck buses, swarms of black London cabs that reminded me of an intrusion of giant cockroaches, and rows of ancient buildings steeped in history, which fascinated me no end. And there wasn't a single skyscraper in sight. During my first few days in the UK, I visited the London offices of WEA/Leeds Music and played them my Tokyo recordings. After they'd listened to them two or three times, I was offered a spot the following week on the British TV show *New Faces*. My immediate response was...

"Umm... Thanks, but no thanks, I've done all that stuff back in Aussie years ago 'n' I haven't come all this way ta start at tha bottom all over again."

As the room went suddenly silent and frowns instantly replaced smiles, I was swiftly shown the door, never to be asked back again. What I hadn't known then, was that the UK 'New Faces' was nothing like the same show back home, where any amateur could get up and make a fool of themselves. The British version was hosted by professionals, and as I would later learn, there was a two-year waiting list just to get an audition date. When I realised that I'd foolishly turned down chance to appear on the show and be known throughout the UK within a week, I could have kicked myself all the way back to Australia. After I eventually tracked down the whereabouts of my producer-friend, Michael Barclay, I was shattered to learn that he had Alzheimer's disease, and was under twenty-four-hour security care in a nursing home on the outskirts of London. My floundering spirit was lifted up again when I met and shared a coffee and friendly chat with Dick Causton, who'd left his post in Japan to take up leadership of the organisation in the UK. It was wonderful to see him again – he always had a magic knack for making people feel better on the inside, even in times of sadness or concern.

DURING THE FIRST few weeks that I lived in London, I stayed at Holland Park with some Aussie friend's that I knew from back home until I eventually found a cheap room in a run-down hotel near Olympia. Masami arrived to join me a couple of days later and was soon able to find a job as a waiter in a small nearby Japanese restaurant. After competing against fifteen professional hairdressers, I was also able to win a position at a well-known London company called 'Wig Creations'. My duties were to shampoo and style pompadour wigs for the British television series *Edward VII*, as well as for another show currently on in London called *Joseph and the Amazing Technicolour Dreamcoat.* The Hollywood actress Marlene Dietrich regularly sent her day-wear wigs from New York Wig Creations, to have them shampooed and restyled, and one day, when I was asked to take care of one of her wigs, WW3 almost broke out. I took it upon myself to add a couple of inches to the height of her hairdo – she hit the roof, almost literally, sending it straight back with a letter of abuse to the company CEO. As a result, I almost got fired on the spot. My British bosses were pompous to the core and outrageously gay to the extreme. By the time that I'd resigned a few months later, they were close to pulling a lot of their own hair out in despair and needing wigs themselves. At our hotel, Masami and I became friends with a grubby middle-aged character named Freddy, who spoke with a strong European accent, was grossly overweight, a heavy chain smoker, and lived in a room that looked and smelt like a rubbish tip. Each time I tried to encourage Freddy to have a shower, he'd pull faces and react as though I'd asked him to get a tooth pulled without any anaesthetic. Freddy may have looked a proper mess, but he certainly knew a lot of influential people around town, including some dodgy folk on the dark side of London. He introduced me to a man named James, who was about to buy a trendy fashion boutique in Brighton on the south coast and who was looking for someone young and trendy to run the business. Freddy had thought that I'd be a perfect candidate for the job. My first meeting with James and his business partner took place in a small pub at the Elephant and Castle. I was officially interviewed for the position, which came with an excellent salary, a yellow sports car that I'd own after a year's service, and a rent-free apartment above the shop with great views of Brighton. I thought that it would do me perfectly while I was waiting to get on my feet musically, so when the job was offered to me, I eagerly accepted.

I'D BEEN CHANTING for over three years, and any past hang-ups that I'd had about my sexuality were virtually non-existent. Gone too were the gruesome feelings of suicide and low the self-esteem brought about by society's homophobic hatred and George's relentless abuse and brutality. The wisdom that I gained from Nichiren's teachings had helped me to develop a much brighter common-sense outlook and understanding of what life is truly all about, allowing me to feel as equally 'normal' as any heterosexual does. The heavy burden of guilt that I'd carried for most of my life due to past religious brainwashing had also been reduced to little more than a distant bad memory. I'd also come to realise that the previous misleading beliefs that I'd blindly tried to support and been taught to obey throughout my life were responsible for helping to bring about utter misery, hatred and confusion between people, as well as some of the most brutal, evil acts ever committed against humanity. Living in the UK where it was no longer against the law to be gay had given me a great feeling of freedom, but even so, there was still plenty of prejudice to deal with, as well as within the gay community itself. In some respects, it seemed that the more gays were being accepted, the meaner and more prejudiced some gays were becoming towards each other. To me, it didn't matter what a person's sexuality was, or what they look like, or anything else about them, I respected them with compassion and the dignity that they deserved. My new golden rule was always to consider the feelings and wishes of others and not to mislead, disrespect or make insincere promises to use anyone just for sex. Just around the corner from where the Buddhist discussion meetings were held in Notting Hill Gate was a well-known gay pub called *The Champion.* Along with some of the other Buddhists, I'd often pop in there for a drink and chat after the meetings – by then, I was able to enjoy a drink or two without losing control. I seemed to have developed a natural cut-off point where I could stop without any problem. It had also become apparent to me by then that my previous overindulgence in alcohol had been more a psychological problem rather than a physical addiction.

Ever since the Hippy Movement and the sexual revolution of the late 1960s, free love and promiscuity in the western world had become rampant. Apart from Syphilis, Hepatitis and Gonorrhoea, which were treatable, most sexually transmitted diseases were of little or no concern to most of us young's, making it a thriving free-for-all lifestyle for anyone who wanted it. I certainly wasted no time in becoming an active member of the highly promiscuous London gay scene, even though it had way more than its fair share of erratic ups and downs, pardon the pun. Some of the gays that I met at the Champion could be painfully kinky. One guy that I took home kept biting me until I couldn't stand it anymore, so I got up, made him a huge meat sandwich, and then asked him to munch on that for a while instead. He was still putting his pants on when he ran out the door. There were also others, who were into much weirder S&M, however, dangerous sex toys, flesh biting and drugs were never my 'thing', regardless of how sexy or good-looking a guy was. I also met my fair share of psychopaths, and some of them were so creepy-scary that they'd make my ding-dong deflate, and my pubes stand on end instead. In gay terms, I don't mind admitting to being 'vanilla'. Most straight people in the world automatically believe that all gays are into anal sex, but that's just silly. I belong to the small minority who prefer to abstain from anal sex, after all, there are plenty of other fun things to do which most people gay or straight do anyway. For many of us gays, even if we found someone compatible back then, we were more often than not unable to make a relationship work for longer than a few weeks or so. It was lust rather than love that seemed to take priority in our minds, and always thinking that there was something better out there and blindly flitting from one short relationship to another to find it. Deep within, I was looking for a commitment, but often the guys that I took more than a casual interest in didn't want to settle down, and those who did usually didn't interest me. For many gays, one-night-stands and hook-ups were as fleeting as a shooting star in the heavens, and any kind of genuine love or romance was virtually non-existent. Consequently, some of our love lives were an endless continuation of frustrations, disappointments and heartaches. My feelings for Masami resulted in all three on the list, with disappointment at the top, because he wasn't gay.

ONE MORNING, while I was having a coffee and reading the daily paper in the main bar of the Champion Hotel, a sudden chill came over me, and I could sense what felt like a seriously detrimental presence. It happened as I was glancing out across the bar area and saw streaks of *darkness* swirling around the patrons, which I thought was cigarette smoke, but after studying it more intently, the swirls appeared to be more like the waves that are visible when using infrared and ultraviolet cameras. Then, just like that, it instantly vanished! Alarm bells went off in my head that something wasn't right, and I was left feeling anxiously unsettled. From that day on, I tried my best to spread the word about Nam-Myoho-Renge-Kyo around the gay community to anyone who'd stop and listen. Years later, I'd start hearing the sad and devastating news about many of my old friends and acquaintances at the Champion, who were either HIV infected or dying from AIDS. It was then that it suddenly occurred to me that my strange vision and eerie feelings that that morning in the Champion had been about the oncoming onslaught of AIDS.

I WAS STROLLING down Park Lane towards Piccadilly Circus early one afternoon and bumped into the London CEO of Leeds Music, whom I'd been trying to get in touch with for weeks. I'd left the tapes of YOU with him to listen to, but he was always out or unavailable. I asked him point-blank if he'd listened to the recordings or read the storyline and all he did was wave his hands in the air as he hurried away, condescendingly grunting something about it not being suitable for the British market. All I'd ever expected from him was a little down-to-earth courtesy and consideration, but his pompous rudeness and disinterest that day left me feeling rejected and deflated. That night, I was suddenly awakened during the early hours by a nightmare about a man in a beige suit struggling in agony to breathe. The images in my dream had flashed on and off like a strobe light and had me feeling so disturbed and worried that I couldn't get back to sleep. I sensed deep within that there was a message in my dream, I pondered on it until daylight, but without coming up with any answers. The CEO of Leeds Music had worn a beige suit, but even so, I still couldn't figure out any connection. When I heard later the next day that he'd died of a heart attack in his office immediately after returning from lunch after bumping into me, it gave me a tremendous shock, and I wondered if my confrontation with him and his rude and negative response may have helped contribute to his death. I chanted for him to be at peace, and for a long time afterwards, refrained from taking the musical to anyone else to listen to – in case they didn't like it! Silly I know, and I now realise that his feelings of ill health could easily have been responsible for his rude response that day. Shortly after that, Masami left his job and took a live-in position at an upmarket Japanese restaurant in Piccadilly. At the same time, I moved out of the hotel and took a temporary live-in caretaker's job at a private school near Holland Park. It was an opportunity to save some money up while I was waiting to start work at the Brighton boutique. While the pay at the school was nothing to get excited about, and the tiny flat provided was only as big as an average small bedroom, at least it gave me the chance to save and was free. While there, I received the uplifting news that the Shakubuku Band had performed songs from YOU during the first-ever Australian NS/SGI Culture Festival, which was held on Queensland's Gold Coast. I also received news that the songs *Yellow Pony* and *Sensei*, from YOU, had been released at around the same time by WEA on a 45 single. Around the same time, the Buddhist members in the UK were talking about the forthcoming grand opening of a new European Nichiren Buddhist Centre in the south of France at a place called Trets. Each participating country was invited to present a thirty-minute show to celebrate the opening, and the UK members were still trying to decide on what they could perform for it. I put my hand up at one of the meetings and offered an edited twenty-minute condensed version of my musical YOU. After a barrage of differences of opinion and heated debating, a vote was finally cast, and my offer was accepted. During the following few weeks of rehearsals, I did whatever I could to help produce the show, but it didn't look like I was going to be able to attend the actual opening because of my new job in Brighton. As that day approached, I accidentally overheard my future bosses discussing the true underlying purpose of the boutique, which was to be a 'front' for drug dealing! Hearing this left me feeling utterly shocked and stunned! I knew right away that if they caught wind that I'd overheard them, my life could be in very grave danger, so when the men turned suddenly and spotted me, I pretended not to notice and gave them the impression that I was still searching the bar for them. I was feeling sick in the stomach from worry when I pulled out of the final rehearsals for the show – especially without giving anyone a reason or warning. Things then went from bad to worse, when the members of the production team became angry and annoyed at me, and then other members commenced giving me nasty looks. It was far too much of a risk to tell anyone the truth of the matter, and that I was being forced to let them down, in case one of them reported it to the police. These men were dangerous drug lords, so I just had to take it on the chin. When my predicament became more than I could cope with, I gave in and confided in my district leader, James Perry. After I told him that I couldn't see my way out of my obligation and would have to start the job, he anxiously disagreed and pleaded with me not to go ahead and do it, warning me that I'd be making a bad cause that would inevitably result in a future equally bad effect. I was already too far in to easily back out, and the risk of the owners getting suspicious and figuring out that I knew about their drug-dealing was terrifying me. When the commencement date for the job was unexpectedly put back a month, I took James' advice to join him and the others at the new centre in Trets. Everyone at the centre seemed to be having a really great time, but for me, it was fear and misery, and for the entire few days that I was there, I spent every spare minute chanting fervently for a solution to my dilemma.

The performances at the grand opening were a huge success and a French TV network team who happened to be there was so impressed with the UK's performance that they requested a repeat of it so that they could film it and broadcast it throughout France. The show's success should have been joyous news for me too, but those members who were still angry at me for deserting them and who kept looking at me with a barrage of unfriendly, cold and scowling faces, made it blatantly clear to me that I wasn't welcome. They even tried to keep the filming a secret from me, and they would have succeeded if it hadn't been for the two principal dancers who'd choreographed the show. Their sincere faith in the Mystic Law, above all else, and their gratitude towards me for writing the show for the UK members to perform, outweighed the selfishness and deceit of the others, even though, as far as I was concerned, they all had a perfectly good reason to feel the way that they did. Disgusted and upset over how I was deliberately left out, the dancers came and got me before the filming commenced, insisting that, of all people, it was me who deserved to be there. I was grateful for their kindness and support, and I felt no anger towards others. I'd probably have felt the same if I'd been them, but I had much more worrying things on my mind, which, for me, completely overshadowed any jubilation and excitement.

I ARRIVED BACK to London the next day and received a fantastic surprise and the best news that I could have possibly hoped for. The Brighton boutique had been taken off the market, and so too was the deal – my prayers had been answered, and I was free from any further commitment. It reminded me a lot of when I'd escaped a similar potential life-threatening fate in Hong Kong after I'd foolishly agreed to transport fake jewellery to India. Thankfully, I'd n come through unscathed yet again. I was aware that my life-threatening situation had been a manifestation brought about by the same negative karma in my life responsible for getting me into all my other similar messes, and I also understood that it was because of my sincere faith in the Mystic Law and my intense chanting to change my situation, which had brought forth the good karma that I needed to overcome my predicament. It's something that I've never taken for granted and I never will...

*Try to imagine there are two casks.*
*One of them contains clear liquid*
*and the other has mud sitting at its base.*
*Now, imagine placing a paddle into each cask*
*and stirring the liquids up.*
*While the clear cask would remain the same,*
*the cask containing mud would become murky.*
*Would paddle be responsible for this outcome*
*or the mud?*
*In a very similar way, each entity of life*
*contains within it an ever–changing, recorded history*
*of all its own past good and bad causes*
*and whenever something from the outside*
*stirs things up, the same result applies.*
*That's why it's so vitally important for each person*
*to take every opportunity to clean up their karma*
*and to bring forth the wisdom that will enable them*
*to avoid making further bad causes.*
*Blaming others or outside influences for the reactions*
*that take place within one's own life is as futile as*
*blaming the paddle or the mud contained within the*
*cask.*
*...Nichiren.*

# Chapter 31

# UFO - PREMONITIONS OR JUST A DREAM?

The man who'd offered me the Brighton boutique deal owned properties all over London. Because I'd left my job and given up my flat to work for him, he felt obliged to allow me to rent one of his empty bed-sitters on the Camberwell Road, at the Elephant and Castle. Apart from my place and the basement flat, the remainder of the old five-story building was boarded up to keep squatters out. Some of my Buddhist friends pitched in and helped me out with a bed, blankets, sheets, crockery and an assortment of cooking utensils, these things that I'd always taken for granted were suddenly vitally important to me. I was flat broke, out of work and had bugger all in the fridge to eat, but even so, I was far too proud to let anyone know about it or ask for help. It wasn't long before my hunger pangs became so strong that I was almost tempted to join the local drunks and tramps in the park across the road on their daily garbage-bin scrounge. Something within was periodically nagging at me to get to work and write a similar book about the teachings of Nichiren, to the story that I'd heard in Tokyo about Johnathon Livingston Seagull. I certainly had plenty of time on my hands, so I borrowed an old donated typewriter from the London Buddhist office and got stuck into it, and titled it 'Peter Kangaroo'. Typing my story down turned out to be quite a challenging task, as some of the keys on the old typewriter didn't work, making it necessary for me to manually press them onto the paper one by one. But there was a positive side to it all, my efforts and concentration and frustration not only kept me from going stir-crazy but helped to keep my mind off food. I was also aware that the effects of the bad karma that I'd previously avoided still needed to come out and be expiated in other ways, and that also helped me persevere. Realising that there's a lesson to be learned from everything, be it good or bad, I chanted stringently each day to bring forth the good fortune that I needed to overcome my adversities and to grow stronger and wiser as a result. My first encouraging signs of improvement happened when a Buddhist friend named Jean turned up in her quirky little three-wheeler car with a big sack of potatoes that she'd picked up along the M4 Motorway. I'd never been so happy to see a potato, or Jean, in my life! While we were hungrily devouring some of the freshly-cooked spuds, Jean mentioned that she wouldn't mind moving into the flat above me if it was at all possible. It was creepy living on the four upper floors all on my own, so I asked the owner who eventually agreed to let Jean move in. Having someone else around made a huge and very welcomed difference, as did Jean's fridge and stereo player, and it was so good to hear music echoing throughout the building for the first time. Day in and day out, as I struggled to type my book out on my trusty beaten-up typewriter and dined on my staple diet of potatoes, memories of my childhood experiences in the outback came floating back into my mind, portraying a perfect setting for my story. It was certainly no walk down easy street, as the trauma and disruptions that I'd endured during my school years had affected my ability to concentrate and comprehend, especially where literature was concerned. I knew what I wanted to say, but how to say it was always challenging. Nevertheless, I soldiered on regardless, full of determination and tenacity, as I kept reminding myself that nothing is impossible, nor was anything going to stop me so long as I could help it. Then things got even better! On Christmas Day, 1975, just as Jean and I were about to sit down to a plate of lovely fried potatoes and onion, a Spanish girlfriend of Jean's showed up of the blue with a big freshly-baked duck and fruit cake. I could have dressed her up as Santa Claus and kissed her! She, the duck and that magical Christmas lunch has remained among my fondest memories of living in London.

During the first week of 1976, my situation improved even more, when I found a job working as a cashier and pump attendant at a nearby petrol station. I'd never pumped petrol before in my life, but at that point, I was ready and willing to do just about anything to earn a wage. The hourly rate was a lot less than what I could have been earning back in Australia, but even so, it still felt fantastic to have an income at last. I filled in any spare moments at work by jotting down ideas for the book, and at night when I got home, I'd add them to the story. Any surplus money that I had each week, after paying the rent and my living expenses, would go on cheap carpet remnants and other bits and pieces from the nearby Camberwell Road Markets until I was eventually able to transform my sparsely furnished bedsitter into a cosy little colourful boudoir. On top of that, any green-stamp coupons that customers at the garage didn't want, I saved up and used to buy a much-needed fan-heater. Soon after that, I was able to rent a colour TV and fill my fridge and pantry with healthy, wholesome foods. Life was getting better and better, until the end of January, when the winter weather turned bitterly cold, and the flat suddenly presented more draughts than a brewery. In a desperate effort to try to keep some of the cold air out, I stuffed damp newspaper into every crack and crevice that I could find and soon had my place looking like the inside of a garbage container. It became too cold to sit still for long at the typewriter, so I rugged up in bed and made notes for the book with a torch under the blankets, while my little heater blew hot air down across the bed from a nearby side-table. During one of my under-the-covers writing sessions, I drifted off and had another mysterious dream. This time I found myself floating up very close behind the tail of a jet airliner as it was taking off. As I observed, I was gently bombarded by masses of specks that looked like translucent particles churning out of the engines as they propelled the plane into the air. Next, I was watching a helicopter flying by, only instead of pushing, it was pulling itself along with its blades acting like arms swimming through the tiny particles. Once the plane and helicopter had faded into the distance, I wondered how flying saucers might function, and in the next instant, one was sitting in a field right in front of me! The craft was made up of two silver saucer-shaped discs that fitted perfectly together face to face – one of the discs spun clockwise and the other spun anti-clockwise. Each disc had three large holes across its inner surface, and I somehow understood that the energy being generated and released from the holes in one disc was simultaneously absorbed magnetically and utilised by the holes in the other disc, as a self-perpetuating power source. I didn't see any windows, but when I moved up closer, I was surprised to discover that the exterior wasn't silver at all, it was a rusty-reddish colour, and on its upper surface were thousands of grooves that stretched around its circumference, similar to a vinyl record. Next, I was inside observing a large circular recess that seemed to be the craft's centre area. Everything appeared to be made out of something similar to aluminium or stainless steel, and there were hieroglyphic symbols that appeared to be touch-control pads embedded into the crafts inner wall surface. As I was observing all this, a message was conveyed to me from where, I do not know, stating that the technology was capable of producing its own gravity and a balanced artificial environment that could be maintained regardless of speed or direction. I wondered what the source of this power could be, and the immediate answer was 'neutron energy'. Straight after that, I awoke to wonder what on earth a 'cosmic neutron' was. Unable to come up with an answer, I hurried upstairs and asked Jean if she could shed any light on it. We both understood what cosmic meant, but like me, Jean had no idea what a neutron was, so she went to a box and pulled out an old English dictionary that she'd inherited and was keeping, in the hope that it would one day become valuable. Flicking through the pages, it was stated in the dictionary that a neutron was a form of cosmic energy that some scientists believed existed but hadn't at that point been able to identify. It appeared to be a similar situation to the present day mystery regarding Dark Matter. Still lost in a maze of thoughts about my dream, I returned to my bed and trusty heater to warm back up and soon fell off to sleep. Later that day, I was doodling on a pad and found myself jotting several things down as random thoughts popped in and out of my mind. After waking up, still sitting on my sofa with the pen in my hand, I read what I'd written and was horrified. In fact, I couldn't believe that I'd written it. Some of what I'd written not only scared the living daylights out of me but made me feel quite nauseous. In my notes, I'd described YouTube to a 'T', secret bases on the Moon that belonged to the US, China and Europe, and several dark and negative things that I'd never even imagined before, including gloomy, terrifying predictions for the future of the world and its inhabitants. Among my notes, I'd written that humankind would eventually be able to transfer people's brainwaves onto a screen and view their thoughts to expose their hidden secrets, and what takes place during their transition from life to death and beyond. My 'jottings' also revealed that, in the future, if people became incurably ill or too old and costly to maintain or were unable to look after themselves, they'd be instantly terminated by way of electromagnetic technology. In other words, atoms that make up the body, or anything else physical, would be instantly dissembled at the flick of a switch, so to speak, and would end up a pile of fine dust. Although some cancers and other 20th century ailments would be curable, far worse diseases would arise and take their place. One such disease would destroy all living body cells within a matter of days, causing an agonising death. I'd also written that a future global epidemic would cause bleeding from the eyes, mouth and ears, while the body rapidly degenerated within a matter of hours, and that there'd be many worse diseases brought about by human-induced neutron energy exposure, and that they'd spread like wildfire, but without any detailed explanations as to what they would be. There were the usual predictions of increasing record-breaking earthquakes, droughts, floods, cyclones, fires, killer tornadoes, and warnings that some of the disasters would eventually destroy whole cities and leave the land barren and reduced to waste, all brought about through the direct effects or side-effects of neutron energy. Prompted by some of what I'd written, in the following days, I proceeded to write a fictitious short story about a French-made 'neutron aircraft' going out of control and crashing in India, with catastrophic results. The 'saucer-shaped' craft had been designed by way of reverse engineering after an abandoned alien spacecraft had been found in the jungle somewhere near New Guinea. The initial explosion of the French-made craft had triggered off an ongoing neutron storm that turned everything in its path to dust. It also caused the earth's magnetic field and gravitational pull to become damaged to the point where everything in the storm's path, living, inanimate, water and air, was dragged into outer space from the earth's crust, leaving the surfaces of the lands grey and barren – similar to the surface of the moon. Avoiding the worst of the upheaval, several of the world's elites, including renowned scientists, doctors, politicians and other influential leaders – most of whom were fully or partially responsible for the destructive outcome, manage to escape to the moon, using a neutron-powered spacecraft.

Soon after, they continue onward towards a previously discovered planet resembling Earth that had never been physically visited. During the long and tedious journey to reach it, they watched some of the video clips that they'd previously chosen to ignore, which were made by citizens concerned about the dangerous situation the world was in. These visions of the future in my story described YouTube to a 'T', which didn't exist until decades later. In the end, I put the whole thing down to the negative side of my imagination. However, it left me with an overbearing feeling that if the ailing situation in the world didn't improve quickly, especially where people's attitudes are concerned, what I'd imagined could one day come to pass. Since that time, several new dangerous viruses have arisen in the world, including AIDS and Ebola, which matches some of my fictitious story, as well as coronaviruses such as SARS, Bird and Swine flu. I now believe that some dreams are like presents that keep us wondering until we open them to reveal what's inside. In other words, the hidden underlying message doesn't become apparent until it becomes a reality. More recently I've wondered if neutron energy could end up being related to CERN or something similar.

WHILE CHANTING to try to clear my mind of these disturbing images my thoughts switched to an entirely different subject, and I found myself recalling when I'd worked at my brother, Denis' company in Australia, and how I'd never felt comfortable there. My job had been to trek around the working-class suburbs of Sydney, to knock on doors of unsuspecting, lonely homemakers, while their husbands were away at work, and then to retrieve as much personal information about their financial circumstances that I could get them to reveal. Amazingly, most of the women were more than happy to spill the beans about everything that I asked. Not every Australian family had a car in the 1970s, let alone a second one for the wife, so a lot of these women were like prisoners stuck in their meagre dwellings. Some of them were pining for someone new to talk to, especially a receptive young man. After I'd ticked the appropriate boxes and passed on their information to my office, the clerks would do a credit check, and those that fitted the necessary criteria would be visited by a company salesman who'd show them irresistible linens, tablecloths, towels, sheets and other exciting wares to brighten their otherwise dull lives. Sadly, most of these women would succumb to the temptations on offer and sign up for the excessively overpriced goods without the knowledge or approval of their hardworking husbands, and without considering any of the possible future consequences. If any of those women went beyond their means and were unable to afford to keep up the repayments, their husbands' employers would potentially get served with a court order to deduct the money owing from the men's wages, which often resulted in a furious row and a potential beating for the wife in the presence of their traumatised children.

Such an outcome would stem from the initial cause, and I couldn't escape from the fact that I was it. Until then, I'd never understood how my day-to-day workplace actions could have ongoing consequences in such a way, let alone that I was responsible. One thing was becoming increasingly apparent to me, my chanting was awakening something from deep within for the first time, which was prompting me to question and analyse everything in my life from a very new and different perspective. I thought about other things, including how sometimes people's lives end up in a mess, after everything that they've worked so hard for in one way or another goes down the drain for some reason or another. I wondered if it could have something to do with how they earn their living – even if they're unaware of it. I recalled how I'd read articles about how some companies, including banks and well-known religious groups, invest money into the production of arms and other similar negative causes, and it reminded me of something significant that Nichiren had taught...

*If the breadwinner of a family makes his or her living by stealing, then all those who benefit from those earnings are unwittingly or otherwise thieves also.*

Suddenly everything seemed to fit into place and make so much more sense to me, and as I chanted fervently and apologetically with sincere regret in my heart for any woman who'd had problems that I'd helped to cause, a wave of overwhelming feelings of anxiety and shame came over me.

ONE EVENING, just before closing time at the petrol station, I served petrol to a customer who mentioned how he was feeling worn out because he'd just finished an all-day rehearsal. Curious to know more, I asked him what he'd been rehearsing for, and when he told me he was an agent that specialised in musicals, I couldn't resist telling him that I'd written a rock musical based on Buddhism. His initial reaction was favourable, and he invited me to bring my manuscript to his home the following day. That night I could hardly sleep from excitement, and although it turned out that the agent wasn't in a position to help me after all, he was able to introduce me to a couple of actors. One of them was an actor/dancer named Christopher, who'd had parts in several well-known movies and theatrical productions. The agent mentioned that Christopher had only just arrived back in the UK from Lebanon, after enduring a gruelling one-month prison term for possession of drugs, and that he'd been forced to eat raw sheep heads to survive. He'd also let Christopher know that I'd written a musical and said that he was eager to meet me and hear all about it. On his way home later that night, with his best friend Ray at the wheel, Christopher casually mentioned that he'd met a singer from Australia who'd written a rock musical...

"Oh, you don't mean Mister Tommy Beaumont, do you?" Ray haphazardly asked with a chuckle. When Christopher answered, *yes*, and wanted to know how Ray knew, a shocked Ray almost ran his car off the road from the unexpected reply.

I'd known Ray in Hong Kong, and like me, he was a singer with a severe drinking problem. I'd not seen or heard from him since I'd first left Hong Kong to go to Japan, and when I returned a year later and tried to find him to tell him about Nam-Myoho-Renge-Kyo, Ray was no longer anywhere to be found. Someone later told me that Ray and his family had moved back to the UK, so I'd given up searching. I could hardly believe my eyes when I answered the door the next morning and found Christopher standing on the front porch with Ray by his side. For the first few seconds, Ray just stared up at me, trying to make out if it was really me, but once the penny dropped, he couldn't stop talking about how different I looked. I told him that chanting Nam-Myoho-Renge-Kyo had helped me to awaken the strength I needed from within to turn my life around. He had no idea what I was talking about, but he was still super-keen to try the chant himself. Christopher, on the other hand, being Irish and Catholic, didn't want anything to do with it, but when Ray received an unexpected benefit a few days later that he believed was a result of his chanting, Christopher soon changed his mind and asked if he could join in and do some chanting with us as well. As time marched on, Ray, Christopher and I became quite a tight-knit team, regularly chanting together in a shared effort to change our lives for the better. We were all gay, but our relationship with each other was purely platonic, and for most of the time, we got along like a house on fire, sharing many happy hours of fun and laughter, socialising and sometimes even performing together.

ONE NIGHT A friend gave me a large alarm clock he no longer needed after I'd mentioned that I didn't have one. On my way home on the bus, it ticked so loudly that I became anxious that people might think that I had a bomb on-board (those were the days that the IRA were very active in London). Early the next morning, I was awakened not by the clock but a barrage of thunderous banging on the main front door downstairs. I suspected that it was Christopher and Ray messing about, but when I opened the door and was greeted by two big Scotland Yard detectives, who were thrusting their ID cards in my face, my legs almost gave way beneath me. The first thing I thought of was the clock on the bus, and that they were from the bomb squad. It turned out to be a routine check after the cops had noticed that the boarded-up building had people living in it. After asking me some personal questions, they informed me that there'd been a brutal murder in my building a year earlier and that a previous tenant had been shot to death on the stairs. It came as a shock, but at least it finally explained why only half the walls were newly painted and why only a small section of the stairway had new carpet. Crawling back up the stairs and into my bed, I was still shaking...

"What a mongrel of a way ta start a day off!" I mumbled to myself as I snuggled back up and tried to erase it all from my mind and go back to sleep.

During the weeks that followed, and I continued working hard at the petrol station, saving every spare penny that I could, I was soon able to buy an old Vauxhall Velox sedan. What a great feeling it was to be mobile again.

# Chapter 32

# DRAGS, DRUGS AND CRAZY HOTEL GUESTS

Ray and a couple of his musician friends, had formed a band, and they all rehearsed acoustically several nights a week in Ray and his wife's living room. After I popped in one night to have a jam, they asked me if I'd like to join the band. I was reluctant to say yes, but after Ray convinced me that he'd be able to get us plenty of work via a London agent friend of his, I agreed to join as an experiment. Ray and his family lived in London's East End, and because I was spending a lot of time at his house rehearsing, I accepted Ray and his wife's invitation to move in with them and their two young sons. It was a kind gesture on Ray's wife's part, but it was soon apparent that Ray wanted me there for support when the truth came out to his family about the lie that he'd been living. He'd only married his beautiful wife to hide his true sexuality from his dad, who was a high-ranking British Air Force officer and a domineering homophobe. Ray's pretentious marriage had produced two lovely sons, but he felt mentally exhausted and fed up with trying to be someone that he wasn't. It turned out that Ray had been planning to 'come out of the closet' and to be who he really was ever since his father had died earlier that year. One day, Ray's wife stumbled out from their bedroom looking shattered and crying uncontrollably. Ray had broken the news about their phoney marriage, and she ended up suffering a complete nervous collapse. I had to hold her down until an ambulance arrived, and hearing her two little boys cry their eyes out as their mother was being strapped onto a stretcher and carried away screaming, felt like a knife ripping into me. It went deeper still when I saw Ray curled up in a corner, broken-hearted and sobbing. The family's pain and suffering should never have existed in the first place, and it filled me with so much disgust and anger that my blood was close to boiling...

"When are all these self-righteous, homophobic, bigots ever gonna learn ta mind their own fuckin' bus'ness an' let people be who they are?" I inwardly growled – my veins almost bursting with my immense frustration and anger.

As I was helping Ray up onto a chair, the vibrations of his tormented soul shot up my arms like a stream of electricity bolts, and as I also tried to comfort the two sons, I shuddered within at the thought of how many other young kids and their mothers are forced to suffer like Ray's family. The many wives, who don't have their love reciprocated by the covertly gay men that they marry only to end up like Ray's poor wife, alone, devastated and with their life in tatters, all thanks to beliefs tainted with evil and based on cruelty, ignorance and stupidity in the name of a so-called 'loving God'. It still breaks my heart to think about how many gay people's lives are being ruined every day because they're forced to suppress who they truly are and live under the idiotic rules that are enforced by these cruel, destructive and illogical believers of lies. Those evil-minded hypocritical 'do-gooders' of this world, who proclaim that this 'loving God' of theirs condemns gays, are in my opinion, among some of the lowest. Then there are the ignorant and thoughtless parents who make degrading, cruel, brainless jokes about gay's, foolishly convinced that by doing this and brainwashing their kids into believing that being gay is a dirty and evil sin, it will magically deter their child from turning out gay. Thank goodness there are now 'true-life-story' movies available such as 'Prayers for Bobby', starring Sigourney Weaver, and 'Boy Erased', starring Nicole Kidman, each presenting an educated example of the harm that's being caused to youth by such anti-gay, religious propaganda. When I think about how many gay people are forced or driven into taking their own lives when this erroneous nonsense is pushed down their throats, it astonishes me that nothing has been done legally to stop it happening. In my mind, it's nothing short of murder committed in the name of a loving God! One thing for sure, there certainly wasn't anything 'loving' about the way that Ray and his family had their hearts and lives torn apart that dreadful day, it was nothing short of demonic. That unforgettable day also marked the end of my stint with Ray and his band.

CHRISTOPHER, the actor, got me a gig in Plymouth working as the male singer in a popular drag show called *Les Girls.* I was allowed to have a feature spot of six songs of my own choice, but my primary role was to mingle with the 'shemales' and sing the male parts to their songs. It was very different from anything that I'd ever done before, and I was more than keen to give it my best shot and hopefully conquer the challenge. In those days, Plymouth was a hugely popular meeting place for sailors, prostitutes, trannies and highly-promiscuous gays. Working with the drag queens turned out to be another educational eye-opener, especially having to squeeze my way through the dressing room before showtime each night. It was like competing in a dangerous obstacle course, with whopping big false rubber tits poking out at me from everywhere, and badly-aimed hairspray shooting like bullets from all directions – all amidst deafening screams of joy, anger or frustration, and it was like 'Priscilla, Queen of the Desert' on acid. Some of the awkward and bulky costumes that the drag queens wore, often had me being pushed and shoved from one side of the tiny stage to the other. By the end of the night, I'd have bumps and bruises all over me. On top of everything else, some of the queens were aggressive, competitive, jealous and hell-bent on having noisy bitching sessions – or even cat-fights. Whenever that looked like happening, I'd be out of their way quick and smart, yet even though it was like working in a loony bin, more than anything else, it was also a load of pretentious good fun, well, for a while, anyway. My popularity soon overtook that of the highly egotistical drag star, Chris Shaw, who ran the show, and he cut my solo performance down to just one song. When that failed to work, and the audience demanded to hear me sing more songs, Chris became furious and fired me, because according to him, I didn't 'suit the show format' anymore. The other drag queens got together and voted to go out on strike, but I talked them out of it, after explaining that Chris's unfair dismissal would surely have its 'effect', which came much sooner than any of us could have imagined. Each night, when the show ended, Chris' routine was to slide down a banister for the grand finale. That night he lost his grip and crushed his 'family jewels', and his painful, bellowing scream of horror could even be heard high above the band and without a mic'. Of course, there was no real 'proof of connection' to what he'd done to me, but it certainly seemed like instant karma to everyone in the show, and it was also an important lesson to be heeded by all of us on the rewards of being deliberately and unjustly unkind to others. I wasn't unemployed for long, on the day after being fired, I was approached by Ronny Potter, the owner of a strip and drag club, called Diamond Lil's, a few doors further down the road, heard about what had happened and invited me to perform there, which I happily accepted. When a lot of the regulars from Les Girls began to defect to Diamond Lil's to see me sing there, Chris Shaw became furiously frustrated and offered me the full three months' pay that I'd have received had I continued working for him, plus a bonus to leave Plymouth immediately and go back to London. I turned him down flat, walked the other way and continued performing on the Plymouth and Cornwall circuits for another six weeks.

PROMISCUITY was rife in Plymouth, and I happily joined in and indulged in plenty of casual sex with various guys there. I even had women hitting on me, and one of them was a beautiful, sexy stripper who knew I was gay but still relentlessly pursued me. She had a handsome young sailor chasing after her, and after she overheard me telling one of the drag queens that I thought the sailor was 'hot stuff', she secretly agreed to have sex with him, but only if he'd agree to a threesome completed by me. We all got tangled up in a very volatile and awkward situation, and the poor stripper finished up lying beside the bed on the floor alone. The grand finale came when the 'very Catholic' sailor knelt beside her in guilt and begged God to forgive him for enjoying sex with a man, even though, under the rules of his beliefs and indoctrination, he'd have 'sinned' by being with a woman out of wedlock anyway.

I spent my final night in Plymouth celebrating my departure with my friend Christopher and a few other close mutual friends at a bar I frequented most nights after show-time. At the bar, I bumped into a heterosexual sailor friend who'd had one too many drinks, so I offered him a lift home. Christopher was 'out of it' as well, and I had to half carry him from the club and then lift him on to the front seat of my car. The sailor was following closely behind and climbed into the back seat. Shortly after we began driving off, the sailor recognised that it was Christopher in the front seat and a violent fight broke out between them. I hadn't been aware that the pair even knew one another, let alone hated each other. They were going at it tooth and nail – literally – with hair, skin, blood, pieces of wig, torn clothing, sequins and buttons flying in all directions, and my car was copping the brunt of it. The sailor had Christopher around the neck and was trying to yank him back over the seat, and Christopher was making a hysterical attempt to escape from his grip, by kicking in my dashboard. I slammed on the brakes, jumped out the car and tried to save both Christopher and my car by attempting to separate the conflicting pair, and almost had a finger bitten off in the process. Fortunately for all concerned, two big coppers who happened to be parked nearby, quickly intervened and dragged them both out, but not before my poor car and finger had suffered some severe and very painful damage. To add to my dilemma, my savings had been stolen from my room the night before, and I didn't have enough money to pay for the repairs and was forced to borrow the £100+ from a friend to get my car fixed so that I could return in it to London.

ON THE DAY that I got back to London, I found a share-flat, a job, a new agent and a cute and cuddly guy to keep me company for the night. My job entailed managing an old, ran down terrace-style hotel called *Robert House*, which conveniently stood directly opposite Hyde Park and the towering Royal Lancaster Gate Hotel (Now known as the London Elizabeth Hotel). The Robert House owner was serving time in prison for running a brothel in one of his other hotels and had put all of his properties into the care of his three sons, with his youngest, in charge of Robert House. Derrick was a twenty-five-year-old Adonis, and he didn't hold back in flaunting it. While he was a nice enough bloke to talk to most of the time, he could also be challenging and unpredictable, owing to his heroin addiction. Sometimes he'd become almost impossible to cope with, especially if he needed cash to buy more drugs and there wasn't any available – which was every other day and then some. Derrick would often creep into the office late at night and steal whatever was in the kitty, leaving us with no funds to run the hotel the next day. There were two other people working for me full time, plus some casual staff who'd help out whenever I needed them, but because of Derrick's expensive addiction, staff members were often not paid on time, and would usually 'down tools' and refuse to work, leaving me to do everything.

MY NEW booking initially agent gave me a list of gigs that were on the outskirts of London. Her policy was to start all new artists on her books in the more remote areas and then book them into more prestigious venues in and around London proper if and when they'd proven themselves worthy. I was fortunate enough to make the London grade within a couple of weeks. At the time, platform boots were the latest trend and all the rage, so in my usual 'I'll outdo everybody' fashion, I went shopping and bought myself a pair of the most extravagant and outrageous boots that I could find for my London debut. I could barely stand up in them, let alone walk, and that night, members of the band had to lay down their instruments to hold me up and then guide me to the microphone stand on stage, which I clung to for the entire show, for fear of falling over. When I'd finished my show, just as awkwardly, I had to be helped back off stage and into the dressing room – the band and audience just about wet themselves laughing. Being the hotel's manager meant that I had to be present whenever large groups of guests arrived, especially from the Continent. This usually happened two or three nights a week, and their planes were seldom running on time, which in turn, made me regularly late for my shows. Even though performing in London in the thick of it was a great opportunity and pleasure, so too was the hotel a huge responsibility, but a rent-free flat and a wage of over a hundred pounds in my pocket each week, which, for the UK, was pretty healthy dough back then, made it all worthwhile. When things got too out of hand and I eventually had to choose between my singing career or the stability and security of my position at the hotel, the hotel was the winner. At my final gig before taking a break from singing to manage the hotel, I was approached out-of-the-blue by two talent scouts from *Safari Records*, who repeatedly offered me a contract to record some love songs for international release. I was extremely tempted, but I ended up turning their offer down. I was going through a silly phase of wanting to sing songs exclusively about world peace. The scouts almost pleaded with me to change my mind, but I stuck to my guns, until they gave up trying, withdrew their offer, and left me missing out on another potentially great opportunity.

I WENT ON TO MANAGE Robert House for about two years after that, and what an outrageous and eye-opening two years it turned out to be. The bills never got paid on time, the telephone and power were disconnected on a regular basis, the laundry company refused to clean the linen, because they hadn't been paid, and on at least two occasions, there was no central heating in the middle of winter. On top of all that, the rented television got taken away and returned almost every other month, again, all due to non-payment. These things would often take place when the hotel was full of guests, and while I can have a laugh about it all now, there was nothing at all funny about it at the time. It really was a major drama, especially spending days on end at the local laundrette, washing dozens of sheets, towels and tablecloths, and getting abused by angry people who were waiting to use the machines that I was monopolising. Back at the hotel, I'd cop another lot of abuse from angry guests, demanding their money back that I wasn't able to give to them. Sometimes Derrick would be so smacked-out on heroin that he'd forget that he'd already sneaked off with the hotel takings and come back for more, usually, in the middle of the night. He'd wake me up and abusively accuse me of taking the money, after which, I'd tell him to go and get stuffed, or worse, and then quit. As regular as clockwork, Derrick would be back first thing the following day, apologising and begging me to stay – it was like an ongoing ritual. I tried many times to get him to chant, but he wouldn't have a bar of it. Because of Derrick's midnight robberies, at breakfast, the staff and I would often be hiding in the kitchen, arguing over whose turn it was to go out and ask a dining room full of hungry guests to pay more money so that we could shop for food for their breakfasts, which they'd already paid for.

The hotel manager before me had reached the end of his rope and walked out, after destroying the records of prepaid guest bookings, and I'd inherited that nightmare as well. One Friday night when the hotel was almost full, a thirty-piece orchestra, who'd prepaid months earlier, all showed up at once demanding their rooms, and it took me until well after midnight to fit as many of them in as I could and to find alternative accommodation for those that I couldn't. I then had to be up at the crack of dawn to make everyone breakfast. The orchestra's agreement stated that they were to have full use of the dining room between 6.00am and 7.00am for rehearsals, and the looks of disbelief on the faces of the other guests as they were all lined up waiting to get in for their breakfasts that morning was priceless – especially when they were subjected to *God Save the Queen* and *There'll Always Be an England* several times over. I was almost literally pissing myself laughing, and by the time the band had finished playing, my eyes were starting to pop out. About a month or so later, the same thing happened again when forty big, butch, macho, muscle-studs, who'd also prepaid for their rooms, turned up from a sporting club, and again when I didn't have enough rooms or beds to accommodate them all, and neither did anyone else nearby. They thought that I was joking when I asked some of them to sleep two to a single bed. As a last resort,

I was forced to hire twenty-five foldaway beds to prevent the 'tough guys' from rioting.

MY MAINTENANCE man Enzo's life revolved around alcohol, drugs, Rock 'n' Roll, smoking pot, drinking more than he could handle and listening as much as he could to the band *Thin Lizzy*. I tried to get him to chant, but like Derrick, he wasn't the least bit interested. As much as I'm ashamed to admit it now, we all got up to some very unethical antics back then in that hotel, including leaving the intercoms switched on in the rooms so that we could listen in on the good looking guests. On some days we'd take turns at the central receiver, flitting from room to room for hours on end doing our illegal eavesdropping. We'd either be sexually aroused, shocked to our toenails or tickled pink to the point of painful, uncontrollable laughter. One night, while we were listening to an older businessman sweet-talking his pretty-faced young male lover, we choked on our laughter when the young man shouted back...

"Just look at the disgusting state of this place – what the hell do you think I am – a cow?"

It was the way that he said it that cracked us all up and we were laughing about it on and off and calling each other a cow for days. We each had a very twisted sense of humour, but mine seemed to be the twistedest. On another night, I put 50 sausages under the grill and left them on a low setting to half-cook for breakfast. When the staff talked me into going to a disco with them, and I forgot to switch off the sausages, mere words cannot describe the expressions of disbelief on everyone's faces when we came back and found the black, cremated mess still smouldering, I was lucky that I didn't burn the hotel down! I was never able to muster up the courage to accept responsibility, so another much-talked-about mystery was added to an already long list of weird and scandalous Robert House unsolved mysteries. No matter what theories or explanations were suggested, nobody could come up with a logical reason for someone wanting to break into the kitchen just to turn all the sausages into charcoal. Well nobody except Enzo, who kept insisting that it was the doings of one of the gay guests to symbolically let us know what he or she thought of the place. When Derrick heard about it, he instructed Enzo to install a new smoke detector in the kitchen without delay. Maybe the lingering smell of the burnt sausages had something to do with it, as normally Derrick wouldn't spend a penny on the hotel, but on this occasion, the prospect of losing his cash-cow money tree was what probably motivated him to take action. I can't tell you how many times I accidentally set the new fire alarm off while burning toast late at night for midnight snacks. Arabs in their nightcaps and long white robes, half-naked prostitutes, quivering drag queens clinging tightly to their precious possessions and wigs, as they were all hurriedly making their ways down the stairs to escape into the street, was always an outrageously hilarious sight to see. I'd either be hiding and watching from my room through a slightly-opened door or the windows, splitting my sides from outbreaks of excruciatingly painful laughter. Watching the guests gathered outside on the street, teeth chattering and their skin turning blue from the bitter cold, while they were all staring up at the hotel searching for where the fire was, made me laugh so hard sometimes that I thought it was going to kill me.

DERRICK PLACED an advertisement in a gay magazine for Robert House, and in no time at all, the hotel gained the reputation of being a gay whorehouse. Many of the colourful and shameless guests that responded to the ad and came to the hotel in droves were kinky, perverted sex maniacs. Derrick even allowed druggies, dealers, prostitutes, pimps, thugs and heaven only knows what other sorts of dubious characters to use the hotel at will. Among other crazy things, it was nothing unusual to arrive back from a night out to find people up on ledges climbing in and out of windows throughout the building. On one overly warm night when I left my window wide open, an Adonis climbed through and hopped into bed with me – I could hardly believe my luck, eyes, or any of my other bits for that matter. After that remarkable night of what turned out to be sheer bliss, I left my window open every night until autumn arrived and my teeth began chattering, but much to my disappointment, nothing like it ever happened again. After a lot of begging and sucking up from my staff member, Terrance, who was far too handsome, sensual and flirtatious to say easily no to, I gave in and agreed to let him use the dining room for his birthday party, and almost a hundred people showed up. Within no time at all, the situation grew completely out of control, and guys were kissing, cuddling, fondling and munching on each other everywhere you looked, including beneath the staircases and even in the linen closets. I tried to sort it out, but it was an impossible task, so, in the end, I gave up trying and took one of them to bed with me instead. The aftermath of our all-night romp didn't go down too well with the highly disgruntled straight hotel guests, who kept on bending our ears for days about the disgraceful 'carryings-on', as many of them angrily put it. The hotel resembled a garbage dump and the clean up took us almost a week to accomplish. I know it all sounds disgusting, but that's how things were back then in one way or another, especially where all-night parties were concerned for many of my generation, both gay and straight.

MOST OF MY live-in staff was chanters, and it was quite common to hear the sound of Nam-Myoho-Renge-Kyo resonating throughout the building, while the guests were left guessing about what the noise was. No one ever seemed too bothered by it, thank goodness, except when a cute, young gay deaf-mute arrived to stay at the hotel and birthday boy Terrance went instantly gaga over him. The guests hearing impediment wasn't going to stop Terrance from trying to teach him to chant and to help enable the young man to hear the words of the chant, Terrance took him up to his fifth-floor attic room and repeatedly shouted Nam-Myoho-Renge-Kyo at the top of his voice through his synthesiser amplifier at full volume. Amazingly, the guest heard it, and so too did I, loud and clear down in the hotel's basement, as I envisaged thousands of people all over London wondering what the hell was going on and ducking for cover. I couldn't stop laughing about that thought for days. Some of the regular guests frequenting Robert House were married women who'd come to London to work the streets until they'd made enough money to pay their bills back home, and some would even bring their husbands and children with them for a little holiday. Businessmen would sometimes come from out of town to shack up at the hotel with their young male or female lovers, using a room for only a couple of hours, which meant that Derrick would make double, sometimes triple, the regular daily room charge. This never failed to put a smile on his face. There were also threesomes, foursomes, and even the occasional wild orgies, and one never knew what was going to happen next. For me, it was an eye-opening walk on the wild side of British family life, and although my outlook where sex was concerned was more liberal than most, I still maintained an ethical and moral code. As long as paedophilia, rape, violence, bestiality, or anyone being forced to do anything against their will, wasn't involved, it was none of my business. Amid all the craziness, Derrick would sometimes do the rounds and give the staff pot to smoke. I'd only ever tried it out once or twice, but because I'm super-sensitive to some medications and drugs, it usually had a bizarre and scary effect on me. One day, to help keep Derrick in his unusually happy mood, I joined in and had a few puffs, but that wasn't enough, Derrick insisted that I puff on it more and more, and it wasn't long before I was so stoned that I forgot about whom and where I was. I also forgot all about a group of guests that were due to arrive that afternoon from America. When the loud doorbell rang, none of us could figure out what the noise was at first, we were all 'somewhere else'. After the 'penny had finally dropped' I dragged myself up the stairs, opened the door and merrily invited the guests into the foyer, but as soon as they were all inside, I suddenly lost it and burst into a fit of loud, uncontrollable laughter. I can still vaguely recall flashes of their angry faces as they yelled abuse at me, but I can't remember a single word that they were saying. When Enzo followed me up the stairs to see what all the loud noise was, and he saw me twisted up in a heap on the floor, laughing myself silly, he fell down laughing hysterically as well. The Americans all left in a huff, never to be heard from again. Unaware that I was an Aussie, they probably went away telling their folks back home that 'the Brit's were a bunch of loonies LOL.

DURING THE MONTHS that followed, I allowed myself to slacken in my faith again after becoming obsessed with my staff member, Terrance. He and I had indulged in sex a few times, and I'd foolishly become besotted and convinced that we were at the start of a potential relationship. As I'd learn later, Terrance had been leading me on for a purpose, and when I'd over responded and by the time he told me that he didn't feel the same way and couldn't reciprocate my feelings for him, my infatuation was already way out of control. His unexpected rejection hit me so hard that I couldn't think straight, let alone do my job and run the hotel. The fiasco reached a showdown after it became apparent that Terrance had taken advantage of my self-inflicted vulnerability to steal my job as the hotel manager. I was so devastated that I couldn't even argue about it. I packed some things, left the hotel and went straight to a shared flat, where I'd kept a room in case of emergencies. Finding it too painful and challenging to cope with while being on my own, and repeatedly churning over what Terrance had done, I took a shower, got dressed and went to a gay bar in Shepherd's Bush that I frequented regularly. While there, I drank several GT's to try to lessen the hurt and began to feel remorseful about walking out on Terrance. I phoned the hotel to see if he was coping okay, and when Enzo, who answered the phone, hesitantly admitted that Terrance was in my bed with a sixteen-year-old Scottish boy that he'd been seeing behind my back for several weeks, I virtually breathed fire down the phone! At that moment, in my mind, I ready to go back, smash down the doors and toss them both out on their miserable arses, but an acquaintance who sitting nearby at the bar, and who'd overheard my conversation, grabbed my arm and held me back from leaving the club until I'd calmed down a bit. Surprisingly, he was a guy that I'd fancied ever since first laying eyes on him several months earlier, and before I became obsessed with Terrance. After giving me a big hug, he invited me back to his place for the night. I was in such a low state that I'd have probably gone home with a woman, just to avoid being alone. He and I didn't get very far before a cop pulled me over for reckless driving and ordered into the front seat of his police car for a breathalyser test. When the apparatus failed to work, and it looked like I was about to be let off with a warning, the arresting officer couldn't find his hat anywhere. I was sitting on it, and it was as flat as a pancake! The moment I saw it, I burst out laughing and that made him as furious as a feral cat. He radioed another police car for a replacement breathalyser and this time, after failing the test dismally, I was arrested. My car was confiscated and I was driven to the Shepherds Bush Police Station in a patrol car, where I failed a second breath test and was asked to give a urine sample. As dawn broke, and the alcohol was wearing off, the reality of my predicament soon brought me to my senses, and along with that came deep feelings of remorse and self-disgust. (Looking back now, it disgusts me, even more, to think that I was such an ignorant, selfish and irresponsible, young idiot to even think of getting behind the wheel of a car in such a state.) After being released early the next morning, I caught a cab to my flat, knelt down in front of my Gohonzon, and chanted earnestly to be able to manifest the strength and good fortune that I needed to face and overcome my latest self-inflicted mess-up. At the same time, I repeatedly promised myself that I'd never let such self-absorbed idiocy mar my life again – and I never have.

I was awakened later that morning by Derrick, who wanted to know my side of the story. After I told him what had happened, he insisted that I return to the hotel and resume my position as manager, promising he'd be there to deal with Terrance by the time that I arrived. A little while later, I entered the hotel through the basement and found Terrance's young lover washing dishes. He didn't have a clue who I was when I asked him where Terrance was and told me that he was upstairs doing the rooms and that he shouldn't be too long. Aware that Terrance would be busy for a while, and since Derrick still hadn't arrived, I popped next door to the shop and bought some cakes to share with his cute young boyfriend over a cup of tea while we waited. The boy was just an innocent party, and I had no animosity toward him whatsoever. When Terrance arrived and found his under-age lover sitting with me, chatting and laughing, his face became distorted with rage, and he demanded to know why I was back at the hotel, screaming in my face that he was now the manager and to leave the hotel immediately – it was as though a devil had possessed him. I was getting up to leave when Derrick arrived and summoned the staff into the office for an urgent meeting. After initially making it clear that he wanted me to manage the hotel, Derrick told everyone present that it would be my decision as manager whether Terrance remained as an employee or not. All of the heart-wrenching chanting that I'd done earlier that morning had allowed me to retake charge of my life, and I no longer felt obsessed with Terrance. It was as though a blinding light had been switched off, allowing me to see things much more clearly. I not only allowed Terrance to keep his job, but I also invited his young lover to stay on at the hotel with him. My next remaining obstacle to overcome was that I didn't have a current driver's licence, and the police had given me a week to produce one. It looked like I was still going to be in serious trouble and that this time there'd be no getting out of it, but I refused to give up hope and kept chanting each day desperately for a solution. Later that week, I received a letter in the mail from the police informing me that they'd dropped the charges. There was no explanation, and I didn't push my luck by asking for one, I just put it down to another inexplicable benefit from my sincere apologetic chanting and left it at that.

I EVENTUALLY sold my old Vauxhall and replaced it with an Italian sports car, but whenever I went out dancing or socialising, I always used taxis. I only had my new car for a few short weeks before it was gone! Being the soft-hearted and forgiving fool that I so often am, I loaned it to Terrance to go to Cardiff with his boyfriend and never saw it again. It broke down on the M4 motorway, and while they were hitching back to London to get some help, the council found my car abandoned, towed it away and impounded it. Because my licence and passport had expired and I'd forgotten to renew the road tax on the car or change it into my name, I was never game enough to reclaim it.

IT WAS Christmas Eve 1976 and Derrick had promised to provide the hotel staff with the makings of a full Christmas dinner. However, when he failed to show up by 5.00pm, and there wasn't any Christmas food in the place, I decided to use some money from the hotel takings and go shopping with that. Tracey, a female staff member, accompanied me to the nearest supermarket, and after standing on the street for almost thirty minutes trying to get a cab, and with just fifteen minutes left before the shop would close, it suddenly occurred to me to try chanting for a taxi. Tracey looked up at me and laughed, but when two vacant cabs came around the corner almost simultaneously, her eyes almost popped out of their sockets...

"Bloody hell!" She gasped, wearing a look utter astonishment.

With only ten minutes left to do the shopping, we had to race around the supermarket like a couple of game-show contestants, throwing anything that took our fancy into our trolleys. When we got to the checkout, we were shocked to find Terrance there with an over-loaded trolley of his own. Derrick had turned up a few minutes after we'd left the hotel and given Terrance some money to go shopping. Between Christmas Day and New Year, and while Derrick was on holiday in Spain, all that we did was celebrate, eat, drink, get high and make love with whoever was available and felt like it. Not one bed got made, no breakfasts were served, and nobody got charged for overstaying. If any guests came knocking on the office door looking for us, we just hid and kept quiet until they gave up and went away. (We were dreadful, I know.) We had so much food leftover that we ended up feeding the guests Christmas pudding well into the New Year.

LATE ONE night, I'd just finished telling Terrance about my strange flying-saucer and neutron-energy dream, when a news flash on the radio announced that America had successfully tested its first *neutron bomb.* Talk about synchronicity, all we could do was look at each other in silent dismay...

# Chapter 33

# CAMBRIDGEMAN

During an urgent Buddhist gathering held at the hotel to discuss Ray's deteriorating family situation, a heated argument broke out between myself and the attending leaders. I'd been advising Ray to move out and to let his wife and children keep the apartment. I'd also tried my best to encouraged him to do all that he could to support them, and to face up to reality by accepting that he was gay. In contrast, the leaders angrily disagreed with what I'd suggested and virtually ordered Ray to face up to his responsibilities as a father and a husband by returning to his family home and chanting to overcome his homosexuality. When I tried reminding them that Nichiren's teaching is about common sense and logic, and that expecting Ray to be someone that he wasn't, was neither, but they completely ignored what I had to say and still insisted on telling Ray to go back home to his wife and kids and to chant to become straight. In the end, because they were 'official leaders', Ray chose to follow their advice instead of mine, at which point, I stepped aside and let them all get on with it.

I HADN'T SEEN or heard from Christopher since leaving Plymouth. We'd had a falling out over the damage that he and the sailor had done to my car, and how I'd been left to pay for the repairs. The last news that I'd heard along the grapevine was that Christopher had given up his Buddhist practice, so it came as quite a surprise one afternoon when he showed up unexpectedly on the hotel doorstep. Christopher told me he'd been on a world cruise with the drag show from Plymouth and although he'd been made a very lucrative offer to remain with the outfit to perform in Australia, he'd turned it down and chosen to return to the UK instead. He said that he wanted to get his practice back on track with the help and encouragement of his fellow UK Buddhist friends. Christopher had a severe drinking problem, which often made him say and do a lot of crazy, nasty and sometimes seriously annoying things. Since he failed to elaborate on what had actually happened to him on the ship, except to say that it was something that made his life a misery, I could only guess that the decision to come back to the UK had been made for him. I invited Christopher to join Ray and me for some chanting that night, and afterwards, we all shared a happy and rowdy reunion. In many ways, it was just like the old times again, but it was also clearly evident to both Christopher and me that Ray was suffering from some serious psychological problems. The next day, we all drove down to Shepherds Bush Green to get a bite to eat, and I got myself arrested again! It was a bitterly cold day, and I needed to pee, so I dashed into the public toilet on the green and found it chock-a-block full of randy men. I'd hardly had time to finish peeing, before a swarm of police burst into the toilet from both entrances, and rounded us all up. Then they swiftly marched us all outside into the park, and while we were stood on parade, people in passing cars were glaring, laughing, and pulling faces and pointed fingers at us – I cringed with embarrassment. After the police had finished interrogating each, they wanted our addresses, but only I stubbornly refused to give it to them. I kept pointing towards my car and telling the police that I'd only popped down the road to get some chicken for lunch and that if they cared to check and have a quick feel, they'd find it still hot on my car seat. That's when the police and everyone else glanced across the park at my car to see Ray and Christopher anxiously peering out of the windows like a pair of worried old maids. There was a loud outburst of laughter, and after taking down my number plate number, they finally and let me go.

ANOTHER GAY disco club that I liked hanging out at most Sunday nights, was down on Talbot Road. One evening, while I was handing my coat over to a new cloakroom lady there, she mumbled something about how I'd 'disrupted her meeting' that day. I'd only seen the woman a couple of times and barely knew her, so I was taken aback about what she'd said. I asked her to elaborate, and she first introduced herself as being a medium. She then explained that she'd held a spiritual meeting in her home earlier that afternoon with several of her paying customers, but the only messages that had come through were about me. Before I had a chance to say anything, she cut in and insisted that I was going to write books. She also mentioned something about my needing to go to Egypt or to get myself an Egyptian cat. By then I was convinced that the old dear had a screw or two loose, so I gave her a quick smile and quickly headed off into the club. When I collected my coat at the end of the night, she was still going on about it...

"If you can't get to Egypt to get a cat, then any cat will do," she yelled as I rushed away through the exit door and left.

The following Sunday night, I was checking in my coat again and she handed me her phone number on a small piece of paper. Then she told me that I had an Eskimo spirit-guide who was always by my side to protect me. I politely pushed the piece of paper into my pocket and left her babbling to herself while I joined my friends inside. When I went to collect my coat at the end of the night, she was still going on about the Eskimo and told me that I shouldn't be concerned if I ever felt a chilly presence around me, as it would only be him! I stepped out onto the pavement to get away from her as fast as I could, and a gust of icy wind hit me square in the face – chilling me to the bone in more ways than one.

MEMBERS OF THE local LGBT+ community were raving about a handsome, young Australian male dentist working at the Notting Hill Gate Dental Practice, and I suddenly felt the need for a check-up or to maybe even have a cavity filled. They sure weren't kidding! This bloke was drop-dead gorgeous, and I already had my mouth wide open before I'd even made it to the chair! So there I was a few days later, lying back in absolute bliss having one of my front teeth crowned when all of a sudden, his tool snapped off and got stuck in my tooth. The sexy dentist then spent almost an hour battling to get it out, and by the time that he'd finished, my jaw was stuck wide open, and half of my head was numb. My dignity had suffered more than anything else. To get a decent grip on the tooth, he had to virtually lie on top of me, pressing his perfectly shaped hairy torso up hard against my forehead, and if I hadn't felt so embarrassed about telling him that I was wearing a wig, I might have even been cheeky enough to ask him to move a little further along and just stay there. His sexy body was gradually dragging my wig off, and each time that I'd let out a loud moan to make him back off a bit, he thought that my moans were because I was feeling pain. Needless to say, he kept injecting more and more anaesthetic into my gum until it felt like a part of my head had gone missing. By the time that it was all over, I'd completely lost my appetite for 'Mr Gorgeous' and couldn't get out of his surgery quickly enough – well at least until next time.

RAY FOLLOWED the advice of the leaders, returned to his wife and kids and chanted fervently to become 'normal', which almost sent him completely out of his mind. He turned up at the hotel one night while I was out and so were the lights because a fuse had blown, and in the darkness, Ray was freaking all the guests out by telling them that he'd seen extraterrestrials coming in and out of the hotel. I got back right in the middle of all the commotion and as I was entering the lobby, Ray suddenly confronted me and screamed into my face that I'd had a lobotomy and that my ability to often foresee the future had been because aliens were controlling me. I didn't have a clue what the word 'lobotomy' meant and I tried my best to ignore Ray's rambling while I repaired the fuse. Then he started telling everyone that I had a mark on my forehead...

"It's hidden underneath his wig, I tell you!" He bellowed like a madman, causing some of the guests to take a second look at me suspiciously.

I was concerned with Ray's worsening mental state, but I had no other choice than to order him to leave the premises and to go home. A few days later, Ray was admitted to an insane asylum, and it always broke my heart to watch him wandering around meaninglessly whenever I went to visit him. He and some of the other inmates would follow each other in continuous circles around a big room, talking to themselves, and some of them even appeared to be having heated arguments with themselves. The Buddhist leaders who'd instructed Ray to return to his wife and kids didn't show up even once, and I was the only one who made an effort to visit and try to comfort Ray. When Ray was eventually well enough to leave the asylum, I brought him back to the hotel and let him stay there free of charge until he could focus better and regain some form of stability in his life. A couple of weeks later, Ray moved into a small flat that I helped him find in Shepherds Bush, but he was still far from stable.

I WAS INTERVIEWING a girl for a job at the hotel one day when Derrick showed up unexpectedly, took one glance at her, and then told me to hire her on the spot. Ruby was her name, and apart from her sexy image, Derrick didn't know a thing about her. Ruby turned out to be a devoted Punk Rock fan and a sex-toy for one or more of the *Sex Pistols*, which soon resulted in the hotel becoming a meeting place for the whole band and several of their off-beat followers. Most of the time, Ruby was drunk, stoned, or both and I felt increasingly intimidated by both her and this new breed of rebellious Punk Rockers. It didn't take long before Ruby was getting plenty of sex from Derrick as well, and she wasted no time in using her orifices to manipulate him and push me out so that she could steal my job as the hotel manager. The showdown happened one afternoon when Derrick turned up and waited outside my room while I was chanting with some friends. When we'd finished and everyone had gone, Derrick fired me on the spot and ordered me to pack up and to get out. He also pointed at my altar and yelled...

"Get that fucking thing out of here too!"

I tried to convince Derrick that it was ludicrous to take his anger out on my Gohonzon by slandering it as he'd done, but that only made him angrier...

"Don't you go trying to push that shit on me, just get that fucking thing out of here today!"

A month earlier, I'd given up my room in the shared apartment after the other flatmate's had left. I had nowhere to go, especially at such short notice, then I remembered hearing that my Buddhist friend, James Perry, had a spare room available and that he wanted to rent out to a fellow Buddhist, so I phoned him to ask if the room was still available. It was, and he told me that I was welcome to rent it for as long as I needed. Being away from the hotel felt very peculiar, and I soon began to miss it immensely, especially the intrigue and excitement that each new day there had brought. It was nothing unusual for me to cross paths with people from my past in the various countries and cities that I visited, especially London. My world had become a very small place indeed, I'd even bumped into the medical student who'd caused me to miss my flight from Brisbane to Singapore after taking me to the Gold Coast. I ran into my old flame, Phillip, the first male that I'd ever had a meaningful relationship with while I was performing in New Zealand's 1964 World Fair. I'd not seen Phillip for at least twelve years, and bumping into him after such a long time was surreal. The spark of physical attraction between us was no longer there, for me at least, but we were still very close in many other ways and as we strolled down memory lane reminiscing the entire weekend, it turned out to be just what I needed in order to keep my mind off the hotel. I'd already enshrined my Gohonzon at James's place, so after I told Phillip about some of the benefits that I'd received from chanting, he was anxious for me to teach him how to do it as well so that he could receive a few for himself. In the meantime, on the same weekend, Ruby overdosed on drugs and was rushed to the hospital, close to death. I found out about it the following Monday morning when Enzo tracked down where I was living and begged me to come back to the hotel and resume my job as manager. Robert House was full to the brim, and Enzo didn't know who else to turn to for help. My first response was to refuse, but with Enzo's persistent pleading, I eventually gave in and returned, arriving back shortly after midday to find the hotel looking like it hadn't had a clean since the day that I'd left. The usual quota of the guests was complaining about dirty sheets and not getting any breakfast, and some were demanding their money back, nothing new there of course. All in all, it was in its usual state of disarray and chaos, and not a lot had changed, except for the worse. While I was busy vacuuming the stairs, a middle-aged man went past and then, grinning, stopped to speak to me...

"You're Tom, the manager, aren't you?"

"Yeah, that's right. Why? Is there a problem?" I asked.

"I told the other young man that you'd be back here today!" He chuckled, before merrily scurrying off up the stairs to his room.

His approach left me feeling somewhat mystified and ill at ease, and I couldn't get his disconcerting words out of my mind, so I downed tools and went looking for Enzo...

"Yeah, that's right! 'e did say that!" Enzo blurted out, suddenly looking bewildered. "'e reckoned ya'd be back 'ere on Mondee 'n' 'ere ya are!"

It turned out that the man, who came from Cambridge, had phoned and booked his room months earlier, only I'd forgotten all about him, and it had been when he'd asked where I was, and Enzo had told him that I no longer managed the hotel, that he'd made his odd, and as it turned out, accurate prediction. The whole situation gave me a gut feeling that something fishy was going on and I instinctively put my guard up. During the next few days, 'Cambridgeman', as we decided to call him, kept inviting me to join him for lunch or to visit the Home Exhibition at Olympia, near Kensington High Street, but I kept turning him down, telling him that I was too busy. Then, early one morning, he crept up behind me in the dining room, and at the same time as he informed me that he'd been instructed to give something to me, he held a silver medallion out under my nose...

"What tha hell are ya on about? I don't want it! Get that bloody thing away from me!" I snapped at him in a panic, quickly moving out of his reach.

It was an Egyptian cat's head, with two shining eyes, and it looked so realistic that my hairs stood up. I felt like they were glaring straight at me, and had instantly connected it to the strange cloakroom woman at the disco. Refusing to give up his quest, Cambridgeman then told me that a young man he'd spent the previous night with had woken up during the night and instructed him to give the medallion to the hotel manager. I was astounded! Except for a brief passing glimpse of the young man when he went up to Cambridgeman's room, I'd never set eyes on him before. Over the next very awkward and uncomfortable few days, Cambridgeman became weirder by the day, and kept following me around, continuously trying to gain my attention. His eyes were hypnotic, and because I was afraid of becoming spell-bound by them, I kept yelling Nam-Myoho-Renge-Kyo into his face for self-protection. Anyone witnessing it would have thought that I'd lost the plot, but it always seemed to stop him in his tracks and daze him for a couple of seconds. It was as though his train of thought had gone off the rails. At the time, I was still having dental work done and had been making good progress until Cambridgeman came along. Since then, I'd been experiencing excruciating toothaches and accompanying painful headaches.

On the night before he was he checked out, Cambridgeman almost begged me to join him for a farewell drink and refused to take no for an answer. I was still freaking out about the 'cat' situation, but I told him that I'd think about it. Ever since my odd encounter with the medium at the gay club, and then the medallion, I'd become so paranoid about cats, that just seeing a comic book or a Tom and Jerry cartoon could have easily unnerved me! It's strange how certain things can sometimes appear in sequence, and that day was no exception. Later in the afternoon, I went to collect my Gohonzon from my rented room at James's place to bring it back to my suite in the hotel and re-enshrine it there. While I'd been waiting for a bus on Bayswater Road near Hyde Park, a large grey cat had jumped up onto the bench and sat down beside me. When it stared straight up at my face as if it knew me or was about to attack, it gave me such a right that I skipped waiting for the bus and ran all the way to James's house instead. On my way back to the hotel, I popped in to visit a friend who lived near James, and when I sat down to have a coffee with him and saw a picture of a snarling cat on an LP cover lying across the table in front of me, my heart almost jumped into my throat! The cat in the picture was sitting next to some spilt milk, and similar to the cat on the bench, it was peering straight at me with evil, hateful eyes. I quickly jumped up, told my friend I had a bus to catch, and hightailed it out of there as fast as my legs could carry me. As soon as I got back to Robert House, the first thing that I did was to enshrine my Gohonzon and then chant in front of it until for the strength to face Cambridgeman and have a farewell drink with him. While I was getting ready to go, sudden severe pain in my head virtually incapacitated me. Refusing to let it get the better of me, I did what I usually do whenever anything like that arises, I chanted fervently and directed healing energy from within my subconscious, to the area of pain, until the discomfort subsided. (When it comes to our health, our subconscious mind can be a potent force once we learn how to connect to it and manipulate it correctly.) An hour later, I very cautiously set off with Cambridgeman to a little gay bar of his choosing in Piccadilly. Being the manager of a gay hotel and a frequent visitor to most of the gay clubs around London, I usually saw a familiar face or two at most of them. On that miserable, wet, cold and bleak night, I didn't recognise a single person, and I felt like a stranger in an alien environment. I was having a sip on a nice cold beer and was just beginning to settle down into the surroundings when Cambridgeman killed the moment...

"You've not seen everything yet, my dear." He said solemnly.

His voice tone and the look on his face instantly gave me the distinct impression that it wasn't going to be anything good. When I asked him to explain, he held his hand up to my face, and on one of his fingers was another Egyptian cat's head with piercing ruby-red eyes. A wave of panic surged through my body, and I felt every hair rise...

"There's gotta be someone here I know," I told myself anxiously, searching the entire bar again for a familiar face.

Cambridgeman was still telling me more about the ring, but I was trying my best to ignore anything that he was saying. There was a sudden break in the crowd, and there was Phillip, my friend from New Zealand, huddled up in a corner and surrounded by a group of guys. I'd never felt so happily relieved to see him! I caught his attention and gestured for him to come over to meet

Cambridgeman, which he did, and then he stayed talking with us until I'd finished my beer...

"I've gotta get back to tha hotel now," I chirped, plunking my empty glass on the bar and quickly scurrying towards the exit door, hoping with everything in me that Cambridgeman would stay chatting with Phillip, but no such luck! He was right behind me every step of the way.

When we arrived back at the hotel, we found Ruby down in the kitchen, preparing a late-night snack. She still looked sickly and weak but appeared to have overcome the worst of her ordeal. I was about to say goodnight and go to my suite when Ruby insisted that we join her for some supper. Adhering to her wishes, Cambridgeman and I sat down and exchanged some small talk, while Ruby prepared supper. When Ruby sat down and joined us, Cambridgeman quickly changed the subject and became engrossed in a conversation with Ruby about *things unknown*, telling her that she'd lived before and offering to give her past-life regression through hypnosis. It was then that I finally realised what had been happening to me all week, and why each time that I'd blurted out Nam-Myoho-Renge-Kyo in his face, he reacted as if a spell had been broken. Everything about that week suddenly making so much more sense to me, as the whole time that he'd been at the hotel, Camebridgeman had been trying to hypnotise me, which had probably also had something to do with my terrible headaches. I wanted to get away from him as fast as I could, so I very assertively told Cambridgeman that I wasn't interested in hypnosis, wished him and Ruby good luck and goodnight, then I was gone! I felt so relieved to have a logical answer to the cause of my aches and pains. After cleaning my teeth, I chanted in front of Gohonzon to bring forth the strength and good fortune that I needed to protect myself from any further effects from Cambridgeman, and by the time that I'd finished, I felt as though my spirit had been cleansed, washed and dried. When Cambridgeman came down for breakfast the following morning and told me that his session with Ruby had failed because my spirit had intervened and stopped them as I was sleeping, I was gobsmacked! I'd been chanting, not sleeping, but after hearing that, at least I knew that my prayers had been answered...

"You're far too strong for me," he announced with a note of surrender in his voice. "They sent me here to you, but I'm afraid it's impossible."

His strange explanation instantly captured my full attention, and I even felt suddenly threatened by his words. I wanted to know who *they* were, but he didn't give me an answer. The way he kept staring up at the wall gave me the impression that he was going in and out of some sort of trance-state. The whole crazy scenario reminded me of my experience in Katoomba, and I could hardly wait to see the back of him. About an hour later, Cambridgeman finally left the hotel, and after saying his final goodbyes to the others who were present, he told me to think of his face if ever I was in any trouble. Not a chance! My greatest desire at that moment was to put his face and everything else about him out of my mind entirely. Little did I know back then that I'd be writing about him all these years later. Going by what Cambridgeman admitted, it appears obvious to me that he'd been competing with my faith to gain control of my thoughts or whatever the whole time that he was at the hotel. In his words, I'd been the reason for him coming to the Robert House in the first place! As for who sent him, I've never found out, nor do I care to. If I hadn't been kicked out of the hotel by Derrick and Cambridgeman hadn't told Enzo that I'd be back by Monday, I may not have had my guard up and may have even succumbed to his influences.

My curiosity got the better of me, and I tracked down Cambridgeman's lover-boy to verify whether or not it was true that he'd told Cambridgeman to give the cat medallion to me. He turned out to be an attractive, young male sex worker, and although he admitted that he'd done what Cambridgeman had said, he couldn't tell me why because he didn't know the reason himself. Feeling more intrigued and mystified, I phoned the cloakroom lady at the gay bar to see whether she could shed any light on it, but before I had time to finish explaining what had happened, she cut in and adamantly advised me to keep in contact with Cambridgeman and to heed whatever he told me. I instantly suspected that they were in cahoots and conspiring against me, and slammed the phone down, vowing never to have anything to do with either of them again.

SOMEONE HAD ONCE said to me that 'wherever evil appears, more evil will follow'. I was cleaning out one of the rooms a couple of days later, and a huge chunk of plaster crashed down from the ceiling, narrowly missing my head...

"SHIT! Don't tell me Cambridgeman's put a curse on me!" I said out loud.

That afternoon, Derrick's father was released from prison and turned up out of the blue. Upon his arrival home, he'd been greeted by a pile of unpaid hotel-expense bills that reached over £20,000 – a small fortune back then. He was on the warpath looking for Derrick and when I told him that I hadn't seen his son for a couple of days, he let me know that he'd put Robert House up for sale and that I wasn't to allow Derrick onto the premises under any circumstances...

"What a diff'rence a few days can make," I thought to myself.

*Once one's good fortune has been exhausted,*
*the only true strategy in the world that can*
*ever change it, is to acknowledge and accept*
*responsibility for the past 'negative causes'*
*that have brought it about and then make*
*new ' good causes' to restore it.*
*...Nichiren.*

*With Mr & Mrs Daisley on my way to London.*

*Marlene Dietrich*
*wearing one of my hair styles.*

*The Grand Opening of Trets South of France.*

*Masami and me in London.*

*Robert House Hotel London.*

*With Ray's band at Hyde Park London.*

Arab hunted by Yard after London shooting was expelled from Britain a year ago.

# TERRORIST WHO SNEAKED BACK

**Daily Mail Reporters**

**AN Arab deported from Britain last year was named yesterday by police hunting the Easter assassin.**

The man, wanted for questioning after the murder of three Yemenis in London on Easter Sunday, slipped back into Britain a week before the attack.

And as an intensive hunt for him went on last night, it became clear that British authorities had known him for three years as a violent Palestinian fanatic.

### Warning

Scotland Yard named the man, who may still be in Britain, as 23-year-old Zohair Yousif Akashe, a Lebanese Palestinian from Beirut.

Officers warned that he iws dangerous and cvould be armed with a .32 automatic handgun equipped with a silencer.

The tripple assassination happened outside the Royal Lancaster Hotel in Bayswater.

**Zahair Yousif Akache**
**A police artist's impression.**

The former Prime Minister of the Yemen Arab Republic, 60-year-old Mr Abdullah al-Hajari, and his wife Fatima, 40, and an Embassy official were gunned down at close range asthe stepped into a maroon Mercedes car.

**The real Zahair Yousif Akache.**

### Booked

Akache is know to have booked into the Robert House Hotel opposite the Royal Lancaster soon after arriving back in Britain. He stayed in Room 11 on the third floor.

Akache, who is believed to have used the names Ahmed Badir and Adel Hassan, paid £5-a-night for the room and booked out shortly before the shootings.

Commander Jim Nevill,

Turn to Page 3, Column 1

## ACROSS THE ROAD...
## THE ROYAL LANCASTER.

# Room with a view of murder...

**FOR** four days before the assassination Zohair Yousif Akache, the man named by Scotland Yard yesterday had this view of the comings and goings at the front of the Royal Lancaster hotel. He watched from the third floor of the Robert House hotel across the road, where Akache rented a three-bedded room. He spent most of his time peering out of his window, which is 84 yards from where the three Arabs were gunned down. Akache did not sign the visitor's book—but neither did many other people who stayed there during Easter. His room—No. 11—was next to the third-floor bathroom, and at the top of the staircase, with its worn carpet.

The beds in the room had rust-covered coverlets, and there was a single light in the centre of the ceiling and floral wallpaper.

Below, left, is the view Akache saw from his window looking towards the Royal Lancaster. The circle marks the spot where the Mercedes parked on the day of the assassination. Below, right, with the Mercedes outlined, is the view from the Royal Lancaster looking to Robert House.

The dotted line marks Akache's line of vision.

*Queen's Silver Jubilee March in London.*

*Ladbroke Grove House where I lived in London.*

*Some of London's other queens out celebrating the jubilee.*

*Passengers free at last after being hijacked by Palestinian terrorists for five horrifying days aboard a Lufthansa 747 jet.*

# Chapter 34

# ROOM WITH A VIEW TO MURDER!

Easter 1977 was fast approaching, and there was no time for any idle-talk or pondering, the hotel had to be brought up to standard and prepared for the onslaught of the usual nagging guests who'd be demanding their prepaid rooms and complaining about the hotel's shortcomings. Oh, if only that had been the only thing to be concerned about. A couple of days prior to Good Friday, Enzo had answered the door to a young Middle Eastern man who was desperate to rent a room for a week at any cost. Enzo tried to convince him that the hotel was booked out for Easter, but the man still refused to take no for an answer. When Enzo called me upstairs from the basement, and I told the young man the same story, it again fell on deaf ears. He seemed nice enough, and he looked neat and clean, but there was nothing that I could do except to suggest that he try somewhere else, but that didn't work either. The young man claimed that he'd tried every other hotel in the area and that there wasn't a single room available anywhere. Enzo cut in and suggested room 11, the room where a part of the ceiling had come crashing down just missing my head, and I suddenly felt like hitting Enzo over the head with a book I was holding, for opening his big mouth. I tried to explain to the man that room 11 was unfit for occupation, but nothing I said could faze him...

"It's okay. It's okay. I'll take it. I'll take it!" He kept repeating anxiously.

After eventually giving in and taking him up to see the room, the first thing that he did was inspect the view from the window and was extremely excited by what he saw, assuring me that the room was perfect. In the end, I had no choice but to let him have it, albeit reluctantly. My biggest concern was for the man's safety if any more plaster came down on top of him, especially while he was sleeping, and I cringed at the very thought of it. While our new guest was away supposedly collecting his things, Enzo and I got busy and did our best to clean up the mess and try to make the room as comfortable as possible. On the following day, I found some fresh lamb chops wrapped up in white butchers paper sitting on the kitchen bench. While I asked around to find out who they belonged to, I made the crucial mistake of asking an elderly

Maori lady who'd been a guest at the hotel for several weeks, and who always appeared to be irritated and on edge about something. She just about bit my head off and accused me of being a racist, picking on her because she was a Maori. She couldn't have been further from the truth if she'd tried, and I let her know it by giving her a right mouthful of my own, which had very little if no effect. She continued carrying on with her accusations and then started accusing me of being 'wicked sinner'. The poor old dear was a practising Mormon and she'd been upsetting the other guests ever since the day that she'd first arrived, often cornering people in the hallways and preaching to them about their dreadful sins. I'd been copping complaints about her every other day but had chosen not to get involved because of her age, and because I felt sorry or her. That is until she launched her racist attack on me.

Some of the staff members and I had been invited to a gay fancy-dress party that night, and I was already running late, so I left the Maori lady alone and ranting to herself, while I hurried upstairs to get dressed up. We were being picked up for the party by someone that we'd never met, so when I heard a barrage of loud banging on the front door, that's who I thought it was. I raced downstairs dressed as a gay, punk version of Long John Silver, complete with makeup, frizzy wig, big false eyelashes, bulging crotch and a colourful fake parrot on my shoulder. When I opened the door, to my surprise, I found two big macho blokes dressed up as policemen. The first thing that I thought was why are they both going to the party dressed exactly the same...

"We've had a complaint from a lady who says she's been violently attacked here, sir," one of them exclaimed – smirking while savouring my get up.

It wasn't until the old Maori woman barged out from the TV room and started ranting to them about me bullying her to get her to have sex with me, that I suddenly realised they were real coppers! The officers were struggling not to burst into laughter when they glanced back and forth at her and then me a couple of times...

"Oh no, madam, I hardly think so – are you sure?" One cop asked as the other nodded in agreement, still struggling to hold back a smirk.

When the cops couldn't get any sense out of the woman, and she started accusing them of being wicked sinners too, they quickly gave up and left. We, on the other hand, were soon off to the fancy-dress party where, by the way, there wasn't a single 'copper' anywhere in sight. We never did find out who the lamb chops belonged to, so, just as with the 'burnt sausages', they became yet another Robert House mystery.

Early on the afternoon of Good Friday Eve, several prospective buyers turned up with the owner to inspect the hotel, which by then had been placed on the international property market listings. During their visit, I was surprised to find the guest from room 11 scurrying about all over the third-floor landing, it was as though he felt trapped and was looking for an escape route...

"It's okay! It's alright!" I called up from the floor below. "They're just interested in buying the hotel, that's all. They're only looking the place over!"

After the men finished inspected room 11, the owner popped back and abused the guest for spilling his drink on the carpet, which triggering instant, intense anger to well up in the guest's face, who looked like he was about to attack the owner physically, until I quickly intervened and calmed him down. I told him that the owner was rude like that to all of the guests, just in case he thought that the owner was racist, which he probably was.

BY THE TIME the sun had gone down, the hotel was fully booked with the usual quota of weird, odd and outrageous guests. Among them, was a large group of New Zealanders, a group of young, trendy Italian males, a pompous and demanding gay couple from Belgium, and a middle-aged South African black woman who was condescending in announcing that she was a princess, and repeatedly accused us in no uncertain terms of being squatters with no right to be charging her a penny. It gave me quite a surprise to see the gay Belgian couple back again, especially after their previous stay, when they left in angry disgust and vowed never to return. I asked them what had changed their minds to make them come back for potentially more of the same, and they told me that they'd never had a holiday with so much absurdity to talk about after they got back home. In other words, Robert House had given them their money's worth just by being quirky and preposterous, and they were back for some more, no matter how rough or inconvenient it was. Little did they know at the time just how much more they'd be getting. The guy in room 11 had checked in without any luggage and always seemed to wear the same clothes. He also appeared to avoid letting anyone else in the hotel see his face, and would usually sneak out very early in the morning and return quite late at night, and never once showed up in the dining room for breakfast. Like the old Maori woman, he too seemed to be continuously agitated and on edge about something. Sometimes I'd have little chats with him late at night when I was doing my final rounds. He was always very polite and friendly, but I could sense that something was wrong in his life, and was waiting for the right moment and opportunity to tell him about Nam-Myoho-Renge-Kyo, which never eventuated. Whenever I began to even hint at anything philosophical, he'd quickly become uneasy and invariably change the subject.

Ever since Ruby's drug overdose, she'd not been turning up on time to prepare the breakfasts, so I had to repeatedly get up earlier than usual to do them myself. When I arrived in the dining room early on Easter Sunday morning, I was surprised to find Mr Room 11 sitting at one of the tables.

As per usual, he appeared to be very anxious about something and asked if he could have a coffee. I was walking towards the kitchen to make one for him, when he jumped up and insisted on helping me, hanging onto my left shoulder and almost pushing me along. I turned my head to ask him to wait at the table and noticed that he was looking back towards the entry door intensely, as though he was expecting someone. Just as we were about to go through the small doorway that leads into the kitchen proper, some of the New Zealand guests stampeded into the dining room, hoping to get a quick cup of coffee before setting off on an early-start coach tour. The moment that they entered, 'Mr Room 11' let go of my shoulder and darted back to his table, but when I brought him his coffee a few moments later, he was nowhere to be seen. After Ruby eventually showed up for work, and I told her off as discreetly and quietly as I could, I threw my apron down and stormed out of the kitchen. While passing through the lobby, I noticed that the large entrance door to the hotel was wide open and a man in a black overcoat standing on the porch with his back to me. I approached him and asked if he had his key to get back in, and when he turned around, I was surprised to discover that it was 'Mr Room 11'. I'd never seen him dressed in anything other than a burgundy sweater and jeans, so from behind, I hadn't even suspected that it was him. He had both hands in his coat pockets and a very angry look on his face, which was quite a contrast from only minutes earlier. I noticed that he also had something bulky in his pocket that was bulging out, and had assumed that it was his camera. When I told him that his coffee was still waiting for him downstairs, he barked at me and ordered me to close the door and to leave him alone. Uncertain if I'd heard him right, or if there'd been a misunderstanding, I asked him again if he had his keys to get back in – and that's when he lost it...

**"YES! YES! I HAVE KEY! NOW! GO! GO!"** He screamed furiously in a threatening manner.

"Talk about people with fuckin' split personalities," I growled, slamming the door in his face and heading upstairs.

After I'd checked all the rooms from the top floor down and had reached room 11, I was surprised yet again to find the room keys lying on the bed. A scary feeling came over me, and I could sense that something wasn't right. I couldn't put my finger on what it was, and then a couple of minutes later, as I was vacuuming the final stairwell, a South African guest came back up the stairs and told me that he couldn't get out of the hotel because the police had cordoned off the whole area...

"Oh, it's prob'ly just another IRA bomb scare, we get a lot o' false alarms 'round here," I said flippantly. "You'll be able to get out soon."

I carried on vacuuming and then begun seeing flashing images of the face of 'Mr Room 11' in my head, how strange he'd been at the front door, how weird his behaviour had been in the dining room, the keys on the bed and how he'd run all over the foyer when the owner was showing the hotel to the prospective buyers...

"Faaarckin' hell! I gulped. "Maybe there *is* a bomb, 'n' it could be right here in room 11!" I whispered the vacuum cleaner, the stairs, the carpet and the walls – shuddering from the very thought of it.

Suddenly a memory flashed through my mind about the Champion Hotel in Notting Hill Gate, and how I was there one night with friends when a bomb exploded right across the road, killing a man. The deafening noise it made had carved the event indelibly into my mind, and the prospect of that happening again in Robert House instantly became more than I could bear. I practically flew down the stairs to the basement shouting out Enzo's name, but he didn't answer, so I shot back upstairs and asked the South African guest if he'd accompany me while I thoroughly scoured room 11. Having someone with me would help lessen my guilt feelings that I'd have for suspecting the occupant if my suspicions turned out to be wrong. As we entered the room, I felt like I was walking on thin ice, and it was such a relief it to only find a couple of empty Camp Pie and coke cans. Returning back downstairs, I finally found Enzo, who looked like he'd just seen a ghost. In an anxious fluster, he told me that three people had just been shot to death in their car right outside Robert House, but before Enzo could finish telling me any other details, I cut him off, and in no uncertain terms, told him that it was the guest from room 11...

"Ya can't just go 'round makin' up stuff like that about someone!" Enzo barked in denial.

"I'm not makin' it up, Enzo, I *know* it!" I almost shouted, convinced that I was right.

The terrifying thought that the man might already be back in the hotel sent me hurtling down into my basement suite to chant for protection, with Enzo following right behind me. While chanting, I side-glanced up towards the high-set window and saw police officers mingling amongst a crowd of people on the footpath above, and my heart skipped several beats. Moments later, Enzo, who'd never been interested in chanting, was squatted down on the floor chanting with me. I was scared stiff, but Enzo was a complete nervous wreck...

"If tha cops ask, we don't know nothin' about it, d'ya 'ear? Enzo nervously demanded as soon as we'd finished. "Let's just keep our gobs shut, Okay?"

I asked Enzo to explain why and he admitted that he'd been breaking the law by collecting Social Security payments while working at the hotel. His confession quickly reminded me that I'd forgotten to renew my passport and that the visa in it was no longer valid...

"Yeah, rightio mate... Our lips are sealed... We don't know nothin'...," I agreed in a nervous flutter.

A short time later, while we were in the kitchen trying to calm ourselves down with a cup of strong hot coffee, a team of Scotland Yard detectives from the Anti-Terrorist Squad stormed in and surrounded us...

"Rightio then lads, what do you pair know?" The cop in charge asked as he held out his badge and the others stared coldly at us in total silence.

It would have been evident to the police that Enzo and I knew something, but we were electrified with fear and could hardly speak...

"I-I th-think it was tha bloke in room 11," I whimpered with a stutter.

"And just what makes you think that then?" Asked the chief detective even more dogmatically and moving closer to peer straight into my eyes.

"I... I dunno, I just think i-it w-was... That's all."

It sounded feeble, but I didn't want to say anything that could jeopardise my agreement with Enzo. In the following few minutes, everyone in the hotel was placed under house arrest. Until the police could confirm whether or not the killer was the guest from room 11 and that the rest of us had nothing to do with the murders, we were all chief suspects. After continuously being questioned all that day and late into the evening, plus being made to sign multiple statements, I'd reached a point where I wasn't sure if I was awake or stuck in the midst of a frightening nightmare. On Easter Monday, the police concluded that the triple murder had been a political terrorist attack and their fingers were all pointing towards 'Mr Room 11'as the probable assassin. The gay Belgian couple certainly got their money's worth, and when the 'African princess' returned to the hotel and was told by the police that she'd been staying in the next room to a suspected political assassin, she became so hysterical with fear that not even the police could calm her down. None of us had believed her when she said that she was a princess, so when an embassy limo, flying her country's flag, pulled up to collect her, we were all dumbfounded. One of the police later informed me that it's not uncommon for high-end 'officials' to stay in cheaper hotels when they're trying to keep a low profile. He also told me that the police didn't want the alleged assassin to know that they'd found out where he'd been staying, and to help confuse the media, they'd based themselves in other hotels around the area as well. They also had plain-clothed police officers hiding out in several street locations, keeping Robert House Hotel under 24/7 surveillance. When I phoned Dick Causton at the London Buddhist headquarters for some much-needed guidance and support, he explained to me that it was due to my karma that I was in my predicament and advised me not to make any personal judgements on the matter, but to abide by the laws of the United Kingdom and to cooperate with the police in every way that I could. I did my best to adhere to Dick's advice, but I didn't feel like cooperating with anybody. I just wanted it all to be over as quickly as possible. When the cops on night duty warned me that there was a possibility that the assassin would return to try to kill the only witness to his identity, namely me, their shocking news sent a chill up my spine that almost had a laxative effect. The detectives gave me strict instructions that if and when the doorbell rang, I was to open the door and try to act normally, promising me that secret police would be standing by and hiding in the background. The thought that I could get shot at any moment had me in bits! I may have had the best protection in town standing by, but every time that fricken doorbell sounded it reverberated through me like a road drill.

I kept thinking about how excited the murder suspect had become when we first showed him room 11. It was no wonder that he was so super keen, as the room had given him a clear view of the main entrance to The Royal Lancaster Hotel, where the former Prime Minister of the Yemen Arab Republic and his ill wife were staying, while she received urgent medical treatment from a Harley Street specialist. The murder suspect in room 11 had access to view their every move to and from their hotel. The BBC Evening News reported that the couple had been murdered as they were leaving their hotel in their official embassy Mercedes and that the assassin had opened the back door and shot the ex-Prime Minister, his wife and their driver at point-blank range, instantly killing all three of them. The assassin was then seen nonchalantly slamming the car door and quickly disappearing into the Hyde Park Sunday Street-Market crowd. All this had taken place within minutes of my last encounter with him on the front steps of Robert House.

The Australian High Commission was closed for the Easter Holiday weekend, which meant that I wouldn't be able to apply for a new passport until the following Tuesday. When that day finally arrived, and Enzo three attempts to submit my passport for renewal, he was repeatedly refused because they needed to see me there in person. With no other option available, I asked Enzo to organise a cab to the front door of the hotel, and then amazingly succeeded to sneak out unnoticed – or so I thought. As the cab drove off and I looked back at Robert House, I still couldn't believe that I'd made it past the gaggle of police without being stopped, and my heart was pounding so loudly that my ears felt like they were popping. As we approached Piccadilly, I had the creepiest feeling that I was being watched and followed, and I fearfully expected a hail of bullets to tear me apart at any moment. By the time that we arrived at our destination, I felt so lightheaded from all the horror thoughts racing around in my head, that I thought I was going to faint. An hour or so later, I sneaked back into Robert House and again couldn't believe that I'd made it unseen. However, before I could reach my suite, I was stopped in my tracks by one of the officers and summoned down to the dining room, where the Anti-Terrorist Squad Chief was waiting to interview me...

"Did you enjoy your little excursion across London town, Tommy, lad?" He asked with a smirk.

I felt numb, and like a naughty little boy who'd been caught playing truant from school, and at first, I couldn't even open my mouth to answer...

"You needn't have bothered, you know," he explained, with a cheesy grin. "You couldn't leave Mother England at the moment, even if you wanted to lad... You're presently a guest of Her Majesty and, just for the record, we knew all about your passport, visa, your family and nearly everything else about you, within the hour or so of meeting you, Tommy boy."

When I'd sensed that I was being followed and watched during the taxi ride, I hadn't been paranoid after all, as the police had deliberately let me sneak out and had kept me under surveillance the whole time. After all, I was still a potential suspect. A couple of days later, the hotel telephone was disconnected for the umpteenth time without any warning. Derrick had taken the phone-bill money out the kitty and used it to pay for drugs. Scotland Yard tried in earnest to get the line reconnected, but the bills had been in arrears too many times already, and British Telecom was fed up and flatly refused the police request. Because there weren't any mobile phones back then, as a substitute, the police brought in walkie-talkies to keep in touch with each other. Newspaper reporters hovered around the hotel like moths to bright light, day and night, continually ringing the doorbell one after the other to try to get information. Their stubborn and inconsiderate persistence only added more painful stress to my misery. Regardless of how scared and upset I was about doing it, I was still required to answer the door every time that someone rang the bell or knocked and pretend to act 'normal'. Meanwhile, a foolish, attention-seeking taxi driver, who clearly enjoyed being in the spotlight, regularly appeared on the evening TV evening news claiming that he'd been a close-range eyewitness to the assassination. He'd helped the police put together a photo-fit sketch of the assassin's face, which had looked nothing like 'Mr Room 11'. When I let the police on duty know that the description by the taxi driver of the suspect didn't resemble the occupant of room 11,I also told them that I thought the taxi the driver was a brainless idiot for not only putting his own life in danger but the lives of his family and friends. In the end, the police asked me if I could help them put together a photo-fit likeness of 'Mr Room 11', but when I tried, I couldn't make the resemblance close enough from what was available, so they took me to see a police artist instead. The procedure took about an hour, and it was like being under a spell.

I have a strong 'photographic memory', and after answering what seemed like a million questions, the artist created a face that looked so much like the assassin that the police were able to identify who he was from where they were sitting in the distance watching. On the following day, the picture was published in the papers, with a warning to the public not to approach the suspect if sighted. Shortly after that, I received a spine-chilling letter in the mail addressed to *The Manager* with words made from newspaper clippings, like a ransom note, which said that the police were wasting their time because the assassin had long since left the country.

Most of my staff had abandoned the hotel in fear for their lives, and who could blame them? I was too afraid to venture upstairs to the rooms for the same reason, so none of the rooms got cleaned for the entire period that the police were there. Every morning, I was summoned to the hotel lounge area, which had been transformed into a temporary incident room, to be given an update. Sometimes I'd spend hours with them afterwards, telling them about Nichiren's teachings, which helped me to keep my sanity. I think they probably realised that, and although they may not have always paid much attention, they were at least polite enough never to tell me to shut up or go away. Some of them would sometimes ask random questions, and one day, one of them wanted to know how roughing up a suspect to get information stood with my view of the Buddhist philosophy. After giving it some thought, I eventually suggested that, in my humble opinion, any adverse action, including what is for the 'good', would still be the result of karma and subject to the strict law of Cause and Effect. This, in turn, led to quite a heated debate, and a couple of the officers became very uncomfortably offended with what I'd said. In the end, we all just agreed to disagree.

I wasn't at all familiar with the Middle Eastern nations, but after what happened at Robert house, I'd certainly learnt a lot about the Republic of Yemen. One of the detectives told me that Scotland Yard was contractually obligated to solve the crime using their very best men, due to an international agreement and the nature and location of the crime, and that some of the men guarding me were also responsible for safeguarding members of the Royal Family, including the Queen. The murdered politician was rumoured to have been responsible for the deaths of thousands of people in Yemen. I didn't know how accurate that was but hearing these things had only made me feel increasingly distraught. All I could do was pray for everyone involved, and as I'd done before, ponder on why so many human beings choose to hate and kill each other.

Early one morning, halfway into the saga, the police informed me that Ruby had been overheard mouthing off in a local pub and telling reporters that the murderer had stayed in Robert House, and she'd also given them my name as the hotel's manager. I felt like strangling the dopey cow! Fortunately, some of the plain-clothes police staking out the pub were able to discredit Ruby's story and prevent it from going to print. The police may have assured me that they'd given Ruby a strict warning never to blab again, but she was yet to be the recipient of my wrath. When she casually strolled into the kitchen, an hour or so late as usual, and humming what sounded like a Sex Pistol song, I lost it and threw a jug of cold milk straight in her face...

"Are you outta yer fuckin' mind? What tha hell are ya tryin' ta do? Get me fuckin' killed, ya brainless arsehole?" I growled through my teeth in a screaming whisper.

For a moment she was too stunned to answer, but she definitely knew that I meant business. Until that morning, Ruby had only ever experienced me as 'Mr Nice and Easy Guy'. I then stormed off, leaving her to clean up the mess, and then things went from bad to worse. The bailiffs turned up with a court order to confiscate all of the hotel furniture due to unpaid bills, and following that, the intercom system, which Derrick hadn't paid for three years, was also about to be confiscated. Luckily Scotland Yard intervened and managed to successfully persuade them all to wait until the investigation was over. After that, once the police finally had put a name to their murder suspect, and the identity of the hotel could be declared to the media, a detective took me to a Knightsbridge restaurant for lunch and brought me up-to-date with the details. He let me know me that the Yemen Government was offering a reward of up to £500,000 (approximately £5 million today) for any information that helped to identify the assassin and that I'd be entitled to some of the money if not all of it...

"I don't want any o' their bloody money!" I told the detective in a panic. "I can't make money outta someone gettin' murdered! You guys keep the money for yourselves, please just keep me and my name out of it!" I pleaded.

He agreed to do his best, and then explained that members of the media from around the world would be bidding for my story and that I could make quite a hefty sum of money from that as well. Again, I made it clear that I wasn't interested, and that no amount of money was worth risking my life over. When I again invited the police to claim the reward for themselves, he told me that the police weren't eligible to accept any money. In the end, he promised sincerely to do everything in his power to keep my name a secret. Looking back now in hindsight, I should have asked the police to give the reward money anonymously to a charity because I'd bloody-well earned it. Within minutes of our arrival back at the hotel, and when members of the British and International Press swarmed in, I had to break speed records in getting down to a basement dugout in time to hide from them before being spotted. As I was squatted amongst the putrid decaying garbage stored there for three weeks, and I held a cloth over my nose to try to cope with the stink, an army of reporters and TV film crews bombarded Robert House as though they'd just joined a gold rush. Once all that was over and done with, and the assassin had been publicly identified and exposed, the police informed me that I no longer needed their protection and were packed up and gone the following day. The newspapers and TV news networks described Robert House as a filthy cesspit, but at least my name never got mentioned. Robert House was no fancy palace, but except for whenever we'd held any of our extended parties, it was always kept reasonably clean and tidy. The around-the-clock vigil at the hotel had lasted for a terrifyingly-long three weeks and being forced to remain under police protection, 24/7, had affected my life dramatically. I was an innocent prisoner, and even going for a short walk down the street or popping into the local pub for a quick beer with friends had been entirely out of the question. When I fully acknowledged how close I'd come to being added to the list of the three murder victims, I shuddered so much that I didn't think I'd ever calm back down. According to what I'd been told by the police, on the day of the shootings, when 'Mr Room 11' had pushed me into the kitchen, it hadn't been to help me with the coffee at all, it had been to silence me permanently before his triple assassination. One of the police also told me that Mr Room 11 was a Martial Arts expert and that he wouldn't have even needed to use his gun to finish me off. Realising over and over again how easily he could have quickly snuffed me out effectively and in silence, remained an ongoing, lingering, sickening thought. The big bulge that I'd noticed in his coat pocket at the front door had been his gun with a silencer attached and ready for his murderous job at hand. If it hadn't been for the New Zealanders arriving at the dining room at the very moment that they did, the police suggested that the killer could have terminated my life there and then. I was the only person who could accurately identify the assassin, so even though I'd tried to befriend him, in his mind, I had to be silenced. Throughout my ordeal, I didn't hear from any Buddhist members, other than a couple of close friends I'd introduced to the practice. This had left me feeling more disappointed and disenchanted with the UK/NS/SGI than ever. Granted, the phone was disconnected, and during the drama, Robert House wasn't an ideal place to visit, but one of the senior members that knew me could have at least sent me a message of support and encouragement in the mail. I got bugger all, not a flipping sausage. From that very sad and miserable awakening, I learnt the hard way never to trust or rely on the organisation for anything, especially its leaders, and to always heed what Nichiren taught...

*Put your faith in the Law and not in the person.*

A few days after the ordeal was over, the hotel owner's son, Derrick, turned up, creeping in through the kitchen, to avoid bumping into his dad, who was still hot under the collar and gunning for him. I made us both a cup of tea, and then Derrick sincerely apologised to me for kicking me out of the hotel in favour of Ruby. He also admitted that he'd made a crucial mistake and that he'd known it as soon as he ordered my Gohonzon out of the hotel, but his selfish ego and stubborn nature had prevented him from backing down and changing his mind. In a strange reversal of roles, *he* was out of the hotel, and my Gohonzon and I were back in. I encouraged him by sharing something else that Nichiren had taught...

*The ground on which we fall is the same ground that we use to pick ourselves up.*

When I invited Derrick to do some chanting with me in my room, he was hesitant at first, but after some friendly persuasion on my part, he eventually agreed to at least give it a try. Afterwards, he told me that he'd always respected me and had held me in high regard, even during our many disagreements and rows. I was touched to hear it, and my heart went out to him. In many ways, he reminded me of a lost and confused child.

ON THE night before the new owners took possession of the hotel, Christopher visited me with his friend Mo, an attractive young woman of Scandinavian descent. He wanted my help in teaching her about the practice, which turned out to be a perfect antidote. Later that evening, when the three of us chanted together, it began to feel just like the good old times again, and then the loud hotel doorbell sounded. I cautiously climbed the stairs and opened the door to find a sinister-looking character of Middle-Eastern appearance staring me in the eye. His demeanour was a touch unfriendly and unsavoury. So, without hesitation, I politely told him that we were fully-booked and quickly closed the door.

# Chapter 35

# CH-CH-CH-CHANGES AND SOME UNAVOIDABLE COMPLAINING

A relaxing fortnight's break in Paris staying with Masami did me a great deal of good! His rooftop apartment directly overlooked the busy River Seine and had unobstructed views of the world-famous Eiffel Tower. Apart from feeling like I was back in the real world, the break proved to be therapeutic in ridding me of a lot of pent-up stress and tension. One of the highlights of my Paris holiday had been a visit to the magnificent Notre Dame, and the heavenly taste of mouth-watering ice cream beneath the famous windmill at Moulin Rouge! After a sad farewell to Masami, a few days later, I flew back to London amid the Queen's Silver Jubilee celebrations and landed just before the first celebratory bonfire was about to be lit. Although Paris had been a cleaner city, it lacked the unique warmth and friendliness of London where most people spoke English, and I was so happy to be back on British soil. 'Her Majesty' wasn't the only queen out celebrating that evening. During my cab ride from the airport, I was kept entertained by the sights of dozens of colourful street parties, filled to their brims with hundreds of outrageous and flamboyantly-dressed characters who were dancing to Donna Summer's amazing new hit song, 'I Feel Love'. It was billowing out of speakers from every direction.

Before I'd left for Paris, Christopher's friend, Mo, had arranged for me to rent a bed-sitter in an old Victorian terrace house where she lived in Maida Vale. My room was located upstairs at the back of the house, with a small kitchen area built into a wall closet beside the wardrobe, a single bed and just enough room for my TV. The view was nothing to get excited about, as my only window overlooked a jungle of unsightly weeds growing wildly in the backyard areas between our building and the terraces in the next street. Hidden amongst the weeds were years and years' of built-up rubbish that had been dumped there, as well as an army of feral cats and heaven only, knows what else. There were also plenty of musicians living in the area, and during the days, those living opposite would hang out of their back windows soaking up the sunshine while playing their instruments at full volume, seemingly competing with each other. While most of them were excellent players, some were atrocious, and whenever they all let rip at the same time, it became a discordant din of what I can only describe as being severe noise pollution. Some of the internal walls in the house were very thin, especially those standing between my room, a shared toilet and bathroom, and another bed-sitter on the other side that was occupied by an Irish guitarist and a Belgian drummer. Each time the toilet was flushed, my wall would vibrate, adding to some of the audible sounds that came before the flush. The guys next door loved their beer and women and made sure that they got plenty of both. Next to them was Mo's flat, which was much more comfortable and spacious. Then, downstairs there lived a gay transvestite with her handsome Norwegian lover and a towering Canadian Punk-Rock drag queen. He would have been close to seven-foot-tall and needed to bend down going through doorways. He also spoke louder than anyone that I'd ever heard.

There were all sorts of weird, wonderful and colourful characters in and out of the building day and night, and most of the time, it was like living in a perpetual out-of-control street party. Sometimes, when everyone played their stereos up loud at the same time, the whole building would vibrate with discord. If the musicians out the back were going full-pelt with their 'volume competition' too, adding more noise to the already unholy racket, the result would be enough to make anyone feel like pulling their head off to escape. At nightfall, most of the musicians were out gigging, the feral cats would take over with their feline choruses of wails and loud, ear-piercing screeches, and I'd usually be hiding my head under the pillows and trying to get to sleep. The Canadian punk-rock drag queen owned a mobile disco business and would frequently return home during the early hours of the morning, out of his head on drugs, and start playing punk music at full volume. That's when Mo would hurtle past my room down to his, bellowing like a madwoman and telling him to shut the fuck up! Mo could be lovingly sweet most of the time, but if anyone pissed her off, she could quickly resemble a woman on the warpath. It was all crazy beyond crazy, but it was also just what I needed to help erase more memories of my Robert House ordeal.

Not long after I'd moved in, the punk-rock drag queen's 90 plus-year-old mum came to visit him for a few weeks from Toronto. She was as deaf as a doorknob, which was probably why her son habitually yelled whenever he spoke to anyone. The poor old dear was utterly disgusted with the place and everyone in it, including her son and me. One night when a threatening storm was brewing, I jumped into bed, put a pillow over my head, and tried to sleep through it. It was the middle of summer, unusually humid, and it was just as I was dozing off that a tremendous flash of lightning accompanied by a massive blast of thunder startled me awake. At the same moment, I saw a pale figure fly through the air and then felt something latch onto my leg through the sheet.

It gave me such a terrifying fright that I almost climbed up the wall, before back-flipping across the bed to the door, and then charging along the hallway towards the Irish and Belgian musicians. When I suddenly burst into their room, their shocked facial expressions, which have remained in memory ever since, was absolutely priceless! There I was, standing buck naked, wig-less and looking like I'd just seen a ghost – then they did too! Suddenly aware of my nakedness, I leapt back out into the corridor towards my room and ran smack-bang into the punk-rock drag queen's old mum as she was coming out of the toilet, knocking her across the hallway and then tumbling down on top of her. As I was struggling to get up and drag my body off of her, she became as hysterical as I was. As I stood with my hands cupped over my crowned jewels, apologising profusely and trying to explain, all she could do was scream her lungs out because she couldn't hear a bloody word that I was saying. Watching her shriek her way down the stairs to her son's room, her long, silver hair flying about in all directions, reminded me of an escapee from a loony bin. I only had just enough time to get my pants on before everyone else in the building rallied around to search my room for what had frightened the life out of me. Mo was first to eventually discover the culprit. It was a feral white cat that must have squeezed through the opening in my window when the lightning struck. The poor little thing was semi-conscious, frothing at the mouth and wedged up in the lining under my bed, where it had clawed its way through. The punk-rock drag queen rushed it to a local vet but, sadly, it had used up its ninth life.

MY DETECTIVE friends from Scotland Yard would still visit me occasionally and sometimes take me out for lunch. The other tenants must have thought that I was a police informant because they became very suspicious and avoided having anything much to do with me. My ex-lover, Terrance, from the Robert House, came to visit me one day and after experiencing the atmosphere of where I was living for himself, insisted that I move into a room in his shared Ladbroke Grove residence, where he'd lived since just before Robert House went on the market. By then, I'd overcome my foolish one-sided 'love' desires for Terrance, and I'd grown to love and care for him like a brother instead. I'd also discovered that, deep down, Terrance was a good person with a huge heart, and that he was a compassionate and caring human being. The house at Ladbroke Grove was an old, four-storey building, with a basement and a small steeple on its top. The owners were a gay couple, who'd been gradually refurbishing it. Compared to the house at Maida Vale, it was like a palace, and I ended up living there for about a year. During that time, I experienced more unexpected and significant changes in my life, some of which were very disturbing due to my ailing relationships with certain leaders and members of the organisation. While I'd been living in the UK, the membership had grown considerably, and the Headquarters in Japan had finally offered to provide the funds for the UK members to buy their own centre. As a way to express their appreciation, some of the members had written and produced a new show called 'All Together Now'. They planned to perform in a London theatre as both a thank-you celebration and a public introduction to Nichiren Buddhism. During the pre-planning for the show, I noticed how much the general attitude in the organisation's activity sector had changed. The warm, relaxed and friendly approach that had existed with similar past performances, when just about anyone was welcome to join in, had been replaced with a business-like seriousness. For example, in earlier times, any members wishing to participate in a show would have been found a place, regardless of talent or ability, but now they were being asked to endure rigorous, scrutinising auditions. To top all that off, it seemed to me that some of the decision-makers were a law unto themselves, as I found some of them to be overbearingly rude, arrogant and motivated more by their egos and self-importance than their down-to-earth Buddhist compassion. And I wasn't alone in my perception, as some of the other members that I spoke to about it were saying the same thing. Even the weekly meetings had become domains of power struggles, with many leaders and lay-members competing with each other each week to see who could round up the most converts. To me, they seemed to be losing the plot by overlooking or forgetting the essential basics, such as taking care of the needs and feelings of those members they already had, the nervous ones who were often shy about coming forward, or who chose to remain in the background. It seemed as though everything was about gaining as many new converts as possible and the goal was to please the leaders, particularly the SGI world leader Daisaku Ikeda. For those of us who didn't join in and follow suit, it was either fall by the wayside or be spoken about as being someone who was 'out of rhythm', or untrustworthy, as we were often termed. I suspect that there were plenty of members who, in fear of being frowned upon or left out, pretended to go along with the flow just to keep 'face' and not be 'judged'. Some leaders could be quite two-faced and deceitful as well. They'd often say one thing in the presence of a leader and the opposite to others less prestigious. Let me be the first to admit that there was still a ton of room for improvement in my life, but because my faith was based solely on the Mystic Law, I had no desire to be favoured nor to deceive for personal gain.

The Japanese man in charge of all the European members back then was Doctor Yamazaki, and whenever he visited the UK to give guidance to the members, many of them would flock to him like he was a visiting rock-star or a new messiah. I was never disrespectful or rude to anyone, but because I refused to go along with the idea that the organisation's 'hierarchy' was to be honoured more highly than others of lower status, I was more often than not frowned upon and increasingly ostracised. Nichiren's teachings and practice are all about equality, and people rubbing together like rough stones to smooth out theirs and each other's impurities to eventually shine. It's a goal that can only be achieved by having pure faith in the Mystic Law and not in any person. I'm sure that if I'd made a big enough fuss of the leaders, and if I'd looked up to them and appraised them as so many other's did, I could have easily climbed the ladder and reached great heights. After joining the NS/SGI, I'd brought many converts into the organisation, which made it awkward and tricky for the powers that be to push me aside easily, but some tried nonetheless. One of the biggest lies that we were tricked into believing was that unless we were part of the organisation, we couldn't practise Nichiren's teachings correctly or attain our enlightenment. Consequently, many of us were reluctant to complain or object for fear of being excommunicated and losing the feelings of confidence and inner-security that we'd gained from our chanting. By no means did I regard myself as being an 'excellent example' or someone special, I've let other people down and didn't always practise what I preached. However, I was never bossy, rude or lacking in compassion or empathy, not even towards people that I didn't particularly like. In my efforts to help others with similar faults, I was always willing to admit my mistakes and shortcomings to explain how chanting Nam-Myoho-Renge-Kyo had enabled me to face and overcome them. Sadly, by exposing myself so openly and honestly there were some, including leaders, who took advantage of what I revealed and used it later to gossip and make me look bad. The main hypocrites who did this never seemed to have the guts or were prepared to admit even the smallest of their faults, in fear of losing face. They'd usually only ever want to share their obvious benefits, such as getting a new job, a new car and stuff like that. Some of the leaders, who took advantage of the honesty of others, also seemed to regard their official positions as a licence to bully people and rudely boss them around whenever they felt like it. There were times when I felt like screaming out that the organisation's leadership was a big pile of 'fuckin' bullshit' and throwing in the towel. The underlying lie that kept me persevering was an immense fear of more visions the 'black-eyed man' returning, plus losing all the security and happiness within, that I'd gained from my chanting. On a far more positive side, a more powerful influence that kept me going was the memory of the extraordinary dream that I'd had in Hong Kong about finding the truth in Japan at the foot of a pointed mountain etcetera. Sometimes I felt as though I'd climbed the mighty peak to pluck the single rose only to discover that I'd lost my sense of smell. In the end, I contributed one song to 'All Together Now', but that was as involved as I wanted to get.

WHEN IT CAME to explaining Nichiren's Gosho, Dick Causton was one of the best that anyone could hope to have as a teacher, and my wish was to learn as much as I possibly could from him. However, during one of our friendly chats, Dick tried to convince me that Daisaku Ikeda was equal to Nichiren in present-day times, in other words, that he was an enlightened being – a Buddha, after which I began having some second thoughts. By then, I'd read several articles supposedly written by Daisaku Ikeda that I'd either questioned or found difficult to accept as being in line with my understandings of what Nichiren taught. For the first time, I couldn't bring myself to agree with what Dick said, and I told him so, explaining that, although I respected Ikeda's wisdom and sincerely appreciated his contribution in helping to spread Nichiren's teachings worldwide, I didn't feel the same way about Ikeda as many of the other members did in their adoration of him, and that my devotion was above and foremost to the Mystic Law. Dick had responded by claiming that my bad karma was influencing my judgement and that if I sincerely chanted enough about it, I'd eventually overcome the obstacles that were controlling my life and see Daisaku Ikeda in the same light as the others. I couldn't agree with that either, and his unsuccessful attempt to reassure me only left me feeling even more confused and alienated. Nichiren wanted people to 'put their faith in the Mystic Law and not in any person', including himself, which I could always relate to. What was Dick thinking that day? After our conversation, it was clear to me that I was not only on a different path to many of the other members but also to my original mentor, Dick Causton. In the past, I'd never doubted Dick's judgement and guidance in the slightest. As remorseful as I felt for doing it, from that day on, I analysed and thought very deeply and carefully about whatever else Dick had to say.

MASAMI HAD fallen in love with a local female member named Vanessa, and after he was finally able to return from Paris to live in London, and stayed with me at Ladbroke Grove, they were finally able to spend more time together. On the night of his 31st birthday, while I spent the night at a friend's place to give them some space and privacy, it turned out to be the special night that their first child, Koichi, was conceived. I'd been in many short-lived relationships, but nothing ever seemed to quite work out, and I was feeling fed up with living a life of promiscuity, uncertainty, failed affairs and endless one-night stands. I wanted so much to settle down in a stable and loving relationship. Knowing that Masami had found true love had, in a strange sort of way, generated a degree of hope and happiness for me as well – for a little while, anyway...

TERRANCE CAME knocking on my door one day, raving on about a new Donovan song that he'd just heard playing on the radio...

"It's all about that Light that you said you saw!" Terrance told me excitedly.

Later that day, he returned with a copy of the record for me to play and listen to. The words took my breath away, and my skin tingled, it was like a message from the beyond, and I must have played it at least ten times to copy down the words. I also wondered if Donovan had been to the Light himself. Here are the words and the link to Donovan's amazing song...

The Light

I Died ….. and I sighed As the chains of the flesh left me.
As the moans and the groans of the friends sending me.
On my way to the Land of the Dead.
I flashed ... that my soul was Unharmed as my earth form, I shed.
That the image of death had been a thought in my head
And the truth is a spirit am I.
I sussed that my life had been a lesson chosen by me.
For to purify my Soul that I may be worthy to shine forth the Light.
The Light – The Light
As I moved ever upward – a Great Light there came.
More feeling than seeing and it filled me with Shame.
Like a Bright Shining mirror reflecting my being.
My present condition of Soul I was seeing.
I Beheld ... Forms of Great Beauty and they shone forth the Light.
With love vibes, they met me and they cast off my fright.
Those great souls of ages long past.
I praised the great souls of the ages who care for our needs.
They lovingly nurture - wisdom's bright seed.
Showing the way to the Light.
I ached for the womb and the earth and another time around.
Seeking circumstances, the best that can be found.
To give me the lessons to learn.
I was born, and through childhood, my soul still remembered the Light.
And through teens, I fought fiercely for my vision of the Light.
Then I saw Mum and Dad had forgot.
The Light – The Light – The Light – The Light.
https://www.youtube.com/watch?v=IBWTIc4G9

*Myo is the unfathomable nature of all life from one moment to the next.*
*It is something that the mind is unable to comprehend and there are just no words that can truly define it. If we try to study our own mind at any given moment we will not see any particular colour or shape to confirm that it exists. But even though this is so, we still cannot say that it does not exist due to the countless thoughts that are continuously happening within it.*
*Life is an indefinable mystery that reaches far beyond the conceptualisation of being and not–being.*
*Even though it cannot be proven to either exist or not exist, it still discloses the attributes of both.*
*It is the mystic entity of the Middle Way that is the supreme and true reality.*
*Myo represents the mystic nature of Life and ho, its manifestations.*
*...Nichiren.*

# Chapter 36

# CO SAN

Vanessa helped get me a job in a large Swiss Cottage supermarket, just north of London proper, serving in the takeaway-food section, and it wasn't long before I had enough money saved to buy a little green, second-hand Ford Anglia, similar to the one used years later in the Harry Potter movies. One night, I was driving across London in it and got caught in a massive traffic jam after several IRA terrorist bombs had gone off in the CBD. Most of central London was at a standstill, and to make things worse, I'd left my wallet at home in another jacket, and I was starving hungry with only 50P to my name. As the bumper-to-bumper traffic continued crawling along inch by inch, and the mouth-watering aroma of delicious hot food from the nearby restaurants filled my nostrils, I was even having fleeting thoughts of gnawing on the steering wheel! In an attempt to manifest some inner strength to help me cope with my nagging hunger pangs, I started chanting. I'd hardly begun, before a sudden hard, loud bang from behind jolted me forward and then slammed me back against my seat. I was convinced that an IRA bomb had gone off right behind my car until I turned to look and discovered that a large prestigious car had crashed into the back of me. I hopped out to inspect the damage and was greeted halfway by a chubby little man in a tuxedo who'd already given my car the once-over...

"Oh, I'm frightfully sorry old chap! Here, take this! Do you think that will cover it?" He half gasped as he handed me a £20 note. (£300 today)

I couldn't see the slightest bit of damage on my car, but I took the money and happily agreed that it would do. I then spent the next hour or so watching the traffic trickle past at snail's pace while I sat comfortably in a restaurant, happily devouring the source of the aromas that had wafted into my nostrils only minutes earlier. It was like switching from a bad dream into a good one.

THE LADBROKE GROVE house was purported to have been built on the grounds of an ancient cemetery, and in it, there was one particular area of the stairway that leads down to the basement, where the resident cat's fur would often stand on end for no apparent reason as it hissed and snarled at 'nothing'.

At first, I thought the cat was picking up the scent of a mouse or some other creature hiding beneath the floorboards. Its odd behaviour reminded me of an experience that I'd had when I was seventeen, and an older man that Mum and I helped care for had just died. We were all gathered in his living room consoling his elderly wife when the couple's Persian cat's fur stood up for no apparent reason as it backed away from the doorway, hissing and spitting as it went. When Mum and the man's daughter raced to another room to gulp down some 'medicinal' brandy to help them cope, I became so freaked out that I almost dived out of a nearby window. Late one night when some Buddhist friends were visiting, the cat at the Ladbroke Grove house did a similar thing, but rather than running in fear, this time I heeded Dick Causton's previous advice and used the 'strategy of the Lotus Sutra' instead. Standing directly in front of the cat, with my heart filled with as much courage, conviction, love and compassion as I could muster up, I softly chanted Nam-Myoho-Renge-Kyo, and by way of positive thoughts, beckoned the universal forces to set whatever or whoever it was free and allow it to continue its journey back home to the Light. Everyone watching must have thought that I'd lost the plot, but the cat soon settled down and remained docile for as long as I continued living there.

ONE OF MY detective friends showed up unexpectedly early one morning and told me that it was vitally important for me to accompany him to the New Scotland Yard Headquarters. When we arrived, he took me on a speedy sight-seeing tour of the building and then led me into what appeared to be a lab, where he asked me to sit down for a moment. Suddenly, there was a huge black and white photograph staring me in the face of a corpse riddled with bullet holes. I immediately recognised the face in the picture as being that of Mr Room 11 and found the photo to be sickening and disturbing. I also didn't appreciate how the detective had gone about showing it to me and told him so. He explained that it was necessary to present the picture abruptly so that he could gauge my initial reaction. As soon as I'd signed a document to verify that it was the body Mr Room 11, I just as abruptly asked him to please put the picture away out of my sight. Mr Room 11 had been the leader of a suicide squad of Palestinian terrorists, who'd hijacked a Lufthansa-747 jet and taken the passengers and crew on a five-day horror trek around the Middle East. I'd been watching the crisis on the evening news and had felt empathy for what the poor hostages must have been going through, but never for a moment had I expected that it had anything to do with the Robert House saga. During the hijacking, 'Mr Room 11', shot and killed the pilot in front of the passengers and then left his body on the cabin floor for over sixteen hours. The horror trip finally came to a violent ending when a crack team of German commandos shot and killed all the members of the terrorist group, including Mr Room 11, and liberated the jet in Mogadishu, Somalia. The German police working on the case wanted to fly me to Germany so that I could identify the assassin's body in person, but I flatly refused. I'd already been through as much as I could bear by then, and I wasn't willing to voluntarily add any more to it. My involvement in the murders had been a draining and deeply disturbing experience. Regardless of rights or wrongs, my only desire by then was to cut all ties with the whole thing. Thankfully the British police respected my wishes, and the German request was denied. Later that day, I found myself thinking about the Law of Cause and Effect...

"Could it be possible that my meetin' up with Mr Room 11, 'n' nearly gettin' killed by him, was connected ta somethin' I've done in my past? I asked myself with a cringe.

I'd thought about the lies that I'd told as a child regarding a man shooting at me, and how I'd called the police and falsely reported seeing two escaped prisoners dragging a woman into the bushes near where I lived. It was all done to terrorise my fathers' live-in lover, Beatty, but even so, that still didn't make it right. I eventually concluded that my present dilemma of being in the wrong place at the wrong time had been karma payback.

I HADN'T SEEN my friend Ray for months, until one day when he showed up out-of-the-blue without warning and looking so dreadful that I hardly recognised him. I was in bed with the flu and felt pretty poorly myself, and seeing Ray looking such a mess made me feel suddenly ten times worse. In the few minutes that Ray hung around, he hardly spoke a word that made any sense to me, so I was none the wiser after he'd gone as to what he'd come for, nor what was going on in his life. That night, a neighbour of Ray's phoned the house, begging for me to get over there immediately. I felt far too sick to leave the house to go anywhere, so I asked Terrance to go for me, and when he arrived and told Ray that I couldn't make it, Ray went ballistic, abusing Terrance and setting fire to his Gohonzon. Had I known that Ray was about to react like that and go so out of control, I'd have dragged myself there, no matter how sick I felt. When Terrance returned from Ray's and told me what had happened, it hit me like a sledgehammer. Terrance was feeling devastated and furious with me for asking him to go in the first place, but I was more concerned d about Ray's state of mind and wellbeing, so I phoned the London Buddhist office and asked for someone to look in on him.

SHORTLY AFTER I'd commenced chanting, I asked Dick Causton where I stood regarding Nichiren's Buddhism and my sexuality, and his answer was...

"If being a homosexual is the source of your unhappiness, Tommy, then you may change and become happier by being heterosexual, but if it isn't, you'll become happier being just who and what you are. As far as I'm aware, there's nothing in Nichiren's teachings about homosexuality at all, or in the teachings of Jesus, for that matter. Therefore, I can only assume that neither of them considered it necessary to even comment on the subject."

Dick didn't show any sign of discomfort with my question, nor did he pass any kind of judgement. His uplifting words of advice not only gave me new hope in attaining dignity as a gay human being but had also helped me to bring forth the inner-strength that I needed to rise above the torments of a cruel and unjust world. Since then, while my sexuality hadn't changed, something else had, especially following the Robert House incident. After years of living the loveless lifestyle of a gay, freelance sex-addict, I finally felt ready and prepared to do whatever it took to achieve the happiness that I'd long dreamed about and to find the lasting love that I yearned for.

It's such a travesty that so many gay people have in the past been forced, and still continue to be forced, to go through their lives hiding their true identity and pretending to be someone they're not, especially those without family support and guidance. Far too many gays have been, and still are, left to learn from the confused and misguided words and actions of others whose lives are just as perplexed, or even more so! This unfortunate outcome, in my opinion, is the main reason behind why there has been so much instability, promiscuity and perverse sexual behaviour in the gay community, which in turn, has resulted in unhappiness, depression, and sometimes suicide, especially among younger gays. Heterosexuals are different, as they usually have the freedom to openly bring their date's home, and when they're ready to settle down, they usually also have the loving support from their parents and siblings to help guide them and give them a chance to share a stable future. Thank goodness he situation today for gays has changed for the better.

Back in 1977, my greatest wish was to share my life with another male who'd help me in my quest to create value towards life, either through my songwriting, music, or storytelling. A tall order, yes, but deep within I felt sure that there had to be someone like it out there somewhere if only I could become worthy of achieving the good fortune that I needed to be at the right place at the right time to meet him. After a year of chanting solidly for this and still getting no real results, I'd given up trying and had started relapsing into my old ways, after I took a job serving in the coffee shop of a local all-male state-of-the-art gay sauna club at Shepherds Bush. The club's environment was very stimulating and erotic, and part of my job was to wander around the large establishment every hour and make sure that no one was having sex in any of the sauna rooms. To do this, I was authorised to open doors without knocking, and some of the sights that I witnessed each day were priceless! One evening, I was delivering coffee to a couple of extremely feminine, gay elderlies, when a young Asian guy walked in the main entrance, and at the moment we noticed each other, our eyes instantly locked! It stopped me dead in my tracks, and the feeling that I felt was like nothing that I'd ever experienced before with another human being – far more spiritual than sexual. He was strikingly-handsome, but it was the magnificent, mystical glow from his eyes that I'd first noticed about him. That moment magnetically entrancing, and as though we'd known each for the longest time and were finally reconnecting. I couldn't tell if he was Japanese or Chinese, even though his long, shiny, jet-black hair flowing freely down his back reminded me a lot of a samurai. As I stood in wonder, one of the older men broke it all by sarcastically asking me if there was to be a chance of him getting his coffee before he was too old to pick the cup up and drink it. A few minutes later, wearing only a white towel, the handsome young Asian came up to the counter, ordered a drink and then introduced himself as Co, explaining to me in broken English that he'd never been to a sauna before. It turned out that a carpenter friend of his who was temporarily working in the sauna doing some cabinet-making had talked Co into coming that evening for a freebie.

It was May 28th, 1978, a special day that would soon become one of the most beautiful, important and significant days in my life. A day that would not only trigger an extraordinary turning point in my life's destiny but also become one of the most valuable and rewarding days of my existence since becoming a Buddhist. Co and I had barely enough time to exchange our phone numbers and addresses before I had to leave him to take care of several customers that were waiting impatiently at the counter to get served, and by the time that I'd finished with them, he'd taken his drink and gone back to his table. Oh, how I wished that I throw down my apron and join him. Things became extremely busy after that, so much so, that I didn't even notice Co leave. The next chance that I had to look for him, he was nowhere in sight, which deeply disappointed me. I can't describe what a wonderfully unexpected surprise I got the next day when Co knocked on my door. After I invited him in, we chatted over coffee and biscuits for the next couple of hours, during which time, it became apparent to me that Co's mind was being intermittently preoccupied with the altar cabinet that housed my Gohonzon. He eventually asked me if I was a member of NS/SGI, and at first, I was hesitant to give him an answer. Then, when I admitted that I was, just as I was expecting, Co responded with what seemed like a look of disapproval. I didn't know how to react or what to say next, and after a few seconds to try to gain some stability in my thoughts, I took the plunge and asked Co what his views were on the organisation. When he answered by relaying an unpleasant childhood experience that took place back in the 1950s when he was a small child, and when some members came to his house to try to get his mother to join the NS/SGI organisation, I was left speechless. When his Mum had refused to join, they'd turned against her and threatened her that she'd die a terrible death in the gutter. As I explained earlier, when the awareness and propagation of the Mystic Law were in their infancy during post-war Japan, although the members meant well, some went about it in the completely wrong way, probably out of desperation and ignorance, and the aggressive approach used to recruit Co's mother is a perfect example of this. I quickly changed the subject and offered to make us another fresh cup of coffee.

In the past, I'd lost potential partners because of my steadfast devotion to my faith, and I didn't want to risk it happening again if I could avoid it. After Co left and went home that day, with deep regret and sadness in my heart and with tears welling in my eyes, I rolled my Gohonzon up and packed my altar away. I felt like I was turning my back on a trustful friend, but I was so desperately serious about Co that I was prepared to do anything within reason to keep him if I possibly could. My plan was to continue my chanting but in secret. Over the next couple of days that followed I noticed that Co was a little aloof, and suspecting that his attraction towards me was possibly going off the boil, I took the leap, faced the guns head-on and asked him frankly if anything was wrong. I was expecting to hear what I most dreaded, *sayonara*, but instead, Co took me by complete surprise by asking me where my Gohonzon was. When I told him that I'd put it away, he reacted with a look of shock-horror, and when he encouraged me to re-enshrine it and to continue on with my practice, I was astounded! The next day, when Co revisited me and noticed that I'd re-enshrined my Gohonzon, he asked to hear me chant for a while. I'd was only chanting for a couple of minutes before Co knelt beside me and blew my mind by joining in, the last thing that I'd have ever thought possible under the circumstances, and I wasn't sure if it was really happening or if I was hallucinating. When we'd finished chanting, I asked Co why he'd knelt down and chanted with me, and in broken English, he let me know that he wanted to share his life with me and to be involved in everything that I did, including my Buddhist practise and propagation of the Mystic Law. I wasn't sure if I'd understood him correctly, or if I'd only imagined what I wanted to hear, but once Co reaffirmed what he meant, by saying it all a second time, his beautiful words were like a symphony to my ears, and my inner-being almost exploded with happiness.

The vibe within the Ladbroke Grove house had become increasingly unpleasant. One day, just after I'd given Masami some requested advice about something, Vanessa pulled me aside privately and virtually ordered me to stay away from Masami because he was 'no longer my concern'. I'd only ever showed respect and care for him, but now that they were about to be married, it appeared that she was becoming overly possessive of 'her property'. To some degree, she was within her rights to say what she said, but she could have been a lot more compassionate about it. Her cold delivery had reminded me of when Beatty and Dad had ordered me to keep away from my little brother Billy. Vanessa's stern warning left me feeling hurt and rejected, and when I told Co what she'd said, he insisted that I come and live with him.

On the same day that I moved into Co's split-level Hammersmith flat, I received another unexpected amazing and totally unexpected surprise, when my ultimate dream was completed after Co took out his guitar and began playing. Until that moment, I'd had no idea that Co could play a musical instrument! By the end of that day, we were busy writing songs together about Australia. Although Co had never been to Australia, it didn't take long at all before he had a real, fair-dinkum feel for the place, especially after I shared some stories with him about my life there. The first three songs we wrote were *Nullarbor Plain*, *Swan River Waters* and *Sydney*.

Co's warm support and love had allowed me to put my resentment towards Vanessa behind me, and just a couple of weeks later, I was best man and chauffeur for hers and Masami's wedding. Once Vanessa had finished decorating my little green Anglia all over with white lace and pink ribbon, we drove off to the registry office, with it looking like a Barbie Doll toy. Co was at my side during the reception afterwards, and later that night, we decided to uproot and move to Australia. In a last-minute attempt to try to get us a couple of free tickets, I offered our 'Australiana' songs to a travel agency in central London, who was seriously considering using them for promotional purposes until the fuel-tanker drivers went on strike, and most flights out of the UK were cancelled. The strike marked the beginning of a national crisis that snowballed and eventually brought Great Britain to its knees.

*Chang-an wrote 'If one befriends another person but lacks the mercy to correct him, one i in fact his enemy.'*

*The consequences of a grave offense are extremely difficult to erase. The most important thing is to continually strengthen our wish to benefit others.*

*Never seek this Gohonzon outside yourself.*

*The Gohonzon exists only in the mortal flesh of us ordinary people who embrace the Lotus Sutra and chant Nam-Myoho-Renge-Kyo.*

*...Nichiren.*

# Chapter 37

# POSITIVES & NEGATIVES

Almost a week into the strike, our travel agent phoned with news of a couple of cancellations and offered us a very cheap flight from Paris to Sydney via Bangkok and Singapore. Accepting would mean that we'd only have two days to pack and get over to Charles De Gaulle Airport in France. We were anxious to start our new life together in Australia, so we accepted. Co's carpenter friend had gone missing after owing Co money and had left behind several pieces of his machinery. With nowhere to store it and to retrieve some of what was owing to help pay for the trip, Co had to sell it for whatever he could get. Having to leave my faithful Ford Anglia behind was the hardest thing that I had to do. I felt like I was abandoning a loving pet or a trustworthy friend. With no time to advertise and sell it, I gifted it to Masami and Vanessa, but within only a couple of weeks, everything under the sun started going wrong with it. I've heard it said that our cars are extensions of ourselves when we're driving them and that after a while the electromagnets holding us and our cars together become entwined. When Masami let me know that my little Anglia had given up the ghost, it was almost like hearing the bad news that someone had died. During the early-morning coach ride to Dover to catch a hovercraft to Calais in France, I gazed out from the window into the moving images and reminisced about my adventures while in London. Remembering why I'd gone the UK in the first place, I felt an uncomfortable wave of guilt and disappointment race through my body for not having made more of an effort, and for losing direction by focussing on other trivial issues. There'd only been one time that I'd come close to a breakthrough with YOU, and that happened one afternoon when I was strolling through the back streets of Soho. I came across a leading theatrical company, and curious to find out more about it, I'd stepped inside for a quick sticky-beak and was lucky enough to cross paths with the company's CEO, who just happened to be passing through the foyer. After I gave him a brief outline of what my musical was about, he invited me into a large conference room to discuss it further in-depth. When he'd finished listening to a couple of the songs, he asked if he could borrow the tape to listen to the rest later when he had more time, promising also to phone me in a few days with his decision. I was ecstatic, and running around like a headless chook telling everyone about it! A week later, the CEO kept his promise to phone me, but the news wasn't what I was expecting. He explained that although he thought YOU was a 'refreshingly new and exciting' concept and that it had a lot of potentials, his company had signed a deal for a big production that was about to open in London. In other words, their plate was full, and his hands were tied...

"If only you'd come to me with this six months ago," he concluded, before wishing me well with the musical and then finishing the call.

Perhaps he was just trying to comfort me, but I chose to believe him to help myself cope with yet another rejection. Deep within, I felt devastated, but as it turned out, he'd told me the truth. A few months later his company's production of *Evita* opened at London's Prince Edward Theatre.

The rough passage across the English Channel to Calais was a waking nightmare. I cursed every single minute of it and swore that I'd never travel anywhere by hovercraft again. The long and gruelling coach journey to Paris that followed added even more salt to the wound. I ended up with a whopping headache and other aches and pains where I'd rarely ever felt them before. We arrived in Paris just after midnight and found the streets chock-a-block full of people trying to get taxis to the airport. As we waited in the very long queue, a young Canadian guy asked if we could give him a lift to the airport. Like so many others at the bus and taxi terminal that night, he was flat broke, hungry and desperate to get out of Europe as soon as he possibly could. When we eventually arrived at Charles De Gaulle Airport, it too was chock-a-block full of desperate people trying to get on flights. Co and I had barely slept a wink for two days, and our plane wasn't due to fly out until 8.00am. We invited our Canadian friend to have a bite to eat with us and then found a quiet spot to sit and wait the hours out. To help fill in time, we told him about Nam-Myoho-Renge-Kyo, and while we were in the midst of explaining some of the basic fundamentals, another young man who'd been lying down quietly behind us on the opposite side of our seat suddenly popped his head up and cut in...

"Is what yer sayin' fer real, man? Does all that chantin' shit really work?"

He spoke with a strong American accent and would have been in his early twenties. He also seemed to be frantically anxious about something, and after I assured him that the chant did work and we all officially introduced ourselves, he told us that he'd been stranded at the airport for over a week, desperately trying to get a flight home to New York City, where his father was lying in a coma after suffering a stroke. As the young American explained, the fear and desperation in his voice and eyes made it clear that he was terrified of never seeing his dad alive again, and my heart went out to him. I couldn't make any guarantees, but I did promise him that chanting Nam-Myoho-Renge-Kyo would give him a positive result of some kind, even if only the strength to cope better. Then, before I could say another word, he was up off his seat and pleading with us to chant with him...

"Can we do some now? Can we do it right here and now?"

The sudden thought of us all being dragged off to the funny farm prompted me to suggest looking for somewhere a bit more private and secluded. While we were searching, the American surprised us all again by letting us know that he'd already been to an NSA/SGI Buddhist discussion meeting in New York City a year earlier. The only reason he'd gone was that he had a crush on the woman who'd invited him, and that's where his focus had been the whole time. Nevertheless, the words of the chant had stuck in the back of his mind. We eventually found a secluded spot to chant amongst some large concrete pipes that we found laying about just outside of the main terminal building. After placing my little my 'British Airways' bag on one pipe, we all climbed up and positioned ourselves 'horseback' on another pipe and started to chant. Things were going perfectly until we were suddenly frightened out of our wits by two French airport security guards, who crept up on us from behind with two huge German-shepherd guard dogs. I tried my best to explain to the guards what we were doing, and how whenever I travel with my Gohonzon, I always keep it rolled up and safely packed in my hand luggage, but they didn't seem to understand anything that I was saying. They probably thought that we were a group of religious fanatics praying to a British Airways bag to get on one of their flights. Once the guards had finished giving us a good looking over, checked our passports, and then poked around in my little blue bag, they went merrily on their way waving their hands about laughing, and leaving us to continue our chanting. Before we parted company with our American friend, I urged him to keep chanting as often as he could, even under his breath if necessary, and to focus on making it back home in time. I also promised that Co and I would do the same for him.

By sunrise, the airport was so crowded that Co and I had to almost fight our ways through the crowd and struggle to stay together until we'd reached the check-in desk. Because it was a cheap flight, we hadn't realised that there was an extremely limited weight allowance. What a shock we got when we were advised that our luggage was overweight to the tune of US$500, a considerable sum back then and almost all the money that we had. If we paid, we'd have left for the other side of the world close to penniless, and if we stayed, we'd risk being stranded in Paris for goodness knows how long, and still end up broke. We needed some time and space to think, so we took our luggage off the scales and moved to the back of the queue, where I chanted desperately under my breath for a solution until I eventually surrendered to the possibility that this time there wasn't going to be any way we'd be able to avoid or overcome our seemingly-insurmountable obstacle. I was searching my mind for alternative solutions when a lady tapped me on the arm and told me that a man further down the line, who was travelling First Class with only carry-on luggage, had offered to let us use his weight allowance for our excess baggage. I thought that I was *hearing things.* I don't know if it was another mystical event, or if the ground staff had suggested it to the man, but whatever the answer was, our problem was solved and we were so happy and grateful! Minutes later, we were airborne and on our way!

Our plane was a Boeing-707, which appeared to have been modified to accommodate extra passengers, and we were crammed in like sardines. The first leg of our journey took us over Southern Europe to a short stopover in Greece at Athens. Peering down and taking in the sights of the beautiful tiny islands that peppered the Mediterranean Sea, as we were arriving and leaving Athens, was a spectacular sight to behold, as they resembled precious little gems adorning turquoise satin. Our next stopover took place in the middle of the night in Kuwait. It was so hot that the air was like breathing in soup, and I remember saying to Co...

"No wonder they're always at each other's throats in this part o' tha world, this heat's enough ta send a marble statue nuts!"

By then I'd become delirious with fatigue. After leaving Kuwait to continue the final leg of the journey to Thailand, and I sat quietly gazing out of the window and eventually spotted what I believed was the sandy western shoreline of India. An hour or so later, I began wondering why we weren't passing beyond it, so I pushed my face hard against the window to try to get a more unobstructed view. What shock I got when I saw an explosion of bright blue light...

**"HOLY SHIT! THEY'RE SHOOTIN' AT US! WE'RE GETTIN' FIRED AT!"** I screamed, causing panic to erupt throughout the cabin.

As the flight attendants struggled to calm all the other passengers down, it was brought to my attention by Co, that I'd mistaken the moonlight shining on the wing edge for the Indian shoreline, and the *explosions* for the plane's night lights that were flashing beneath the wing. If dirty looks could kill, I'd have been dead in my seat then and there. One of the distraught passengers presented me with a bottle of Ouzo as a gift, which was probably to help calm me down or put me to sleep. I then spent the remainder of that awkward and uncomfortable flight hiding my face in shame and embarrassment. We finally arrived in Bangkok, just after daybreak, to find the airport crawling with Thai soldiers carrying machine guns. My first thoughts were that a war had broken out while we'd been up in the air, but it turned out to be their standard security measures. The moment we arrived in our hotel room, I made a beeline for the shower, where, as well as myself, I hand-washed our underwear and then used what little energy I had left to hang our underwear over the front of the box air conditioner to dry. A few hours later, I was awakened by a strange spluttering noise. I checked to see if the noise was coming from Co, and then scanned the room. What a surprise I got when I looked upwards and noticed a virtual iceberg hanging from the air conditioner, spluttering away for its life with our underwear frozen within it. It took Co and me most of the afternoon to hack away the ice with wire coat hangers, as we desperately tried to retrieve our underwear from the ice before the hotel staff noticed it and presented us with a bill for the damage.

EARLY THE NEXT morning, we set out on a walk across Bangkok, relying on a map that turned out to be highways only, and ended up totally lost. The sky had turned jet-black, and then before we knew it, deafening roars of thunder filled the air and a bombardment of lightning darted down upon the ground in all directions. In the next instant, the heavens opened up and released an avalanche of water that almost instantly created a flash flood. As Co and I quickly waded knee-deep through the fast-rising water towards a bus shelter that we could see in the distance, I mentioned to Co that there could be cobra snakes swimming amongst the debris. The very thought of it had us charging through the water like a pair of ship propellers. After reaching the bus shed, we quickly jumped up onto the seat and waited anxiously for the storm to pass and the water to recede. Once we were able to resume our trek and leave those imaginary 'snakes' behind, we backtracked to where we'd come from. By the time that we reached the safety of our hotel, it was well after midnight, and the next day, instead of walking and risking getting lost all over again, we caught a cab to do our sightseeing and struck up a friendship with its driver, who was a gentle old soul named Charlie. He only had one tooth, his face was heavily lined and weather-beaten, and he could hardly speak a word of English, but even so, we still managed to communicate in our usual friendly way. Charlie's old taxi and its worn-out suspension had seen far better days, but he and his cab ended up making the remainder of our stay in Bangkok a bouncy, bumpy delight, and an unforgettable adventure that we absolutely loved.

I WANTED TO leave Charlie something special to remember us by, so before vacating our room, I'd chanted to find a way to somehow introduce him to Nam-Myoho-Renge-Kyo. We had three hours to kill before we needed to be at the airport to check-in, so I asked one of the hotel interpreters to ask Charlie to take us to a cheap restaurant along the way for some traditional Thai food. When we rolled up to a big old tin shed in the middle of a field, I at first thought Charlie was playing a joke on us. A middle-aged woman, who looked like one of the farmworkers, hurried out to the car and greeted us with a big friendly smile. She then ushered us all into the shed, which turned out to be a make-shift Thai restaurant. As we perused the menu, Charlie indicated that he wouldn't be eating anything due to Ramadan and fasting, which I knew nothing much about at the time, but it did seem to me to be an appropriate opportunity to try to tell Charlie about the chant, so that's what I did. I wasn't getting very far because of the complexity of it and the language barrier. Then the woman preparing our food, who'd been listening in, wandered across to our table and told that she chanted Nam-Myoho-Renge-Kyo. Following that, as we watched and listened to her explain it to Charlie in Thai, and noticed his face light up, I felt certain that the synchronicity had been the result of my chanting that morning. Once we'd finished eating, the same lady let us know that the Bangkok Airport staff was rigorous and didn't allow anyone through with even a kilo over the limit. Her daunting and unexpected warning brought on an attack of instant indigestion. While we were waiting to check our luggage in, I could hear Co chanting softly behind me, and even though I doubted whether it would work this time, just hearing Co chant about it of his own volition filled my heart with joy. Co wasn't completely convinced about the practice, but he was certainly becoming optimistic due to the proof that he'd already witnessed and experienced. Just then, something unbelievable happened! While everyone else's luggage ahead of us in the queue had been placed upon the scales and weighed, when we arrived at the scales to weigh in ours, the guy behind the counter whose job was to lift the luggage off the scales and onto the rollers, stepped across the scales, picked up our luggage and carried it directly onto the conveyor belt. Co and I were so astounded that we couldn't even get our words out to answer the check-in clerk's questions. We were even more dumbstruck when the next person's luggage was placed on the scales and weighed. I realise that all this may sound pure BS or ridiculously far-fetched, and that's okay, but anyone who chants Nam-Myoho-Renge-Kyo consistently will full-heartedly agree that chanting these words can often produce synchronicity and benefits beyond belief. I've since wondered if Charlie may have known the guy behind the check-in desk and had asked him to help us out. The universe works in mysterious ways, so whatever way it may have happened, for us, it was still an amazing and very uplifting and mystic experience.

A FEW HOURS LATER, we disembarked at the Singapore terminal, where we were unexpectedly confronted with yet another obstacle. I'd completely forgotten that long hair on men was against the law in Singapore and that the 'hair Nazis' were always on the prowl. Co's hair wasn't only way down past his shoulders, but before leaving London, he'd had it highlighted, and that made it unmissable. When Co and several other young Asian men were asked to step aside to have their hair cut, it came as a daunting surprise to both of us. As I saw one sad-faced young man after another hurry out from the shearing shed, holding his head down in embarrassment, all that I could do was inwardly chant for Co to somehow be able to keep his. I can't express in words what a surprise we got when the barber stuck his head around the corner and told Co that he could proceed through without losing his locks! I've since wondered if the laws for men to keep their hair cut short had been changed by then and that it longer applied to foreign tourists. During the taxi ride to our hotel, the driver insisted on pulling over at brothels and trying to sell us on the idea of paying for sex with girls. In the end, to stop him from doing it, I had to threaten to flag down a police car and report him.

It was six years since my last visit to Singapore, and I was flabbergasted at how much the skyline and the character of the city had changed, so much so, that it was barely recognisable. All the rows of little shanty-town markets along Orchard Road, where I'd often enjoyed bargain hunts, had disappeared and had been replaced by skyscrapers, concrete roads, tiled pavements and perfectly manicured gardens. Gone also were the rickshaws and beeping taxis that would chase people up and down the streets for a fare. It may have looked impeccably neat and sparkling clean, but at the expense of the city's heart and soul, as we soon discovered. Prior to leaving London, I'd accompanied Co to the Australian Embassy to help him fill out a visa application for Australia. While we waited in the queue, I became so angry and disgusted with the rude and arrogant way that some of the staff members were speaking to the foreigners ahead of us, that I lost my temper and gave the staff members a mouthful of my own, then dragged Co out before we got around to submitting his application. Uncertain of how long it would take for Co to get a visa at the Australian embassy in Singapore, we used what little money we had very sparingly and stayed at the cheapest motel that we could find.

AUSTRALIA WAS in the grip of a telecommunications strike which made it almost impossible to contact my family and let them know where we were. With so much spare time on our hands, Co and I did a lot of chanting in the hope that it might speed things up, but when things only got worse, not only Co began losing hope, I fell into a state of despair as well, especially when our money had almost run out and we could no longer afford to pay for our room. Later that afternoon, we were leaving for the telephone exchange to make another attempt at contacting my family, when a beautiful, black South American entertainer that we'd befriended at the motel, spotted us and invited us to join her for a farewell drink in her room. She was leaving that night to do shows in Denmark and wanted to know if things had improved for us. I was in the midst of giving her a brief update, when her American boyfriend, whom we hadn't realised was there, came out from the bathroom and handed me a US one hundred dollar bill...

"Maybe this'll help you guys out 'til ya can get back on yer feet," he said, smiling through his strong southern American accent.

He was a tall and handsome Texan and he held a high-ranking position on an off-shore oil rig. As we were leaving, he handed me one of his Singapore business cards...

"If you guys get stuck 'n' need some more money, just take this card 'n' show it ta my office people here 'n' they'll fix ya up with whatever ya need."

As Co walked back to our room, I felt as though we'd just been rescued from a runaway train by Superman. Early the next morning, just before we were about to chant, I told Co about how, when I'd first arrived in the Far East, I'd met several people employed by the British and Australian Governments. Their jobs had often come with a large apartment, and some of them were very hospitable and happy to have some company every now and then. Since we still didn't know how much longer we'd need to remain in Singapore waiting for Co's visa, I decided to try my luck at chanting to meet one of them there – a pretty outrageous expectation, considering that we didn't even know anyone. Nevertheless, I was still determined to give it a darn good shot anyway! Imagine what a surprise it was later that day when our phone rang and an SGI Singapore women's leader asked me if I'd be willing to help explain the chant to an Englishman. We'd left our hotel number with her a few days earlier when we visited the Centre to chant in front of Singapore's main Gohonzon. She explained that a young American woman named Kathy, who'd only been chanting a short while, had travelled from Europe just to teach her British fiancé, Phillip to chant. I was delighted to do whatever I could to help. I'd not long put down the phone and had begun explaining the request to Co before Kathy was outside our motel honking her car horn. She wanted to invite us to join her and Phillip at his house that evening for a barbecue.

Phillip was a young bank manager in his early twenties, who lived in a spacious house set in a tropical wonderland of colourful flowers and lush greenery. His extra-large living room extended the entire length of the house, and leading off it was five bedrooms that each had its own private ensuite. That night, as we enjoyed a delicious meal on the patio under a warm, star-filled Capricornia sky and hit it off with Kathy and Phillip famously, Phillip invited us to move into one of his spare rooms free of charge and to stay for as long as we needed. Co didn't understand what Phillip was saying at first, but once I explained it in simple English, he was so surprised that it took him another few seconds to get the right words out in English to accept Phillip's invite and say thank you. We stayed at Phillip's house for the next three weeks, and what a contrast it was compared to living in our tiny motel room. Phillip not only proved to be the perfect host but also a great friend. Even after Kathy had returned to London, he still took us on numerous outings, including road trips up through Malaysia's dense rubber plantations that seemed to stretch out forever. On one such occasion, he took us on an unforgettable fishing-boat ride out to an uninhabited tropical island just off the coast of Malaysia. What an extraordinary experience that turned out to be. While Phillip was away scuba diving on the other side of the island, Co and I stripped naked and spent most of the day skinny dipping in the warm, crystal-clear water. Between dips, as we lounged around, soaking up the sun, we gorged on the luscious, local, tropical fruit that we'd brought with us. It was all so magical until I caught sight of a large black fin sticking up out of the water and gliding through the surface only meters away from Co. I had to almost scream my lungs out literally to get above the noise of the sea to warn him...

**"CO, GET OUT! GET OUTTA THA WATER QUICK! NOW!"**

Safely back on the beach, and beginning to calm down after Co's close encounter of potentially being shark fodder, our little 'taste of paradise' came to an abrupt ending when a violent storm snuck in from behind the island and the open sea that instantly created a living nightmare. There were moments when we thought our numbers were up, as the hot sand blasted everything in its path, and debris and rubble flew through the air like missiles. Some of the palm trees were bent almost horizontally to ground level. Co and I took shelter behind a pile of big rocks and hung on for dear life in absolute terror. With one hand gripped to a large chunk of rock and the other clamped over my head, how I ever managed to keep my wig from shooting off and heading north to China, I'll never know. As giant waves pounded relentlessly onto the rocks and beach, and the angry sky lit up from a barrage of forked lightning, we were soon forced to retreat into the jungle to take better cover. Then, as suddenly as the storm had come upon us, it was gone!

When Phillip resurfaced from his scuba diving adventure, he wasn't even aware that there'd been a storm. Being exposed to the sun all day had certainly taken its toll on me, my skin felt like it was on fire. The next big, daunting challenge we had to face was getting to the fishing boat through the 'shark playground'. The sea was still far too choppy for the fishing boat to come in closer than about 50 meters from the beach, so it was either swim and climb aboard or get stuck on the island until the next high tide – which none of us was willing to do. Little did we know at the time that, along with sharks, saltwater crocodiles also infested the area. Just thinking about this now, makes me shudder even more than I did back then. The rough journey on-board the boat to the mainland for me was like a jagged roller-coaster ride through a raging fire. My sunburn hurt so much that I had to struggle to control of my emotions and not let out a barrage of painful screams. By the time we got back to Phillip's, my sunburn was so severe that I had to be helped from the car and into the house. On the day before we'd gone to the island, I'd purchased tickets at the local cinema for us all to see *Close Encounters of the Third Kind,* which had only just been released. Phillip and Co ended up seeing the movie without me, and when they got back home, Co woke me up and told me that a giant spider had raced around inside Phillip's car. I just brushed it aside and thought that he was trying to get me back for frightening everyone with a rubber toy spider that I'd bought in Bangkok. When Co mentioned the spider again the next morning, my curiosity got the better of me, and I hobbled out to take a look inside the car for myself...

**"BLOOOOOODY HELL!"** I hollered in horror, slamming the door shut.

A giant black, furry spider leapt from the front dashboard onto the back window ledge in a single bound, and my two feet went up and down like a jackhammer. We'd learn later that it was probably a rubber-tree spider we'd picked it up on our way back from the island. Even a tiny spider can freak me out, so if I'd seen one even half the size of the one in the car and had been with Co and Phillip that night, I'd have gone mental and could have potentially caused an accident. At the end of that day, and when Phillip had returned home from work, we all mutually agreed that staying home because of my sunburn had been a blessing in disguise.

TWO LOVELY YOUNG girls from the Buddhist Centre would often visit us to join us in some chanting, and one day, after we'd finished a session, and I was telling the girls about some of the fantastic things that had happened so far since leaving London, Co cut in and flippantly remarked that it could have all just been a coincidence and nothing to do with the chanting. Until then, things had been going almost miraculously for us, and it seemed as though nothing too bad could go wrong. Co's comment was a big disappointment to me, and it sounded arrogant and ungrateful and I told him so. I also told him that I hoped his thoughtless words wouldn't affect his chances of getting a visa. Co just smirked and shrugged that off, but he soon wiped the grin off his face the next day when we went to collect his passport and visa from the Australian Consulate. Co's application had not only been denied, but several big refusal stamps had been plastered across three pages of his passport. My first thought was that he had a criminal record or that he'd been in trouble, but that wasn't the case at all. Co asked the woman at the counter for an explanation as to why he'd been rejected, and when she told him that he wasn't entitled to one because he wasn't an Australian, I stepped in and ranted and raved until two men came out from the rear section of the office and gestured for me to follow them along a hall and into a private office. Along the way, I noticed them slyly smirking at each other and immediately became suspicious. Once in their office, I asked if Co had done anything wrong to be denied his visa in such a rude manner, and after a prolonged pause, one of them eventually decided to speak...

"Nothing," he answered with a smug look on his face.

I was so dumbfounded with the answer that for the next couple of seconds I couldn't even think straight enough to speak. I then demanded to know why so many giant refusal stamps were necessary. Their answer this time was that it had merely been a personal and essential decision, none of which made any sense to me at all. At that point, I was becoming increasingly pissed-off with them. I asked them to explain exactly what their *essential decision* was all about, and the only answer I got for that was more sneering and smirking, followed by even more meaningless drivel...

"It's a bit like telling someone to wear a certain coloured tie or not."

I angrily ordered him to elaborate and received another sarcastic grin. Then I was almost pushed back out to the reception area. Along the way, I swung around and called them a pair of brainless arseholes and told them that they were so full of bullshit that it's a miracle trees haven't started growing out of their skins. I also threatened to report them as soon as I got back home to Australia, which didn't make a scrap of difference. Their decision was final, regardless of what I had to say. That horrible day left Co and me with no other choice than to go our separate ways. We tried to get on flights that were leaving at around the same time, but that wasn't possible. Co's plane to Osaka was scheduled to depart at 10.00am and mine to Sydney at 10.00pm. Parting with Co was one of the hardest things that I've ever had to do. As I stood by a window watching him walk across the tarmac and then board his plane, I felt like my whole body was being ripped in half – as though a part of me was dying. Minutes later, Co's plane ascended into the clouds and was soon out of sight, and that's when I felt an even greater surge of despair engulf me. I began panicking within from the painful thought of never seeing him again, and the fear that our separation would change all the magic that we'd shared – all thanks to the outdated, cruel, heartless and illogical religious-based laws of Australia at the time. While Australia had come a long way since its wild colonial years, when people could be legally hung for just stealing a ration of bacon, it still had a hell of a long way to go...

"No wonder so many people are turnin' their backs on Western religions," I thought to myself in anger, as I slowly started to wander away from the window – my legs almost buckling beneath me.

If we'd had enough money, we could have flown back to London or gone somewhere else safer where we could remain together in peace, but that would have broken Mum's heart. She and I hadn't seen each other for over four years, and she was eagerly looking forward to my return. I took a taxi back to Phillip's empty house, and the first thing to greet me was Phillips beautiful garden that Co had admired and loved so dearly. Only now it had changed into a powerful source of pain, so much so, that I could hardly bear to look at it. More tears welled up in my eyes when I glanced down and spotted the little rows of sugar ants that Co had so often enjoyed watching, as they busily carried their huge loads between the paving stones. It all became too overwhelming, so I called another cab and went straight back to the airport, where I remained for the rest of the day pining for Co, and feeling wave after wave of deep sadness. While there, I reminisced about different things, including what had happened to a young man named Tony that I'd once worked with during my teens. Similar to Co, he was one of the most gentle and caring human beings that anyone could ever wish to meet, and everybody in the company loved him dearly. When his wealthy mother found out that Tony was gay, and proceeded to turn his life into a waking nightmare, by following what many doctors recommended was a successful treatment for curing homosexuality, the world as Tony knew it ended. With the support of Australia's Christian-based judicial system, she forcibly had him admitted to a mental institution, where the hospital staff locked him up and virtually destroyed Tony's spirit. Each day they strapped him to a chair and charged his body with electric shocks whenever a photo of a naked male was displayed on a screen. They also pumped him full of drugs until he didn't know who or where he was anymore, and when poor Tony was eventually released, the previously bright, intelligent and caring young man that he'd always been and whom we'd all loved and cared for, had been transformed into little more than an unrecognisable and unintelligible vegetable.

It was time to board my plane home. In just a few short weeks, I'd endured a life-changing ride on an emotional rollercoaster that was now only barely hanging on to the rails.

# Chapter 38

# HURTFUL CONFRONTATIONS

During another long and gruelling overnight flight, this time on a rattly DC10, I struggled within to prepare myself to act as cheerfully as I could upon my arrival. I was torn apart emotionally. One minute I'd feel waves of joy from thoughts relating to reuniting with my family after so many years. The next minute there'd be an explosion of sad disappointment and heartache. My joyful dreams of arriving home and starting a new life with Co by my side were as distant as they'd been so close only days before. Waiting to greet me at Sydney's International Airport were Denis and Gay, my niece, Alicia, my nephew, Rodney, and Billy's new wife, Lynette, whom I'd never met. (I've chosen the name Lynette to protect her privacy). When they spotted me coming out from the arrivals gate, the stunned looks on their faces clearly depicted that my dishevelled appearance wasn't at all what they were expecting. I was jet-lagged, distraught and still suffering from the after-effects of sunburn – I must have looked like an over-baked carrot. With all the turmoil that was going around in my mind, everything seemed like a distorted dream. Seeing Mum shortly afterwards, was almost incomprehensible. She was still quite active for her age and, like always, remained young-at-heart, but she'd become so much frailer. To celebrate my return home, she'd been busy the entire week baking cakes and tasty delicacies, and by the time that we'd sampled her irresistible treats, we were all just about fit to burst. During the days that followed, I continued to do my best to hide my painful inner-torment, especially from my family, but it was obvious that they could tell something was wrong. They kept asking questions, particularly about where Co was until, in the end, I gave in and relayed the whole story.

Australia had changed so much that I felt like a tourist in my own country. Most of my nieces and nephews had grown into young adults, my stepsister, Glynis, had separated from her husband, John, and was living as a single mum with their three children, Beatty, her mother, had died from cancer shortly after I'd left, as had my mother's partner, Eric, who'd provided for Mum and me for many years, and Adrian, the bass player of the long-disbanded Shakubuku Band, had married a beautiful secretary that he'd met at MCA, the production company that had signed up YOU. While I'd been away, Denis and Gay had received their own Gohonzon but had since given up the practice altogether. Part of the reason was that I'd selfishly and irresponsibly let them down by not returning when I'd promised, plus I still hadn't paid them back the money they'd loaned me to get back home from America, which I eventually repaid threefold. Something else that wouldn't have helped was how certain leaders in the organisation that Denis and Gay had confided in had relayed their private matters to other members. Sadly, Denis had mistakenly based his conception of the faith on the actions of the 'person' rather than on the *Mystic Law*, as Nichiren had taught. Be that as it may, I'm more inclined to believe that the main reason for my brother's angry resentment and abuse towards Buddhism, especially in my presence, was, and still is, more to do with his ailing relationship with me. After I started chanting, I started developing strong opinions of my own, and unlike in the past, I no longer agreed with everything that Denis thought, said and did, and I still don't. One of the major differences between us is that, unlike Denis, who bullies his way through any disagreement and rather than admitting he's ever wrong, rubbishes whatever I have to say with a mouth full of abuse, I respect his right to have his own opinions, even when I don't agree with it. In recent times, I've come to realise and accept that most members of my family and I are polar opposites. In other words, we perceive, think, respond and react to things on completely different levels, particularly where Denis and I are concerned, who's constantly on the prowl for an argument, and having a conversation with him is always like a walk across thin ice. Be that as it may, I'll always be grateful for all that he's done for me in the past.

After years of chanting and studying the teachings of Nichiren, I've come to believe that our family, friends and acquaintances never come about by chance and that fundamentally nothing is ever entirely someone else's fault. I also believe that what we encounter during our life's journey, including our relationships with others, can help us grow stronger and wiser, or if we so choose, defeat us and sometimes cause us to end up a failure.

Unlike what I'd become accustomed to in the UK, it was so disappointing to discover that homosexuality in Australia was still a highly illegal offence and that people were still being imprisoned for it. I also discovered that it had been apparent to the consulate officials back in Singapore, that Co and I were a gay couple, and that the size and amount of refusal stamps in Co's passport were a secret code to indicate that he was gay and an 'undesirable', in case he went to another country to apply for his visa there. The 'certain coloured tie', referred to by the officials, simply meant gay or straight. For the first few weeks that I was home, I stayed with Mum at her newly-built government apartment, about forty kilometres southwest of the city. The closest shops were about half an hour's walk away, and the bus service to and from Liverpool was minimal. It came as quite a shock to me, especially after living right in the heart of London for so long. When I learnt that Mum had continued to chant each day, it gave my spirit a much-needed boost. She'd already experienced enough actual proof in her life to convince her to keep it up – her trust in the Mystic Law had become unshakable, even though she continued to do all of her other prayers as well, especially to her little statue of St Anthony. Our dear friend Akiko would often visit Mum and me and sometimes drive me to meetings that were being held at the new Buddhist Centre, just west from the CBD in Arncliffe. The centre was also where I first experienced the wrath of some of the members that I'd known before leaving for the UK, who were also upset because I hadn't kept my word and returned when I'd said I would. Some were rigidly untrusting, judgemental and very cold-hearted towards me, and their unforgiving attitude soon had me feeling resented and alienated. It was hard to believe that they were the same people. Unfortunately for them, they'd failed to acknowledge and appreciate the fact that I'd not only invited new members to join the organisation in Australia but also in the UK and several other countries. On top of that, they failed also to consider or appreciate that I was only human and entitled to my imperfections the same as them or anyone else. While I was at the centre one day, Lynette's older sister, an NS/SGI women's leader, officially informed me that it was during a pilgrimage to Japan by some of the Australian members, and after they'd performed my song Sensei when President Daisaku Ikeda had decided to provide the Australian members with the money to buy the Centre at Arncliffe. Even though her body language gave me a distinct impression that she resented having to tell me, I still appreciated hearing something nice about me for a change. As the following weeks went by, and I continued trying to make up for my past shortcomings, some of the members still couldn't find it in their hearts to forgive me, and some even went as far as gossiping and spreading lies about me. Needless to say, their ongoing rejections and slander soon became extremely distressing, until in the end, it was only my sincere faith in the Mystic Law Itself and my deep determination and belief that Co and I would one day be reunited, that kept me from falling apart. It was also the fact that the vivid premonition I'd had in Hong Kong six months prior to learning about Nichiren Buddhism, had since become a reality, that helped give me the strength to keep up my faith, no matter what.

BILLY AND LYNETTE hadn't long returned from their honeymoon in the US, and were still in what I'd mistakenly thought was honeymoon mode. Lynette turned out to be quite a modern Milly, and it wasn't long before I discovered that, like some of the other new and younger members that had joined the organisation during my absence, she too could be bossy, dogmatic, rude and self-righteous. My shaky relationship with Lynette came to a very nasty crunch one Saturday night after I'd spent an enjoyable sunny afternoon happily relaxing in the garden of a successful producer/songwriter, negotiating plans to re-launch my singing career by recording two of his songs on a single. When he and his wife had invited me to stay on and discuss it further over dinner, and I'd phoned Lynette to let her know that I wouldn't be able to come to a party she'd invited me to that night, she adamantly refused to accept it and virtually ordered me to be there. I tried to explain that it was a very important business dinner, but she still refused to listen and didn't want to hear another word about it. In the end, to try to keep the peace, I gave in and agreed to turn up, albeit begrudgingly. As I was about to put down the phone, Lynette shouted out for me to invite Barry, a friend of mine that I'd previously introduced her to at the Buddhist Centre. She and Billy lived out in the western suburbs at Blacktown, quite a long drive from the Eastern suburbs, and by the time that I arrived, the party was well underway. The first thing I saw when I walked in the door was Barry kissing and caressing Lynette in a dark corner of their dimly-lit living room. I quickly turned to look the other away to try to deal with the shock of it and then saw Billy dirty-dancing with a scantily-dressed female in the opposite corner. To top it all off, neither Billy nor Lynette appeared to be the slightest bit perturbed at what each other were doing. For the next few moments, I wasn't sure if what I'd seen was real or a hallucination. It hadn't the first time that I'd seen Lynette kissing other young men, but this time, the thing that shocked me the most and made me feel overwhelmingly guilty, was that I'd invited Barry. How I wished I'd stuck to my guns and not allowed myself to get pushed into coming – even worse, be tricked into inviting Barry. I soon made my feelings of regret and disapproval disturbingly clear by glaring at them both to the point of making them feel as disillusioned and uncomfortable as I felt. Lynette soon became fed up with me watching her and stormed off to bed, and following that, Barry became a loud-mouthed drunk and extremely agitated towards me. Catching me unaware, he lunged at me while I was sitting on the arm of the sofa with a mug of coffee in my hand, and then locked one of my legs with his leg, pushed me backwards across the arm of the sofa so that I couldn't defend myself, and then attacked me with a barrage of clumsy punches. Billy soon grabbed him by the scruff of the neck and threw him out of the house, after which I spent the remainder of that night of horror licking my wounds and pining for Co, while I waited impatiently for dawn to break so that I could find my way back to Mum's place in the light of day. I was finally getting up to leave when Lynette charged out from their bedroom acting like a woman insane and abused Billy for breaking one of her mugs. At first, I thought that she was only *having a laugh*, it was only a cheap, two-dollar mug from Woolworth's. When I realised that she was serious and then tried to explain that it was me who'd broken the cup, she wouldn't listen to a word of it and just kept screaming her head off at Billy. Raising my voice to get above hers, I again let Lynette know that the broken mug was my fault and that I'd buy her a new one that day. Still refusing to listen, she instead, swung around and told me to mind my own fucking business and to get the fuck out of her house. It was the final straw and I let her have it, by accusing her of being a disgrace to her marriage and a deceitful, sneaky low-life for tricking me into inviting Barry for all the wrong reasons. At that point, her older sister, who'd been asleep in the spare room, raced out screaming at me to get out of the house immediately. As I strutted towards the door, car keys in hand, I span back around and told Lynette's sister that she didn't even have the wisdom and compassion to lead a blind man away from treading on dogs shit, let alone to be a leader representing Nichiren Buddhism. My angry and insulting words sent her further into a state of rage, and like a spoilt brat throwing a tantrum, she stamped up and down on the floor, repeatedly screaming for me to get out of the house, which by then, I was more than happy to do. Billy followed me out to my car and apologised for what had happened and also let me know that his marriage to Lynette had been on the rocks for some time, which at least made sense as to why they were slow-dancing up close with different partners – if only I'd known before I'd agreed to attend the party! Later that day it occurred to me that the real reason behind Lynette insisting that I come to her party and why she wanted me to invite Barry, was to utilise the current animosity toward me, by using Barry and me as scapegoats to end her deluded marriage. Like a silly fool, I'd fallen for it hook, line and sinker. I also realised that Lynette would use what happened to lead everyone into believing that I was the cause of the breakup. When Billy came to see me at Mum's place the next day and explained that, although he and Lynette were 'a couple of rough diamonds', they'd been lead to believe that by chanting together about it, things would work out for them, I could hardly believe what I was hearing...

"You and Lynette may've been chantin' an' doin' all sorts've Buddhist activities 'n' stuff, but tha way ya've both been disrespectin' yer marriage is as stupid as settin' fire to yer house 'n' not expectin' it ta burn down! If ya'd been followin' Nichiren's guidance correctly, instead of spendin' so much time 'n' effort tryin' ta show good face ta impress the leaders, perhaps yer marriage might've worked out – or even better, ya might've summoned up enough wisdom not ta get married in tha first bloody place!"

Although Billy listened, I don't think he heard a single word that I said, and just as I'd expected, within days, rumours were rife around the organisation that I'd destroyed Billy and Lynette's marriage, which in turn, added more strength to the rest of the gossip and lies being told about me. Then things got even worse! Another member named D (Real name excluded for privacy), whom I'd helped introduce to Nichiren Buddhism before I left for the UK, offered to rent me a spare room in his Lakemba flat, about fifteen kilometres southwest of the city. Public transport in the area was abundant, and taking up his offer would also mean that there'd be more opportunities for socialising and finding employment. Since the novelty of being back home had worn off, and Mum and I were starting to argue again, without viewing the flat, I accepted D's offer, believing that it would be a perfect opportunity to get on with my life and to build a home for when Co eventually arrived. However, the moment that I walked into D's flat, I felt like spinning around and racing straight back out the door again, I'd seen cleaner pigsties! He hadn't done any washing for months, if ever, and there were piles of dirty clothes and bed linen stacked up on top of his broken-down washer that virtually reached the laundry ceiling. The smell would have been competition for a skunk, and when I questioned D about it, his answer was that it was easier to buy new sheets every few weeks than have all the added bother of washing them. With no other choice than to try to make the best of it, I spent my first week cleaning up and tidying. Each day I carried two large garbage bags full of dirty sheets by foot to the local Laundromat, which was almost a kilometre away, then spent hours washing them, before lugging them all the way back again. Sadly, my hard work and efforts were entirely unappreciated. No sooner would I have the place looking shipshape before D would have it back to looking like a rubbish tip again. I'd also eventually soon learn to my dismay that D had made it his mission to sneak around behind my back and run me down to anyone gullible enough to listen and believe his nasty exaggerations and lies.

D was a gossip and a sensationalist, and couldn't resist the temptation of spreading around anything that he'd heard about other people's private lives, which he'd usually twist around or add more to. D thrived on making things look more shocking or worse than they actually were, and took full advantage of my unpopular status in the same way that Lynette had done. Eventually, his continual stream of blatant lies, half-truths, gossip and slander created more and more resentment and anger towards me, even from people that I'd never met, which had no doubt been his intention. Some members that D told lies about me to, had wholeheartedly believed him and judged me without even bothering to find out if any of it was true, or had merit. Sadly, unbeknownst to them, while my bad karma was being expiated, thanks to their gullibility, theirs was rapidly increasing. In Buddhist terms, it was a perfect example of 'professing to adhere to Nichiren's teachings' as being one thing, but 'putting them into practice and creating value', as being quite something else.

Finding a job turned out to be a bigger challenge than I'd anticipated, and being unemployed and stuck amongst D's squalor, lies and backstabbing, soon became a state of ongoing torture. Had it not been for my continuous strong faith in the Mystic Law and Co's loving and comforting words of support and encouragement during our regular phone chats, I don't know what I would have done – but there was a price to pay. Compared to today's crazy cheap prices for overseas calls, back then they cost a small fortune. Therefore, by phoning Japan almost every other day in my usual state of despair, I ran up a massive phone bill that I couldn't afford to pay. D had a field day with that one. I'd find out later that he'd told members nationwide about it, running the bill up even higher himself in the process. That is, until something quite extraordinary happened that could have been a 'miraculous' coincidence, or something far more 'mystical'. A significant technical disruption within the phone company caused thousands of people's statements to get wiped from the computer account records, and D's was one of them! And boy, didn't he have a struggle trying to get his head around that one?

TO HELP KEEP myself occupied and focused, for the first time since I'd started writing it in the UK, I got stuck back into finishing my story about 'Peter Kangaroo". And just as it had been during the initial draft, these were challenging and difficult times, but even so, I soldiered on regardless and finally got it finished. Billy had become a qualified sign-writer and an excellent commercial artist while I'd been abroad and helped me out by doing most of the illustrations for the book – which everybody loved. When a non-Buddhist friend expressed interest in Peter Kangaroo and offered to pay the cost of printing five hundred copies, I was over the moon, until my cloud nine was reduced to a cloud zero. The printer disappeared on a drug binge and spent all the money that I'd paid him up front, without starting on any of the work, leaving me with no choice than to put everything on hold until I could find a job and earn enough money to pay for the printing all over again somewhere else. The disappointing outcome added even more weight to the heavy burden that I was already carrying, particularly in regard to my many angry and negative thoughts towards D. Sometimes I'd chant for up to two hours a day, just to try to maintain my inner-self-control and manifest the wisdom that I needed to retain a degree of optimism, plus the strength that I needed to challenge the fundamental reason for my predicament – my own bad karma! Once the anger and disgust that I'd felt for D had subsided enough to be changed into pity and compassion, as well as feeling sorry for D, I felt gratitude towards myself for not being the one that had been making all the bad causes.

WHEN LYNETTE'S sister had screamed at me at the party and ordered me out of the house, had she known the truth behind my anger, perhaps she may have been less supportive of Lynette. I've jumped the gun and reacted to things without knowing all the facts plenty of times myself, and that may have even been why it had happened. After all, our good and bad karma is constantly manifesting like the ticks on a clock does. If I were to find myself in the same or a similar situation today, I'd simply mind my own business, turn around and walk straight back out the door. I've also learnt through past experience that those of us who choose to practise Nichiren's Buddhism and to propagate the Mystic Law, are destined to dig up and expose even some of our worst karma content. Therefore, it's only natural for our respective bad karma contents to clash and cause discord and disruption between us. We were all young, crazy back then and had so much to learn and change about ourselves, particularly our outlooks on life in general, which is what practising Nichiren Buddhism is all about. My bad experiences with Lynette, her older sister and others, were proof that our bad karma was being brought forth and exposed to us to see it for what it was, and to give us an opportunity and a choice to do something about changing it. Therefore, the sufferings, misconceptions and wrongfulness that we'd endured or created, was never on else's fault but our own. I've also come to understand that my shortcomings and obstacles in life have all acted similarly to the bumpers in a pinball machine – each bump directed or redirected me towards my ultimate mission in life, which is to learn to stand alone and to awaken both myself and others to the supreme importance of life's 'Mystic Law' above all else.

# Chapter 39

# BEST REUNION OF ALL

Yearning to make some new friends outside of the organisation, I joined up with a club consisting of a small group of gay people, who held Friday night social meetings every second week in Liverpool, about forty kilometres west of the city. Being involved in the NS/SGI for so long, I'd almost forgotten what it was like to socialise generally with non-Buddhists, particularly other non-Buddhist gays. Escaping from the judgemental eyes of certain members of the organisation was like taking a holiday, and each Friday night get-together was like a breath of cool, fresh mountain air on a hot summer's day. It was always such a lot of sincere and honest good fun. At one of the gatherings, I met a young lesbian named Leslie, who was a Martial Arts student and seriously into several other sports. She'd noticed the words Nam-Myoho-Renge-Kyo inscribed on a medallion that I was wearing around my neck and questioned me about it. When I told her that I chanted the words each day to activate my Buddha-nature and to help generate and send out good energy-vibrations from myself towards all life on Earth, Leslie was instantly interested and soon took to chanting like a duck to water. At another of the gatherings, I met a young guy my own age named Johnny, and after spending most of the evening chatting with him, discovered that we shared a lot of things in common. A few days later, Johnny popped in to visit me at D's flat, and when he saw first-hand the conditions that I was living under, offered to rent me his spare room – I immediately accepted! While I was preparing to move away from D's, a terrible tragedy struck. Ever since Billy separated from his wife, he'd been living with our step-sister, Glynis, and often drove her children to school on his way to work. Meanwhile, the children's father, John, was living with his girlfriend, Mary, and her young daughter, Michelle, just across from D's apartment. They'd built a very close bond with a young lad named Keith from Queensland, and although I'd only ever met him once or twice briefly, he'd given me the impression that he was an amiable and kind young man. I was in the midst of carrying some of my stuff into the living room when I suddenly heard someone outside screaming. In the next instant, there was a succession of loud thumps on the front door, so I quickly opened it to see what was going on and found Mary bashing on the security screen and crying hysterically. Between her screams, she kept spitting out something that sounded like she was telling me that Billy and the kids had all been killed, which soon sent me spiralling into a sudden state of horror and shock! Helping Mary across the living room to the sofa, and doing my best to console her, was like being caught up in a real-life living nightmare. Once she'd calmed down enough to speak a bit more clearly, it became apparent that her friend Keith had been tragically crushed to death while trying to stop his car from rolling backwards down a slant at a petrol station. Even though I understood that Billy and the kids were all okay, I was still in a state of shock and extremely confused. A neighbour had already phoned John at his work to let him know, so as soon as he arrived and took over, I darted straight down the hall to my room and chanted to try to get my head together. My mind was racing all over the place, so much so, that I could hardly even focus on my Gohonzon. I suddenly saw an image of Keith in my mind's eye, standing beside an entrance to an amber tunnel that curved upwards, similar to how a trumpet does. I've used the term 'mind's eye' because I now believe that our mind can sometimes project inner images outward, in a similar way to how a projector shines images out onto a screen, only rather than a 1D image it's a 3D hologram, or at least that's how it seems to me. Keith's peaceful and almost angelic appearance had an instant calming effect on me, and then I began to see thousands of specks of light whizzing upwards into the tunnel from all around Keith, like sparks rising up from a fire. At the same time, I somehow sensed that Keith knew exactly where he was and to where he was going. He relayed a short message to me telepathically, concerning a baby, a dog and an elderly couple, none of which made much if any sense to me. Then, just like that, Keith became a speck of light and ascended into the tunnel along with all the other bits.

Moving into my room at Johnny's place the following day felt like stepping out of a dark place and into fresh air and sunshine. Johnny kept his flat and its contents so squeaky-clean and tidy that I was scared to touch anything for fear of spoiling it. Johnny proved to be really good company and did all that he could to make me feel welcome, comfortable and at home. Being an electrical engineer by trade, Johnny held a high-ranking position at an electronics manufacturing company. Before moving in, I'd specifically informed Johnny of how serious I was about Co, and we'd agreed that if anything should ever happen sexually between us, it could only be a casual fling without strings. Within a few days, I found myself a well-paid job as a credit control clerk in a towel-rental company and was soon able to buy a cheap car. It felt so good to have some wheels again, even though I only had the car for a week before a drunken Telecom technician completely wrecked it. He was on his way home from a Christmas party in his official Telecom van and ran straight into the back of my car while it was parked. Telecom was anxious to keep the story from getting into the press, so the first thing the following morning, a rep was at my front door offering me a cheque for ten times the value of my car. Keeping my mouth sealed, I put my hand out, took the cheque, and then went merrily went on my way and treated myself to a much better car for a Chrissie and birthday present.

My lesbian friend, Leslie, had continued to chant and would often pop in and do some chanting together with me, and it wasn't long before we had Johnny joining in with us as well. One day, when I was visiting John and Mary and was chatting with a man who'd known Keith well, I told him about Keith's messages, and he reacted with a look of utter amazement! He told me that an elderly couple Keith had often run errands for and walked their dog, had loved him like a grandson. He was also certain that the baby in the message belonged to Keith's adopted sister, and that Keith had loved it dearly. I wasn't sure what to make of it at the time, and it played on my mind for months. Although Keith's vision had only lasted a few short seconds, after hearing his friend's reassuring explanation of what I'd seen and heard, I felt absolutely confident that Keith was happy and at peace. Going by some of the similar experiences that I've since had, I now believe that Keith was communicating with me to get a final message through to those that he loved.

Early one morning, Johnny and I woke up feeling drained and bewildered. Over breakfast, I told him about a dreadful nightmare that I'd had regarding the Shah of Iran and a foreign army invading Australia, which had taken place in a chain of short flashes. Johnny's immediate response was let me know that he'd had a similar nightmare himself. In my dream, I'd seen a young man standing on a pedestal surrounded by a group of young students dressed in Middle-Eastern attire. They were loudly cheering him on, and then I saw the Shah of Iran running for his life from one country to another, seemingly trying to hide from someone or something. Then it all changed, and I was suddenly standing at the foot of a tall skyscraper with important documents in my hand that I felt compelled to deliver to the top floor. There were angry people waiting in the foyer, I could see their eyes peering out at me cat-like from dark corners, and I somehow knew that they were there to prevent me from getting through. Suddenly Johnny appeared in front of me and acted as a decoy while I sneaked into the building from another entrance unnoticed. With a look of disbelief, Johnny cut in and told me that he'd seen a tall building in his dream too and that the papers in my hand had lists of instructions on how to help heal the world. He felt certain that they were my songs and writings about World Peace.

In the next part of my dream, I was observing the world from a high altitude and heard some of the loudest and thunderous noises that I'd ever experienced. There were also spurts of something black and fiery shooting up from the ground somewhere in the Middle-East. I then saw several blotches expanding on the west coast of America and in parts of Europe. In the next instant, there were more flashing images of the young man on the pedestal again, only this time, he sounded much louder, and the crowd around him had entered into a deafening wild frenzy. Leaving all that behind, I escaped through what I can only describe as being a portal of some kind – if such things exist. Then I was suddenly all the alone on a very long stretch of road in the blazing red Outback of Australia. All along one side of the road, stretching either way as far as the eye could see, was a barbed-wire fence, and somehow I understood that Australia had been divided into two and that I was standing on the wrong side of the fence. Up ahead in the distance were troupes of foreign soldiers standing up in jeeps and on the backs of trucks with guns pointed in every direction, and heading southward directly towards me. Following behind them were tanks with bigger flags waving in the wind, and as they all rapidly moved closer, I started frantically searching for an opening in the fence, but there wasn't any! As a last resort, I got down on my knees and dug like a mad dog to escape beneath the fence, only just making it through in the nick of time to hide behind a nearby bush and watch the fearsome intruders passed me by. The next thing that I knew, I was floating in a void of complete silence and peering across a field at an elderly lady who had snow-white hair. She was sitting in the distance on a beach chair by the sandy shoreline of a raging sea and was surrounded by beautiful virgin meadows in varying shades of green. The soft, long grass that was growing closest to her seemed to be dancing with the breeze, and there wasn't the slightest sound to be heard – it was similar to watching a silent movie. I slowly drifted across towards her and was shocked to discover that it was my mother's dear old friend Witty, who'd gone missing while I'd been in Europe. She relayed a penetrating message to me telepathically to let me know that what we were looking at was the potential future outcome of humankind unless we quickly change our ways. I got the clear impression that humankind was on a path of self-destruction and moving rapidly closer to the original 'source', where everything ends up and starts all over again. Witty's strange and penetrating message had me feeling worried and confused. When I floated out into the waves, I became even more worried and confused. Masses of tiny specks of energised matter that I somehow understood would one day grow into cells and develop into the new replacement for humans were all around me, and I got the feeling that humans had made the same journey many times before, but each time had failed to advance beyond the pitfalls of greed, anger and stupidity.

Johnny interrupted for a moment to tell me that he'd seen an old lady in his dream too, but hadn't known who she was. I'd never before heard of dream-sharing, let alone experienced it, but I've since read that it's not all that uncommon. On my way to the office that day, I was a bundle of nerves. I kept asking myself if the dream was a warning that I was meant to act upon. I eventually made an attempt to contact *The Sydney Morning Herald* newspaper from a public phone booth to let someone about it, but at the moment they answered, I lost my nerve and hung up. It was too far-fetched to tell anyone, and my brother Denis would've almost had an orgasm ridiculing me over it. Later that day, I told Mum about my dream, which prompted her to set about searching for Witty. Amazingly, she found her a couple of days later in the Alzheimer's ward of a nursing home, which, of all the places that it could have been in Sydney, was right around the corner from where I was living. Mum visited Witty at the nursing home the next day and found her sitting up in bed surrounded by chocolates. For as long as we'd known Witty, she'd always been quite a 'character', and nothing had changed in that department, except that she didn't have the faintest idea who Mum was. It turned out that Witty had stolen all the chocolates from the other patients after scolding them for taking the chocolates from her, and nobody could remember anything about any of it because they all had Alzheimer's. Mum and I had a good laugh about the funny side of it, and the more we thought about it, the louder we laughed. Sadly, I never had a chance to visit Witty myself, as on the day following Mum's visit she passed away peacefully in her sleep – no doubt surrounded by chocolates – what a delightful way to go!

When the Gulf War erupted a decade or so later during the 1990s, news that the oil fields had been set alight instantly brought back memories of the dream I'd shared with Johnny, and I feared the worst, which thankfully didn't eventuate. Looking back now, I'm inclined to think that part of the hair-raising dream could have been a glimpse of what's still yet to come. Considering how the world has deteriorated since then, I'd say that anything could be possible. By way of an invasion of Australia by Indonesia, Russia, India, or more importantly, China, who's since become a significant power, our shared nightmare that night could potentially become a reality any day now.

AS A CONTRIBUTION towards helping to make Australia a better and safer place for us all to live, I recorded a self-penned song entitled, *The Hungry Kids*. Members of The Atlantics, a band who'd enjoyed enormous success in the 1960s with their huge hit surfing instrumental *Bombora*, were kind enough to both produce the record and play on it. In my song, I encouraged fellow Australian's to reach out and to communicate with the nation's youth more, especially those who were homeless and living on the streets. Back then, Australia didn't have much of a street-kid problem, but I'd been inspired by another dream to write a song predicting that it soon would if we didn't act quickly enough. Among other things, my lyrics warned of kids dying from drug abuse and violence in every city and town around the country, and that the potential of it becoming a reality was already right on our doorstep. I took the finished product to one of Sydney's top record companies to ask for their help in getting the record released and promoted, offering also to donate any royalties to a worthy charity that helped homeless people. The CEO's ignorant attitude and rude, dismissive rejection shocked me so much that I was lost for words...

"Who the hell do you think you are, coming here writing lyrics like that about Australia!? Do you seriously expect the Australian public to put up with that sort of offensive rubbish!?"

While living in the UK, I'd picked up a slight accent, and the CEO must have mistaken me for a Brit criticising Australians. The song only got played on FM radio a few times, and was never officially released – if only the Internet had been available back then! Now that my lyrical prediction has become a present-day reality, I sometimes wonder if that foolish CEO has ever looked back and thought about what he said to me that day – probably not. Had my song been given a chance, it could have at least made more people aware of the growing problem of homelessness, drug abuse and delinquency in Australia, and also might have motivated some people to take early action to help prevent the worst of it from happening. I guess we'll never know the answer to that for sure, but at least I have the satisfaction of having tried. On a more positive note, I eventually saved enough money to get a hundred copies of 'Peter Kangaroo' printed, and it was such a thrill to see it finished finally! A lot of people that I knew bought copies, but due to my lack of schooling, my writing skills were far from professional, and the book was never officially published. However, rather than feeling a failure, I chose instead to challenge the outcome by studying hard to improve as an author, and to one day rewrite the story and take it to a higher level.

IT WAS MUM'S 70th birthday, and I decided to give her a big surprise party with a difference. VCRs and video cameras were relatively new and novel at the time, so I hired one of each for the special occasion and invited most of my siblings and their spouses to come along, but just as I'd expected, my eldest brother, Fred, and his wife, Edna, didn't even bother to show up. Fred had never directly said anything regarding my homosexuality to my face, but he'd certainly had plenty to say about it to others behind my back. His severe homophobic hang-up about it was something that I could only smile about and pity him for, especially considering he had an excessive and perverted foul mouth and a severe gambling and drinking problem that my family and I had to accept and put up with for decades. Although Fred had always let me down in his role as a big brother, I'd never disrespected him in any way, nor had I deliberately said or done anything to embarrass or upset him, so having him despise me for simply being who I truly was had always hurt, but at least, by then, I'd become used to it. We spent most of the party filming and then playing it back in bits as we all laughed hysterically at ourselves. It was a real treat for those members of my family who'd never seen themselves on TV before. Mum seemed to be having the time of her life until I presented her with a cake that had a large number '70' on it. With a sudden surprised and embarrassed look on her face, she'd smirked and then quickly looked away. Since then I've found out that Mum had been telling porkies about her age for years, it was actually her 74th birthday!

Johnny had been trying harder than ever to make my stay in his flat as comfortable as he possibly could, and even though he knew that I loved Co and that I wanted to spend the rest of my life with him, he was still having difficulties in accepting it. Johnny had become overly besotted and wanted a relationship with me himself, and after we discussed it and I reaffirmed that a relationship with him was out of the question, he started taking drugs and coming home from work drunk – which only made us both more miserable. Johnny was a handsome guy and oozed sex appeal. He also had a vibrant personality and was also an excellent keyboard player – the kind of guy that I'd always dreamed of being with. Had I not already met and fallen so deeply in love with Co, I would have happily reciprocated. I spent Christmas Day feeling heartbroken for Johnny, sorry for myself, and wishing that I'd never had a fling with Johnny in the first place. I was also dreading what the potential future consequences of it would turn out to be.

A couple of days later, I received an unexpected last-minute invitation in the mail from a recording studio in the nearby suburb of Canterbury, to attend a New Year's Eve party they were having. I'd recorded at the studio once or twice in the past, and knew the owner of the studio was as gay as a peacock in drag. I'd also heard along the grapevine that his parties were always over-the-top, outrageous, totally hot and fascinating, and definitely not to be missed. When New Year's Eve arrived, I decided to put on my glad rags to go and dance the night away. More than anything else, I was hoping that it would help to get my mind off my increasingly awkward situation at home with Johnny. When I arrived at the studio, I found the place chock-a-block full of loud and colourful people. Among them, were 'flaming' drag queens and lots of other outrageously dressed and highly flamboyant people. Among them was a celebrity gay clairvoyant by the name of *Mr John*, whom I'd often seen on TV. He'd been hired to entertain the guests by predicting their love life for the following year ahead and was busy tucked away in a dark corner, surrounded by several tall drag queens dressed in feathers and sequins, telling them their fortunes one by one. It reminded me a lot of the tiny dressing room at Le Girls back in Plymouth. After watching and listening to one queen after another shriek and squeal out in rapturous delight, I was unable to resist getting my own fortune told, even if only just for the fun of it. Mr John was asking people for items belonging to the person that they wanted to hear about, and as it turned out, I was wearing a locket that Co had sent me from Japan for Christmas, so I handed it to him, and then took a deep breath and hoped for the best. After Mr John held the locket in the palm of his hand to read its vibrations, he then went on to impress me beyond belief! In a semi-trance-like tone, he told me...

"A young man with long black hair loves you very much. He's Asian, and at the moment he's separated from you by an ocean... You miss him with all your heart, and he misses you too, but you needn't worry because he'll soon be here with you, and together you'll both combine your talents to contribute towards peace... That's because it's your eternal destinies to do this and always to be together."

Mr John's description of Co was spot-on! I felt so amazed and excited that I almost let out a shriek and a squeal of my own! His prediction left me feeling convinced that Co was definitely coming, and by the time he'd finished, I was already mentally preparing for Co's arrival. Mr John couldn't have previously known who I was, let alone anything about Co, and neither did the producer or anyone else in the room. None of them knew that Co even existed, as they were all total strangers to me. With only a few short minutes left before midnight and the beginning of 1980 almost upon us, Mr John's prediction was exactly what I'd needed to hear to start the New Year off with a heart full of hope and optimism.

DURING THE FIRST week of 1980, our good friend, Phillip that Co and I stayed with while we were in Singapore, gave me a huge surprise by showing up on Johnny's doorstep totally unexpectedly. It was Phillip's first visit to Australia, and he wanted to see everything that he possibly could, so Johnny invited him to stay with us in the flat, and I offered to be his faithful tour guide. Earlier that day, I'd told Johnny that it might be a good idea for me to start looking for somewhere else to live, and in a desperate effort to encourage me to stay, Johnny remained on his best behaviour the whole time that Phillip was with us. On the day before Phillip was due to leave, Co phoned to let me know that he had a new passport and that he'd finally got his visa to enter Australia, adding that all he needed was to save up another thousand dollars to be able to get here. Phillip had overheard our conversation and quickly got up and took the phone...

"Co, I'll send you the money tomorrow! Just give me your bank details and consider it done!"

I was almost dancing up and down for joy when Johnny's face suddenly sunk like the Titanic...

"You must bring Co to stay here! There's plenty of room!" Johnny offered anxiously later that evening.

The last thing that I needed was to have Co and Johnny under the same roof, as it would have spelt disaster with a giant 'D'. At the same time, I also didn't want to hurt Johnny any more than he was already hurting, nor did I want to seem ungrateful. I sat down and explained to Johnny as nicely as I could that I needed to be with Co alone. Then, early on the following morning, I found a flat just down the road and moved in. When Mum and I went to meet Co at the airport a few days later, I was so nervous and excited that I didn't even recognise him. Luckily, Mum had seen photos of Co and was the first to spot him pushing his way through the crowd towards us. Because Co hadn't mentioned that he'd had his hair cut short, I'd been concentrating on finding his long, streaked locks. At the moment Co caught sight of me waving at him, he built up speed and hurried towards us. Mum was almost as excited to see him as I was.

Years earlier, I'd written to Mum from Hong Kong to let her know that I was gay, and it was such a huge a relief when she wrote back and told me that it made no difference to her whatsoever – that I was still her son, regardless of my sexuality, who I loved or chose to share my life with. She'd also added that God made us all individuals and that her love for me was unconditional and unchanging. Mum's acceptance and support back then had meant the world to me, I felt like an enormous weight had been lifted from my shoulders. Seeing Co's beautiful smiling face that day, and the joy that I felt inside as he raced up and hugged me, is a magnificent and wonderful memory that will always remain strong in my heart. For so long, I'd been praying and daydreaming for this day to come, and when it finally arrived, it felt so surreal and dream-like that it was a struggle to conceive that it was actually happening. Although distance and time had separated us, we were able to just pick up from where we'd left off, and it almost instantly felt as though we'd never even been apart. It really was a wonderful blessing to have Co back in my life and by my side again, but our love for each other was still far from out of danger. Homosexuality in most parts of Australia remained illegal, which meant that we needed to be on our guard at all times, especially in public. Within a couple of days, our efforts to be careful almost turned to paranoia after we discovered that a policeman and his family were living on the floor directly below us.

A STAFF MEMBER where I worked, by the name of Anne, had been on leave for several weeks since her daughter was tragically killed in a school-bus accident. When she finally returned to work and I was officially introduced to her, I was astounded to discover that she was married to one of the salesmen that my brother, Denis, and I had worked with years earlier at the bed-linen and tablecloth company. The job I'd quit because of a gut feeling I had about something not being right with what my duties entailed. Anne was still in mourning, and it was clear to see that she was struggling to cope, so I refrained from mentioning anything about the death of her daughter. A few days later, I gave Anne a copy of my book, Peter Kangaroo, in the hope that the positive, philosophical messages in it might help her to deal a little better with her loss. During the few months I'd been employed by the company, I'd managed to clean up an enormous amount of their outstanding 'accounts owing', some of which had gone unpaid for several years. The sales manager had noticed my achievement and were impressed with how well I was able to deal with the public. So much so that he offered me a position in the company's sales team, which included a new company car, a much higher salary and several other attractive fringe benefits. When I mentioned this to Anne, she totally freaked out...

"NO! NO! NO! TOMMY! DON'T GET INVOLVED! It's not worth it! It'll only bring you bad luck and unhappiness! Don't do it!"

The first thing that came to my mind was my book, Peter Kangaroo. Had she read something in it that got through to her in some way? Or did she know something dodgy about the job that I didn't know? I never found out, I didn't want to ask for fear of upsetting her more, but one thing was definite, the idea of me joining the sales team was well and truly out of the question!

*Co in London just before we met.*

*In Singapore on our way to Australia.*

*Just after Co finally arrived in Sydney.*

*Co and Mum on our way to visit George.*

*Co admiring George's wonderful artwork.*

*Mum and Co sightseeing on Sydney Harbour.*

*Co first meets Akiko with me in the background.*

*Kerry and Gerry.*

*Dino, me, Kitty and Co starting our new life together.*

# Chapter 40

# MODERN FAMILY

After hearing that my brother, George, had been released from prison, just as I'd done with my stepmother, Beatty, I confronted him to put an end once and for all to the hatred that I'd previously held for him. Other than Mum and my two elder sisters, my other siblings didn't appear to want anything to do with George, and you could have knocked me down with a feather when he invited Mum, Co and me to visit him at his country home over the Easter Holiday Weekend. After living in highly populated cities such as Los Angeles, Hong Kong, Tokyo and London for so long, driving through the New South Wales countryside turned out to be an exciting, eye-opening experience. Co was spellbound by the unique wide-open spaces and homesteads dotted here and there across the beautiful carpet of green landscapes, enjoying sights that he'd only ever seen in books or on television.

Although George looked older, he was still as handsome as ever, and unlike me, had a full head of hair – albeit silvery-white. During his long stretch behind bars, he had discovered and then developed a previously-unknown talent, and had become a successful artist. A major TV network had already produced and aired a documentary on his work, as some of his paintings were also selling in other parts of the world. I found it almost inconceivable to think of him as being the same person that caused me so much suffering. During that weekend, I also found myself gazing at some of his creative works and asking myself repeatedly how, with such an evil and violent past, could George have possibly expressed such exquisite beauty and done it with so much sensitivity and passion. I didn't mention anything about the past with George, as that was not my intended reason for the visit. My only desire had been to clear the hate that I'd accumulated towards him from within my life. George and the new lady in his life, Dawn, were very friendly, hospitable, and welcoming, and as we were leaving to return to Sydney, invited us to come back and stay with them again another time, but I chose not to take them up on their offer. I'd achieved my goal of making my peace with George and that's all that mattered. Besides, he and I were on very different paths, and I felt that it was far wiser to keep some distance between them. I thanked them, bid them farewell and just left it at that.

I hadn't seen George's second-eldest son, Kerry, who was about three years younger than me, for almost fifteen years. Ironically, he'd also turned out to be gay and was living with his boyfriend, Gerry, on Sydney's North Shore. Two weeks later, they visited Co and me, and we all soon became great friends. Although Kerry and Gerry were as different a chalk and cheese, they couldn't have been more perfectly suited. Gerry was a 'straight-acting', well-educated, a business-minded type, and thrived on bush walks and nature, while Kerry was 'camp' to the hilltops, fun-loving, care-free and a dedicated follower of fashion. He was also a party addict and would usually spend his Friday and Saturday nights dancing from dusk till dawn beneath the bright, flashing disco lights of the bumper-to-bumper gay clubs along Oxford Street, a renowned gay area in the city. Whenever we all got together, Kerry and I would usually end up doubled over with laughter within minutes of seeing each other, and sometimes without even knowing what we were laughing at. Kerry could pull some of the most hilariously funny faces at times, and it was common for him and me to be rolling around in hysterics, even during some of our more serious conversations.

AFTER WE FOUND out that it was much easier to get a resident visa in New Zealand, Co and I decided to go and apply there instead. If successful, it would mean that Co would be able to use his New Zealand visa to live and work in Australia as well – it seemed the perfect solution. We wanted to raise as much money as we could for the move, so we sold the car and furniture and then rented a room in a very cheap, rundown hotel on one of the back streets in Kings Cross. I soon found a job in a classy fish and chip takeaway beneath the well-known, prominent-landmark-Coca-Cola sign located at the top of William Street, and Co managed to find a part-time, cash-in-hand job at a nearby Japanese restaurant, working as a waiter and chef's assistant. I was only working at the takeaway for a week before the owner offered me the manager's position, which included a substantial wage increase. Co was able to extend his tourist visa for another three months, so we decided to stay in Australia a bit longer and earn as much money as we could before heading off to the land of the long-white-cloud. After I accepted the promotion, I took a couple of days off to find a more suitable place to live, and to make our search easier, we bought a cheap, old car that had been hand-painted mat black, which made it less noticeable, especially at night. The first day we went house hunting in it, we had three near-misses with cars that almost ran into us, and by the end of that nerve-wracking day, we decided to get rid of the car ASAP. We weren't far from Mum's place when we called it quits, and decided to pop in for a short visit with her before driving back to the Cross. As we were approaching the busy Hume Highway, near where Mum lived, I received a profound warning of impending danger from that same familiar voice that seems to come from within and usually always proves to be correct. By then, I'd learned not to dare ignore the voice, so I quickly stopped the car and asked Co to tighten his seat belt up as tightly as he could, while I did likewise. Back in those days, seatbelt's needed to be adjusted manually. Co gave me a strange look and wanted to know why? I tried to explain about the voice, but he just grinned, tightened his belt and basically treated it like a joke. It was quite a while before we were able to enter onto the highway to join the steady flow of afternoon traffic heading west, and when we finally did, the bright glow of the setting sun made it almost impossible to see more than a few meters ahead. Stretching along the centre of the six-lane Hume Highway, was a wide concrete edged median strip, and just as I was manoeuvring across to the middle lane to use the medium strip's edging as a guideline, Co let out a horrifying scream of terror and threw his hands up over his face...

**"LOOK OOOOOUUUUUTTTTT! LOOK OOOOOUUUUUTTTT! "**

I instantly froze with fear! Flying through the air towards us from the opposite side of the medium strip was a shiny projectile that I thought was a plane about to land on the highway. Instinctively I hit the brakes and then **BAAANG!!!** As our car was being violently mangled, Co and I were thrown in every direction, and all I could see in front of me were what seemed to be millions of tiny lights flickering amidst momentary blankets of darkness. After everything came to a sudden ending, my biggest concern and fears were for Co's safety. I was terrified that the car would burst into flames at any moment, and when I couldn't get my door to open, I became so panic-stricken and disorientated that I tried to squeeze my body through the door's twisted window. Fortunately, Co's door hadn't been damaged, but he kept shouting for me to come over to his side to get out, his voice sounded like it was coming from miles away and his words didn't register or make any sense. Before I knew what was happening, Co had hold of my arm and was tugging me across the seat to his side, and eventually dragged me out of the car.

Two teenage boys, speeding in a sports sedan and coming towards us from the opposite direction, had hit the edge of the other side of the median strip and become airborne, and our car had served as their landing strip. The initial impact had pushed the front of our car through to the dashboard and almost onto the front seat. After their airborne car had spun around and smashed my side of our car in, it continued on and smashed the boot in as well, leaving the car a total wreck from end to end. I was initially too stunned to feel any pain, but the moment that I stood up, it hit me all at once, and my head throbbed so severely that I thought it was going to explode. Onlookers helped me to the curb, where I sat for several minutes with my head in my hands and moaning, waiting for an ambulance to arrive. Co was also moaning, as my head had bashed into his ribs on impact. We were both in a fair bit of agony, but at least we were alive! By the time the ambulance arrived, a crowd of spectators had gathered around us and were anxiously looking on. As the ambo was running his hands and fingers up the sides of my face and head, he suddenly stopped and gasped. My hairpiece had come loose, and his fingers became caught up under it and caused it to pop up. There was also a sharp intake of breath from the pale-faced onlookers, who must have also thought that the top of my head had come off. Later, when we were interviewed by the police at the hospital, they told us that my fast reaction in braking had stopped our car just short of having our roof torn off, and potentially our heads with it. Hearing this left me feeling more grateful than ever for the 'warnings' that I'd received from the unknown *voice...*

"I'm so glad I listened and was alert enough to hit the brakes when I did," I told myself.

The tenant of one of the houses that we'd inspected earlier in the day, was returning to live in Italy and was about to have his gorgeous little Border-Collie dog put down. We weren't interested in renting the house, but we jumped at the opportunity to save the dog and offered to adopt him before the Italian's left the country. A few days later, I remembered the dog and suddenly realised we were already two days past the pick-up date. Co quickly ran upstairs and flagged down a taxi, with me hobbling behind him as fast as I could on my crutches. I can't put into words the enormous relief that I felt when we arrived at the empty house and found our new pet pooch sitting alone on the porch waiting for us. He was a bit unsure about of us at first, but after a couple of little snarls, he soon felt the love that we had for him, and off he marched with his caring new owners.

Our application to lease an old semi-detached house on Canterbury Road in Hurlstone Park had been approved by then. So, on our way back to the Cross in the cab, we stopped off at the agent, picked up the keys, and along with our new family member 'Dino', moved in the same afternoon. Luckily, we were able to buy some cheap furniture from a nearby second-hand shop before closing. Mum later gave us a little kitten she'd named 'Miss Kitty', and once the cat and Dino had overcome their differences and made friends, we all happily settled into our new home and became yet another typically gay, 1980s modern family.

# Chapter 41

# SINCE THEN

It's been over forty years since that wonderful and very memorable night when I'd first met Co, and many more extraordinary changes have also since taken place, including odd experiences, significant dreams and more messages from the mystery *voice* within. One of the recent messages that have since had a significant effect on the world is the unsolved disappearance of Flight MH 370. At the very same moment that I first heard about the missing plane, via a TV news flash, two words simultaneously popped into my mind – *mystery* and *mystic.* As we all now know, it's since turned out to be one of the modern world's greatest mysteries. The only explanation I've so far been able to come up for the word *mystic* is something other-worldly or extraterrestrial. Perhaps even some sort of universal phenomenon that we still know little or nothing about. I, like so many other's who've witnessed UFO activity, also suspect that cover-up could be in the works. Maybe in the far-off distant future, human space travellers will discover the remains of MH 370 on another Earth-like planet. After all, stranger things have been found right here on Earth, including discoveries of the remains of dinosaurs, neanderthal's, along with many other mysterious and unusual ancient artefacts.

Among some of my many lucid dreams was an alarming one back in 1990 that depicted what later ensued in New York on September 11th, 2001. That dream was accompanied by a profound message, that 'the system as we know it will never be the same again'. I've also faced my fair share of obstacles and have had plenty of disappointments to confront, challenge and overcome, including more close encounters with death. Be that as it may, I'm gratefully happy to say that the two most essential things in my life that have continued to grow stronger and improve each day are the love and affection that Co and I feel for each other, and our shared faith and trust in Life's Mystic Law.

Nichiren's states in his writings, that we each contain a copy of the entire universe within our own lives and that our bodies are physical replicas of the Earth. In other words, 'Dust to dust, ashes to ashes and life to life'. After years of pondering on how Nichiren's explanation could relate to my near-death experience back in 1970, I've finally concluded that some doctors' analysis of NDEs could be closer to the truth than even they realise, but on a very different level. For example, the difference between our physical and spiritual self, such as the matter which our body is made up of and the energy (life-force) that creates it, holds it together and propels it into action, is quite thought-provoking, to say the least. Let's say that we were to fall or jump from a skyscraper without a parachute. Our body would inevitably end up a mangled heap and die. That's because, like all other forms of matter in this world, our body is controlled and restricted by Earth's environmental limitations, and that's also the reason that we need an artificial, 'earth-like' environment, to physically leave the Earth and travel into space. To the contrary, we can easily imagine in our mind what it's like to fall from a skyscraper and hit the ground or even dream about it, without suffering any physical injury at all. That's because our life-force or our mind if you prefer, contains the entire universe, and therefore, isn't restricted by any of the Earth's environmental limitations, nor anything else physical in the universe. As a matter of fact, or spiritual self doesn't appear to have any boundaries or restrictions at all. For this reason, and after seeing a photograph taken by Hubble in 2003 of the Cone Nebula, and then in 2009 a video titled, 'Hubble Space 3D', which resembled my lightning-induced journey to the Light almost to a 'T', I've now concluded that my trip to the beautiful 'Light' back in 1970 was a journey into my deepest subconscious. Seeing the Hubble Space video had also added more credibility to what Nichiren writes about each of us containing the entire universe within. To have reached that distance and back in a couple of minutes have also left me in doubt about light being the ultimate speed, especially when it comes to the immense elasticity of LIFE. I now believe that anything is possible, and that's why I'm also convinced that the journey I took that night was a journey across the universe within myself.

ON A DIFFERENT note, although I've had many opportunities to achieve stardom in my singing career, owing to my karmic circumstances and reckless choices, it has never fully eventuated. Even so, I have no regrets, and that's because I now consider all of the successes, failures, sufferings, mistakes and disappointments that I've endured or enjoyed in my life to be important and necessary steps that I needed to fulfil my destiny and discover my true mission in life, to help awaken as many others as I'm able to the awareness of Mystic Law. All of the past good and bad knocks along the way have also helped make it possible for me to be in the right place at the right time, and in the right frame of mind, to meet Co, and then to maintain a loving, fulfilling and long-lasting relationship with him. When I compare my life with some of the people that I've known, read or heard about, who've reached their dreams to become megastars but have failed dismally in achieving lasting and fulfilling love and happiness in their personal lives, I wouldn't trade what I have with any of them. I'm also deeply grateful for whatever it was that I did in a past life to have been so fortunate in this one. I only wish that everyone else could enjoy a similar experience to mine in their love-lives. For many of us born into this chaotic world of suffering, it's often been a tough and rough journey, especially during this present crucial age of rapid growth and chaotic changes. It appears that we've all arrived here just in time to experience the greatest revolution in the history of humankind – 'the grand awakening and awareness of Life's Mystic Law'. Or to put it more simply, the switching-on of the most significant light of all, our inner light to our enlightenment! As I've mentioned before, one of the many valuable lessons I've learnt along the way is that not everything that goes wrong in life is destined to have an adverse outcome. To elaborate on this, I often use the following example; if we were to slip over on our way to a bus stop and break a leg, we'd consider it as a bad thing. However, if the mishap prevented us from being at the bus stop in time for a truck to run off the road and kill everybody waiting, our broken leg would instead be considered as being a miraculous benefit or blessing. When things are not to my favour, I always compare it with how much worse things could be, or how much worse things are for someone else.

FOR MY BROTHER, George, to have experienced some of the return effects for the pain and suffering that he'd caused others to endure, it appears that his children had to pay the hefty price. Tragically, his first and eldest son, Little George, contracted a bone disease when he was twelve years old, which left him partially disabled for life, then his little daughter and eighth child, Belinda, died at the age of four after accidentally setting fire to herself while playing with matches, and then years later, his second eldest and his favourite son, Eddy, was accidentally knocked off his motorbike by a car and then killed instantly under the wheels of an oncoming truck. Following that, George's third son, Kerry, who was my favourite nephew, tragically succumbed to AIDS, and following that, a couple of months later, Kerry's partner of ten years, Gerry, tragically hung himself in a house that they'd bought when Kerry was sick. In and around all of this devastating misfortune, one of George's daughters-in-law was decapitated in a car accident, and then a grandchild died from cancer. What a heartbreaking and sad string of events for one family to endure, particularly for my sister-in-law, Hazel.

During 1981, our dear friend Akiko suddenly died, whose unexpected death came as a tremendous shock to Co and me, as it did for so many others who knew and loved her. I was finding it extremely difficult to accept and come to terms with, until one day, while I was chanting for her to be at peace in the universe, her beautiful vision appeared in my minds-eye, and I saw her standing on a winding pathway upon a long, silvery-white cloud, smiling down and waving me goodbye. Even now, it still seems like she was actually there, and she looked so vibrant and excited, that it was impossible not to feel happy for her.

In 1988, Mum phoned me early one morning to admit that she'd helped push Dad into Beatty's arms, by not showing him enough affection and attention. It was a strange thing to hear Mum admit, as she'd never accepted the blame for any of it. She also spoke about other things that surprised me, and it now appears to me that her subconscious was letting her know that her time on Earth was coming to an end and was giving her a last-minute chance to set a few things right. Two months later, along with thousands of others both young and old, Mum succumbed to a severe outbreak of the flu and returned home to the Light. Shortly after Mum's passing, Co and I experienced some 'beyond-the-grave' evidence that soon had us convinced that she was still very much with us in spirit. It happened when a workman was jackhammering the ground around the pool area of our newly-built house to prepare it for tiling. Our large living room doors were wide open at the time, and when a large grey bird landed a meter away from the worker and merrily walked straight past him and into the living room, totally unaffected by the noise and vibration of the jackhammer, we were astounded. After the bird had finished inspecting inside the house, it walked back outside, checked around the yard, and then flew off, never to be seen again. The workman, who had by then stopped jackhammering, told us that he'd never witnessed anything like it before in his life. Fortunately, I was able to catch a lot of what took place on video.

In April 1995, after suffering a long and painful illness, my eldest brother, Fred, succumbed to cancer, and then a year later, in May 1996, my youngest brother, Billy, succumbed to cancer as well. I didn't get to see Fred before he died, he wouldn't even talk to me on the phone. No surprises there of course, other than making hateful comments behind my back about my homosexuality and my relationship with Co, whom he referred to others as being a 'fucking Jap poofter', Fred had never shown any interest in me at all. After he died, I prayed for him to find some peace and dignity to come back within his next incarnation, but for the above reasons and a few others, I chose not to attend his funeral. Fortunately, my relationship with Billy was a far more brotherly one, and even though, as most siblings do, we had our differences, we still cared about each other. Billy lived with his wife, Ned, and their four young sons near a popular beach resort in Coffs Harbour, which was about 400 Kilometers south of the Gold Coast where Co and I were living. We'd already driven down to visit them for a couple of days in February of 1996, and it had been wonderful to be with them all again, especially after such a long period of not seeing each other, which, by the way, hadn't been by choice. We'd had very little to do with the boys ever since Ned became a Jehovah Witness, after which Co and I were suddenly no longer permitted to spend time alone with them, even though we'd been in the boys lives ever since day one. The fact that a mob of, what I now consider to be hypocritical, fanatical and evil-minded strangers had brainwashed Ned into creating a wall of distrust between the boys and us, because we were gay, had broken our hearts.

Billy was receiving chemotherapy at the time of our visit and was barely recognisable, but he still managed to put on a brave and happy face. Since Billy's first marriage to Lynette had ended, he hadn't done much if any at all chanting, so I drove him up to a quiet spot overlooking the Pacific Ocean and got him to do some with me there. In May 1996, and just as we were about to leave and visit Billy and his family for a second time, Mary phoned to give us an update on Billy's worsening condition and wanted to prepare us for possible adverse news. Her detailed description was so gut-wrenching to hear that it sent me into an instant state of depression. As memories of my early childhood came flooding into my mind of happier times when Billy and I were closer, I almost fell to pieces. I'd always been able to protect him and keep him safe, and the fact that I no longer could, felt like a painful fire was burning in my heart. As much as I missed Mum, I also felt so grateful that she'd been spared from going through the heartache and trauma of seeing Billy and Fred deteriorate and suffer as they did.

While all of these thoughts were firing all around in my mind and I stared blankly out across the living room, a tainted image of Billy's ailing face developed in my minds-eye and took priority in my thoughts, and that made me feel suddenly worse. In the next instant, completely out of nowhere and like a light suddenly switching on, an apparition of Billy was standing directly in front of me across the room, that seemed to be made of glass, porcelain, or perhaps it was light? He had a big friendly grin on his face, and his left eye was twinkling like a tiny TV screen showing waves upon a miniature ocean – his face beamed with joy and good health. Then, just like that, he was gone! Billy's apparition had been a complete contrast to the image that I had of him in my mind's eye, only a second before he appeared, and I can still remember it as if it only happened yesterday. I remember wondering if Billy might have had an 'out of body' experience and had come to me for help. During her call, Mary had mentioned that a doctor had visited Billy earlier in the day, and had predicted that he only had a couple of weeks left to live if that...

"Maybe he's already dead?" I thought, as I hurried down the hall towards our prayer room – glancing at the clock along the way, which showed 11.00pm.

Little did I know as I was chanting for Billy to be relieved of his suffering and allowed to return back home to the Light, that he'd started the journey and was probably already there. Early the following morning, Ned phoned to tell us that Billy had died at 11.00pm the previous night, around the same time that I'd seen his apparition. After her call, I felt a sudden rush of relief, joy and severe sadness permeating my senses all at once...

"Could Billy have come ta show me he's safe 'n' okay?" I asked Co, who was stood at my side.

Before Billy died, it had been raining non-stop for well over a week, and by the time that we were ready to leave for his funeral, a severe flood had developed, blocking all the roads leading to Coffs Harbour. I tried to get seats on a plane but to no avail, due to the flood, they were already booked out. Being prevented from attending Billy's funeral should have devastated me, but it didn't, as there wasn't a doubt in my mind that Billy was alive, wide-awake and happily existing somewhere else. On Father's Day, a few months later, I received even more significant proof of this during a vivid dream. In the dream, I was in a park and Billy was standing directly in front of me again, only this time, instead of a hologram, he was of physical form, or so it seemed. As we were conversing by way of thought, I unintentionally found myself floating up close to Billy's face. It was like looking at his skin through a powerful magnifying glass, and I could see streams of tiny particles moving around in perfect unison. Then a single, striped bed mattress appeared standing upright beside me. I automatically thought that Billy used it to lay on under the shade of a large eucalyptus tree that was gently swaying ahead of us in the background. While I was examining the mattress from its top to its bottom, I came across a large rip about halfway down. Billy appeared to have noticed my surprised reaction and waved his hand over the mattress to make it disappear. Just then, a random thought crossed my mind about Denis's bullying and noisy temper tantrums whenever he doesn't believe or agree with something I say or suggest, or when he didn't get his way in an argument. Billy was suddenly sitting on a pile of animated dirt in a pose similar to Rodin's statue of 'The 'Thinker', and relayed a simple but very powerful message to me that I believe was meant for everyone...

"If people only knew what a stupid mistake and waste of time and effort, it is to fight and argue with one another."

Billy's awareness and wisdom appeared to have elevated to a much higher level than it ever was here in this physical world. It was as though he'd awakened to a whole new understanding and awareness of life. After I awoke from the dream, I remained laying on my pillow and pondering it all, especially the mattress...

"Nah – it prob'ly meant nothin' 'n' just happened cuz it's Father's Day 'n' I've been thinkin' about him a lot," I told myself, very unconvincingly.

I shared the details of the dream with Co over breakfast and then phoned Mary to ask if she'd seen or heard from any of Billy's boys, as it was their first Father's Day without him, and I was concerned to know if they were coping okay. I'd barely had time to say hello to Mary before my 'call waiting' started to beep. It was Billy's eldest son, Jamie, and he sounded groggy. I asked him if he was okay and what he told me, hit me like a rock! Jamie had been woken up during the night by loud noises coming from his dad's art studio at the back of the house. The two family dogs had broken in and torn a gaping hole in a striped mattress that Billy had lain upon under his living room ceiling fan during the final few weeks of his life. Jamie insisted that the dogs had never done anything like it before.

OVER THE YEARS, I've often left my body while sleeping and travelled to places far away, including the outer edges of space, where I'd sometimes cross paths with people that I've known in the past but who'd since died. These dreamlike experiences usually took place prior to me waking up in a pool of sweat and gasping for air. In 2000, I underwent an overnight sleep-lab test and was diagnosed with severe Sleep Apnoea. According to the test results, I was averaging up to eight episodes of Apnoea p/h. Most times, my oxygen was dropping to dangerous levels that were low enough to cause death. Since then I've concluded that a lot of my past 'out-of-this-world' dreams have taken place during Apnoea episodes. Since my diagnosis, I've used a C-PAP to help prevent further incidents, but even so, I still sometimes experience similar adventures, but without the accompanying sweat and gasping for air.

TO AVOID DELIBERATELY adding more crazy stuff to my life, until 2007, I'd refrained from having anything to do with psychics, but all that unexpectedly changed, when I was randomly approached by a woman whom I'd never laid eyes on before and was told private things about my mother and family that she shouldn't have possibly known. After she accurately described Mum and the circumstances of her death, she relayed several astounding messages to me, including that Mum wanted me to know that she was very proud of me. She insisted that Mum was with her baby son, but couldn't make out what his name was. Fred and Billy were adults when they'd died, but I mentioned their names anyway, but the woman shook her head and said it was neither of them. Racking my brain to try to think of any babies in the family that had died, it suddenly occurred to me that Mum had lost her first child, Teddy, from cot death. Withholding any details, I mentioned his name...

"Yes! Yes! That's him!" She affirmed without even a moment's hesitation. "He's right over there with your Mum." Everyone present looked to where she was pointing, which happened to be in the direction of our Gohonzon.

The woman turned out to be a professional psychic and invited me to attend her weekly séances, which I declined. I was grateful for the messages from Mum, but that was as far as I wanted to get involved. A few weeks later, almost the same thing happened all over again, when I crossed paths with another woman I'd never met before, who also turned out to be a professional psychic. She'd applied for a position in my office, and in the middle of the interview, she suddenly cut in told me that my father was present in the room and that he now 'understood everything'. When she described him to a 'T' and told me personal things about him that I'd long forgotten, I was astounded! She then told me that he wanted me to know that he was deeply sorry and that he was proud of me and loved me very much. For a moment, I felt like a little boy again, reliving some of my infant years when my father had loved me – it was a struggle to hold back my tears.

It's been thirteen years now since my meetings with those clairvoyants, and so far, nothing like it has ever happened again. Rethinking about Dad's message has me wondering if he was referring to my homosexuality by letting me know that he 'now understands everything'. If only I could be sure of this and that he was also letting me know that, regardless of my sexuality, he still loved me. As for why he'd felt 'so sorry', well, that's a difficult question for me to even to begin to address, as there are so many potential answers. For one thing, when I was a small child, he may have noticed certain aspects of my character and personality that pointed in the direction of me becoming homosexual. Perhaps that might have sent him over the edge and was the reason behind why he treated me with so much cruelty, hate and contempt. Perhaps in death, he'd been forced to face the consequences of his past deeds, and to experience the sufferings that he'd inflicted upon me, including all the cruelty, torment and heartache that he'd allowed George to bring into my life – sufferings that potentially could have killed me. The distorted beliefs of the Catholic Church instilled into people's minds back then could have easily made my father feel like he was getting punished. After all, he'd not only been saddled with a *black* sheep, namely George, but a *pink* sheep as well. I suspect that his life would have been extremely complicated and challenging to deal with, just as it still is for those who continue to be brainwashed and controlled by the same evil religious dogma today. Something else that's since occurred to me relating to what I endured under George's care – could it have been George's deluded way of taking out his revenge because of what had been done to him by other males during his many periods of incarceration? Or could his malicious hatred towards me have been his way of trying to deal with and camouflage his own underlying homosexual desires, which can sometimes be the case? Maybe I'll get all the answers after I go back to the beautiful Light. No hurry though, as I still have more I'd like to do here yet.

When George died in 2007, I sincerely prayed that he'd expiated the hate that he'd brought into the world and that his future incarnations would be much happier, loving and peaceful for him – as well as anyone destined to become connected to him.

# Chapter 42

# AFTERTHOUGHTS-IDEAS-OPINIONS & SOME TRIVIAL STUFF

For reasons including a lot of backstabbing, abuse, bullying and lies, and because some members of my family have never entirely accepted my homosexuality or my choice of practising Buddhism, I've chosen to live the past twenty years of my life without most them being a part of it. Similar lying and backstabbing have also caused me to distance myself from SGI, especially since I was excommunicated in 1993 by the then Australian leader, Dr Tom Tei-Tei. The showdown took place while I was at a leader meeting in Queensland, and after I'd angrily objected to how, rather than promoting world peace, he and many of the other SGI leaders were coaxing and manipulating lay-members into participating in a damaging and degrading battle against the Nichiren Shoshu Priesthood. Dr Tei Tei's equally angry response was to adamantly remind me that SGI had spread the practice of Nam-Myoho-Renge-Kyo throughout the world, to which my answer was, 'if chanting Nam-Myoho-Renge-Kyo didn't produce the actual proof that it does in people's lives, SGI couldn't have spread it further than the Vegemite on a sandwich'. With that, Dr Tei Tei became enraged, told me that SGI didn't need me anymore, and then ordered me to go. As I've mentioned before, I now believe that any negative situations I experienced while I was a member of NS/SGI, were meant to happen in order for me to grow stronger and to eventually learn to stand alone, and to achieve my real mission in this life, which I believe is to do all that I can to help awaken and reawaken others to the importance of Life's Mystic Law above all else.

## NS/SGI DISPUTE VERSUS THE SUPREMACY OF THE LAW.

PLEASE REST ASSURED that it's neither my wish nor my intention to denounce any of the Nichiren organisations. Rather, my aim is to try my best to explain some important and often overlooked issues in defence of the dignity of the Mystic Law. Please also keep in mind that the following explanation is of my own humble opinion and shouldn't be taken as the entire truth, as there are so many other facets and dimensions that need to be addressed and questioned.

## SLANDER OF THE LAW

THE UNFORTUNATE and highly disruptive dispute for power came to a head in 1990, when SGI's President, Daisaku Ikeda, was officially demoted by Nichiren Shoshu's then High Priest, Nikken Abe, who'd long been trying to disband SGI and bring its membership under the control of the Priesthood. From what I understand, Nichiren Shoshu had relentlessly objected to SGI's modernistic propagation methods, particularly the idolisation of Daisaku Ikeda and other senior SGI leaders. Following Ikeda's demotion, millions of devoted SGI supporters around the world joined forces in massive hate and slander campaigns against Nikken Abe, who eventually, retaliated by excommunicating the SGI organisation world-wide. Nikken's shocking and unprecedented response only served to add more fuel to the fire and triggered off a far greater and angrier global conflict that divided the many millions of members who chose to support either side. Smoke coming out of the fiery conflict soon caused media frenzy to erupt, resulting in reports of the fight being presented to the public on a daily basis by the various news networks and sources around the world, including CNN and The New York Times. Adding even more fuel to the fire, many of the reports were highly exaggerated, erroneous or completely fake.

For me and others of the same mindset, witnessing Nichiren's beautiful philosophy being twisted and polluted to the point of giving the general public an incorrect and distorted view of what Nichiren's teachings are truly about, was a heart-wrenching and torturous ordeal. For many of us who'd chosen not to take sides or participate in the dispute, it was either get kicked out of SGI or be ostracised into leaving voluntarily. Topping all that off, a desperate kill-or-die campaign was launched to try to keep hold of any members who were feeling confused or uncertain about what was going on and what they should do about it. Those of us who believed that protecting the dignity of Life's Mystic Law was above and foremost, and who wanted no part in the fight or who'd left because of it, were declared enemies of SGI. In a relentless effort to try to prevent others from following our lead, many of the organisation's leaders and their devoted lay-supporters spread vicious lies and demeaning propaganda about us. In my opinion, instead of dragging everyone into it as they did, the debating and fighting that took place between the leaders should have been kept among themselves and sorted out privately. Had they been thoughtful, caring and responsible enough to have done this and chanted together for a solution, I sincerely believe that they'd have eventually overcome their differences, or at least would have reached a far less damaging compromise. If I sound angry here, I apologise, as the truth is, I feel more deeply frustrated, disappointed and sad about it than anything else. SGI is one of the wealthiest organisations of its kind in the world, and I'm sure I'm not alone in wondering if there may have been an underlying ulterior motive at work that far exceeded the importance of protecting the dignity of the Mystic Law – that is was more about a fight for power.

In his Gosho, Nichiren repeatedly appraises the Mystic Law as being the ultimate of 'all that is, ever was, and ever will be'. Be that as it may, there are many members on both sides who, while professing to be Nichiren's followers, unwittingly or otherwise, are more inclined to consider their leaders as being the most important aspects of their faith. Worse still, some of them feel that it's right to condemn and lie about those of us who've chosen to practise Nichiren Buddhism independently. Also in his Gosho, Nichiren encourages us to chant Nam-Myoho-Renge-Kyo and teach it to others to the best of our ability, which also seems to have gone by the wayside and been ignored. Some SGI leaders have even gone as far as threatening lay-members to remain with the organisation and support its leaders, or else lose their chances of ever achieving their enlightenment. I know it sounds similar to Christian fear-mongering, but I for one can verify that it's true, as I received the same erroneous warning several times myself, especially after began losing confidence and trust in the SGI.

According to what I've read and studied in the Gosho, Nichiren mentions nothing about the importance of an organisation in order to receive benefits from chanting Nam-Myoho-Renge-Kyo. And nor does he say that one needs to exist in the first place, let alone all the misleading rules dictating that members should adhere to an organisation's so-called leaders and blindly accept everything that they think, say and do. However, Nichiren did, leave a very clear warning that his followers should never put their trust in anyone simply because of their high rank, material wealth, good looks or position in the secular world, including priests and other influential leaders. He strictly encourages people to put their trust (not faith) only in a those who express sincere faith from their hearts in the Lotus Sutra (Mystic Law), regardless of how unimportant, unattractive or humble such a person may appear to be.

I WAS TAKEN BY surprise in 2001, when, out-of-the-blue, Dr TeiTei phoned me and then visited me to sincerely apologise for having excommunicated me from SGI ten years earlier. After letting me know that he thought I was a decent person, he then explained how, while he'd been SGI Australia's leader, whether he liked it or not, he'd been obligated to obey any instructions sent to him from the SGI Headquarters in Japan. In other words, in an indirect way, he was admitting that he'd been instructed to get rid of any members found to be stirring up trouble by opposing SGI's fight against Nichiren Shoshu's head priest, Nikken Abe. Shortly after Dr Tei Tei's visit, he passed away, and I was left to wonder if he'd sensed or known that the end of his life was nearing, and if his apology and confession to me that day had been something he'd felt compelled to deliver while he still could. Of course, I'll never know the answer, but his powerful and unexpected apology had certainly recharged my heart with a new sense of hope and confidence. I say this because over the years I've often struggled to get my head around how some people who claim to be devout followers of Nichiren's teachings, are able to justify and brush aside their double-sided attitudes and actions in their daily lives so easily. In particular, how they can sit in front of a Gohonzon and the truth that it represents, chant for world peace, and then at the same time, live their lives creating, telling, listening to and relaying hurtful, damaging opinions and lies about others. The only answer that I've ever been able to come up with that makes any kind of logical sense to me is that their faith is deliberately or unwittingly being directed towards the 'person' and not the Law – the exact opposite of what Nichiren taught.

Shortly after Nichiren first chanted Nam-Myoho-Renge-Kyo on Mount Minobu, he instructed those gathered around him not to make a fuss over him or put him up on a pedestal in any way, shape or form. In his Gosho, 'On Attaining Buddhahood', he clearly states that a Buddha exists because of the Law and not the other way around and that the only difference between a Buddha and a common mortal is that one has reached his or her enlightenment.

While none of us can claim to be without fault, with so many members on either side of the dispute placing their leaders and the politics of their organisations at the top of their honours list, I'm not surprised that there's been a worsening state of natural disasters and economics, particularly since 1990, in Japan and other parts of the world. The Covid-19 pandemic, and how quickly its brought the world to an almost standstill, reminds me of something else that Nichiren mentioned about how, although the lion is king and all the other animals are afraid of him, a tiny parasite or worm can easily enter its bowels and eventually devour him. Perhaps Covid-19 will be humankind's final warning directly from Nature. If we fail to wake up and realise that the most important thing in life isn't winning a contest for fame, fortune and power, but to respect all LIFE in general, and since killing and eating the flesh of other sentient beings has so often been the source of deadly viruses, perhaps putting an end to that would be a major first step towards a less dangerous and far safer tomorrow.

*If the minds of living beings are impure, their land is also impure, but if their minds are pure, so too is their land. There are not two lands, pure or impure in themselves. The difference lies solely in the good or the evil of each of our minds.*

I've included this piece from the Gosho for a specific reason, as it appears to me that in parts of the world where the values of life and the environment are being exploited, ill-treated, misused, disrespected and abundantly polluted, there also appears to be a similar corresponding amount of poverty, injustice, crime, sickness and ever-increasing natural disasters. Of course, I could be wrong about some of this, but the country that I do know a little bit about is Japan, the special place on Earth where, according to what I've read and now believe with all my heart, on April 28th, 1253, Nam-Myoho-Renge-Kyo, was first revealed by Nichiren Daishonin. Not long after, he sent a letter to the Japanese Shogunate, warning them that an invasion of Japan from the west was imminent and that serious changes needed to be set in motion urgently. His warning was ignored, and then, between 1274 and 1281, his prediction came to pass when Japan was unexpectedly attacked by weapons utilising gunpowder, a substance that was accidentally discovered, developed by Chinese alchemists, and then used as a weapon by the Mongolian Empire in an attempt to conquer Japan. Around seven hundred years later, at the end of WW2, Japan also became the very first nation to experience the horrific effects and unbearably cruel sufferings caused by gunpowder's big brother, namely the Atomic Bomb, the forbearer of what has now developed into a monstrous threat to all life on Earth. The Hiroshima and Nagasaki bombings had taken place during the same period that the awareness and propagation of Nam-Myoho-Renge-Kyo re-emerged and begun to spread to other countries. By the late 1960s, millions of Japanese and thousands of other nationals throughout the world had converted to Nichiren Buddhism and joined Nichiren Shoshu/SGI. At the same time, Japan had begun to prosper and eventually succeeded in achieving one of the highest standards of health, lowest rates of crime, and to become the manufacturer of some of the best quality products ever made, including cars and electronics.

Up until when the NS/SGI leadership conflict came to a head, everything for Japan seemed to be getting better and better. However, ever since 1990, Japan seems to have changed direction and has been on a downhill spiral for the worse, plagued by continuous natural disasters, an unstable and sagging economy, rising rates of crime, ill-health, and more recently, a severely damaged nuclear plant that remains a threat to everyone and everything on the planet. Although for many people, Japan is still a very exciting and enjoyable place to visit, for some people, it's become a scary and potentially dangerous destination. This saddens me, as the Japanese people of today are among some of the most beautiful and peaceful people in the world. Personally, I believe that the downward spiral of Japan and other parts of the world parallels with another of Nichiren's predictions...

*Wherever the Law is slandered, the land will always react accordingly.*

The ongoing fight between SGI and Nichiren Shoshu has caused a great deal of slander towards the dignity of the Mystic Law. It's not only brought about immense disrespect and ridicule towards Nichiren's teachings from outsiders but has also frightened away others who'd known little or nothing about the teachings before all the fighting started. Sadly, this poisonous conflict still continues to this day.

During the early years of my practice, if any of us members ever became engaged in a dispute with each other, Dick Causton, would encourage us to sit together and chant about it until we'd reached a mutual and peaceful solution. Dick's gave us excellent advice that seldom failed to achieve a good outcome, but when the dispute between Soka Gakkai and Nichiren Shoshu erupted, Dick appeared to have also had a sudden change of heart by wholeheartedly encouraging the lay-members to take sides and to chant for SGI and Ikeda to win – he also published a book with this message of advice. I remember thinking at the time that it was the epitome of hypocrisy, and it deeply saddened years later when I realised that, just as it had been for Dr Tei Tei in Australia, Dick had probably also been pressured into adhering to what SGI Headquarters in Japan had demanded of him, and forced to agree to things that, in his heart, he didn't want to. I was shattered even more in 1995, and when the dispute was in full swing after I received the devastating news that Dick had unexpectedly passed away during a medical procedure. Although Dick wasn't perfect, he was an extraordinary and exceptional human being with a tremendous desire, gift and the ability, to help encourage many people, including some of the most deluded, to challenge and improve their lives. To me, he was a compassionate and wise human being who always did his best to help bring peace and harmony among others, and he was respected and loved by anyone who got to know him. After a lot of thinking and prayers about what happened to Dick, I eventually concluded that the universe may have taken him back home early to protect him from doing any more damage to his good karma, good name and his excellent and well earned good reputation.

Concerning matters regarding Nichiren Shoshu and its Priesthood, the only problems that I've experienced personally are their rigid refusal to consider suggestions for any changes that are presented to them by lay-believers. Rather than listening to what we've had to say, what we think or how we feel towards the way that Nichiren's teachings should be taught in the West, visiting priests have insisted on only adhering to the wishes of the High Priest, in a similar way to how many SGI leaders adhere to Daisaku Ikeda. Nichiren Shoshu's ancient method of practice and its priests' adamant refusal to adapt to other cultures and catch up to the 21st Century, for some of us, has been frustratingly difficult to cope with and accept. In fact, it wouldn't surprise me if the same problems have reigned supreme within the Priesthood's dispute with SGI.

In his Gosho, Nichiren left instructions that his teachings should be taught in accordance with the place and the time. From my personal experience, this hasn't usually been the case with priests visiting Australia, who've like I said, chosen to ignore requests for adjustments and insisted on continuing to present the teachings following the Japanese culture and tradition, which hasn't always gone down well here. Hopefully, this will change in the future, and Nichiren's teachings will be taught in the way that he wanted, 'according to the place and the time'. I certainly hope and pray so and that it will happen sooner rather than later.

Also in his Gosho, Nichiren warns about how the only people capable of destroying his teachings are those who claim to represent them while twisting their true meaning around to mean something else. Well, this certainly 'rings a few bells' from some of what I've seen and heard over the years. To elaborate, just because someone claims to be a Nichiren Buddhist and holds an official leadership position in an organisation, doesn't automatically mean that they can be trusted or that they've reached their enlightenment. Realising and expiating our bad karma in this increasingly difficult world of suffering is a lifetime job, and there'll always be shortcomings along the way for all of us, regardless of how long we've been chanting. Some leaders and lay-members contain the kind of karma that often motivates them to unwittingly or otherwise create disruption and disharmony. It's an outcome that can easily happen, particularly when the Mystic Law isn't given the top priority, and it can easily arise on all levels. Be that as it may, it's also a necessary evil to help with the achievement of Kosen rufu (peace and harmony life and the environment), as we first need to dig up and expose our bad karma to see and understand it before we can do anything about improving or changing it. Whether we chant the words Nam-Myoho-Renge-Kyo or not, it's only by adhering to what the Mystic Law represents, above all else, that we can ever successfully change our poisons into medicine. In other words, we need to respect the presence of the Mystic Law and all that it represents in our own and all other life.

The organisations are made up of people from many different walks of life, and some often lack in experience when it comes to being responsible for the welfare of others. Unfortunately, some of these members are given leadership positions long before they've had enough time to learn and absorb even the basic fundamentals of Nichiren's teachings, and it can easily cause problems and chaos, not only for a leader concerned but the members under his or her care. It's something that I witnessed time and time again while I was a member of NS/SGI, especially when new and uninformed leaders attempt to live up to the expectations of their status by giving those under their care incorrect or substitute answers to questions that they have no idea how to correctly answer. The best advice that I can give to anyone who doesn't feel comfortable about something they've either heard, read or been told regarding Nichiren's teaching, is to ask their respective leader or someone else in the organisation, to verify the answer they've received by pointing out where it's written in the Gosho, but whatever you do, don't be foolish enough to let yourself become a victim of someone else's karma, by allowing your faith to suffer because of it. And always keep in mind that no one is perfect and that mistakes are sometimes meant to happen in life to help us to grow in our faith, and indeed, life in general. Having said all that, I'd like to also assure you that among the SGI and Nichiren Shoshu believers, there is an abundance of beautiful and compassionate human beings, all working hard and doing their best to overcome their shortcomings and to help make this world a better place to live for everyone and everything in it. My purpose in telling you all this hasn't been to encourage anyone to leave their organisation or refrain from joining one, as I can personally testify that attending meetings to learn and help others learn about Nichiren's teaching, is a very rewarding, fulfilling and worthwhile cause. It's also a valuable opportunity to hear about the experiences of others, which can often encourage and motivate others to grow stronger in their faith, but only if the most important things being discussed are directed towards the importance of Life's Mystic Law and not the organisation's politics and hierarchy.

Co and I will always be grateful to NS/SGI for making it possible for us to discover and learn about Nam-Myoho-Renge-Kyo in the first place. We continue to consider ourselves as being unofficial members of both groups, even though these days, we're just a couple of independent Buddhist, grooving along to the rhythm of life, and doing our best to keep in step with the beat by explaining Nam-Myoho-Renge-Kyo to the best of our ability to anyone who'll listen. We do not desire to be leaders and consider ourselves as being only as valuable and worthwhile as the compassion and sincerity we're able to express from our hearts allow. I also have no desire for personal fame-like recognition, should my book ever become a success.

Although some of what I've written and shared in my life's journey may seem a bit over-the-top and too outrageous for some readers to believe, hopefully, it will at least be entertaining. I also hope and pray that my story will serve to help others, especially those who've experienced similar happening in their life's journey. Having said that, the one thing that will not be difficult to accept and believe is the beneficial result that you'll receive from chanting Nam-Myoho-Renge-Kyo, regardless of who, what or where you are.

In his Gosho, Nichiren tells us that the universe is teaming with other worlds, which, like Earth, have their own rivers, forests, mountains, suns and moons etcetera. And that there are more stars in the heavens than there are grains of sand upon the Earth – an estimate that many of today's scientists agree with and support. Nichiren also assures us that there are countless other conditions of life that exist, some of which reach far beyond our present ability even to begin to imagine. In his Gosho's titled, 'The Four Debts of Gratitude', Nichiren describes this world as being a Saha world (World of suffering), a place of opportunity, where each of us has a chance to recognise and eliminate our bad karma, by manifesting the wisdom to make good causes to replace it with good karma. He also states that achieving such an outcome won't be at all easy, that our bad karma will try to influence us to go the other way and to inevitably make more bad karma instead, and make things even more difficult for ourselves and others around us. Nichiren concludes with a warning that our accumulated bad karma, if not challenged and changed, has the potential to destroy this world of opportunity. Observing the mess we humans have made of this planet thus far, I'd say he hit the nail squarely on the head with that one.

## MY THOUGHTS ON CHRISTIANITY.

I'VE OFTEN BEEN told by Christians that my faith in the Law is wrong, that it's the Devil's trickery and that I need to devote my life to Jesus as my saviour, otherwise, regardless of how much good I do in this world, I will surely end up in Hell. In a similar way to how Jesus taught that the Kingdom of Heaven is within us, Nichiren taught that enlightenment is within us. In other words, both are the same premise, but no matter how many times I try to explain this to extremist Christian fear mongers who thrive on threatening people with their hard-line propaganda, they refuse to listen to a word of it. The reason being, either through fear or ignorance, they're unable to consider thinking beyond the walls of their dogmatic misinterpreted doctrines. I say 'misinterpreted' because, over the years, the followers of both Jesus and Nichiren have split apart into many groups – all claiming that their interpretation is the correct one. Consequently, an ongoing onslaught of injustice, heartache, bullying, confusion, abusive conflict and confusion have more often than not ensued. Considering there was only one Jesus and one Nichiren, this never should have happened in the first place.

According to what I was taught as a Christian, the lessons that Jesus gave were written down by other people and not until quite a long time after his death. Among the authors responsible were the same disciples of Jesus that had abandoned him when he was arrested, and who'd denied even knowing him. Nichiren wrote down his teachings himself, and most of what he wrote still remains intact today at the Head Temple, Hoando, in Taisekiji. While Jesus taught the Law of 'reaping what we sow', Nichiren referred to it as being the Law of Cause and Effect and declared to be one of the three major fundamental Laws of all Life.

Rather than shouting out Jesus' name in praise, I believe he'd have much preferred his future followers to use his example as a compassionate, forgiving and loving human being to represent him and what he stood for. Of course, I realise that a lot of people refuse to believe that Jesus even existed in the first place, but whether he did or didn't, it's clearly evident to me that someone exceptional existed, in order to be able to successfully change and replace some of the hate and evil in the Old Testament with the love, compassion and forgiveness that he tried so hard to teach. To believe that by appraising Christ's name and condemning others with alternative faiths and views, is enough to score points and earn a place in Heaven, is to me, not only illogical but utterly ludicrous. In my mind, it's as silly as going around praising and calling out the company name that you work for, rubbishing other companies, doing no actual work, and then expecting to receive a pay-cheque at the end of the week. Whether we choose to believe in the stories relating to Jesus and Nichiren or not, the one common thing that clearly stands out is that they were both trying their best under extremely difficult circumstances to rectify and improve the cruel and distorted teachings of old. For many years, I believed that the story about Jesus appearing three days after his death was a fictitious tale, created to add strength to his greatness, but all of that completely changed when my brother Billy appeared in front of me at the same time as he'd died 300 kilometres away. I've now come to believe that Jesus was one of several outstanding human beings born into this world of suffering, with an important mission to accomplish, and that he'd been stopped in his tracks by the evil-minded hierarchy of his day, who murdered him to stop him from bringing them, and other slanderers of the truth, down to the same level as everyone else, so that they could be seen and judged for what they really were. The disastrous result we now have is a mixture of the leftover hatred from the Old Testament, that Jesus was prevented from addressing, blended in with the love, compassion and forgiveness that he spent his life teaching. Instead of poison being changed into medicine, the opposite has been taking place, and the medicine has instead been contaminated with poison. I believe this is why so much discrepancy exists among the various 'so-called' Christian sects. The fact that so many people who claim to be Christians continue to fail to recognise and acknowledge this, makes it even sadder. A good example is the many Christians who condemn homosexuality in the name of Jesus Christ, even though he didn't mention a single word about it! Then there are the foolish parents who claim to live by the code of love, compassion and forgiveness, but at the same time condemn, punish, or disown their gay children, because they're unable to pretend to be someone they're not meant to be. Such parents may have a lot to answer for if a day of reckoning turns out to be true. For a perfect example of what I've been saying here, please watch this video...

https://www.youtube.com/watch?v=zwmbAFNZ5lI

## NOW BACK TO MY STORY

2007 TURNED OUT to be a life-changing year for Co and I. During the first Buddhist lectures that I attended in the early 1970s, I'd heard that Nichiren chose not to eat the flesh of other sentient beings and that he'd only ever worn furs and skins that came from animals that had died naturally. I questioned some of the SGI leaders and Nichiren Shoshu priests about this and was told that it's now okay for Nichiren Buddhists to eat meat, which, I have to admit, had always seemed a hard pill to swallow. Since leaving the organisation and doing more research on this and other similar things that I'd been told, I've discovered that not everything I was told about Nichiren Buddhism has been the truth, and being assured that it's 'now okay' to kill other sentient beings, steal their skin and eat their flesh is certainly one of them. I can only guess that this lie was and still is deliberately told to make it easier to draw new converts into the organisation, who will help contribute towards its ever-growing wealth. For those interested in knowing, Nichiren did not say that it was okay to kill and eat the flesh of other sentient beings, and while I'm on the subject of 'marketing' for rapid growth, from my personal experiences and the experiences of others that I've known, SGI avoids talking or writing about anything to do with the 'supernatural', particularly experiences submitted by its members. I can only assume that this is also done to prevent any walls of ridicule from getting in the way of their membership growth. While I admit and accept that some of the experiences that I've shared in my book sound like absolute BS, I'm not afraid to go out on a limb and tell the truth, regardless of how strange and unbelievable some of it may seem. I also feel confident that anyone with similar experiences, of which there are many, will understand mine perfectly.

After years of trying to ignore where meat and chicken come from and trying to convince myself that it grew on trees, the reality finally caught up with me after a friend of ours recommended a YouTube video entitled 'The Earthlings'. However, because we prefer not to watch anything that depicts violence for entertainment, we were reluctant even to look it up, but that all changed in 2007 when I felt suddenly compelled to address my lifelong addiction to eating meat and chicken. I admit that delicious steaks, juicy chops and crispy fried chicken had always given my taste buds a delightful treat, but I wanted to make a bigger effort towards following Nichiren's fundamental example as a *person*. I decided to quit procrastinating and to make some serious decisions, so Co and I sat down and watched 'The Earthlings', which, to our combined shock and horror, turned out to be one of the most gruesome, cruel and upsetting videos that we'd ever seen. What broke the camel's back, was a disturbing scene towards the end of the video where tears roll down the cheeks of a terrified bull as it struggles to push back against the other animals behind it that are being forced to push it forward. The poor, creature gave us the distinct impression that it knew exactly what it was in for, and I could almost hear and feel its terrified spirit reaching out from the TV screen and begging for help, just as any human would if their life was on the line. We could clearly see that the poor, defenceless bull desperately wanted to stay alive, and as tears welled up in my eyes, something that I'd read in Nichiren's writings sprung into my mind...

*If the breadwinner of a family earns a living from thieving, then all those who depend on the breadwinner's earnings are thieves also.*

I was overcome by a state of deep regret and shame when everything clicked into place and suddenly made perfect sense, and I was awakened to the fact that by eating meat, I was just as much a killer as the slaughter-man. In other words, I may as well have cut the poor creature's throat myself. Since that dreadful night of horror, Co and I have remained steadfast vegetarians. I also now believe that, just as humankind has moved forward from cannibalism and slavery etcetera, which were all once considered to be righteous and commonly accepted, we humans now need to take the next giant leap forward and rise above our desires to kill, eat' and enslave our other non-human sentient beings. At Bible studies back in my childhood, I heard scary stories about how people sacrificed animals to prove their love and obedience towards God. One story was about Abraham, who'd been asked by God to offer own his son, Isaac, as a sacrifice. Apparently one of God's angels stopped it from happening at the very last moment. I still fail to understand why a loving God would ask those that he loved to make such violent and cruel offerings, just for God to feel powerful and honourably obeyed. Even a loving human parent wouldn't expect or ask such a thing of their children, so why a loving God? If this and other similar stories recorded in the Bible are true, then it seems to me that the authors of the Old Testament weren't writing about a loving God at all, and were possibly members of an advanced alien race here to experiment and mess around with the bodies and minds of humans. Some of today's electromagnetic and technological wonders have often had me wondering if we may be catching up with those critical days of creation, recorded in the Old Testament of the Bible. Especially now that we've discovered DNA and how to manipulate it, as well as how we now use body cells to repair and replace damaged body parts. Doctors have even figured out how to bring humans back from the brink of death, even when there's no sign of life, and how to help the blind to see and the deaf to hear etcetera. The Bible tells us that the lifespan of the first humans was reduced from several hundred years to three scores and ten, and today's scientists are very close to reversing this limitation as well. The Bible also tells us that everything was stopped or ended by a flood and the destruction of Sodom. It also tells us that angels who were sent here to do work for God, became so enchanted by the human females' beauty, that they abandoned their allegiance to God, married whomever they fancied and then produced 'exceptional' offspring, who then were able to reach adulthood before God knew about what was going on and was able to put an end to it. If it's true that the God described in the Bible knows, hears and sees everything, then why did it take so long for God to realise what was going on? Secondly, if everything that's recorded in the Bible is God's word, then how come Jesus had to change and rectify so much of it? These are questions that none of us can accurately answer without creating stories of our own to compromise.

In accordance with the rules of this physical world, Jesus and Nichiren, like all other sentient beings, first needed to be conceived, born, then needed to eat, drink, urinate, defecate, wash, sleep communicate, discover, create, and so on and so forth, and unless they die beforehand, eventually reach maturity, old age, sickness and death. Without the underlying workings of Nature, Cause and Effect and Communication, the Law which Myoho-Renge-Kyo represents, nothing past, present or future, could exist. Therefore, for anyone to consider the Law as being second to a 'person' or the work of the Devil, as so many Christians have claimed, is just too ludicrous and illogical even to merit thinking about. I personally believe that the real meaning behind the quote below is more to do with the unlimited human mind potential than the workings and existence of the physical human body...

*Let us make humankind in our image, in our likeness, so that they may rule over the fish in the sea and the birds in the sky, over the livestock and all wild animals, as well as all the creatures that move along the ground.*

Everything in the world is moving faster and faster, so much so, that it's becoming increasingly difficult to try to keep up with it all. Thanks to our greed and stupidity, and the decisions and actions of many of the world's past and present teachers and leaders, we're now like sitting ducks, as the saying goes, stuck on a speeding planet with maniacs at the wheel. We must turn our attention towards improving and developing our wisdom and showing more respect for the environment and each other. It's the only way for us to survive and keep what we've already got. As I mentioned earlier in my story, chanting Nam-Myoho-Renge-Kyo enables anyone to tap directly into the source of their wisdom and to bring it forth. The present devastating effects of the Earth's changing climate may be our final warning to change before it's too late.

*The first of the five precepts is not to take life, and the first of the six paramitas is that of almsgiving. The ten good precepts, the two hundred and fifty precepts and all the other rules of conduct begin with the prohibition against the taking of life.*

The above piece from Nichiren's Gosho is yet another reason we need to stop killing, stealing, eating the flesh and using the skins of other sentient beings, as regardless of how hard we pray unless we quickly wake up and stop the killings of our other sentient beings and all the other harmful stuff that we do to each other and contribute to our environment, we're done for, and one doesn't need to be a scholar to see what's potentially coming.

## SOMETHING LIGHTER TO FINISH ON.

OTHER THAN writing songs and making some home recordings with Co at the helm producing and creating the music, the only public performances that I've done after returning from England and since the car accident, have been very low key. However, once this book is finished and published, we are planning to update YOU and add a few new songs. Over the last few years, Co and I have volunteered at a large rest home, chatting, playing games and doing whatever we can to keep the residents entertained and happy. We also sing their favourite old songs with them, which gives us a tremendous buzz, especially seeing them all enjoying themselves. It was very challenging and confronting at the home first, but after we'd grown more accustomed to it and were told by the residents' how much joy we bring to their lives, it soon became a very fulfilling experience. In fact, I can honestly say that going out of one's comfort zone to bring happiness to others without expecting anything in return is among the most rewarding and fulfilling gifts that anyone can give or experience, which enhances everything else that you do in your life, and I sincerely recommend it to everyone!

I'd also like to mention how sincerely grateful I am for all the changes that have been made in Australia and some other parts of the world regarding people's attitudes towards homosexuality. I feel particularly grateful for the wisdom, understanding and tolerance expressed by the younger and far more worldly generations, straight and gay, who've helped make it possible for younger gays to be free to be themselves and live their lives as equal human beings. I'm part of the baby boomers generation, and 60 years ago I couldn't have imagined even in my wildest dreams that homosexuality would one day be decriminalised, let alone that Gay Marriage would become legally acceptable in many forward-thinking countries. Along with so many others who've suffered through the horror years of legalised homophobic hatred and abuse, I too get emotional just thinking about it.

Two of the most significant benefits that I've received in my life since I've been chanting Nam-Myoho-Renge-Kyo have been the mystery 'voice' that's guided me through difficult circumstances, often just in time to save my life, and the beautiful companionship, support and unconditional love that Co has always given me. I'm also very happy and grateful to report that so far Co's health has been good, even though mine hasn't been quite so smooth. After a couple more close shaves with death due to illnesses, including a heart attack in 2001, I'm also deeply grateful to still be alive and kicking to hopefully be able to do more good in the world, particularly as a result of this book, written for that very reason.

There are also several well-known celebrities that chant Nam-Myoho-Renge-Kyo, including, Tina Turner (As depicted in her movie 'What's Love Got To Do With It), Herbie Hancock, Boy George, Orlando Bloom, Sandy Shaw and rock's wild child, Courtney Love, just to name a few, who's often publicly declared that it's the only practise that's helped her to control her inner demons. It was also pleasantly and unexpectedly surprised when I first heard Olivia Newton-John singing about Nam-Myoho-Renge-Kyo it in her beautiful song, 'Let Go Let God'...

*https://www.youtube.com/watch?v=6CZ0XJqWRr4*

Regardless of who or what you are, or what your beliefs are, please try chanting Nam-Myoho-Renge-Kyo, and give yourself a chance to experience the incredible and powerful difference it can make to your life.

Finally, from my heart to yours I sincerely thank you for reading my story and hope that your future is blessed with an abundance of peace, love, wisdom and happiness...

*"Misfortune comes from one's mouth and ruins one, but fortune comes from one's heart and makes one worthy of respect."*

*"There are two types of illness, minor and serious. Early treatment by a skilled physician can cure even serious illnesses, not to mention minor ones. Karma also may be divided into two categories: fixed and unfixed. Sincere repentance will eradicate even fixed karma, to say nothing of karma that is unfixed"*

*"A passage from the Lotus Sutra reads that it is 'the most difficult to believe and the most difficult to understand'. Many hear about and accept this sutra, but when great obstacles arise, just as they were told would happen, few remember it and bear it firmly in mind. To accept is easy; to continue is difficult. But Buddhahood lies in continuing faith."*

*"When one chants the Daimoku (Nam-Myoho-Renge-Kyo) bearing in mind that there are distinctions among those who embrace the Lotus Sutra, then the blessings one gains will be equal to Shakyamuni Buddha."*

*"Each of you should summon up the courage of a lion king and never succumb to threats from anyone. The lion kings fear no other beasts, nor do its cubs. Slanderers are like barking foxes, but Nichiren's followers are like roaring lions."*

*...Nichiren.*

Nam-Myoho-Renge-Kyo

Printed in Great Britain
by Amazon

59110123R00223